Mill Hill Saturday: 1770 —

Dear Solander our [...] Friend Doc.r Franklin proposes to make us a Vissit Next Week — my Son & I request the favour you will be of the Party — Doc.r Franklin sayes any Day next Week will Suite Him, but it will be most convenient to Us if Fryday or Saturday will be so to you —

Pray step over to the Doc.r & concert measures with Him for I have presumed so farr, as to Say, you would wait on Him for that purpose & the sooner the better — In hopes of the pleasure of seeing you both I am Sincerely yours

Collinson

"Forget not Mee & My Garden . . ."

Frontispiece *Peter Collinson. J. Miller. Engraving from John Fothergill,* Some account of the Late Peter Collinson . . . *London, 1770. The Linnean Society of London.*

The book on the left is Hortus Cliffortianus *by Carl Linnaeus, 1737, opened to an illustration of the plant Linnaeus named in Collinson's honor,* Collinsonia canadensis. *The plant on the right is Pinxter-flower, an American azalea.*

Front Endpaper *Left:* Peter Collinson to Benjamin Franklin, *August 12, 1753; right:* Peter Collinson to Daniel Solander, *October 17, 1757 (?) (APS).*

PETER. COLLINSON.
F.R.S. S.A.S.
ACAD. REG. BEROL. et SVEC. Soc.
Ætat: LXXV.

"Forget not Mee & My Garden . . ."

SELECTED LETTERS, 1725-1768
OF PETER COLLINSON, F.R.S.

edited and with an introduction by Alan W. Armstrong

AMERICAN PHILOSOPHICAL SOCIETY

Independence Square   Philadelphia   2002

MEMOIRS OF THE
AMERICAN PHILOSOPHICAL SOCIETY
HELD AT PHILADELPHIA
FOR PROMOTING USEFUL KNOWLEDGE
VOLUME 241

ISBN: 0-87169-241-4
US ISSN 0065-9738

Library of Congress Cataloging-in-Publication Data
Collinson, Peter, 1694–1768.
"Forget not mee & my garden. . ." : selected letters of Peter Collinson / Alan W.
Armstrong, editor.
p. cm. — (Memoirs of the American Philosophical Society held at Philadelphia for
Promoting Useful Knowledge, issn 0065-9738 ; 241)
Includes bibliographical references (p.).
ISBN 0-87169-241-4 (cloth)
1. Collinson, Peter, 1694–1768—Correspondence.   2. Plant collectors—
England—Correspondence.   3. Naturalists—England—Correspondence.
4. Merchants—England—Correspondence.   I. Title: Forget not mee and
my garden.   II. Armstrong, Alan W., 1939–   III. Title.   IV. Memoirs
of the American Philosophical Society ; v. 241.
Q11 .P612 vol. 241
[QK31.C65]
08 s—dc21
508'.092 B]   2001022121

for MCA & SMA

Magnolia Lauri folio, Subtus Albicante.
The Sweet Flowring Bay.

Coccothraustes cœruleus.
The blew Grofbeak.

Sweet Flowering Bay (with Gross Beak). Mark Catesby, from Collinson's copy of Natural History of Carolina, Florida and The Bahama Islands. *2 vols. London, 1730–1747 at Knowsley Hall, Vol. I, plate 39. Courtesy of the Earl of Derby, Knowsley.*

Contents

Illustrations

(numbers refer to letter numbers)

Introduction

"Forget not Mee & My Garden. . . ," the 27 year old Peter Collinson wrote his Maryland friend George Robbins in 1721. "If you have any Shells, Curious Stones, or any other Natural Curiosity Remember Mee. I want one of your Humming Birds which you may send dry'd in its Feathers, and any Curious Insect."[1] And so with Collinson's letters for the rest of his life—importunings, thanks for rarities received, introductions to people and plants, cultivation instructions, queries, encouragements.

His letters are vigorous and enthusiastic, filled with excited descriptions of new discoveries and how-to-do-it advice. He often wrote in haste, standing up at the shipping desk in his fabric merchant's shop in London, snatching time from business to write: "This comes from behind the Counter. You know what a shop Is to write under no Interruptions, but I am used to It & my friends are so good to Excuse all my Blunders."[2] He referred to himself and his Virginia planter friend John Custis as "Wee Brothers of the Spade."[3] Thanking Linnaeus for naming a plant after him, Collinson observed, "Something, I think, was due to me from the Commonwealth of Botany, for the great number of Plants and Seeds I have annually procured from abroad, & you have been so good as to pay it, by giving mee a Species of Eternity botanically speaking, that is, a name as long as Men and Books endure."[4]

More than seven hundred and fifty of his letters survive (192 follow) to more than seventy-five correspondents (27 are represented here). He corresponded with the leading scientists and collectors of his time—Carl Linnaeus, Benjamin Franklin, Sir Hans Sloane and Sir Charles Wager; many of the nobility including the 8th and 9th Lords Petre, the Earls of Jersey and Bute, and the Dukes of Richmond; colonial officers and gentlemen such as the Penn proprietors, Cadwallader Colden (Deputy Governor of New York), John Custis, and William Byrd II of Virginia; and inspired amateurs like John Bartram and others of those "Curious in our Way"[5] in the North American colonies, Germany, Ireland, Russia, the West Indies, Holland, Switzerland, Italy and Sweden.

He wrote about plants, butterflies, British imperial interests, electricity, weather, fossils, earthquakes, snakes, wars, terrapins, cures for gout and rabies, red Indians, astronomy, premiums to encourage colonial productions, the migration of swallows, magnetism, and now and then a Quaker homily. He did not mention music or slavery.

Collinson's letters display a clear sense of his own achievement, a temper, and the forward manner that helped make him such a successful collector. Writing thanks to Sir Hans Sloane in the 1730s for a present of shells, Collinson asked for a few more: "If I mistake not I remember to have seen you have a great Number & Variety of Duplicates in a Cabinet that stands on the Left Hand as I went into the Roome where the Mummy lies."[6] His letters reflect his pride in his nation and of English achievements—for example his December 10, 1762 note to John Bartram: "Now my dear John, look at the map and see by this glorious peace [of Paris] what an immense country is added to our long, narrow slip of Colonies."

He was remarkably healthy. Aside from a few bouts of gout, his 76 years were energetic without interruption. As for what he looked like, according to his friend John Fothergill, "His stature was below middle size, and his body was rather corpulent; his habit was plain, having been bred a quaker; his aspect kind and liberal. . . .[7] Another contemporary, Richard Gough wrote of him in a private memorandum, "He remarkably hardy and wore thin wastcoat in winter."[8]

After his death, the *Annual Register* reported

> When he was in London he applied to the business of his counting-house; when in the country, he was almost continually employed in his garden, observing and assisting the progress of vegetation, which equally contributed to his pleasure and his health.
> He was in the highest degree fond of both flowers and fruit. Of fruit he always made the principal part of his meal: and his house was never without flowers, from the early snowdrop to the autumnal cyclamen.[9]

He hated heat and he loved food. On September 17, 1765 he complained to Linnaeus, "I do assure you I have had little pleasure of my life this summer, for I cannot bear heat. I have longed to be on Lapland Mountains." On the subject of food, "The North American Ursus I have often eat of it in England & think it is the most agreeable tast of all Flesh. My friend a Merchant had large young Bears brought over every year & fatted them with and Sugar. It is really fine Eating & the Fatt is whiter & finer than the Fatt of Lambs."[10] He annotated his copy of Philip Miller's *Gardener's Dictionary* with a list of "melting Peaches," their size and characteristics.

A plain man of limited education and large enthusiasm, Collinson was born in London on January 28, 1694 and raised by a gardening grandmother in Peckham. His limited means and his Quaker heritage that precluded his taking the Test Oath meant that he could not go to an English university (in his time affiliated with the Anglican Church). He chose instead to go into his father's business of selling quality fabrics to an elite domestic market and exporting them to the British colonies. It was a good business in the 1730s, '40s and '50s, but it declined with the trade disruptions of the Seven Years War and the impending American Revolution. Collinson was not well-off when he died.

He taught himself through his friends and his reading. His library included most of the natural histories available and published in his time, along with biographies, travel accounts, gazetteers, geographies, mythologies, books on antiquities, astronomy, and practical science. He used his books hard and marked them for reference. Typical is the annotation in his copy of Pliny's *History of the World:* "It is plain from this romantic account they knew not the origin of asbestos—nor the country from whence it came & yett knew how to manufacture it. I have paper made with it by Ben Franklin of Philadelphia who sent me several sheets of them."[11]

His scientific interests were recognized early. At 34 Collinson was elected to the Royal Society under the sponsorship of Sir Hans Sloane. He served it for 40 years (fourteen as a member of the council), introducing in their own names the discoveries of others, including his American correspondents Franklin and Bartram and arranging for publication of their letters to him. He wrote often for the new *Gentleman's Magazine* (the *New Yorker* of his time) and contributed to the Royal Society's *Philosophical Transactions* and to other journals.

Friendship came easily to him, face-to-face and through letters. His business acquaintance with the gentry and the nobility, his American planter customers, his Philadelphia friends, ship captains, and his mercantile correspondents all helped expand his collections as he sought curiosities of every description. Many the captain who carried home in his cabin packages of seeds and nuts, shells, bulbs, ginseng roots, sprouting skunk cabbages, hatching turtle eggs, dried birds packed in tobacco dust. His zest for collecting held strong all his life. Three months before he died he wrote a friend, "Pray if any thing new or odd occurs Lett me know."[12]

The ranks of the Curious grew during Collinson's lifetime, a reflection of the nation's peace and its growing profit from colonial trade. Collecting and research benefit from a climate of prosperity, and there were many who could afford science in the 18th century. Support for colonial expansion and development went hand in hand with the impulse to exploit natural history as much for the sake of pure science as to render science useful to trade and industry. Collinson grew up with Robert Boyle's "General Heads for the Natural History of a Country, Great or Small: Drawn out for the Uses of Travellers and Navigators" (1666) and John Woodward's 1696 *Brief Instructions for Making Observations In All Parts of the World*. His early letters to John Bartram are filled with brief instructions of his own.

Shared curiosities often bridge differences in age and class and they did for Collinson. Consider his warm friendship with Sir Hans Sloane, an educated man 34 years his senior and physician to the Queen. Sloane delighted in the younger man's talent for observation and discovery, and he found Collinson's enthusiasm charming, just as he enjoyed having his treasures openly admired—all the more gratifying when the admiration carries a hint of honest envy as Collinson's did.

It was Sloane who introduced Collinson to the Royal Society. On the docks and in the coffee houses where stocks were traded and rarities displayed alongside the latest New World cargoes, commoner met nobility and gentry on level ground as they exchanged observations and specimens, but the Royal Society was the club of the most sophisticated philosophers. The entrée Collinson gained there was crucial.

An enthusiast himself, Collinson was an indefatigable broker of enthusiasms. He recognized the achievements of others and helped to further them. For all he was a determined collector eager to add to his garden and cabinet, he was unselfish and seems to have defined himself in promoting the ventures and discoveries of his imaginative friends, frequently through the Royal Society.

His promotion of Benjamin Franklin exemplified his inspired patronage: "Collinson is the most important single person in Franklin's scientific career. He was responsible for Franklin's initial activity in electrical science; his encouragement was equally responsible for its continuation."[13] In 1753, at Franklin's request, Collinson used his influence with "those at the helm" to get Franklin appointed deputy postmaster-general of the American service.

He helped to popularize Linnaeus's system of plant identification and championed the interest of Linnaeus's protégé Daniel Solander (later to sail with Banks as Naturalist aboard the *Endeavour*) to become curator of the British Museum. His greatest triumph was the introduction and re-introduction of more than 100 American plants through the efforts of his American collector John Bartram. Also, he sent some good plants west: pear scions, peach stones, melon seeds, and, to Bartram what we know today as our kitchen rhubarb with instructions on cooking and this note, "Eats best cold." [14]

Here is how his friend Cadwallader Colden described Collinson to a friend in London,

> I have lately fallen into a literary correspondence with a Gentleman, who is curious in several branches of the natural History of America, & I am told has an exceedingly curious collection of that sort, as well as the most compleat Garden of American Plants that is in great Brittain. It is the more extraordinary by his being a Merchant, who seldom apply themselves to any study that no way tends to advance their trade. He seems to me to be a man of Generous principles & universal Benevolence. . . .[15]

Writing about himself to Colden, Collinson observed, "I hate to be idle, and think all time surely lost that is not usefully employed; for which reason clubs, taverns and coffee houses scarcely know me." [16]

Although Collinson traveled extensively around England, he left it only once and never visited America. As he wrote John Bartram,

> It is with pleasure when we read thy Excursions (& wish to bear thee Company) but then it is with concern that we reflect on the Fatigue thee undergoes, the great risks of thy Health in Heats & Colds but able all the Danger of Rattlesnakes. This would so curb my Ardent Desires to see vegitable Curiosities that I should be afraid to venter in your woods unless on Horseback & so Good a guide as thee art by my side.[17]

Among his wealthy and aristocratic friends he encouraged large-scale planting of American evergreens which he described as "another means of painting with Living Pencils." [18] He was, however, not a landscape architect but a gardener and propagator. Individual flowers from his garden were often painted, but no painting or drawing of his garden is known, and while many of his contemporaries remarked on the extent and range of his collection, none described the arrangement of the whole as remarkable.

In later years he described in a private memorandum his introduction of exotic plants and perfection of propagation techniques as his greatest contributions. "My Publick Station in Business brought me acquainted with Persons that were natives of Carolina, Virginia, Maryland, Pensilvania and New England. My Love for New & Rare plants putt mee often on soliciting their assistance for seeds or plants from those Countries," he wrote, but "What was common with them (but Rare with us) they did not think worth sending. . . . Neither Money nor Friendship would Tempt them. . . ."

Then John Bartram was introduced "as a very proper Person for that purpose, being a native of Pensilvania with a numerous Family. The profits ariseing from Gathering Seeds would enable him to support it."

The introduction worked and Bartram turned out to be an inspired collector. Collinson arranged subscriptions for the five guinea boxes of Bartram's seeds (packets of 105 varieties of trees and shrubs in each). His careful records show more than one hundred subscribers including collectors in Ireland, Scotland, France and Germany during the period 1740–1767. Of course "Transacting this Business of procureing Foreign Seeds brought on mee every year no little Trouble, to carry on such a Correspondence attended with so much Loss of time, viz. In keeping Accounts, writing Letters with Orders, Receiving and Paying the Collectors Money, Difficulties and attendance at the Custom House. . . & then disperseing the boxes to the proper owners, etc. etc.

"Yet all this trouble with some unavoidable Expence attending it did not discourage mee for I willingly undertook it without the least grain of profit to my self in hopes to improve, or at least adorn my Country. . . I had Public Good at Heart. . . ."

His trouble didn't end with distributing the boxes and paying Bartram. For one thing, Bartram didn't always want cash, so Collinson had to act as banker, and often Bartram wanted goods that Collinson had to obtain and ship. And then, "[A]fter I had supplied the several persons. . .with Seeds, the next was pray Sir how and in what manner must I sow them, pray be so good Sir as to give me some directions, for my Gardener is a very ignorant Fellow." [19]

With the exception of Franklin, Collinson met few of his American correspondents. He depended on their "Speaking Letters in that Silent Language [to] Convey their most intimate thoughts to my Mind." [20] What is remarkable is how intimate *his* letters are—his dismay at the death of his best friend, Lord Petre; his joy when a dry root takes life; his pleasure at "the peep of a new thing"; his gusto for tastes and fragrances; his terror of snakes and delight when the mud turtle Bartram sent climbs his stairs; his happiness for his friends. His operating principle seems to have been, What I gave away I kept. Meanness wasn't in the man. He was animated all his life by a sense of wonder. He was a dirt-under-the-nails gardener.

Late in life he reflected, "I often times Stand with Wonder & amazement when I View the Inconceivable variety of flowers, Shrubs & Trees now in our Gardens & what they was 40 years Agon, and in that Time what quantities from all North America have annually been Collected by My Means and procuring. . . . Very few

Gardens, if any, excells Mine att Mill Hill for the Rare Exotiks which are my Delight." [21]

He died on August 11, 1768, "seized with a stoppage in his Water which could never be remedied." [22]

This selection is intended to provide a convenient picture of his interests and influences. The letters are presented essentially as he wrote them (or from drafts and copies where the original could not be located). In their sometimes sprawling, scrawling incoherence his letters reflect what Collinson told many of his correspondents: "I am vastly Hurried in Business and no Leisure." Subjects were interrupted when a customer came into his shop or a new thing came to mind, and often a letter was left open for days before the ship that would carry it set sail. Many of his postscripts are longer than the basic letter, and postscripts to postscripts are not uncommon.

His capitalizations and spelling are erratic. Where sense required, the editor has discreetly modernized spellings, inserted dropped words, eliminated underlinings and added minimal punctuation. Collinson's dashes have been replaced with paragraphs, commas, and periods. Interpolations are given within square parentheses. His "Old Style" datings and Quaker spellings of the months have been modernized and their placings standardized at the beginning of each letter.

A brief biography of each addressee appears at the foot of the first letter to that person. Plant identifications have been included where reasonable certainty permitted, but as Collinson wrote Bartram in 1735, "a Compleat History of Plants is not to be found in any author." [January 20, 1735. ALS:HSP] That remains true. For the identifications we have made we have relied on Mabberley, D.J., *The Plant Book . . .* (2nd edition), Cambridge University Press, 1997, and Bailey, L.H. *The Standard Cyclopedia of Horticulture.* New York, 1928. Dr. Ann F. Rhoads, Senior Botanist, Morris Arboretum of the University of Pennsylvania, checked the identifications we attempted.

Martha Armstrong, G.D.R. Bridson, Gina Douglas, and R.G.C. Desmond helped identify subjects for illustrations and locate images. We sought illustrations Collinson might have seen by artists he knew and patronized and, in some instances, supplied with subjects: Mark Catesby, Georg Dionysius Ehret, George Edwards, Philip Miller, Moses Harris, and William Bartram. The American Philosophical Society, Hunt Institute for Botanical Documentation, The Linnean Society of London, the Library Company of Philadelphia, the Royal Society, and Lord and Lady Derby of Knowsley Hall kindly allowed us to use images from their collections without fee.

Dr. John Edmondson, Curator of Botany, Liverpool Museum, and Mrs. Carole LeFaivre-Rochester of Philadelphia proofed the text for the most egregious errors. Those that remain are the editor's.

NOTES

1. PC to George Robins, October 6, 1721: MdHS (not included here).
2. PC to Franklin, April 12, 1747: N-YHS.
3. PC to John Custis, December 15, 1735: AAS.
4. PC to Carl Linnaeus, May 13, 1739: LS.
5. PC to John Bartram, August 16, 1735: HSP.
6. PC to Sir Hans Sloane, [ca. 1730]: BL.
7. *The Annual Register, or a View of the History, Politics, and Literature For the Year 1770.* 5th edition, London, 1794, p. 57.
8. Autograph memorandum, Cambridge Univ. Library.
9. *Annual Register, op. cit.*
10. PC to Carl Linnaeus, October 26, 1747: LS.
11. Plinius (Caius Secundus, the Elder). *The Historie of the World,* 2 vol. in 1, First Edition in English, 1601; vol II, p. 4: APS.
12. PC to John Player, May 19, 1768: Glos. Rec. Off (not included here).
13. Cohen, I. Bernard: *Benjamin Franklin: Experiments,* Cambridge, Harvard University Press, 1941, p.15.
14. PC to John Bartram, August 16, 1735: HSP.
15. Cadwallader Colden to Captain John Rutherford, *Colden Papers* 1743–47, p. 15: N-YHS.
16. PC to Cadwallader Colden, March 7, 1741: N-YHS (not included here).
17. PC to John Bartram, February 3, 1736: HSP.
18. PC to Philip Southcote, October 9, 1752, Draft: LS.
19. "An Account Of The Introduction of American Seeds Into Great Britain, By Peter Collinson," Autograph Memorandum: Natural History Museum, Botany Library, London.
20. PC to John Bartram, December 10, 1762: ALS:HSP.
21. Autograph Memorandum copied at the foot of the Appendix in PC's copy of Philip Miller's *Gardeners Dictionary* (8th edition) at the National Library of Wales, Aberystwyth. Also quoted (in a slightly different form) in Dillwyn, L. W. ed. *Hortus Collinsonianus: An Account of the Plants Cultivated by the Late Peter Collinson, Esq., F.R.S.* Swansea, 1843, p. vi.
22. William Logan, Jr. to his father, in Philadelphia, London, August 14, 1768: HSP.

Acknowledgments

Dr. Whitfield J. Bell, Jr., then American Philosophical Society Librarian, planted the idea of this book and for twenty-five years patiently cultivated it. As an editor of *The Papers of Benjamin Franklin,* he wrote one of the footnotes about Collinson: "His penmanship was loose and careless, and his capitalization and punctuation are the despair of the transcriber who must divine what he produced and meant." (*Franklin* III, 116)

Gina Douglas, librarian and archivist at the Linnean Society of London, helped with transcribing and annotating the letters to Linnaeus, tracked down other letters, researched obscure references and ran down innumerable queries. Mr. G.D.R. Bridson, bibliographer and researcher with the Hunt Institute for Botanical Documentation, Pittsburgh, read the manuscript, made suggestions, and suggested the illustrations. Mr. R.G.C. Desmond, historian, formerly librarian, Royal Botanic Gardens, Kew, offered suggestions, technical and editorial advice, and filled many gaps, as did Dr. John Edmondson, Curator of Botany, Liverpool Museum, Liverpool. The late Edmund and Dorothy Berkeley of Charlottesville, Virginia, helped select as most representative the letters to Bartram included here. The late Joseph and Nesta Ewan, formerly of the Missouri Botanical Garden, St. Louis, and Professor George Frick, of the University of Delaware, Newark, furnished leads and bibliographic support. The American Philosophical Society of Philadelphia supported my work as one of its Library Research Associates and financed it with generous grants from its Michaux Fund. In compliance with the terms of the grant a file of the letters I found (with transcriptions) has been deposited with the American Philosophical Society.

Lady Jean O'Neill, of Lymington, England, author (with Mrs. Elizabeth P. McLean, Garden Historian, Philadelphia) of a forthcoming biography of Peter

Collinson, has been my partner in locating and selecting letters. She provided information about Collinson's life and helped with the notes. Her discovery of Collinson's annotated copies of several editions of Philip Miller's *Gardeners Dictionary* at the National Library of Wales has proved very useful. Elizabeth McLean also contributed plant identifications, answered many questions and offered a number of valuable suggestions.

Many people helped the project along: Edward C. Carter II, Librarian, Roy T. Goodman, Assistant Librarian, Beth Carroll-Horrocks, formerly Manuscripts Librarian, Robert S. Cox, current Manuscripts Librarian, Stephen Catlett and Murphy D. Smith of the American Philosophical Society Library; Martin Antonetti, Curator of Rare Books, and Karen V. Kulik, Associate Curator, Smith College; Peter D. Hingley, Librarian, Royal Astronomical Society, London; the late Edwin Wolf 2nd, then Librarian, John Van Horne, current Librarian, Ms. Wendy Woloson, Bibliographer, and Ms. Erika Piola, Curatorial Assistant, the Library Company of Philadelphia; Dr. R.W. Kiger, Director; Dr. James White, Curator of Art and Principal Research Scholar, Ms. Anita Karg, then Manuscript Librarian; Miss B. G. Callery, then Librarian, Ms. Charlotte Tancin, Librarian, Mr. Michael T. Steiber, then Archivist, Hunt Institute for Botanical Documentation, Pittsburgh; The Right Honorable The Earl of Derby and Mrs. Amanda Askari, Keeper of Collections, Knowsley Hall, Prescott, Merseyside, England; Edwin Bronner, retired librarian, the late Michael Freedman, librarian, Barbara Curtis, and the late Miriam Jones Brown of the Haverford College Library; James E. Mooney, first as director of the Historical Society of Pennsylvania and later as librarian, The New-York Historical Society; Isabel Kendrick, research assistant, The Royal Commission on Historical Manuscripts, London; G.R.D. Allen of the Royal Society for Encouragement of Arts and Manufactures, London; Porter Aichle, then of Bryn Mawr College; Peter Parker, formerly director of the Historical Society of Pennsylvania; E. Charles Nelson, formerly of the National Botanic Garden, Dublin; H. J. McArdle, librarian, Botany School, Oxford University; the late Ralph Sargent, Gummere Professor of English at Haverford College; C. Helen Brock and Peter I. Gautrey, Cambridge University; Dr. Grenville Lucas, OBE, formerly Deputy Director and Keeper of the Herbarium and Library, Ms. Sylvia M. D. FitzGerald, formerly chief librarian and archivist, Royal Botanic Gardens, Kew; Albert E. Sanders, curator of Natural Sciences, The Charleston Museum, Charleston, South Carolina; the late Anna Wells Rutledge, Charleston; Dr. David Moltke-Hansen, director, and Margaretta P. Childs, field archivist, South Carolina Historical Society, Charleston, South Carolina; Roy A. Rauschenberg, Ohio University, Athens, Ohio; the late Edmund and Martha Bray, formerly associated with The Academy of Natural Sciences, Philadelphia; the late Charles van Ravens-waay of Wilmington, Delaware; R. M. Peck and Thomas Peter Bennett formerly of the Academy of Natural Sciences, Philadelphia; Hugh S. Torrens, Department of Geology, University of Keele; Judith M. Diment, formerly Botany Librarian, Dr. Malcolm Beasley, Botany Librarian, Judith Magee, Assistant Botany Librarian, and Julie M.V. Harvey, Entomology Librarian, The Natural History Museum, London; Amy R.W. Meyers, curator of American art, and Carrie Haslett, Research Associate, The Huntington Library, San Marino, CA; and the staffs of Friends Reference Library, London, The Wellcome Institute Library, and the Royal Society, London.

R. Barry Borden of LMA Group, Merion, Pennsylvania, gave valuable computer advice; Angelene Zarnowsky of Philadelphia and Susan Grant of Ardmore, Pennsylvania patiently managed corrections and notes; and William T. Windsor, of Media, Pennsylvania compared the editor's transcriptions to xeroxed copies of Collinson's letters. Mary Anne Hines of Gibbsboro, New Jersey checked the notes, filled in holes, and prepared the indexes.

Special thanks to Carole LeFaivre-Rochester, Editor emeritus, Mary McDonald, Editor, the American Philosophical Society, and to Adrianne Onderdonk Dudden, the book's designer.

Sarracena *(and Frog). Mark Catesby. From Collinson's copy of* Natural History of Carolina, Florida and The Bahama Islands. *2 vols. London, 1730–1747 at Knowsley Hall, Vol. II, plate 69. Courtesy of the Earl of Derby, Knowsley.*

Short Titles and Abbreviations

AAS	American Antiquarian Society, Worcester, MA
APS	American Philosophical Society, Philadelphia
Brett-James	Brett-James, Norman G. *The Life of Peter Collinson.* London: Edgar G. Dunstan & Co., [1926]
Berkeley and Berkeley	Berkeley, Edmund and Dorothy Smith Berkeley, eds. *The Correspondence of John Bartram.* Tallahassee Press, University of Florida, 1992
BL	The British Library
Bodleian	Bodleian Library, Oxford University
BPL	Boston Public Library
Coll. Phys	College of Physicians of Philadelphia
DAB	*Dictionary of American Biography*
Desmond	Desmond, Ray, ed. *Dictionary of British and Irish Botanists and Horticulturists.* London: Taylor & Francis, 1994
DNB	*Dictionary of National Biography*
DSB	*Dictionary of Scientific Biography*
EB	*Encyclopedia Britannica.* Edinburgh, 1771
Erlangen	Universität Bibl. Erlangen
Fothergill	Fothergill, John. *Some account of the Late Peter Collinson . . .* London, 1770
Franklin	*The Papers of Benjamin Franklin.* New Haven: Yale University Press, 1959–

Frick	Frick, George F. "Peter Collinson" in *The Dictionary of Scientific Biography*. New York: Scribners, 1971, Vol. III, p. 349–51
FRL	Friends Reference Library, London
Glos. Rec. Off.	Gloucestershire Record Office
Gray	The Gray Herbarium, Harvard University
Haverford	Haverford College Library, Haverford, Pennsylvania
Henrey	Henrey, Blanche. *British Botanical and Horticultural Literature before 1800*. Oxford, 1975
Hindle	Hindle, Brooke. *The Pursuit of Science in Revolutionary America, 1735–1789*. Chapel Hill, 1956
HSP	Historical Society of Pennsylvania, Philadelphia
Hunt	Hunt Institute for Botanical Documentation, Pittsburgh
LC	The Library of Congress
LCP	The Library Company of Philadelphia
LS	The Linnean Society of London
MaHS	Massachusetts Historical Society, Boston
MdHS	Maryland Historical Society, Baltimore
NHM	Natural History Museum, London
N-YHS	New-York Historical Society, New York
Oxford	Oxford Universtity
PC	Peter Collinson
PMHB	*Pennsylvania Magazine of History and Biography*
PRO	Public Record Office, London
RSA	Royal Society for the Encouragement of Arts, Manufactures and Commerce, London
RS	The Royal Society, London
Swem	Swem, Earl G. *Brothers of the Spade: Correspondence of Peter Collinson, of London, and of John Custis, of Williamsburg, Virginia, 1734–1746*. Worcester, Massachusetts: American Antiquarian Society, 1949
UPa	University of Pennsylvania Library
VaHS	Virginia Historical Society, Richmond
Yale	Yale University Library

Chronology of some events in Peter Collinson's life

1694	Born January 28
1696	Went to live with grandmother
1711	Working in father's mercery shop
1722	Begins catalogue of his plants
1724	Marries Mary Russell
1728	Elected Fellow of the Royal Society
1735	Linnaeus visits PC's "museum" in Grace Church Street, London
1737	Elected Fellow of the Society of Antiquaries
1739	In a letter to Linnaeus PC acknowledges the naming of *Collinsonia canadensis*
1742	Lord Petre dies
1747	Elected Fellow of the Royal Society of Sweden
1748	Peter Kalm visits and describes PC's garden at Peckham
1749	PC moves to Ridgeway House, Mill Hill (having spent two years transferring his plants from Peckham)
1753	Mary Russell dies
1757	Franklin visits PC
1763	His brother and business partner James dies
1765	Retires from business
1768	Dies, August 11

"Forget not Mee & My Garden . . ."

1 ❧ TO HANS SLOANE

ALS:BL

[circa 1725]

Hans Sloane

    I am heartyly Sorry I happen'd to be so Engaged when you was so Kind to Call on Mee, but I hope you'l please to Consider Mee as a Trades Man in hurry of Business which prevented Mee paying the Respect I would a done.

    I have had Lately come 50 Bottles of Curious Creatures in Spirits & Severall other Curiosities. If thou'l please to do Mee the Favour of Another Visit any Morning I hope I shall be att home & Disengaged to Wait on thee, which is a pleasure I am very fond off & will be particularly Acceptable to thy Sincere Friend.

P. COLLINSON

Thursday
Letter came in a [box] of Mine from Carolina.

HANS SLOANE (1660–1753), FRS, pupil of Tournefort, physician to Queen Anne and to George I, made Baronet in 1716. At the start of his career he served as physician to the governor of Jamaica, 1687–89, studied its natural history and returned with eight hundred species of plants from which he prepared *Catalogus Plantarum quae in Insula Jamaica . . .* , 1696. He became secretary (1693–1712), then president (1727–41) of the Royal Society; acquired the land on which the Chelsea Physic Garden was located, and in 1721 transferred it in perpetuity to the Company of Apothecaries. He wrote *A Voyage to the Islands Madera, Barbados, Nieves, S. Christophers and Jamaica with the Natural History of the Last,* 1707–25. In 1732 he became one of the promoters of the colony of Georgia. He was the chief patron of British botanists during the first half of the eighteenth century. See Reveal, James L., and James S. Pringle, "Taxonomic botany and floristics," pp. 157–192. In: Flora of North America Editorial Committee (ed), *Flora of North America north of Mexico* Vol. 1. New York, 1993, p. 160.

Sloane was Collinson's earliest influential friend, an ardent collector who recognized in Collinson a kindred spirit and supported him, introducing him to influential friends and promoting his election to the Royal Society, which significantly expanded PC's range of acquaintance.

In *Some Account of the Late Peter Collinson . . .* John Fothergill described Collinson as "one of those few who visited Sir Hans at all times familiarly, and continued so to do to this latest period; their inclinations and pursuits in natural history being the same, a firm friendship had early been established between them." [London, 1770]

A noted physician and philanthropist, Sloane was said never to have refused a patient who could not afford to pay. At his death he bequeathed to the nation his extensive library and natural history collections (including an asbestos purse Benjamin Franklin sold him on his first visit to London in 1725 [See *Franklin* I, 54]), on condition that his estate be paid £20,000 for materials which had cost him more than £50,000. This was the foundation of The British Museum.

Collinson was mentioned in Sloane's will and invited to his funeral. (See Collinson to Gronovius, March 24, 1753.) "Why he was not elected one of the curators of the British Museum was a matter of wonder to many of his acquaintance. He was one of the founder's most ancient and intimate Friends, a contributor to this collection, acquainted with the subjects, and had done more towards promoting researches into natural history than perhaps most of his contemporaries; but he had no greater ambition than to collect what knowledge he could, and to render this knowledge subservient as much as possible to the good of mankind." [Fothergill, *Some Account . . .* , pp. 15–16. And see Kippis, Andrew. *Biographia Britannica,* 2nd ed. vol. IV. London, 1789, pp. 34–42.] Notwithstanding this "well-known disappointment" (DNB), Collinson maintained a life-long interest in Sloane's collection. (See Collinson to Watson, October 5, 1762.) (DNB; de Beer, Gavin. *Sir Hans Sloane and the British Museum.* London, 1953; MacGregor, Arthur, ed. *Sir Hans Sloane.* London, 1994.) In the many references to the Museum in his correspondence, Collinson gives no hint of disappointment. (See for example his letters of March 24, 1753; April 29, 1757; and October 5, 1762.)

Opposite page: Sir Hans Sloane. Sir Godfrey Kneller, 1716. Royal Society

2 ❧ TO MARY COLLINSON

ALS:BL
Rotterdam, July 27, 1728

My Dearest,

Thine gave Mee more satisfaction than I can Express. The very sight of thy Dear Characters made my heart Leap for Joye, but when I read the Contents, where Love & Tenderness flows in every Line, how did my Soul Spring to thee in Extasies of Love.

I struggle Dayly with contending passions, a strong Desire to see thee, & yett now I am on this Side the Herring pond a few fine Towns & a fine Countrey Lies Near us. We have meet with some of our Country Folks & Bro. Michael's Acquaintance[1] & to Morrow wee sett forward for Antwerp & so Round to Calais & Dover Home. Wee left Amsterdam & went by Coach to Utrech the finest Country in all Holland. Vast number of fine Seats & Gardens afforded us agreeable Entertainment & here is fine Waterworks, Grottos & Cascades. Wee left this & went to Targou [Ter Gouw—now Gouda] where is a fine Church Recon'd to have the Most & finest painting on glass in the world.[2]

Pray my Dear tell Brother James[3] I Rec'd his long kind Letter & will write to him next post. Wee are all Very well & hearty and of the Sober party.

I kiss thy hand. Vale PC

The places where Wee shall Stay will be so uncertain & our Stay so Short that I can't fix any place for thee to Direct too on this Side the Water, but I hope to Meet with one of thine att Ed Warrys att Dover. Pray my Love fail not. PC

Pray Lett Bro Jemmy see those Letters of mine that Relate to my Travels.

I am glad to hear all friends are well. My Dear Love to all from my Dearest thy most affectionate husband.

P. COLLINSON

MARY RUSSELL COLLINSON (1704–1753), PC's wife. They married in 1724. This is the only surviving letter to her, written in the course of the only trip Collinson is known to have made out of the country. No portrait is known.

1. Michael Russell, PC's brother-in-law.
2. Probably Sint Janskerk or Groote Kerk near Gouda.
3. James Collinson (1695–1762), PC's brother and business partner, also referred to as Jemmy.

3 ❧ TO WILLIAM BYRD II

Contemporary transcription: Westover MSS, VaHS
[circa 1730]

Col. Byrd, kind friend,

I'd the pleasure of yours June 14th per Captain Boswell, & am glad to find mine contain'd any thing worth your notice. I wish the success may answer both our expectations. I shall be glad to hear of the prosperity of your vineyard, & which sort of grape succeeds best. Why should it not with you as well as at the Cape of Good Hope, but there must be a time for all things & different climates require different management. At the Cape where the wind perpetually blows a tempest, the vines with great care are run on stages close to the ground, & kept constantly tied and indeed the pains they bestow is very well recompenced by the excellent wines they produce.

But I am yet of the mind that at the time a year that your natural country grapes are ripe, if a person that was a judge was to mark those that were most elegant for size & flavour & soon after take cuttings & plant in a fresh generous soil & regularly cultivated, I can't help thinking but they'd be much improv'd & being natural to your climate & seasons would produce better than foreigners & perhaps may yield a wine peculiar for strength & flavour. I had this year a letter from North Carolina where amongst many curious remarks on the produce of that country the author says that he saw & eat grapes growing wild, as large & as good as any he ever eat up the Streights [of Gibraltar]. I hope I may depend on him; if so, what a noble produce that province would yield if rightly cultivated. I cou'd be glad you'd make the experiment of a quarter of an acre with the best & choicest of your country grapes. That wou'd be enough to see the produce.

William Byrd II. Sir Godfrey Kneller. Virginia Historical Society

WILLIAM BYRD II (1674–1744), FRS, planter, author, colonial official, born in Virginia, educated in England, returned to his family's estate, "Westover," in Virginia in 1693. He served in the Virginia Council of State, and in 1728 was appointed one of the commissioners to run the dividing line between Virginia and North Carolina. Byrd had extensive frontier holdings, was interested in western expansion, and was one of the first to warn of French designs on the Ohio Valley. He wrote *The History of the Dividing Line,* *A Journey to the Land of Eden, A Progress to the Mines,* and *An Essay on Balk Tobacco,* none of which were published in his lifetime. (DAB)

William Byrd II's correspondence is reproduced in *The Correspondence of the Three William Byrds of Westover, Virginia—1684–1776,* edited by Marion Tingling. Charlottesville, The University Press of Virginia for The Virginia Historical Society, 1977.

ALS:BL

Friday [circa 1730]

Dear Sir Hans,

It is my Duty to return you many Thanks for your Last kind present of Shells. Please to remember that they are bestow'd on One that knows how to Value them not only for their Rarity but for the Sake of the Donor, who I shall always remember with the greatest Esteem, and In Gratitude I ought So to Do, For you have favour'd Mee with your Friendship & have always been my Patron.

But my Dear friend amongst the Great Variety that you gave Mee before & now, To make my Collection Compleat some Specimens of Spotted Rhomb is wanting, or the Rhombus Reticulatis of Leister No 39.[1]

If I mistake not I remember to have seen you have a great Number & Variety of Duplicates in a Cabinet that stands on the Left Hand as I went into the Roome where the Mummy lies.

I Rely on your Goodness & Candor to pardon this Freedome & if I am Mistaken or my Memory Fails Mee pray Excuse Mee.

I have you Frequently in my Mind and am Fearfull least the Hurry and Fatigue of Removeing is not to much for you. Pray be mindfull of your own Health & Ease & do nothing to prejudice Either.

My Hurry of Busines will be over in 2 or 3 Weeks, then I shall do my Self the pleasure to Wait on you.

I am with the Greatest Regard & Respect, Your Affectionate Friend

P. COLLINSON

---

1. Martin Lister (1638–1712), FRS, physician and conchologist. Published *Historia sive synopsis methodica conchyliorum.* London, 1685–1692. The work is divided into sections of types of shells and within each section the plates are numbered

Right: Rhombis Reticulatis. *Martin Lister,* Historia sive synopsis methodica conchyliorum. *London, 1685–1692. #39. The Library Company of Philadelphia.*

Opposite page: "The Monax or Marmotte of America." George Edwards, A Natural History of Uncommon birds and of some other rare and undescribed animals, quadrupeds, reptiles, fishes, insects, etc. *London, 1743–1751. Vol 1, plate 104. In his preface Edwards mentions Collinson as one of the "generous Encouragers of this Work." The Library Company of Philadelphia.*

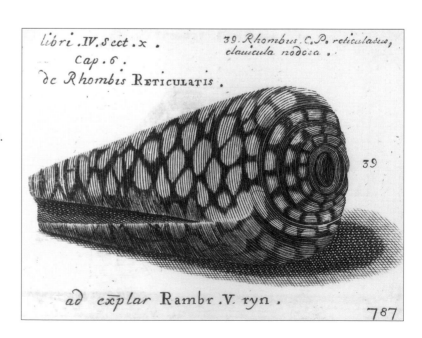

ALS:BL
[circa 1730]
Monday

Sir Hans

The Bearer conveys to you Just Imported from Virginia a Creature not Discribed by any writers of those Countrys. It Seems to be between the Rat & the Squirrel. It is called Monac and is Reconed One of the Seven Sleepers [*Marmota monax,* woodchuck].[1] Att or Near His time of Sleeping He Sheads his Hair. He Requires to be kept very Warm & Fed with all Sorts of greens, Aples, Carrots, Chesnutts etc. If he is putt in a Large Squirrel box filled with Hay for as he grows naked he grows very Tender.

I wish it may be acceptable.

From yours

P. COLLINSON

I hope you have Received from Lady Wager a She Posham with three young ones.

1. Years later Collinson annotated the illustration of "The Monac of North America" in his copy of Mark Catesby's *Natural History of Carolina.* [1743] as follows:

The only Natural Historian that has mentioned this animal that I ever mett with is Lawson in his History of Carolina who only mentions any quality peculiar to it.

About September he made his retreat into a hole he had made in a corner of the cellar. There he made his bed with everything he could pick up of things that the servants happened to drop there. He continued sleeping till about March.

From thence he was call'd one of the seven sleepers. How the number seven came in I can't say.

This animal was brought mee alive from Maryland. I gave it to Sr Hans Sloane & [it] lived with him many years and became a domestic animal, run up and down stairs like a catt or dog but loved the kitchen best for the sake of the cook's favours. Lived on Bread, roots & greens, call'd the Gound Hogg of Monac or seven sleeper from Virginia 1733. Is neither rabit, rat, nor squirrel & has some propertys of each.   P.C.

[Autograph Memorandum Signed; Knowsley]

ALS:FRL
London, March 27, 1732

Dear Friend

Thy Long Expected kind Letter came Safe to my hands and It is a pleasure to Mee to hear of thy Welfare & of the kind reception thee Mett with amongst Friends & that Brotherly Love the Badge of Decipleship a Bounds. May the god of Love Shead it more & more Abroad In the Hearts of all Men but in particular those of Our Society, for where this is Wanting all pretences to Religion are vain.

I am Glad to learn of thy Success with last years Seeds. Considering the Dry Season thee has fair'd better then Our Curious Gardeners about London.

We are now in Great Want of Rain for the Gardens & for the Summer Corn. I never remember the Like, The Ponds & Ditches quite Empty. All Last Week the Sun & Air was as Warm & warmer then Sometimes in June.

This Last year prov'd very kindly for Grapes. Was not Ever remembered to be Ripen'd to greater perfection In England.

A Gentleman of my Intimate acquaintance from the Fourth Year of planting a Vineyard of Two Acres made Eight Hogsheads of Excellent Burgundy without any Art but pure Juice of the Grape, which those that was Good Judges in wine was glad to give Him Twenty Guineas a hogshead. I have tasted It Several Times & have not often tasted better Burgundy from France. For this had the Richness, Colour & Flavour of Fine Burgundy & He made besides from same Spot a good hogshead of Rich White Wine.

Abundance of Gentlemen have planted Vineyards in Our Southern parts. The Wines from Abroad are so Adulterated that it is a Great Discouragement to private Gentlemen to Send for them, which Encourages them to plant Here & to know what they Drink. Many Others Besides that I know have made fine Rich Good Wine Last Year.

There is Lately come from Alleppo in Turky Some Berries of the Juniper it is Call'd, but I take it to be a Sort of Cypress by the Figure of the Berry & the Number of Seeds in Each Berrie.

I have sent thee a Few & a Few Ever Green Oke Acorns. They Endure Our Winters Here very well but must be Sown where they are to Stand for they Will not bear Removeing.

In the Winter whilst young may be Easily Protected by Covering them with Pea Straw which Lies Hollow. Is not Subject to Rott so is Even Better then Common Straw.

The juniper may Require some protection the First Year but I conclude it pretty Hardy. Besides thee'l find some Mixt Pine Seeds from South Carolina which I wish is not to tender for your climate.

A Curious Gentleman from Maryland [Richard Lewis] Sent Mee a Poem of his own Composing which att the Request of my Intimates was printed Here.[1] I Doubt not but thee'l find it very Entertaining being Interwoven with many diverting Incidents & Fine Reflections.

I am Straightened for Time being not willing to miss so favouraable an oppertunity of Conveyance by my Neighbor Robert & my pens bad which obliges mee to Conclude. Thy very Sincere & Loving Friend

P. COLLINSON

My Dear Molley Joyns with Mee in Send Love & Respects to thee. My Grandmother
Mary Russell has been so bad for Severall Months that I am afraid shee will not gett over
It. M: Plumstead is pretty near her time. Her Dear Love waits on thee.

THOMAS STORY (1670?–1742), Quaker preacher and lawyer. At William Penn's request Story went to Pennsylvania in 1698 and stayed for sixteen years. He was chosen the first recorder of Philadelphia, was a member of the Council of State, Keeper of the Great Seal, Master of the Rolls, and in 1706 was elected mayor but paid a fine for declining to serve. He was interested in forestry and late in life planted large numbers of English and American trees on his property at Carlisle. (DNB)

1. Richard Lewis (c. 1700–1734), Maryland schoolmaster and clerk of the Maryland General Assembly (1732). He wrote "Proposals . . . for founding an Academy at Annapolis" which envisioned an institution that combined the intellectual training of his alma mater Eton and more practical education in trades and husbandry. The poem referred to is: "A Journey from Patapsco to Annapolis, April 4, 1730," first printed in the *Pennsylvania Gazette* May 20, 1731, then in the *London Weekly Register* Jan. 1, 1732. Collinson may be referring to its publication in the *Gentleman's Magazine* II (March 1732): pp. 669–671.

Lewis also corresponded with Collinson on scientific topics and had letters on the Aurora Borealis, earthquakes and insects published in the *Philosophical Transactions* in 1732–1733.

7 ❧ TO THE LIBRARY COMPANY

ALS:Gray
London, July 22, 1732

Gentlemen

I am a Stranger to most of you but not to your laudable Designe to erect a publick Library. I beg your acceptance of my Mite: Sr Isaac Newtons Philosophy & Philip Millers Gardening Dictionary. It will be an Instance of great Candour too accept the Intention & Good Will of the Giver and not regard the meaness of the Gift.

I wish you Success & am with much Respect,

Yours, P. COLLINSON

The Library Company of Philadelphia was founded in 1731 by Benjamin Franklin and a group of his friends as a subscription library.

On November 7, 1732 Joseph Breintnall (see footnote 1 to Jan. 24, 1734) sent the following letter (composed by Franklin) acknowledging Collinson's:

Your Goodness in assisting Mr Hopkinson in the Choice and purchase of our Books, and the valuable present you have so generously made us, demand our most grateful Acknowledgements. . . . Every Encouragement to an Infant Design, by Men of Merit and Consideration, gives new Spirit to the Undertakers, strengthens the Hands of all concern'd, and greatly tends to secure and establish their Work. . . . We wish you every kind of Happiness and Prosperity, and particularly that you may never want Power nor Opportunity of enjoying that greatest of Pleasures to a benevolent Mind, the giving Pleasure to others. (*Franklin* I, 248–249)

Collinson served as The Library Company's unpaid London agent for twenty-two years until a new secretary complained (because postage was expensive) of his sending parcels of seed, cloth, and used clothing to John Bartram in the Company's trunks.

After Collinson died, Benjamin Franklin wrote Collinson's son

Michael:

[A]s you may be unacquainted with the following Instances of [your father's] Zeal and Usefulness in promoting Knowledge, which fell within my Observation, I take the Liberty of informing you, That in the year 1730, a subscription Library being set on foot in Philadelphia, he encouraged the same by making several very valuable Presents to it, and in procuring others from his Friends; And as the Library Company had a considerable Sum arising annualy [sic] to be laid out in Books, and needed a judicious Friend in London to transact the Business for them, he voluntarily and chearfully undertook that Service, and executed it for more than 30 years successively, assisting in the Choice of the Books, and taking the whole Care of Collecting and Shipping them without accepting any Consideration for this Trouble. The Success of this Library (greatly owing to his kind Countenance and good Advice) encouraged the erecting others in different Places, on the same Plan; and it is supposed there are now upwards of 30 subsisting in the several Colonies, which have contributed greatly to the Spreading of useful Knowledge in that part of the World, the Books he recommended being all of that kind, and the Catalogue of this first Library being much respected and followed by those Libraries that succeeded. During the same time he transmitted to

Bartram's house and garden. William Bartram sketch in Peter Collinson's common-place book of images at Knowsley Hall. Courtesy of the Earl of Derby, Knowsley.

the Directors the earliest Accounts of every new European Improvement in Agriculture and the Arts, and every philosophical Discovery. . . .

Franklin to Michael Collinson, February 8, 1770. *Franklin.* Vol XVII, pp 65–66.

8 🦬 TO JOHN BARTRAM

ALS:HSP
London, January 24, 1734

My Good Friend John Bartram,

I am very much Oblig'd to thee for thy Two Choice Cargos of plants which Came very Safe & in good Condition & are very Curious Rare & Well worth my Acceptance. I am very Sensible of the great pains & many Tiresome Trips to collect So many Rare plants Scatter'd att a distance. I shall not forget It, but in some measure to Show my Gratitude tho not In proportion to thy Trouble I have sent thee a small token, a Callico gown for thy Wife & some Odd Little things that may be of use amongst thy Children & family.

They Come in a Box of Books to my Worthy friend, Jos Breintnall [1] with another parcel of Wast paper which will Serve to wrap up seeds &c. and there is Two Quires of Brown & one of Whited Brown paper which I propose for this use & purpose & will save thee a great deal of Trouble in writing, That Is, when thee Observes a Curious plant in Flower or when thee gathers Seed of a plant thee has an Intention to Convey to Mee a Discription off, on both these Occasions, thee has nothing More to do then to gather Branches or Spriggs of the plants then in Flower with their Flowers on and with their Seed Vessells fully Form'd, for by these Two Charisticks the Genus is known that they belong too.

Then Take these and Spread them between the Sheets of Brown paper Laying the Stems Streight & Leaves Smooth & Regular & when this is Done putt a Moderate Weight on a Board the Size of the paper. In Two Days Remove the Specimens into the Other Quire of Brown paper, keeping the Weight on, & then In a Week or Two, being pretty Well Dryed, convey them thence Into the Quire of Whited Brown paper. Thus when now & then thee observes a Curious odd plant thee may treat it in this Manner by which thee will Convey a More Lively Idea then the best Description, & when thee Gathers Seeds Mark the Same Number on the Seeds as thee Marks it In the Sheet where the Specimen Is, only writeing under it the Country Name. So once a year Returne Mee the Quire of Whited Brown paper with the dryed Specimens Tied Fast between Two Broad Boards & then I will send some More in their Roome. When the Sheets of paper will Hold it, putt one, Two or Three Specimens of the Same plant in the Same sheet So they will but Lay smooth by each other.

Besides what I have further to propose by this Methode is thy own Improvement in the knowledge of plants, for thou shall Send Mee another Quire of Duplicates of the Same Specimens. I will get them Named by Our Most knowing Botanists & then Returne them again which will Improve thee More then Books, for It Is impossible for any One Author to give a General History of plants. Lett the specimens be of the Length of the paper.

Thee canst not think how well the Little Case of plants came being putt under the Captains Bed & saw not the Light till I sent for it, but then Capt Wright had a very Quick

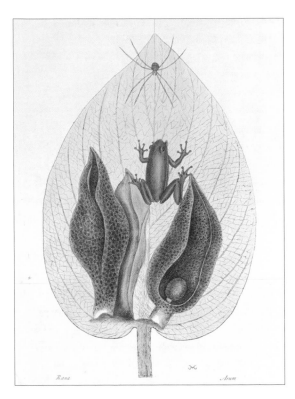

Symplocarpus foetidus, *Skunk weed. Mark Catesby.*
From Peter Collinson's copy of Natural History of
Carolina, Florida and The Bahama Islands. *2 vols,
London, 1730–1747 at Knowsley Hall, Vol II, plate
71. Courtesy of the Earl of Derby, Knowsley.*

*Catesby noted, "The introduction of this most curi-
ous plant, with innumerable others, is owing to the indefatigable attachment of Mr Collinson, who, in the
year 1735, received it from Pennsylvania, and in the
Spring following it displayed itself in this manner at
Peckham."*

passage & it was putt on board In a Right Month for when plants
are down in the Ground & in the Mid Winter months they may be
Stowed any where. But it must not be attempted any time this side
Xmas.

The Warmth of the Ship & want of Air had Occasion'd the
Skunk Weed [*Symplocarpus foetidus*] to putt forth Two Fine Blossoms very Beautifull. It is of the Arum genus. The Cedum is a
very Rare pretty plant, the Leaves finely Vein'd. It came very fresh
& Green. Thy Herb Two Pence [*Lysimachia nummularia,* Creeping Jenny loosestrife] was very Acceptable. I have had It formerly,
but I lost It. It is a pretty plant.

The Cane-wood is pretty Common in Our Gardens. It goes
Here by the name of the Virginian Guelder Rose. The two Laurells [*Kalmia*] was very Fresh & Lively, & the Shrub Honesuckles
[deciduous azalea] which I had formerly from So Caroliny flower
very fine but in Two or Three years went off. Neither our Soil or
Climate agreed with It. But yours perhaps from the Northward
may do better. The Laurell & Shrub Honesuckle are plants I much
Value.

I wish att a proper season Thee Would procure a Strong Box
2 feet Square & about 15 or 18 Inches Deep, but a foot Deep in
Mould will be enough. Then Collect half a Dozen Laurells & half
a Dozen Shrub Honesuckles & plant in this Box, but be sure make
the bottome of the Box full of Large Holes & Cover the Holes with
Tiles or oyster shells to Lett the Water draine better off. Then Lett
this Box stand in a proper place in thy Garden for Two or three
years till the plants have taken good Root & made good Shoots. But
thee must be Care full to Water it in Dry Weather.[2]

I wish that thee would not fail to putt 3 or 4 Specimens of the
Sprigs of the Laurell with the flowers fully Blown (for I Long to
see it) in the paper Transferring them from one to another as I
have Directed. As my design is not to give thee More Trouble so a
few Specimens will Content Mee.

I have Further to Request thee to putt up a little Box of plants (yearly) In Earth such
as thou finds in the Woods that are odd & uncommon.

What Thee Observes of the Frost to be sure had the effect thee Describes. I once Remember one like it in England but the Effects was not so severe.

I hope next year thee will be Able to make Some collections that may make thee some
Returns.

The White Flowering Bay [*Magnolia virginiana,* Swamp Bay] is a plant that grows In
Moist places. The leaves are Long, of a Bay Shape and of a Silver Colour on the back of the
Leaves. It bears a fine Large White flower Like the Water Lillie with a Fine perfum'd
Smell which is succeeded with a Seed Vessel of a Cone like Figure. I have a plant that
Flowers finely In my Garden. It is in abundance of places in Maryland, but weither it is
found More Northward I can't say. It is a fine plant to adorn thy Own Garden. But give
Thyself no trouble about It. And as the Firr & Cypress Cones are not found Near thee Wee

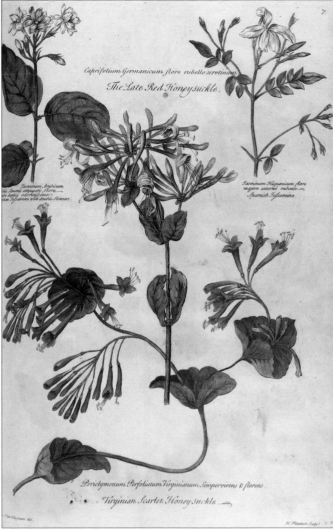

Above left: Kalmia angustifolia, *Sheep laurel" (Chamaedaphne). Mark Catesby. From Peter Collinson's copy
of* Natural History of Carolina . . . *at Knowsley Hall,* Vol II, plate 98. *Courtesy of the Earl of Derby,
Knowsley.*

"*The noxious Qualities of this elegant Plant lessens that Esteem which its Beauty claims; for the Deer feed
on its green Leaves with Impunity; yet when Cattle and Sheep, by severe Winters deprived of better Food, feed
on the Leaves of these Plants, a great many of them die annually . . .*

"*After several unsuccessful Attempts to propagate it from Seeds, I procured Plants of it several Times from
America, but with little better Success . . . till my curious Friend Mr. Peter Collinson, excited by a view of its
dried Specimens, and Descriptions of it, procured some Plants of it from Pennsylvania, which climate being
nearer to that of England, then from whence mine came, Some Bunches of Blossoms were produced in
July 1740 and in 1741. . . .*"

Above right: Shrub Honesuckle— "Virginia Scarlet Honeysuckle." *Georg Dionysius Ehret. Philip Miller,*
Catalogus Plantarum . . . , *Plate 7, American Philosophical Society.*

will wait for some More favourable oppertunity to Collect them. Send First Those Seeds that are Near thee.

The Box of seeds came very Safe & in Good Order. Thy Remarks on them are very Curious but I think take up to Much of thy Time & thought. I would not make my Correspondence Burdensome but must Desire thee to Continue the same Collections over again & to prevent Trouble only Number the papers & give the Country Name or any Name thee may know it by. Again, then keep a List of them by thee with ye Number to the Names & when they Come Here those that do not Come up, Wee have only to write to Thee for the Same Seed to such a Number to send over again.

As I designe to make a present of part of these seeds to a very Curious person[3] I hope to procure thee some present for thy Trouble of Collecting.

I am thy very sincere friend.   P. COLLINSON

JOHN BARTRAM (1699–1777), Quaker farmer and self-taught botanist, lived on the Schuylkill River near Philadelphia. Through Dr. Samuel Chew, a physician in Maryland and Philadelphia, and Joseph Breintnall (whom he assisted by collecting and identifying local plants), Bartram was introduced to Peter Collinson in the early 1730s. The two never met, but their correspondence over thirty-four years forms one of the great records of enduring friendship and eighteenth century natural science. Collinson read a number of Bartram's letters to the Royal Society and arranged for some to be published in the Society's *Philosophical Transactions*. Bartram was largely responsible for providing the North American plants Collinson introduced into cultivation in England. Through Collinson's efforts Bartram was named King's Botanist in 1764 with an annual stipend of £ 50. (DSB; Berkeley and Berkeley, *The Life and Travels of John Bartram*. Tallahassee: University Presses of Florida, 1982). No portrait is known for a certainty.

Berkeley and Berkeley give this as the earliest surviving letter from Collinson to Bartram and date it 1735. The year is not legible. The editor believes it was written in 1734.

1. Joseph Breintnall (d. 1746), Quaker merchant in Philadelphia, secretary of the Library Company 1731–46, sheriff of Philadelphia 1735–38, described by Benjamin Franklin as "good-natur'd, friendly . . . a great Lover of Poetry, reading all he could meet with, and writing some that was tolerable; very ingenious in many little Nicknackeries, and of sensible Conversation." He recommended John Bartram to Peter Collinson as "a very proper person" to furnish seeds and plants. He was an amateur naturalist, sent leaf impressions to Collinson (two volumes of his excellent leaf impressions are at the Library Company of Philadelphia) and wrote Collinson about the aurora borealis and his reaction to a rattlesnake bite. (*Franklin* I, 114)

2. Collinson was a pioneer in working out techniques of live plant transportation and methods of shipping seeds and bulbs. See PC to Bartram January 20, 1735; June 19–28, 1735; February 3, 1736. More generally, see Ellis, John. *Directions of bringing over seeds and plants from the East Indies . . . in a state of vegetation*. London, 1770; and Some *Additional Observations . . . for the benefit of our American colonies*. London, 1773. See also, Desmond, R. "Transportation of plants" in *The European Discovery of Indian Flora*. London, 1992, pp 309–22; and "The problems of transporting plants" in *The Garden: a celebration of one thousand years of British gardening*. Victoria & Albert Musem, London, 1979, 90–104.

3. Probably Robert James, 8th Baron Petre (1713–1742), FRS, English Catholic, Collinson's dearest friend and, briefly, Bartram's most important patron. Petre maintained extensive gardens at Ingatestone and later at Thorndon Hall in Essex which included a great number of foreign trees and shrubs. John Hill helped arrange his gardens; his gardeners included James Gordon, later a celebrated nursery man at Mile End, and John Miller, Philip Miller's brother. Petre is generally credited with introducing *Camellia japonica* L. into cultivation in England. He was among William Houstoun's subscribers for a 1732 trip to the Spanish American colonies to collect plants to take to Georgia for cultivation. Linnaeus named *Petrea L.* in his honor. (Desmond; Henrey) See also Collinson to Bartram July 3, 1742. No portrait is known.

Opposite page: Magnolia virginiana, *Sweet flowering bay. Mark Catesby. From Peter Collinson's copy of* Natural History of Carolina . . . at Knowsley Hall, *Vol I, plate 39. Courtesy of the Earl of Derby, Knowsley.*
"*This beautiful Flowering Tree is a Native both of Virginia and Carolina, and is growing at Mr. Fairchild's in Hoxton and at Mr. Collinson's at Peckham, where it has for some years produced its fragrant Blossoms, requiring no protection from the Cold of our Severest Winters.*"

9 🐌 TO JOHN RUSSELL, 4TH DUKE OF BEDFORD

Draft ALS:LS
May 16, 1734

Noble Friend

You seeme to Intitle Mee to this freedome by the great Friendship & Favour you have shown Mee, the sending Mee my Late Worthy Friend Dr Lloyds Legacy.[1] It is an Instance of Great Justice due to his Memory and of great Confidence in Mee. I shall always retain a gratefull sence for this favour. Do wish it was in my power to retaliate otherwise then by my sincere thanks.

But it is my Misfortune in my Sphere of Life that I can contribute but little either to your profit or your pleasures unless by my Experience in plantations & Gardens. All that I know in these Matters are devoted to your Service and you may with Freedome Command Mee who am with Great Respect yours

PC

JOHN RUSSELL, 4th Duke of Bedford (1710–1771), an early subscriber for John Bartram's boxes of seeds. Maintained a famous garden at Woburn, Bedfordshire. See PC to Russell, April 12, 1759.
1. Probably Robert Lumley Lloyd, D.D. (d.1730), rector of St. Paul's, Covent Garden, a patron of horticulture and the owner of a famous garden at Cheam in Surrey. At his death Lloyd left his estate at Cheam to the Duke of Bedford. We do not know what the legacy was. (Henrey)

10 🐌 TO HANS SLOANE

ALS:BL
London, June 20, 1734

Sir Hans,

I Presum'd It might not be unacceptable to you & the Rest of the Gentlemen [Fellows of the Royal Society] to see a Sloth. It is well preserved. It came last from Jamaica, but I conclude is no native of that Island because [it is] not Mentioned In your Natural History.[1]

Mr Edwards[2] has taken a Draught of It. With it come the Horns of a Stagg from New England, which project forward & are quite Different from our English Deer.

I am Very Much Yours   P. COLLINSON

There is also Two pair of Row Bucks Horns from the Highlands, which may be a Rarity to them that have not seen them before.

1. *Catalogus Plantarum quae in Insula Jamaica . . .* London, 1696.
2. George Edwards (1694–1773), FRS, artist, ornithologist, and librarian of the Royal College of Physicians. He revised Mark Catesby's *Natural History of Carolina,* 1754, published *A Natural History of Uncommon Birds, and of some other rare and undescribed animals, quadrupeds, reptiles, fishes, insects, etc.* London, 1743–1751, and *Gleanings of Natural History.* London, 1758–64. Collinson is mentioned in several of his descriptions as having supplied the subject.

Sloth. George Edwards. Gleanings of Natural History. *London, 1758–64. Plate 310. Collinson supplied the subject. The Library Company of Philadelphia.*

John Custis ("Tulip" Custis). Artist unknown. Washington and Lee University archive, Washington–Custis collection.

ALS:AAS
London, October 20,1734

Kind Friend
Mr John Custis

I am Infinitely Oblig'd to you for your kind present But what much Enhances the Obligation, on my side, Is that being an Intire stranger you shou'd take so much pains to Gratifie Mee. I can't Enough commend the Methode you took to Convey this Rare plant[1] to my hands by sending the seed by one ship & the plantt by another the seed came safe & the box with the plant.

It wou'd have given you pleasure to see the Contending passions of Joye and trouble Exert themselves by Turns. You may be sure I had Joye Enough to hear the box was Come but when I rece'd It & not one remains of a Leafe appear'd How my heart sunk & all my hopes Vanish'd but then again when I turn'd the mould out, to see such a fine sound root, what an Exult of pleasure. How often I survey'd It and anticipated the Time of its growth, by Imagineing what Class & what sort of Flower & Leafe, such an odd Root must produce.

You'l Excuse this Wast of your time & paper on these sallies but as they are the Natural Effects of one that is a fond Admirer of all plants from your Country I couldn't help giveing you a specimen of my Tast, I have now only one Request to make to putt it in my power to Gratifie you with any thing our World produces. As a small token of my Gradetude for your Favour I desire your acceptance of a Box of Horse Chestnuts [*Aesculus hippocastanum*]. Why this Name is Imposed on this Noble Tree I can't saye for no Horse that I ever heard will Eat the Nutts or Delights more in Its shade then any other Tree tho' I am told in Turkey from whence they came they give the Nutts in provender to Horses that are Troubled with Coughs or are short Winded but I have not heard that it has been used Here. The Botanicall Description Is that It hath Digitated or finger'd Leaves. The Flowers which consist of five Leaves are of an Anomalous Figure opening as it were with Two Lips, there are Male & Female upon the same spike which when fully Blown [flowering] make a specious shew being a Noble Beautifull Large spike of flowers and always Stand at the Extremity of the Branches. The female Flowers are succeeded by nuts which Grow in Green prickly Husks. [See Simpson, Alan. *The Mysteries of the "Frenchman's Map" of Williamsburg, Virginia.* Williamsburg: Colonial Williamsburg Foundation, 1984.]

Mertensia virginica, "Mountain Cowslip." Mark Catesby. From Peter Collinson's copy of Natural History of Carolina . . . at Knowsley Hall, *Vol II, plate 101. Courtesy of the Earl of Derby, Knowsley.*

"This plant was sent by Col. Custis From Virginia & Flowered in the Garden of Peter Collinson att Peckham in Surry the Beginning of Aprill 1735."

Terebinthus Indica Theophrasti Pistachia
Discordis.
Pistachia Nut

19.

Pavia Boerh
Scarlet Horse Chesnut

Sylvestri folio
incano.
ster or Wild

Nau Huysum del.

H. Fletcher Sculp.

Scarlet Horse Chestnut. (American) Georg Dionysius Ehret. Philip Miller, Catalogus plantarum ... *Plate 19—American Philosophical Society*

This Tree makes an Early Noble shade it putting forth in February & March & is the first Green of any Timber Tree here. Its Growth is singular for the whole years shoot is commonly produc'd in Three Weeks. There is a great Regularity in its Growth their under Branches being Naturally Extended the succeeding ones Decreaseing Gradually to the Top do forme a Natural obtuse pyramid, the Flowers being att the End of the branches are very Conspicuous & yield a Delightfull prospect. Rows of these Trees planted before your Houses next the street att Williamsburgh woud have a fine Effect. I hope you'l Excuse this prolix account but as this Tree is a stranger perhaps it May not be Unacceptable & the subject I am upon draws my penn further than I Design'd. They are very Good natur'd Trees. Grow in any soil and in any place. Sett some nutts where they are to stand to Grow to Maturity soone as for the Rest plant them in Quarters to be Removed. Plant the nutts about 2 feet assunder for the Leaves are Large & Require Roome. Please to give a few to my Good Friends Sir John & Mr. Isham Randolph[2] to whome pray my Respects & If the whole Quantity come Good to my good friend Colonel Byrd. I thank you for both Your Obligeing Letters and am with abundance of thanks for your kind present with much
Respect Yours   P. COLLINSON

Sett the nutts as soone as they come to hand, There is In the Box besides some peach stones of the Double Blossome peach which att the time of flowering is a most beautiful sight and att the Top is some Almondes. They make Excellent Tarts which a pinn can be thrust through them. First stew them, then putt them in Crust with sugar. The Green shell, & Brown shell & Cornell [cherry] being all Tender have an agreeable Rellish together. There's Two or three plants in your country I should be glad off viz the Dogwood Tree & a sort of Laurell or Bay that

Left: Dogwood (with Mock Bird). Mark Catesby. From Peter Collinson's copy of Natural History of Carolina . . . at Knowsley Hall, *Vol I, plate 27. Courtesy of the Earl of Derby, Knowsley*

Below: Chionanthus virginica, *Fringe Tree. William Bartram. From the album of Collinson's prints and drawings at Knowsley Hall, page 45. Courtesy the Earl of Derby, Knowsley.*

bears bunches of Flowers not much unlike the Laurus Tinus it is by some Improperly Called Ivy and if the sheep Eat It Kills them.

If Three or 4 of Each of these plants about Two feet high was Collected & then provide a Box Two feet square & Deep, make Large Holes in Bottome to Lett out the Water. A foot Deep in Earth is sufficient to Cover the Roots. Water them at planting and send them by some of the Last ships, for if they come Over in the Summer Months they are Generally Burnt up for want of Water. And if it is Convenient send by any of Mr [John] Hanburys' ships who is my Intimate Friend.

I shall be oblig'd to you as soone as this comes to hand if you will procure these plants & sett them as above advised, then sett the box in the shade giveing it Water as wanted & send by Autumn ships.

Please to Putt some Chinquapin Nutts in the Earth in the Box, sett it full, but if you have roome Left then please to putt 3 or four Young plants in their stead with the Dogwood & Flowering Bay, Laurel or Ivy.

I have sent severall sorts of seeds I wish they may be acceptable and if nott please to Lett Mee know what will.
Yours
P. Collinson.

Pray have you in Virginia, no spring or summer flowers with Bulbous Roots.[3] Pray putt some in a Box of Earth for Mee against another year. Another flowering shrub which grows with you which I very much Want Wee call it heare the Fringe Tree [*Chioanthus virginicus*] for the Flowers are white and so Lacerated they seem Like a Fringe or shreds of Holland or narrow scraps of white paper. I have seen it Flower In England but it is scarse Here.

JOHN CUSTIS (1678–1749), handsome, wealthy, eccentric Virginia planter, born in the colony, developed a great interest in gardening.

This is the first of twenty-three surviving letters Collinson wrote Custis, presented, with those of Custis to Collinson which survive in draft in the Custis letter-book, in Swem, E. G. *Brothers of the Spade: Correspondence of Peter Collinson, of London, and of John Custis, of Williamsburg, Virginia, 1734–1746.* Worcester: American Antiquarian Society, 1949.

The trees survived and show up as equally spaced dots at the Custis site on the "Frenchman's Map"—a billeting map drawn in 1782 by a French soldier after Cornwallis's surrender. The map is in the Colonial Williamsburg Foundation Library.

Horse chestnuts were introduced from Istanbul into Vienna in the second half of the sixteenth century. They were first described in a letter from Istanbul to Pier Andrea Mattioli which he published in 1561. See Lack, H. Walter, "Lilacs and Horse Chestnuts: Discovery and Rediscovery," *Curtis's Botanical Magazine,* Vol 17, Part 2, May, 2000 pp. 109–120.

1. The mountain cowslip, *Mertensia virginica,* (L.) Pers. Virginia cowslip, true lungwort, Roanoake bells, "a beautifull out of the way plant and flower," as Custis described it to Collinson in an undated draft letter written after Custis received the chestnuts Collinson sent him under cover of this. See Swem, pp. 39–40. In one of Collinson's memoranda, ". . . Mountain cowslip. Banister and Plukenet . . . Miller's sixth species, a most elegant plant, was entirely lost in our gardens, but I again restored it from Virginia by Col. Custis; flowered April 13, 1747, and hath continued ever since [1765] a great spring ornament in my garden at Mill Hill." [L.S.]

2. Sir John Randolph (c. 1693–1737), planter, shipmaster, merchant and public official of "Dungeness" on the James River, Goochland County, Virginia, and Isham Randolph (1685–1742) also a planter and merchant; represented Goochland County in the General Assembly. (Berkeley & Berkeley)

3. No tulips, hyacinths or daffodils are native to eastern North America; however, early botanists included the iris among "bulbous roots." Custis sent Collinson "Indian" iris in 1735, perhaps *Iris verna.* (Swem, p. 44)

12 ❧ TO JOHN BARTRAM

ALS:HSP
London, January 20, 1735

My Good Friend,

I now do my Self a further pleasure to Consider thy Curious Entertaining Letters of November 6. I am only afraid In doing Mee a pleasure so much Time was loss'd which wou'd turne to a more profitable account in thy own affairs.

Thee writes for some Botanical books and indeed I am att a Loss which to recommend for as I have observed a Compleat History of plants is not to be found in any author. For the present I am pswaded the Gentle Men of the Library Company att my Request will Indulge thee the Liberty when thee comes to Town to peruse their Botanical Books. There is Miller Dicy[1] & some others.

Please to Remember those Solomons Seals that Escap'd thee Last year.

The Great & Small Hellebore are grat Rarities here so pray send a Root or Two of Each next year. Please to Remember all your sort of Lillies as they happen in thy Way & your Spotted Martigons will be very acceptable. The Divils Bitt or Blazeing Star [*Liatris spicata*] pray add a Root or Two and any of your Lady Slippers [*Cypripedium*].

My Dear friend I only Mention these plants but I beg of thee not to neglect thy more Material affairs to oblige Mee. A great many may be putt in a Box 20 Inches or Two feet square & 15 or 16 inches High & a foot in Earth is Enough. This may be putt under the Capts bed or Sett in the Cabin if it is sent in October or November. Nail a few small Narrow Laths cross it to keep the Catts from Scratching It.

If thee could procure some Layers of the Woody Vine with variegated Leaves [not

Above: Helleborus niger. *Georg Dionysius Ehret. Hunt Institute for Botanical Documentation*

Right: Cypripedium, *Lady's Slippers (with Ground Squirrel). Mark Catesby. From Collinson's copy of* Natural History of Carolina . . . at Knowsley Hall, *Vol II , plate 72. Courtesy of the Earl of Derby, Knowsley*

"This curious Helleborine was sent from Pennsylvania by Mr. John Bartram, who, by his industry and inclination to the searches into Nature, has discovered and sent over a great many new productions, both animal and vegetable. This Plant flowered in Mr. Collinson's garden in April, 1738."

identified] It would be acceptable. Also a Root of the Aristolochia which is of such Sovereign Remedy for sore Breasts would be well worth haveing.

I hope Thee had Mine per Cap Davis with a Box with Seeds in Sand & 2 parcells of Seeds per my good Friend Isaac Norris Jr.[2] One percelle I sent after Him to the Downs but weither He was Sail'd or no before it came to hand I can [not] say, but by the List Inclosed thee will know if they are Come to hand, or if He had them.

Podophyllum peltatum, *may apple (with The Turtle of Carolina). Mark Catesby. From Collinson's copy of* Natural History of Carolina . . . at Knowsley Hall, *Vol I, plate 24. Courtesy of the Earl of Derby, Knowsley*

Pray what is your Sarsaparilla? The May apple [*Podophyllum peltatum*] is a pretty plant, is what I have had for some years sent Mee by Dr Witt.[3] It flowers well with us, but our Summers are not Hott enough to perfect its Fruite.

The pretty Humble Beautifull plant with a Spike of yellow Flowers I take to be a Species of Orchis or Satyrion. What sort of Root it has thee hath not Mention'd. If it is taken up with the Earth about the Roots it will certainly Flower the first if not the Second year. I wish thee'd send Mee two or Three Roots if there is plenty.

The Ground Cypress is a singularly pretty plant. If it bears berries or Seeds pray send Some and if it bears flowers or Seeds pray send some Specimens in both States.

Pray send Mee a good Specimen or Two of the Shrub 3 foot High that grows by the Water Courses [not identified].

The Shrub that grows out of the Sides of Rocks Sometimes 5 or 6 foot High bearing Red Berries hanging by the Husks is Call'd Euonymus, Spindle Tree or prick Wood. Wee have the Same plant with a Small Difference. Grows plenty in England.

Your Wild Senna with yellow flowers is a pretty plant. Send Seeds of both this and Mountain Goats Rue.

Thee need not collect any more of the White Thorn berries that has prodigious long sharp Thorns It is what Wee call the Cock Spurr Thorn. I had a tree last year that had att least a Bushell of Berries, but Haws of any other sorts of Thorns will be very Acceptable.

Pray send Mee a Root or Two of Cluster bearing Solomons Seal. It [is] in all apperance a very Rare plant, as is the panax.

Pray a Root or Two of Joseph Brentnals Snake Root.

Pray send a Root of the Grassey Leaves that bears pretty little blew flowers [*Sisyrinchium,* blue-eyed grass] that is good against the obstructions of the bowells.

When it happens in thy Way send Mee a Root or Two of the Little Tuberous Root Call'd Divils bitt which produces one or Two Leaves yearly.

I only bearly Mention these plants not that I Expect thee to send them. I dont Expect or Desire them but as they happen to be found accidentally & what is not to be meet with one year may be anon.

It happens that your Late Ships in the Auttumn come away before a great many of Our Seeds are Ripe & the Spring I dont approve as the best Season to send them. But as it rarely happens otherwise I have taken a Methode to send Some in paper & Some in Sand. After thee has picked out the Largest which must be Instantly Sett for very probably they was Chilled comeing over, when It is my Case as it often happens takeing the following Methode I have raised a great many pretty plants out of your Earth. I lay out a Bed 5 or 6 feet long, 3 foot Wide. Then I pare off the Earth an Inch or Two Deep, then I Loosen the bottome and Lay it very smooth again and thereon (if I may use the Term) I sow the Sand & Seed together as thin as I can. Then I Sift some good Earth over it about half an Inch thick. This bed ought to be In Some place that It may not be Disturbed & kep'd very Clear from Weeds for several seeds come not up till the second year.

I have putt some Hard Shell'd almonds of my own growth & some Soft Shell'd from Portugal. They are easily distinguished. The almond makes a fine pie taken whilst a pin can be run through them, for you eat Husk, Shell & Kernell altogether. They must be first Codled over a Gentle Fire & then putt in Crust. I Query wether young peaches would be as good before the Shell is hard.

I have putt in the Sand some Vine Cuttings and Some of the great Neapolitan Medlar which Wee always graft on White Thorn & so must you. As soone as these Cuttings come to hand Soake them all over in Water for 24 Hours & then plant the Vines (the Earth being well Loosen'd) as deep as only the uppermost bud of the Cutting may be Level with the Earth. Water them in Dry Weather. These Seldome fail growing. The Grafts after Soaking may be Laid in the Earth or in a Moist place till grafted which should be Soone.

I hope thee will take these Two Long Rambling Epistles in good part. They are writt a bitt now & then as business will permitt. Lett Mee heare from thee att thy Leisure wich will much oblige thy Real friend

P. Collinson

Sent to I Norris in the Downs

pimpernella Saxifraga
Galeaga Goats Rue

Calamintha
Caryophellata Avens
Pigellium Flea wort
Gordium
Imperatoria
Eryngium
Ferula gabanifera

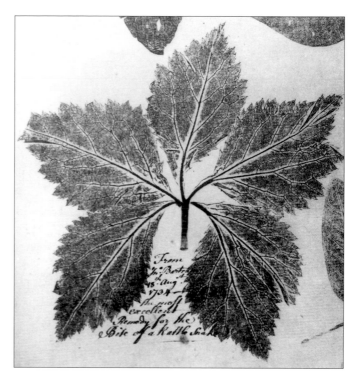

"Joseph Brentnals Snake Root," Sanicula canadensis. *Joseph Breintnall annotated this leaf print: "From Jn Bartram 18th Aug 1734. The most excellent Remedy for the Bite of a Rattle Snake." The Library Company of Philadelphia*

Send a quantity Seed of the Birch or Black Beach. It seems to be new. Send Mee a good Root of the Swallow wort or Apocinon with narrow Leaves & orange Colour'd flowers [not identified] & of the pretty Shrub called Red Root[4] and of the Cotton Weed or Life Everlasting & some more Seed of the perannual pea that grows by Rivers [prob. *Lathyrus palustris,* marsh pea]. This year or next or next after as it happens pray send Mee a Walking Cane of the Cane Wood.

1. Philip Miller (1691–1771), gardener at the Chelsea Physic Garden 1722–1770, receiving and introducing plants from all over the world. He probably had more influence on gardens and gardening than any man of his time. His *Gardeners Dictionary,* went through eight editions in his lifetime and became the standard reference on both sides of the Atlantic. In the seventh edition (1759) Miller began to use the Linnaean system of classification, and in the eighth (1768) Linnaeus's binomial nomenclature. PC presented the first edition (Volume 1, 1731, volume 2, 1739) to the Library Company. No portrait is known.

In 1730 Miller wrote *Catalogus plantarum: A catalogue of trees, shrubs, plants and flowers . . . which are propagated for sale, in the gardens near London.* London, A Society of Gardeners, 1730. In it he refers to PC as one of the "many curious gentlemen which at present are carrying the Spirit of Gardening to a considerable height."

In 1743 PC wrote Joseph Breintnall, "I have a Favour to Begg of the Gentlmn of the Library Company which I perswade my Self they will not refuse Mee (being as I apprehand no ways Inconsistent with their Constitution) and that is to admitt my Worthy & Ingenious Friend John Bartram on Shulhil [Schuylkill] an Honorary Member without any present or Future Expense, as it will reflect a great Honour on the Society for takeing Notice of a Deserving Man who has not that Effluence of Fortune to be a Subscriber But who has a great Genius which may be Greatly Improved by haveing a free Access to the Library, whose gratefull Disposition is such that I am perswaded In returns for so great a Favour He will Contribute all in his power to Make a Usefull & profitable Member.

"My Good Friend Had I Leisure the Above Should be better Digested, but Such as it is be so kind to Communicate It att a suiteable oppertunity to the Gentlmn with my Respects. What I ask is common in almost all Societys, Especially in the Royal Society, where Ingenious Men of Slender abilitys or Foreigners are thus Distinguish'd by becomeing Honourary Members." (ALS:HSP, February 24, 1743)

The request was not granted.

2. Isaac Norris, Jr. (1701–1766), Philadelphia-born merchant, militant pacifist, leader of the Quaker party and speaker of the Pennsylvania Assembly. He visited England in 1735, which explains the reference toward the end of the letter, "Sent to I Norris in the Downs . . .". (DAB)

3. Christopher Witt (1675–1765), self-described in his Will as "a practitioner of physick," James Logan's doctor, English-born scientist and tinker of Germantown, a Rosicrucian who dabbled in the occult and was "regarded as a Magus and used to cast nativities."

(Brett-James) He attached himself to a mystical Pietistic group on the Wissahickon called "The Women of the Wilderness," made clocks and musical instruments, pursued astronomy, astrology, "the black art of hexing" and the search for the elixir of life. He once sent ginseng to Collinson with the report that "Indians would go for three, four or five days without food by keeping a bit of the root in their mouths." He trained young men to be physicians and issued the first American medical diploma. He developed the second botanical garden in America (the first belonged to his neighbor, Francis Daniel Pastorius) and made a botanizing trip to Virginia in 1747. Based on annotations in Collinson's copies of Miller's *Dictionary* we know that by the mid 1720s Witt was sending plants to Collinson, including "those fine Lady's Slippers, which make my mouth water" (Collinson to Bartram, February 3, 1736), and the Snake-root (Collinson to Bartram, June 6, 1736, not included here).

None of Collinson's letters to Witt have been located. Bartram knew and visited him (see Bartram to Collinson, June 11, 1743, reprinted in Berkeley and Berkeley).

Witt loaned Bartram books and gave advice about botany and magic-making. Bartram accepted his botany but of the latter he wrote Collinson, "When we are on the topic of astrology, magic and mystic divinity, I am apt to be a little troublesome by inquiring into the foundation and reasonableness of these notions." He turns up frequently in Collinson's letters to Bartram (see particularly Collinson to Bartram, February 3, 1736). In May, 1765 Collinson wrote Bartram, "I lament the loss of my oldest correspondent, Dr Witt. What was his age [90]?" (DAB; Hocker, Edward W. "A Doctor of Colonial Germantown." *Germantown History* II No. 8 (1948); Hedrick, Ulysses Prentiss. *A History of Horticulture in America to 1860.* New York: Oxford University Press, 1950, p. 85; Barnhart, John Hendley, *Biographical Notes Upon Botanists.* Boston: G.K. Hall, 1965.

4. Probably *Lachnanthes tinctoria.* In a later letter to Bartram Collinson wrote, "I am in doubt about the red root, dont know what it is unless the pecune, an Indian name. I dont find a Specimen." (ALS:HSP, July 22, 1740, not included here) "Pocoon" or "Puccoon" was the Indian name for the bloodroot or *Sanguinaria canadensis* L., a perennial, not a shrub. Bartram's "red root" is actually *Ceanothus americanus* L., or New Jersey tea, a plant he later described as "red root from the color of bark of the root. It grows 3 foot high. A pretty bush bearing fine white flowers."

Berkeley and Berkeley date this letter 1736. The year is not legible. The editor believes it was written a year earlier.

13 ❧ TO THE LIBRARY COMPANY

ALS:HSP
January 24, 1735

Gentlemen:

Inclosed are Bills of Lading and parcells for your Order for Books which I hope will prove to your likeing, but as I have formerly observed, if my Bookseller does not use you Well, I am under no Obligation but will go where you direct.

Your bill for Eighteen pounds Is paid & carried to your account.

The Bill of parcells some what Exceeds your Commission but as it is not a great deal I hope it will be of no Consequence. Inclosed is your accot Currt.

I beg no more may be said about my Trouble as Commissnr. You will oblige Mee not to mention it again. I do assure you I have no Mercenary Views, but if my Little offices merit but yur acceptance, it will be a pleasure to your Well wishing Friend.

PS Gent. I believe you was not apprehensive how many nos of Salmon Wilos[1] was printed. Thought fitt to advise you of It. If you approve them they may be had next Cargo. Shaws Abridgmnt of Boyle[2] is out of print but is to be had for 3:10:0, which being a very advanced price did not send it without your Orders. Inclosed is a proposal for Reprinting the Turkish History.[3] If you approve it, I will subscribe for you. Yours PC

1. Possibly Salmon, William. *Botanologia, The English Herbal.* London, 1710.

2. Peter Shaw (1694–1763), physician and author, edited *The Philosophical Works of the Hon. Robert Boyle, Abridged,* 3 vols. London, 1725.

3. Kantemir, Demetrius. *History of the Growth and Decay of the Othman Empire,* 2 vols. London, 1734–35. The Library Company has only the first volume. Since its publication antedates Collinson's letter, neither he nor the Library Company is listed among the subscribers.

14 ❧ TO JOHN BARTRAM

ALS:HSP
London, February 12, 1735

Dear Friend John Bartram

Tho I am vastly Hurried In Business and no Leisure Yett the Many Instances of thy regard for us Obliges Mee to Steal Time to say Something further to thy kind Letters.

I am glad the Roots in a Box by Cap Wright came to hand & was acceptable. I Rece'd the Box of Berries Fresh & in Good Order. The Sarsifrase was a fine parcel & the Cherry Stones & several others are what Wee had not before. I sent them to Our Noble Friend [Lord Petre].

The Leaves of that Golden Rod are finely scented. Pray have Wee any of the Seed? Now Dear Friend I have done with thine of the 9th of Sepr & now I shall only tell thee I have Rece'd thine of Novemr 18, Decem 1 & the 9th & thine of the 10th with the Invoices.[1]

Captain Savage has been Exceedingly kind & Obliging. Pray when Thee sees Dr Flexner [not identified] give my Respects to Him & thank Him also.

I have gott all the Boxes on Shore but No 3 & 4 which are the Large Boxes. The Seeds in No 2 was nicely pack'd & Came in Good Order but the 12 pticuler Sorts in that Box are Mostly New & Curious.

SELECTED LETTERS OF PETER COLLINSON ❧ 27

The Box of Specimens with the Seeds came very Dry, Safe & Well. I think thee has Discharged that affair very Elegantly & gives us great pleasure & Convey to us Stronger Ideas of your plants then can be Described & Saves a great Deal of Writeing. I shall att my first Leisure send thee their True Botanical Names & I shall send thee more paper. But one Quire a year will be Sufficient.

The Box of Insects was very prettyly & Nicely putt up & Described, but pray Chain up that unruly Creature the Smith [moth] that He may do Us no More Damage next time. I shall have some Fresh Requests to make as to Insects which by Inclosed Instructions [not found] thee may Learn thy little Boyes to Catch & I will Reward them.

Thee will Heare att Large from Mee when I have oppertunity to Discourse with thy Noble patron.

All the Things thee wrote for I shall send, the Small things by Israel Pemberton[2] & the Box of Nails per Cap Savage or some other Ship which I am not yett Determined, but I shall acquaint thee with It.

Butt I almost Forgott thy Noble present of plants which came very Safe & Well to all appearances & Contains a many Curious plants.

This year pray rest a Little from thy Labours. I shall only ask of thee one Sett of plants & that is all the sorts of Ladies Slippers thee happens to Meet with if not far to Fetch for I Expect none from the Doctor [Witt]. He has Indeed sent Mee a few Seeds but they are fine Sorts, the 2 Large Jacea or Blazeing Starr & 2 sorts of Seeds of Martigons & Clinopodium, [*Satureja,* savory] a fine plant.

Above: Sassafras. Mark Catesby. From Collinson's copy of Natural History of Carolina . . . at Knowsley Hall, *Vol I, plate 55. Courtesy of the Earl of Derby, Knowsley.*

"*This tree will bear our Climate, as appears by Several now at Mr. Collinson's at Peckham . . .*"

Right: Pink lady slipper. Georg Dionysius Ehret. Natural History Museum, Botany Library, London. Ehret painted the subject in Collinson's garden, at Millhill, June 28, 1761"

I have gott a Box of Chesnutts in Sand & some Spanish nutts & some of our Katherine peach stones. It is the Last & a Large peach that ripens with us in October, but will sooner with you. It is a hard, Sound well flavour'd peach, none better, & Clings to the stone, 17 & as many apricot stones, & In the Little Box that the Insects Came In are some Seeds. The China Aster [*Callistephus chinensis*] is the Noblest & finest Plant thee ever saw of that Tribe. It was Sent by the Jesuits from China to France & from thence to us. It is an Annuall. Sow it in Rich Mould Immediately & when it has half a Dozen Leaves transplant in the Border. It makes a glorious Autumn flower. There is White & purple in the Seeds.

The Lebanon [cedar, *Cedrus libani*] Cone with a knife carefully pick out the Seeds. Sow in a Box. Cut Large holes in the bottome & cover with Shells in sandy Light Mould. Lett it only have the Morning Sun.

I sent 2 percells of the Aster for fear by sowing Late it should not ripen seed. I have sent the Dr [Witt] Some.

I am my Dear friend with Hearty acknowledgment for all thy pains & Trouble & thy many favours, in hast, thine Sincerely
P. Collinson

The Spanish Chesnutts &c Comes in a Little Box in Sand committed to the Care of Israel Pemberton.

Wee have been Largely Supplied with Chinquapins [*Castanea pumila*] from Virginia but I Designe thee shall have the Credit & profit of them, for our Noble friend knows nothing but they came from thee. I can Easily be

Above: Callistephus chinensis, *the China Aster. Artist unknown. The Wellcome Library, London.*

Left: Castanea pumila, *Chinquapins (with Cuckow of Carolina). Mark Catesby. From Peter Collinson's copy of* Natural History of Carolina . . . *at Knowsley Hall,* Vol I, plate 9—*Courtesy of the Earl of Derby, Knowsley*

supply'd from that Country, so give thy Self no further Trouble about them, for I know they grow not near you to the perfection they do in that Country.

Butt one thing Dear John I must Request of thee. Our Curious Bottanists are sadly perplext about the Difference between the Red & White Cedars. Pray be so kind to gather 3 or 4 specimens of each sort of the Size of the paper, Branches with their Leaves, & when Dry'd send by First opertunity the Size & Height of each Sort & their Uses & a few Berries of Each Sort by way of Sample. The Red wee have but Want Seeds of the White Cedar.

One of my Curious friends is writing a Book & wants to Insert the Cedars Red & White & Show their Differences which is not perticulary Described by any Author.[3] So pray be Exact & thee'll much oblige Thine   PC

1. These invoices do not survive, but from this reference we may date the beginnings of Bartram's supplying plant material on a commercial basis.

2. Israel Pemberton (1715–1779), prominent Quaker merchant of Philadelphia.

3. Johann Jacob Dillenius, who was revising William Sherard's *Pinax*. See Collinson to Linnaeus, October 26, 1747 and April 10, 1755.

15 ❧ TO JOHN BARTRAM

ALS:HSP
London, March 1, 1735

Kind Friend John Bartram,

I am now just Return'd to Town from paying a Visit to a Noble Lord [Petre], my most Valuable & Intimate Friend. One of my proposals I sent thee last year to Collect the Seeds of your Forest Trees was for Him as He is a Universal Lover of plants. I presented him with a Share of the Seeds thou Sent Last year which was very Acceptable as he is a Man of a Noble & Generous Spirit. He very Rationally consider'd thy pains & Trouble in Collecting them & Desired to make thee some Returns & Left it to Mee. I thought a Good Suite of Cloths for thy Own Ware might be as Acceptable as any thing So have sent thee Ones with all appurtenances Necessary for its makeing up which I hope will meet with thy approbation & help in some measure to Compensate for thy Loss of Time.

My Noble Friend Desires thee to Continue the Same Collections. Send the Same Sorts over again & what New Ones happens in thy Way & Sent att the Same Time a year & in the Same Manner will do very well. Please to look in my other Letter for my further remarks on this head.

All the seeds was in good order except the All Spice Seed which was musty. Perhaps that was Owing to the Dampness of the Roots putt up for Sr Hans Sloane. For the future putt up no Moist thing with the Seeds but send them in a Little Box by them selves.

If thee can Compass to Send 30 or 40 Sorts of your Herbaceous seed Every year it will be Sufficient. As to Invoice of Forest Tree Seeds their Quantity & Price is fix'd, So thee knows what thee Does. Thee has had great Luck hitherto In sending the seeds in Good Order. I hope the Like will attend thee in the Forest Tree Seeds. I Refer thee to my Letters on that Head sent with the Catalogue [not found].

Left: The Small Mud Tortoise. George Edwards. Gleanings of Natural History, *Vol I, plate 166. The Library Company of Philadelphia.*

"It hath a small dusky tail, with a sharp horney point; the use of which is, I believe, by turning it downward in its progression on inclining muddy banks, to stop its motion at pleasure. It is said, when living, to have a strong musky smell. I imagine this might be a young one. . . .

"It was sent from Pennsylvania by Mr. Bartram to my worthy friend Peter Collinson, Esq. F.R.S. who on all occasions is ready and willing to oblige me with the use of every new subject he receives from foreign countries." and underside— "tail turned round when in this position," Collinson noted in his annotation. William Bartram. From Collison's album of prints and drawings at Knowsley Hall, page 119. Courtesy of the Earl of Derby, Knowsley

Below: The Great Mud Tortoise from Pennsylvania. William Bartram. From Collinson's album of prints and drawings at Knowsley Hall, page 117. Courtesy of the Earl of Derby, Knowsley.

Collinson liked turtles. There are fifteen images of them in his picture album at Knowsley Hall, many by William Bartram.

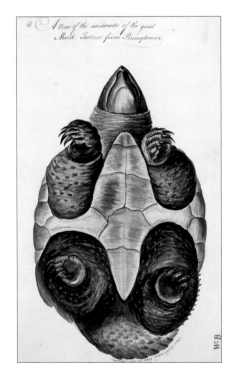

As our Noble Friend will be always Gratefull I hope it will Encourage thee to go on, but yett I would have thee so proceed as not to Interfere with thy Publick Business. Indeed the Forest Tree Seeds I hope will bring Money to thy pocket So the time spent in makeing The Collection cannot be Said to be Lost or Misspent.

There is Inclosed 3 Sorts of Seeds which happened to be Mislaid, but if they fail I will Endeavor to Recruite another year. I hope thee hath Mine per Capt Richmond with a parcell in the Library Companys Trunk & a box of Seeds in Sand per Richmond.

I heartyly Wish thee and Thine Health & prosperity & am thy Real friend

P. COLLINSON

Pray give no body a hint how thee or thy Wife came by the Suite of Cloths. There may be Some with you may think they Deserve something of that Nature.

The Druget is pack up in Brown paper Directed for thee to the Care of Jos Breintnall in a Case of Goods of Capt. Wrights.

If thee Observes any curious Insects, Beetles, Butterflies &c they are Easily preserved being pin'd through the body to the Inside of a Little Box when it is full, Send it nail'd up & put nothing within in it & they will Come very Safe. Display the Wings of the Butterflies with pins & rub off the Down as Little as possible. When thee goes abroad putt a little Box in thy pocket and as thee meets with the Insects putt them in and then stick them in the other Box when thee gets homes.

I want a Terapin or Two. Putt them in a box with Earth & they will come safe. They will live a long while without food.[1]

1. Collinson had a long interest and many adventures with terrapins and turtles. He wrote John Bartram on June 28, 1763, "It is something Singular & I dare Saye the first attempt of the kind but the Mud Turtle had clambered up a whole pair of Stairs out of my Hall into the next floor. Led by what Instinct I don't know, but there was no water upstairs. . . . A few Weeks agon Wee Caught the Great Mud Turtle thou formerly Sent Us—It is much grown & so fierce Wee was much Diverted with It." [ALS:HSP]

16 ❧ TO JOHN BARTRAM

ALS:HSP
June 19–28, 1735

Dear Friend John Bartram

I was well pleased with thine of March 2d & am glad to heare that Some of the Seeds was acceptable. I shall Endeavour to send what I can in thy List, but as they grow very Wide from London I can't propose to send all. But when I make Excursions into the Country shall Endeavour To be Mindfull as they fall in my Way.

This year Better Luck attends thy Seeds. A great many are Come up and are very Curious, but thee art not to wonder if Some Fail, which is principally for want of your Heat, tho Wee Endeavour to supply that Defect with Hott beds which are but precarious without Manag'd with Great Skill to be sure the natural Heat & Soil is most suiteable for Vegitation. If With Care a 3d part Grows it is well.

Please to go on Collecting as Seeds happens to be in thy Way, only observe to Number them as I before observed & make a Name to that number that thee may know them by & then Wee shall only write for those that Miscarry. But there is this further to be observed, that Some Seeds come not up the first year as several of those thee first sent Mee are Come up this Spring.

Thee observes you have Linaria & Mullen grows wild with you. If you have Variety of Sorts, pray send Some of Each. Perhaps it may be Diferent.

Now my Kind Friend I come to give thee some accot of the Tub of plants by Captain Wright, which being sent in a right Season succeed Well & gives Mee great pleasure. I have Six Sorts of the Ferns &c grows. Some are very Different from Ours. I admire them Much. I have the Cluster and Thorough Leav'd Solomans Seal grows Well as doth both Sorts of Hellebore. The Small kind is new & Very Curious as also the Dittany and Golden Rod.

The Dragon & Indian Turnip both grow & are fine plants. The Skunk Weed putt forth 2 fine Blossoms. The Laurells, Dwarfe Service [*Amelanchier spicata,* shadbush] & Hone-Suckle thrive Well and are fine plants. Pray send Mee 2 or 3 HoneSuckles. There is Different Colours. Some are Deep Red & Pale Red Flowers. But the Sedum so finely Vein'd in the Leaves is a very Ticklish plant, will neither grow in the Shade or in Our Sun. It is a very pretty plant which I much admire & yett I am afraid Our Climate Will not suite It. When thee sends Next send 2 or 3 plants & and I will try Different Ways. The penny Wort I hope will Do. In so fine a Collection only Pocoone which I have but I want that with a Double Flowers and the Devils Bitt or Blazeing Star which has failed & Smooth Leafe & Rough Leafed Solomons Seal.

I shall only Observe when thee sends another Tub of plants that a foot Deep in Mould is Enough for Herbaceous plants & that thee Make Holes in the bottome an Inch Diameter & Cover with Shells to Dreane the Water. The Tub thee sent was very Wett & if the plants had Lain Long or had Much Wett would have Rotted for Want of Larger Vents.

Please to Remember Red Lillie.

Right: Rhododendron—Georg Dionysius Ehret. In Trew, Plantae Selectae, *Plate LXVI. The Linnean Society of London.*

Below: Rhododendron periclymenoides, *Pinxterbloom, Azalea. Georg Dionysius Ehret. Natural History Museum, Botany Library, London*

Rattlesnake—William Bartram. From Collinson's album of prints and drawings at Knowsley Hall, page 127.

Collinson's annotation: "Wm Bartram—The Rattle Snake taken uppon the banks of Gr Eg harber River." Courtesy of the Earl of Derby, Knowsley

Pray has thee again Mett with the Hermaphrodite Flower? I have read of It by those that Describe North America. Should be glad to see the Flower but if that Can't be please to send Mee a Dry'd Specimen In paper as I formerly Directed & the Flower of that pretty Wood Cedum before Mention'd. Any plants thee Wants to know the Names send over the Speciments & I will Returne them Nam'd.

I hope the Cullimanco & Druggett [wool fabrics] are Come to Hand & prove acceptable. The First I sent to thee Care of John Breintnall[1] & the Drugt in Cap Wrights Goods by Capt Reves.

Inclosed is a paper relating to the Bite of the Rattle Snake. Please to give Mee thy opinion of It.[2]

There is no Doubt but Spruce, Firr & Pine Cones & their Variety's will be very acceptable & Do Well. I hope that this year Will prove a Good Seed Year. If any pretty Insects remember Mee.

In a Box by Captain Wright is the following Roots:
    2 Cyclamens with Seed to them. Sow it Carefully.
    2 Squills
    2 Male Peonys
    Double pilewort
    White Melody Gladiolus
    Double White Sarsifrage
    1 great Snow Drop
    Double Snow drop
    1 great Colchicums
    Hyacinths
    Wood Anemones

Some Small bulbs of the Fiery Red Lillie & Divers Sorts of Seeds in the Sand. 4 Hyacinths of Peru Lay uppermost in the Box. Variety of offsetts of Tulips.

I have heard that your Severe Winters have kill'd the Cyclamins & Hyacinths of Peru. It may be Safest to plant in potts or tubs & house them in the Winter, but if they are planted in the Ground It must be in the Warmest place & pretty Deep & in the Winter Cover them Well with Pea Straw which I find better than any. The Squills Come from a Warm Country, will not Endure Severe Cold but ought to [be] planted in Potts to be Housed the Winter or Else great Care taken of them. They Love to Grow in Sea Sand with a Mixture of Light Rich Mould.

[On a separate sheet but probably sent with the foregoing:]

Friend Bartram   June 28, 1735

I had besides putt in the Box 2 doz 1/2 Ranunculas. In Sever Weather the Beds should be Cover'd with a Good Heap of Pea Straw but taken off in the Day if the Sun shines to give them Air. Plant them in a South Shelter'd aspect. They must be taken up Ev'ry Year when the Leaves Dries Away & planted again Early in the Spring, but these if there is the Least appearance of buding must be presently planted. But if not putt them in a paper bag or box & keep them very Dry & Look often att them to see they dont Mould for that kills them, and then plant them when the severest of your Weather is over.

Thine,

P. COLLINSON

1. John Breintnall, possibly a relative of Joseph Breintnall who owned property in Philadelphia (PMHB), or mistakenly identifying Joseph.

2. Possibly "Conjectures on the Charming or Fascinating Power attributed to the Rattlesnake . . . by Sir Hans Sloane" *Philosophical Transactions* XXXVIII (1734): 321–331.

The earliest letters between Bartram and Collinson are missing, but the first we have, Bartram to Collinson, July, 1733, is a query

about rattlesnakes. Bartram had found one near Germantown, dissected it, and was curious about its teeth. Collinson's answer is missing, but he thought and wrote about rattlesnakes with horror and fascination all the rest of his life. In 1765 he published "Remarkable and Authentic Influences of the Fascinating Power of the Rattlesnake Over Men and Other Animals, with Curious Particulars . . ." in *Gentlemen's Magazine* Vol. XXXV, pp. 511–514.

17 ❧ TO JOHN BARTRAM

ALS:HSP
London, August 16, 1735

Kind Friend John Bartram

I had the pleasure of thine of June 13 & am pleased the Things was Acceptable. I have Sent the Little Box of Seeds to our Noble Friend [Lord Petre]. What he Raises I have always Share off.

The Large Invoice that I sent thee was for Him. I hope this will prove a good Seed year that thee may be able to send a Cargo which will produce thee some Money Here.

The Water Beach or Button Wood is known Here by the Western Plane & is in great plenty Here & Makes a Noble Tree. Thee Need not send any for it is Raised plentifully by Cuttings. Butt as for the Linden or Lime Tree for ought I know may be a Stranger So pray send Some Seed.

There is Two Captains, Richmond & Wright whom I Love & Esteeme & will take Care of anything for Mee. If it is a Suiteable Time send what thee Canst by them. What is in Casks or Boxes tell them I will pay Freight for, but Little Matters they are So kind to bring Free.

I am Mightily pleased with thy account of the Sugar Tree. Pray send Mee a Little Sprig with Two or Three Leaves Dry'd between a Sheet of paper & if thee Canst the Blossome. Wee Imagine Here It is a Poplar or Maple, but when Wee see the Flower or Seed Vessell Wee shall soone Determine.

The Red Shrub HoneSuckle I have had from So Carolina. It flowered & Throve well for 3 years & then went off. These are Ticklish plants and will not Do unless they are Removed & Stand to be well Rooted before Wee have them. I never saw so Milk a white before. Please to procure Some of Each & plant for Mee. Thou will have Recourse to my former Letters. It is Indeed an Instance on thy part of great Respect to keep them that are much fitter for another Use. However I Except thy Love & Value thy Friendship.

My Valuable Friend John White[1] who is Curious in our Way Carried over the Best Collection of Pears that I believe ever came from England. If they Come Safe and thrive, att My Desire He will oblige thee with Buds or Cions att proper Seasons. Pray Wait on Him with my Respects & ask the favour.

As for Plums, Nectarines & apricots, I may send thee some Grafts in the Spring, but it is my Firme opinion if they was buded or Grafted on Peach or Almonds which are Stocks that produce the Juices freer then any other they would Succeed much better. I should be glad thee'd Try that I may know the Event.

If the Frost has such an effect on your Vines which I could scarcely Believe in so south a Latitude to us you must do as they Do in Germany. When the Frosts Sett In Dig Holes round the Vines & Lay the Last years shoots In & Cover them with Earth to preserve from the Frosts & att Spring take them up again & then Prune them for Bearing.

I am glad to Hear that the Medlar grows. Is the Large Neapolitan Sort which produces a Large Fruite? Dr Witt at German Town wants it much. I sent Him Some att the Same Time but whether He has any Luck I can't tell.

I shall be Carefull to Send the Seeds thee Mentions & what others I can Collect.

My Kind Friend I Heartily Wish thee & thy Good Wife Health & prosperity. I am thy Real friend P. Collinson.

I have not seen my Garden for near Two Months. Haveing been a Long Journey In to Cornwall & Devonshire, so that what Condition thy fine plants are In I Can't say.

1. Possibly John White (fl. 1740s), a successful Philadelphia merchant who returned to live in England in 1741. (PMHB)

18 TO JOHN CUSTIS

ALS: AAS
December 15, 1735

My Worthy Good Friend Mr Custis

Before mee are your Many kind Letters In which you have taken a world of pains to Informe mee, Great Trouble you have had in makeing Collections to Enrich my Garden, & very Curious presents you have sent Mee. When I sum up all these repeated Instances of great Friendship, the Ballance Due on my side is so great, the Obligations so many that when I Reflect on them I am Confused & att a Loss What Returns to Make. I am really Asham'd to receive when I cannot Equally Give. These are my present Circumstances & unless you'l be so Indulgent to Compound with Mee, I must soone Become a Banckrupt but that I may not prove the Worst of Debtors, I wou'd gladly make some Composition In hopes of future Credit. For this End & purpose I have Committed a Case of plants to the Care of Captain Bowling [Bolling] who has promissed to Carry them in the Cabbin. Inclosed is a Catalogue [not found]. I have Endeavour'd to send such as I believe are not Very Common in your Gardens. I wish they may Come safe & prove worth Acceptance.

I shall take Notice of your obligeing Letters In Order & begin with yours of march 25th. As you desired I sav'd some Double Tulips till I could keep them out the Ground no Longer the ships going so very Late, & they was sprouted so Much I was obliged to plant them. Those that was In the Ground have shot their Green Leaves above the surface but I hope to take the Chance of some Late Ship & send them. Our Tuberoses are not yett Arrived from Italy, but I shall take the First oppertunity. In South Carolina the Italian Tuberoses Increase prodegiously as no doubt They will with you, & if planted pretty deep in Good Rich Mould & in the Winter Cover'd with pea Halm or straw to keep them from the Frost.

The Jerusalem Cowslip is a plant In very Little Request in Our Gardens, which Is Reason I can't att present procure it to send It. Your pretty Mountain blew Cowslip is of the same Family there being a great anology between them. With the Tulips I will send some Gurnsey Lillies.

Now my Dear Friend I come to Consider yours of July 3rd: & thank you for the Tub of Laurell plants, the boxes of pocoone & silk Grass. The Laurell was in tolerable Case but severall seem'd rotted with too much Moisture for want of Holes in the Bottome. The Boxes wanted Holes, yett the Pocoone & silk Grass Roots was in good Case for Captain Friend took great Care of them. I know the great Difficulty that attends sending plants on board strange ships but if it was suiteable to you on any of Mr. [John] Hanburys ships I can

Sanguinaria canadensis, *bloodroot, "peccoon." Georg Dionysius Ehret. Natural History Museum, Botany Library, London.*

be well accomodated being known to all the Captains & his Intimate Friend. I can have the priviledge of the Cabbin which is the only place to Convey Our Cargo In with safety. But this I shall submitt.

The parcell of seeds was very acceptable In particular the Yoppon or Carolina Tea [*Ilex vomitoria*]. I have Two plants in my Garden but I have more Friends to Oblige. Locus, Red Budd, Persimmon of all these I have Large Trees in my Garden but they do not seed with us. But the Persimmon I never saw bear Fruite before In England till this year. But the seeds of all these plants was very acceptable for It Furnish'd Mee with an opportunity to pleasure my Distant Friends In England, Holland & Germany. I shall be obliged to you for more of the yoppon, & if the other sorts can be procur'd with Little Trouble please to add some of the Rest for tho' I have Enough already myself, yett I think there is no Greater pleasure then to be Communicative & oblige others. It is Laying an obligation & I seldome fail of Returns for Wee Brothers of the Spade find it very necessary to share amongst us the seeds that come annually from Abroad. It not only preserves a Friendly Society but secures our Collections, for if one does not raise a seed perhaps another does & if one Looses a plant another can Supply him. By this Means our Gardens are wonderfully Improved In Variety to what they was Twenty Years agon.

The seed you Call Indian frill Wee call Cana Indica [*Canna indica*] or Wild Plaintain or Bonana from some Resemblance in the Leafe. With us it is perannuall by securing the Roots from the Frost & Comes up Ev'ry Spring.

I have 3 sorts of pecoone in My Garden, One with a Verry small Flower One with a Large single Flower & One with a Double Flower but I was glad of yours. Perhaps it may prove a Variety.

Now my Dear Friend yours of August by poor Captain Cant is before Mee. No Doubt but have hear'd He has a sad Turbelent passage & in a sad Condition putt into Ireland. All the Fine Cargo that with such pains you had been Collecting are all Loss'd.

The Fringe Tree may be raised from the Verry Good seed you sent Mee and perhaps the Laurell Butt the Ivy never Will. The seed is so fine & small that it will not keep Hei-ther. It would have Rejoyc'd my Heart to have seen it in Flower. What the perle Tree is I don't know. Chincopins I never could raise from seed but now you have taken an Effectu-all Method to do It by sending the Nutt in sand. I have Receid one Large Box of Hickerys Honey Locust, Ivy & Laurell seed & One small One by Captain Spelman for which you shall have my particular thanks & Notice as your Kind Letters come in Course.

I have a Strong Inclination to think Pistacioes Nutts will grow with you. They grow in Many Gardens In England for some years, [torn]. You may Try them in 2 or 3 Aspects in shelter'd places. When the severe or sharp Frosts approaches cover them the First year or Two with pea Halm or pea straw which I find best of all covering for it Lies Hollow & Light.

I have sent you some Dates for a Tryall. In the West of England near the sea they will stand in the Gardens. Sett the stones in the Warmest place under some Wall or pale in a south Aspect & shelter in the severe Weather.

Mr. Catesby[1] tells Mee there is a very pretty plant that He calls sorrell Tree [*Oxyden-drum arboreum,* sourwood] that Grows between Williamsburgh & York. Some seed will be Acceptable.

Sorrel tree, Oxydendrum arboreum *(with Cattering Plover). Mark Catesby. From Peter Collinson's copy of* Natural History of Caro-lina . . . at Knowsley Hall, *Vol I, plate 71. Courtesy of the Earl of Derby, Knowsley*

I had Lately given Mee a Cone of the Cedar of Lebanon. The Tree it was gather'd from was 36 feet about. I have Divided it In halves & sent you one the other to a Curious friend in Pensylvania [John Bartram]. Thee seed lies between the Chives which must be carefully pull'd off with a Knife. If it is soak'd in Water a few Hours it will open. Sow the seed in fine sifted sandy Mould not exposed to the Midday sun & hour or 2 is sufficient in the Morning. I have procur'd a Root of Jerusalem Cowslip & Double Rockketts to be planted with the Rest in the Box. I have yours of Sept. the 5th, 10th, 25th & 26th which shall have my particular notice by the first oppertunity. I am my Friend with Great sincerity & Truth Yours   P. COLLINSON

1. Mark Catesby (1683–1749), FRS, naturalist, artist and author, collected in Virginia and the West Indies from 1712 to 1719, returned to England, came back to collect in the Carolinas and Florida in 1722. He published the *Natural History of Carolina, Florida and The Bahama Islands.* 2 vols, 1730–1747 for which he drew and engraved the plates.

Catesby gave Collinson a copy (now in the library at Knowsley Hall, near Liverpool) which Collinson inscribed on the title page: "This edition of this noble work is very valuable, as it was highly finished by the ingenious author who in gratitude made me this present for the considerable sums of money I lent him without interest to enable him to publish it for the benefit of himself & family, else through necessity it must have fallen a prey to the booksellers. Peter Collinson FRS SAS ARS Sveccia Socius." In several descriptions accompanying his plates, Catesby notes that he was drawing from live specimens provided by PC.

After Catesby's death his *Hortus Britanno-Americanus* appeared (1763) dealing with eighty-five trees and shrubs, most of which had already been described in the *Natural History.*

In his introduction to the 1767 edition of *Hortus,* John Ryall wrote, "[V]ery little regard was had [to these plants] at our first settling those countries; nor indeed was any considerable step taken towards introducing these strangers into England till about the year 1720, since which time, and through the laudable application of a few persons only, many kinds of American plants, and particularly forest trees and shrubs, have been procured and raised from thence.... A small spot of land in America has, within less than half a century, furnished England with a greater variety of trees than has been procured from all the other parts of the world for more than a thousand years past."

See Frick, George F. and R. P. Stearns. *Mark Catesby, The Colonial Audubon.* Urbana: University of Illinois Press, 1961, and Meyers, Amy R.W. and Margaret Beck Pritchard. *Empire's Nature: Mark Catesby: New World Vision.* Chapel Hill: The University of North Carolina Press for the Omohundro Institute of Early American History and Culture and the Colonial Williamsburg Foundation, Williamsburg, 1998.

No portrait is known.

19 🦋 TO JOHN BARTRAM

ALS:HSP
London, February 3, 1736

Dear Friend John Bartram,

I am vastly Obliged to thee for thy many kind Favours which I shall answer in Course, but if it is Irregular, I can't help taking Notice of thine of the 18 September In which thee thinks I have neglected to take notice of thy Favour by young Israel Pemberton, which thee Certainly must misapprehend or Else my two Letters (in answer to that), per Capt Cox Augst 16 & per Capt Green are not come to hand for I keep a regular Account of Letters & by whom answered so can't mistake. Thee should not suspect thy Friend but suspend thy Resentment till thee art Certainly informed how things happened. Thee may assure thyself thee shall not fail of Suitable and grateful returns from me. Phaps I may be slow but I am sure.

The Box of seeds by Israel [Pemberton] came safe & was very acceptable to thy Noble

Friend, The terrapins which I designed for him had bad luck. Some died, others the sailors stole, but Israel made all the amends he could & gave me one that he had. He is a very ingenious, kind, good-natured Lad.

I was pleased to hear the few things proved worth your acceptance. I hope this year to send thee something as a reward for thy trouble which is more than I can imagine, but thee may felicitate thyself that the pains thee has taken is not for those who are insensible of it & who will make suitable returns, though not equal to thy deserts.

Thee writes for Cions of pears. If my good Friend John Whites Collection Came safe He has the best we have in England. No doubt for my sake he will Oblige thee with some Cions.

I never heard it was Insects that annoyed your plums Apricots & Nectarines. If they are att the Root, Water that has tobacco Leaves soaked in it will kill them by making a Bason round the tree & watering it frequently with this water.

I was amazed to hear that the Frost in your Latitude kills the vines in the Winter. You must use the German Method. Dig a Trench or hole close to your vine & therein Lay the young shoots & then cover them with Earth, wch protects them from the Frosts, & when they are over, take them up again & prune them.

Pray how fares it with your wild Country vines? I am strongly of Opinion they will be best to make a vineyard because they are habituated to your seasons, but then it will much Depend on the skill of the pson that chooses the Vines to propagate. When they are ripe a knowing pson in grapes should ride the woods where they grow & select out those that have good qualities as good bearers, best-flavoured fruit, large berries, close bunches, early ripeners, & mark the trees so as to know them again & from these take cuttings for a vineyard. In all wild fruite there is a remarkable Difference. When these come to be cultivated (as all fruites were once Wild & have been improved by culture) who knows but you may make as pretty a wine fit for your own drinking & to serve your West India neighbours as Madeira or any other peticular country wine.

I am pleased to hear the Medlar [*Erataegus azarolus*] Grew. It is the great sort from Naples.

Please to remember as I formerly desired to get some strong plants of your Ivy or Bay that thee sent me some Specimens of & plant in a Box to Stand a year or two or three till it Flowers in the box, and some of your shrub White & Red Honesuckles. These are ticklish plants to keep Here.

I now come to answer thy kind letter of September 9th per Budget. I am pleased to hear thee art acquainted with Dr. Witt, an old Correspondent of mine and has sent Mee Many a Valuable Curious plant, but I am afraid the old Gentleman has been too cunning for thee. Those fine Lady's Slippers [*Cypripedium*] which makes my mouth Water have slipped beside it. The Doctor says he would have sent them Mee but that He was afraid they were spoiled in bringing home for want of proper Care to wet the roots by the way.

This accident brings to my mind a very pretty Method by which plants will keep fresh 3 or 4 days on a Journey, take 3 or 4 largest ox Bladders, Cut off the Neck high, & when a plant is found take it up with Little Earth to the roots, put this into the Bladder, then put water in the Bladder to Cover the Roots, then tie up the neck of the bladder close round the stalk of the plant leaving the Leaves, Flowers &c without. Large plants won't do so well but several small plants may be put in a Bladder. When tied hang it to the pummell or skirts of the saddle or any other convenient way thee may choose. If the water wastes add more. Thus plants with little trouble may be kept a long while fresh. It is always best if water can be had to add it immediately at taking up the plants.

But these fine Lady's Slippers, don't let Escape, for they are my favourite plants. I have your yellow one that thrives well in my Garden but I much want the other sorts. Pray show the Doctor no More, but I find thee has taken the hint thyself. Don't say any thing I have writt. Neither shall I take any notice of thine.

It is with pleasure when we read thy Excursions (& wish to bear thee Company), but then it is with concern that we reflect on the Fatigue thee undergoes, the great risks of thy Health in Heats & Colds, but above all the Danger of Rattlesnakes. This would so curb my Ardent Desires to see vegitable Curiosities that I should be afraid to venter in your woods unless on Horseback & so Good a guide as thee art by my side.

Thy Expedition for the Curious Tree in the Jerseys [*Ceanothus americanus,* New Jersey tea]. Truly shows an Indefatigable Disposition in thee to oblige us here. I hope thee will not fail to find some Gratitude in us.

The seed is exceeding Fresh but such as I never saw before, of a pleasant tast some thing like Juniper berries. I wish thee had Discribed the Tree to us, but what would have saved thee that pains would have been to send us two or three specimens of the Leaves or Branches of a size proper to Inclose between a sheet of paper & then have told us wether it sheds its Leaves or is an Evergreen & what blossoms it has. Do not go on purpose but when ever thee goes that way pray procure some.

The Leaves of the Sugar Tree are very Informing and are a great Curiosity, but Wee Wish thee had gather'd Little Branches with the flowers on them & some Little Branches with the keys on them. The seeds of this Tree which by the Leaves & keys is a Real Mapple. I cracked a many of them & not one has a kernel in them which I am surprised. Whether they were not fully ripe, thee canst best Judge, but so it is. Wee must Desire thee next year to make another Attempt & Send us some Specimens. Its bearing white Blossoms is an Elegance above any other of this Tribe that I know off, for Wee have two sorts in England, a Major which is comminly Here call'd the Sycamore and the other is a Minor less every way & both bear bunches of greenish Blossoms succeeded by keys like those thee sent. From they assured friend,

P. Collinson

20 ❧ TO JOHN BARTRAM

ALS:HSP
London, February 20, 1736

Resp Friend

I have Sent the Goods as under which I hope will Mett with thy approbation and as there was no Direction Either to Quallity or Quantity I have done to the best of my Judgmt. When I have setled with Our Noble Friend who takes all the Cargo to his own Acct I will advise thee of the ballance.

Young Israel Pemberton to whome Thou art much oblig'd att my Request has pack'd up thy Goods with His which consists of 5 percells vizt:

1 parcell with Quallity binding Silks, Combs, Girdles with some other things.

1 parcell with the Garlick & Cambrick [linen]

1 parcell being a fine Sagathie [serge] for Lineings for a Summer Coat & Breeches for thy Self

1 parcell being a summer Gown & Hood for thy Wife &c

1 parcell being Camletes [a light fabric of silk and hair] &c for Coats for thy Children or Wast-coats for thy Self.

What Ever Thou Finds is not charged in thy Bill of parcells is presents for thy Self, Wife & Children. Receive it in Love as it was Sent. I shall write thee fuller on all Matters the first Leisure.

I have procur'd From my knowing Friend Phillip Miller, Gardener to the Physick Garden att Chelsea belonging to the Company of Apothecarys 69 Sorts of Curious Seeds and some others of my own Collecting. This I hope will Convince thee I do what I can and if I Lived as thou does always in the Country I should do More, Butt in my situation it is Impossible. Besides, Most of the plants thee writes for are not to be found in Gardens but growing Spontaneously Many Miles off & a Many Miles from one another. It is not to be expected I can do as thou Does. My Inclination's good but I have affairs of Greater Consequence to Mind, and as I have observed to thee before, & I do Request thee not to suffer any thing thee does for us to Interfere with thine.

Indeed for the Cargo thou sent there was some reason for the makeing it thy Business because thee will have some Gratification, but in thy other Curious Colections which is done purely to oblige us pray give thy Business the preference, but if in the Course of that without neglect of It thou can pick up what thou thinks will be acceptable wee shall be obliged to thee & Study some Requital.

So for the Future no More Censure Mee for not sending the one Sixth part Thee wrote For for the Reasons above.

But yett Transmitt Mee yearly what thou Wants, & any thing in my power or my friend Millers will be always att they Service. & if I send thee the Same thing 2 or 3 Times over thee must Excuse it & place It to the Multiplicity of affairs that Fill my thoughts & not suspect my care, and Then Thee Will Deal Kindly & Friendly & Lovingly with they Friend,

P. COLLINSON

All of these seeds come in Joseph Breintnalls packket.
[List of fabrics, buttons, ruff, and combs sent deleted]

I presume what is more than for thy Own use thee will Dispose of amongst thy Neighbors.

I shall not forgett the Cask of Nails, but I promised to send it by Capt Savage, which In Gratitude I ought to Do for his Great Civility, but if He does not Speedyly returne I shall then alter my Mind.

Pleas to call on Jos Breintnall for Seeds. They come in the Library Companys parcell by Israel Pemberton. Should sow them immediately.

The Orpine Seed must be very Slightly Cover'd. Perhaps if it was Scatter on the Mould in a Midlin Shady place it may do better & then covered with Earth.

ALS:HSP
London, March 12, 1736

Dear Friend

On the other Side thou will see thy Acccount Drawn out with as much Exactness as I could Collect it From thy Invoices. I have Endeavor'd to Do Justice between thee & thy Noble Employer [Lord Petre]. I have shown it to him & He approves of It and has Ordered Mee to give thee Credit for £18:13.3d.[1] Part of it has been sent to thy Order, and for the Ballance thou may draw a Bill on Mee or Order it in Goods which suites thee Best. His Lordship paid Freight & all charges on the Seed being willing to give thee all the Advantage for thy Encouragement.

The things for thine & thy Wifes Ware are a Joynt present from Mee & His Lordship for thy other Seeds and plants & specimens &c.

As Lord Petre Desired to see thy Letters they are all there. He admires thy plain Natural Way of writing & thy observations & Descriptions of several plants. For Want of them I shall only take notice of thy proposal in One of them for an annual allowance to Encourage & Enable thee to prosecute Further Discoveries.

Lord Petre is very Willing to Contribute very Handsomely towards it. He will be Tenn Guineas and Wee are in Hope to Raise Tenn More. This Wee think will Enable thee to Sett apart a month Two or Three to make an Excurtion on the Banks of the Skullkill to Trace it to its Fountain. But as so great an Undertaking Requires Two or Three years & as many Journeys to Effect it, so wee must Leave that wholy to thee.

But Wee do Expect that after Harvest & when the Season is that all the Seeds of Trees & Shrubs are Ripe thou will Sett out and them that happen not to be ripe when thou goes they may have attained to Maturity when thou Comes Back.

Wee shall send thee paper for specimens & writeing and a pockett Compass. Expect thee'll keep a Regular Journal of what occurs Every Day and an Exact Observation of the Course of the River which with a Compass thee may Easily do.

It will Wee apprehend be Necessary to take a Servant with thee & Two Horses for your Selves & a spare one to carry Linnen, provisions and all other Necessaries. If the spare Horse and the Mans Horse Had Two panniers or Large Basketts on Each Side they will be very Convenient to Carry paper to take specimens by the Way & to bring back the Seeds.

Thee may Make a Good Many Little, Midlin & Large paper Baggs to putt the Seeds in & be sure have some good Covering of Skins over the Basketts to keep out the Rain &c. Take some Boxes for Insects of all Sorts with the Netts, and on thy Returne some particular plants that thee most Fancies may be brought in the basketts if there is Roome.

Thee Need not Collect any more Tulip Cones, Swamp Laurell Cones, Hickery, Black walnutt, Sassifrax, or Dogwood, Sweet Gum, White oke Acorns, Swamp Spanish oke, nor Red Cedar Berries.

Butt all other sorts of Acorns, Firrs & pines, black gum or black Haw, Judas Tree, Persimmon, Cherries, plums, Services, Hop tree, Benjamin or All Spice [*Lindera benzoin*], all the sorts of Ash, Sugar Tree Wild Rose, Black Beach or Horn Beam, all sorts of Flowering & Berry Bearing Shrubs, Honey Locust, Lime Tree, Arrow wood, a particular Locust, Guelder Rose.

Frutex Corni foliis conjugatis, floribus instar Anemones stellatæ petalis crassis rigidis colore sordide rubente cortice aromatico. Catesb. Msst

Lindera. *Georg Dionysius Ehret. Hunt Institute for Botanical Documentation.*

Not any thing can come amiss to thy Friends and in particular to thy True Friend

P. COLLINSON

February 5th, 1736

Lord Petre   Dr   to John Bartram

	£	s	d
No 1 Box			
250 Hickery	1		2 : 6
30 Long Walnutts	5		2 : 6
1 peck Sassafrax	5		
No 2			
550 Common Hickery	1		5 : 6
3/4 qrs peck Dogwood	5		3 : 9
2 pecks Red Cedar	5	10	
500 Sweet Gum Cones	5		1 : 5
500 Swamp Laurell Cones	5		1 : 5
100 Spruce Cones	5		
200 Chesnutt Acorns &c	2		

No 3

1 peck Dogwood Berries	5		
500 Swamp Laurell Cones	5		1 : 5
1000 Spruce Cones	5		2 : 10
500 Gum Burrs	5		1 : 5
1500 White oke Acorns	1	15	
700 White Hickery	1	7	
600 Sweet Hickery	1	6	
2000 Swamp Spanish Acorns	1		1 :
2000 Black Walnutts	1		1 :
1000 White oke Acorns	1	10	
400 White Hickery	1	4	
1200 Swamp Spanish oke	1	12	
300 Sweet Hickery	1	3	
1500 Tulip Tree Cones	5		3 : 15
1000 White & black Walnutts	1	10	

By Haberdashery, Linnen &c per Bill	6 : 9 : 2
By Cask of Nails	5 : 1 : 7

	11 : 10 : 9
Due to thee	7 : 2 : 6

The Cask of Nails is ship'd by the St George, Capt Lindsay. I shall write thee by Him and Inclose Bill Loading & pay the freight which must be deducted out of the Bill 7:2:6.

Dear Friend, as thee has given Mee many Instances of thy Curious, Speculative Disposition it has putt Mee on Enlarging thy knowledge in Natural Inquiries as the Earth is filled with wonders & Everywhere is to be seen the Marks & Effects of almighty power. Most things was made for the Use of & pleasure of Mankind, Others to Raise our Admiration and astonishment as in particular what is call'd Fossills, being Stones Found all the World over that Have In them the Impression or Else the Regular Form of Shells, Leaves, Fishes, Fungus, Teeth, Sea Eggs and Many other productions.

That thee may better apprehend what I meane I have sent thee some specimens in a packett of paper for Specimens of plants for Lord Petre with some Seeds & pocket Compass. Captain Savage has promised to take Care of the parcell.

In the Course of thy Travells or in Diging the Earth or in thy Quarries possibly some sort of Figur'd Stones [fossils] may be found Mixed or Compounded with Earth, Sand or Stone & Chalk. What use the Learned make of them is that they are Evidences of the deluge of which thee may Hear More when [illegible]

I hope Israel Pemberton is Safe arrived & the Little Box with Chesnutts and all the other parcells with my Letters & the Box of Insects are Come Safe. Pray dont forgett as soone as possible the specimens of Red & White Cedar & a few White Cedar berries.

1. We get some idea of the value of these shipments when we note that Bartram's credit balance with Collinson at this point— £18:13:3d—amounted to more than a third of the annual Royal pension of £50 Collinson arranged for Bartram in 1764.

ALS : Bodleian
July-August 1736

Dear Doctor

This Day I Sent a Box by John Bow Coach from the Bull in Holborn what plants I could spare. It will be too Late to Send over this year to Mr Spreckleson [not identified] for the Rare Ficoides you Mention. Pray putt Mee in Mind of it Next Year Lest I forgett. I have Sent 2 Cape Gladiolus I am reduced to 2 plants of the Echim Masinum, One Strong plant & the One very Weak. If my Strong plant bears Seed you shall be Sure of Some Next Year. The Ficoides that I have not I hope to procure from Chelsea [Physic Garden]. I have Rec'd the Money of Mr. Monk [not identified].

My Indefatigable Friend John Bartram in Pensilvania has taken an Expedition of 140 or 150 Miles In Search of the White Cedar [*Chamaecyparis thyoides*]. I press'd Him to Satisfie us in perticular Relateing to this plant & if it had been twice as farr he would have done it. I will give you part of his Letter:

I Engag'd an Owner of part of a Cedar Swamp for my Guide without whome I could hardly have found It, Wee travel'd about Twelve Miles beyond the Inhabitants over Desarts of Sand & Such deep Mirery Swamps that Sometimes both Wee & our Horses had much a Do to gett Out. The Sand Lies in Ridges 40 or 50 or 60 poles over & the Swamps Lie between which are the heads of Rivers & Brooks but So thick Sett with Shrubs & Bushes about 10 poles Wide yt We had great Difficulty in passing these Swamps. Att Last Wee came to the Head of (Egghar-

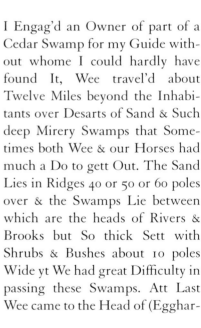

Johann Jacob Dillenius. Artist unknown. Copy of portrait in Oxford Botanic Garden. The flower is Sprekelia formosissima. *His scarlet cheeks fortell his death from apoplexy. The Linnean Society of London.*

bour River) where the great Cedar Swamp Began containing many hundred Acres Chiefly produceing White Cedar but In Some Dryer places, Silver Laurell or Bay Maple, Holley, & Sarsifrass & About the Edges Some pines, but I Observed no Red Cedar. The White Grows only in Wett places often Knee Deep in Water in Wett Seasons. They grow Near together the Small Ones within a foot or Two of one another. A White Cedar of Two Inches Diameter will be 20 feet high, the Larger Trees Grows att 10 or 20 feet Distance which Makes them grow very tall. A Tree of Two feet Diamr att the Stump will be 80 or 100 feet in Heighth and 30 or 40 feet without a Limb. The Soil were they gro I take to be Clay but the Surface is a Matt of Roots all Interlac'd one with another which Intangles the Leaves & Rubish & makes a Bogg. The Bark of the Root is Red which gives a tincture to the Waters that runs from them but the Tast is good & sweet. Our Ceterach & Sarsparilla grows att the Roots where the Sun is rarely Seen. So thick is the Shade above the Leaves is not near so Long and prickly as the Red Cedar. The Fruite is Coniferous Seed very small. To Satisfie your Immediate Curiosity I Inclose a Small Specimen, but this Second of Last June, I cutt down a Large Tree for to Send you Larger Specimens which I shall Send by first oppertunity.

Now dear Dr I think by what Mr Dudley[1] Says & My Friend Bartram who has used Great Dispatch to Informe us, thee art now fully Quallified to Sett Mr. Ray[2] and all Curious Inquirers Since In a Clear Light respecting the White & Red Cedars, the White by its Seed Vessell Here Inclosed appear to be a True Cedar, but what is call'd the Red Cedar are only Junipers or Savins.

Dr Linneus has been to see Mee and intends You a Visit Soone.

I am affectionately yours,   P. COLLINSON

This Day I receiv'd my Friend John's Letter. He tells Mee he was then going up to the Blew Mountains to See for Rare Plants & Seeds.

JOHANN JACOB DILLENIUS (1687–1747), German-born botanist employed by William Sherard (1659–1728) in 1721 to assist with his updating of Caspar Bauhin's *Pinax* of 1623 (never completed; the manuscript is in the Bodleian Library, Oxford), and by William's brother James to catalog the plants in his garden at Eltham, published under the title *Hortus Elthamensis,* 1732, which Dillenius both wrote and illustrated: "The most important book to be published in England during the eighteenth century on the plants growing in a private garden . . ." (Henrey). Among other works he prepared the third edition of J. Ray's *Synopsis Methodica Stirpium Britannicarum,* 1724 and *Historia Muscorum,* 1742. He was the first president of the Botanical Society (of London), was elected FRS in 1724, and upon William Sherard's death and the bequest of Sherard's herbarium and botanical library to Oxford, Dillenius was in 1734 appointed the university's first Sherardian Professor of Botany. (Henrey; DNB)

Although this letter is not dated in Collinson's hand (someone has written July 31, 1736 in the upper left margin of the first page), we do know that on August 28, 1736 Collinson thanked Bartram for "the account of the expedition to the Rattlesnake Mountains." The references to "what Mr Dudley sayes" and Linnaeus's visit also serve to place the letter in 1736, since Collinson refers to the Dudley letter in his to Bartram of June 7, 1736, and Linnaeus made his only visit

to England in 1736, when he visited both Collinson and Dillenius.

1. Paul Dudley (1675–1751), FRS, American-born jurist, graduated Harvard 1690, read law in the Middle Temple, and was called to the bar in 1700. In 1702 he received a commission from Queen Anne as Attorney-General of the province of Massachusetts Bay and became Chief Justice in 1745. "When off the Bench he would often be seen conversing familiarly with the commonest people, having his hands upon their shoulders." An accomplished naturalist, and interested in local antiquities, he contributed papers to the Royal Society. Although Collinson once wrote Bartram that he had no friends in New England, he often referred to "Mr. Dudley of Roxbury." (DAB)

2. John Ray (1627–1705), FRS, English botanical and zoological systematist, variously described as "the father of English natural history" (Desmond) and the "Aristotle of England." (DSB) He produced *Historia plantarum* in 3 vols., 1686–1704. His contribution to botany was a system of classification, later superseded, which produced order out of unsystematic descriptions. He applied similar principles to the classification of insects and the classes of the vertebrates. Ray also wrote on English proverbs, obscure words, voyages and travels, and other subjects, the best known of these works being *The Wisdom of God manifested in the Works of the Creation,* 1691, many times reprinted. (DNB)

ALS:HSP
London, August 28, 1736

Dear Friend John Bartram,

   I Rec'd thy Entertaining Letter & the Acc't of thy Expedition to the Rattle Snake Mountains which His Lordship [Lord Petre] now has So can't In particular Answer it. It was very Well thought to putt the Small Specimen of Cedar with the Little Cones in the Letter. My Friend sayes It is a True Cypress haveing the figure & Properties of the Common Cypress but the Cone Exceedingly Less.

   The plant thee Gather'd Last year near the Mountains That has the appearance In Leaves & Flower of Mallows, but by the pticular Figure of the Seed Vessell it is call'd an Abutilon [*Abutilon,* flowering maple]. There is another Species that much Resemble Mallows, but their Seed Vessell being Like a pod. Its Call'd Ketmia [*Hibiscus trionum*].

Abutilon, *flowering maple. Georg Dionysius Ehret. In Trew,* Plantae Selectae, *plate XC. The Linnean Society of London*

Hibiscus, Ketmia. *Georg Dionysius Ehret. In Trew,* Plantae Selectae, *plate VI. Natural History Museum, Botany Library, London.*

I did not Send thy Goods by this Ship because I'm in hopes by the next which sails in 2 or 3 Weeks to save the Freight.

Pray send Some Acorns of the Narrow leaved Okes, Cones of Tulip Tree, a Specimen in Flower of the Sugar Maple, and the Seed, Flowering bay Cones & what Ever Else thou thinks well of Timber Trees & Shrubs &c.
I am thy Real Friend
                    P. COLLINSON
Inclosed is some Fresh Seed of our True Cowslip. Scatter the Seed on the Ground in a half Sandy place but don't Cover it.

Send More Black Walnutts, Long Walnutts and both Sorts of Hickery Acorns, of all Sorts Sweet Gum, Dog Wood, Red Cedar Berries, All Spice, Sarsifrax. These will be acceptable to the Duke of Richmond,[1] & Lord Petre will Like Some More.

Pack all the Seeds the

Same Way as last Year for they succeed very Well, a few Excepted.

The Acorns & Sweet Gum and Indeed Most of all the other Seeds are finely Come up.

The Greatest Difficiency is in the poplar or Tulip Cones & the Sugar Tree. Not one of the Sarsifrax nor Cedar berries appears but I presume they Lie Two Years.

Thy Kind neighr James Logan[2] is so good as to Order Mee to Buy thee Perkinsons Herbal[3] if I can have it for 25 Shillings. He has shown a very Tender Regard for thee in his Letter to Mee. It may Look Gratefull Every Now & than to Call and Inquire after thy Good Friend Logans Welfare. He is a Great Man in Every Capacity & for Whome I have the Highest Value.

Dear Friend I thought when I began to Write but 2 or 3 Lines but I go on scribling till the paper Confines Mee. Thine   P C

1. Charles Lennox, second Duke of Richmond (1701–1750), Collinson's dearest friend after Lord Petre, maintained a Sussex estate called Goodwood, famous for its plantings of foreign trees including cedars. See Collinson to Lennox, March 29, 1748 and to Benjamin Cook, October 1, 1759.

2. James Logan (1674–1751), Irish-born Quaker, Colonial scholar, statesman, scientist and author, came to Philadelphia in 1699 as secretary to William Penn. He was Chief Justice of Pennsylvania (1731–1739) and as president of the Council acted as Governor of the Colony for two years after the death of Governor Gordon in 1736. He corresponded with Linnaeus and was interested in the theory of sex in plants. In his Philadelphia garden he studied the fertilization of maize which he recounted in a letter to Collinson (November 20, 1735). Collinson presented Logan's experiments to the Royal Society and caused his account to be printed in *Philosophical Transactions* XXXIX (1736): 192–5. These studies were published in Leyden, 1739, as *Experimenta et meletemata de plantarum generatione nec non canonum pro inveniendis refractionum . . .* and were translated by John Fothergill and published in London, 1747, as *Experiments and considerations on the generation of plants.* (DAB)

3. Parkinson, John (1567–1650). *Theatrum botanicum.* London, 1640.

ALS:HSP
London, September 20, 1736

Friend John

I writt thee by Capt Pearce and I have not much to Add but to acquaint thee that I have sent a Case of Glass as per bill Inclosed. I could not Gett the Quallity binding to my Mind to Come by this Ship, it being a Narrower Sort then is sold Here. I was oblig'd to get it made on purpose and One Man made it So Ordinary that I was Oblig'd to returne them & then I had to find a Man to begin again. Att Last I Meet with one to undertake it. I hope He will Do it to my Mind. I will send it by first oppertunity & then will Close thy Acco't.

I have After Some Inquiry Mett with Parkinsons Herbal which I have bought for 25s by the Direction of My Good Friend J. Logan. He Designs it as a present to Thee. It may not be amiss att a Suiteable Time to Wait on Him, but take not the Least Notice that I gave thee this Hint unless He Should ask thee & then tell him freely.

I have the pleasure to tell thee that the Noble Marsh Martigon [*Lilium superbum L,*] Flower'd with Mee which thou sent this spring. It is a delicate Flower.

I have sent in a Trunk to J. Breintnall a paper parcell for thee being Apricot, Nectarine & Some fine peachs & plums Stones of the best Sorts. These Fruites I apprehend will succeed better From Seed then by Grafting unless on peach Stock. Sow them in a proper place. If where they are always to stand it may be better, but if they are Removed I apprehend if apricots, plums & Nectarines was planted on the Margin of a River or on the Side of a feeding Spring where they may be always supplly'd with Moisture to their Fibres they would not be so apt to shrivel & Drop their Fruite in the very hott Weather.

I have further to Request of thee as thou on thy own affairs art oblig'd to Traverse the Woods to take all oppertunitys to make observations on the Rattle Snake or Indeed any other Snake & that Birds, Squirrels &c are found in their Bellies is notoriously known but the Question is how they Came there, Weither the Snake Laying Perdue [hidden] on a sudden Darts on her prey & Bites It & then Lays on the Spot Expecting the Effect of her poisonous Bite will att Last bring the Little animal down Dead to her Devouring Jaws.

Lilium canadense, meadow lily— "Noble Marsh Martigon."
Georg Dionysius Ehret. The Natural History Museum, Botany Library, London.
"Flowered in the garden of Mr. P. Collinson August 1744."

"New Lily." Mark Catesby. From Collinson's copy of Natural History of Carolina . . . at Knowsley Hall, *Vol II, p 116. Courtesy of the Earl of Derby, Knowsley.*

Collinson wrote on the back, "This New and Pretty Lillie come up with a Very Hairy Head before it opens it Flower. Was sent by J. Bartram from Pensylvania. It flowered June 7, 1740."

Sir Hans Sloane and a Great Many others are of the Opinion and by an Ingenious Letter from a Curious person in your Citty[1] their opinion is very much Confirm'd.

But then on the other Side of the Question I have Reced from my Ingenious Friends J Breintnall & Dr Witt very pticular accounts of the power it has over Creatures by Charming them Into its very Jaws.

Possibly some accidental Discovery may be made when it is Least thought on. It will require a Nice & Exact observation to Determine this Matter. If thee knows any thing of thy own knowledge please to Communicate it. The heare Say of Others can't be Depended on. The Common & Long Received opinion of Charming is so Riveted in peoples Imagination that unless they will Divest themselves of It they may not Easily Distinguish to the Contrary.

Pray has thee hear'd or Observed that a Certain Species of Locust returns Every Fifteenth year. I have been Inform'd of Such a thing from New England.[2]

I want very much to be satisfied about the Sugar Maple as to its Flowers if they are White as thee has Inform'd Mee before. Please in the Spring to gather Some Specimens When in Flower and send Mee & be very pticular In thy remarks on It.

Wee have Raised a pretty many fine plants from the Tree in the Jersies. It is a Real Lotus or Nettle Tree and is a Native of your part of the World. Is found in Virginia and in other parts. Parkinson knew only of one Sort which is the European with black Fruite, butt Wee have in the Gardens Two Sorts from your part of the World Distinguish'd by the Colour of their Fruite.

Inclosed is the Bill Parcells for the Glass and the Receipt for it on Board. I got Lawrence Williams to enter it with his Goods to save thee Expence of Shipping Charges.

I have been Twice with the Capt to pay the Freight but being a Small Box His Mate had not given him a Memorandum of It. So I hope if He takes any thing It will be but a Small Matter.

So that thee has nothing More to Do Either to go thy Self or Gett thy Friend Breintnall to Carry the Receipt and Ask for the Box Marked as per the Inclosed paper which was my Directions for shipping It.

Dear Friend John, I am thy Real Friend, P. COLLINSON

---

1. Possibly John Kearsley. See Collinson to Bartram, December 10, 1737.

2. Collinson was long interested in locusts. He read papers on them to the Royal Society on December 10, 1737, and again on February 23, 1764, and published "Some Observations on the Cicada of North America, collected by Mr. P. Collinson, FRS" in *Philosophical Transactions* LIV (1764): 65, giving credit to "my ingenious friend John Bartram" for the observations reported.

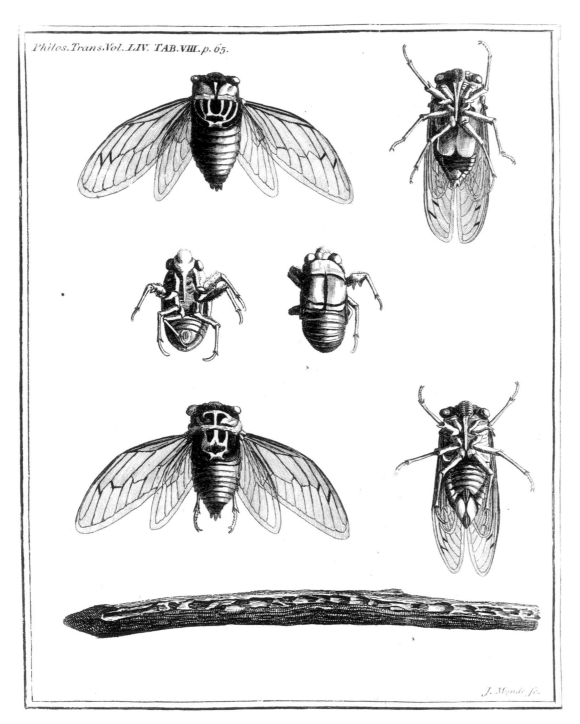

Cicadia—engraving published in Philosophical Transactions *LIV (1764): 65. American Philosophical Society*

ALS: AAS
London, December 4, 1736

Mr Custis

As I know you are a Lover of Rarities it always gives Mee pleasure when I think I can oblige you that Way or Indeed in any other.

I have Just now rec'd from the professor of the Botanic Garden att Petersburgh[1] the Inclosed seeds. They appear to Mee very Fresh and I have known by Experience that Mellon seed will keep Good 3 or 4 years and Wee Esteem 2 years old the best for sowing being more productive of Fruite than New seed.

If you Look into the Map and see the Northern Latitude of Petersburg or Muscow one wou'd reasonably conclude such Delicious Fruites are not to be expected in that Climate. They are Indeed beholden to a more Souther situation for their production, being brought in the seasons by Water up the Wolga from Casan and in particular the Water Mellons from Astracan which Lies near the Mouth of the Wolga on the Caspian sea. These Water Mellons are much Famed. I wish the seed may prove Good that I may have your Opinion of them and if they are any Ways Different from those you have already and some seed. The Calmuc Mellon seems to be an uncommon sort by its Length. I beg Your Observations and some seed of Each sort for you have Tenn Times the Chance of their comeing to full Maturity then Wee can Expect.

If the Cucumber is Different pray send some seed.[2] I would advise to sow half the seed att one sowing and the other half a Little while after for fear of accidents. I wish you may Raise one of the Siberian Cedars, But is more a pine by the seed. I had a sight of the Cone, it is the figure of a Midle size pineapple or annanas, and has att the Head of the Cone a Brown Hard Excrescence in Imitation of the Crown on the Fruite of the pineapple, I mean thee sort growing in the West Indies which are now grown very plentifull in most Curious Gardens with us.

I have taken the Very next ship that sail'd. Hope these will gett early enough to be sown the first of the season.

I am my Dear Sir Yours

P. COLLINSON

3 sorts of Muscovy Mellons
1 sort of Muscovy Cucumber
1 sort of Calmuc Mellon with fruite 2 feet long
1 sort of Astrican Water Mellon
Siberia Cedar or pine
Affrican Mellon seed
Italian Melon
Sir Charles Wagers Melon

1. Johann Ammann (1707–1742), Swiss, FRS, professor of botany and natural history at the Imperial Academy of Sciences at St. Petersburg, 1733–1741.

2. In 1738 Collinson wrote Sir Hans Sloane: "I sent Some Turk Cucumber Seed . . . to Col Custis which produced Such Wonderfull Large Fruite that Surprised all that Saw Them. The account is as follows:

"There Grow this Summer 1737 in the Garden of Mr Daniel Parke Custis . . . a Cucumber of the Turky kind which Measur'd above a yard in length and near 14 Inches Round. What is Very remark It Grow three Inches in Length in One Night. Several Others Grow on the Same Vines near as Large as this." (undated ALS: BL)

ALS:AAS
London, March 21,1737

Dear Mr Custis

I have the pleasure to tell you that the seed of the fringe Tree is now comeing up & your Mountain Cowslip is now in flower. These are Living Memorials with many others of your great kindness. The Chinquapins You sent last year by the help of a Little Art are a finger high & yett I beg your further assistance this year, for it is a Tree Wee are in great Want off amongst our Curious plants, and you above all others are so very happy In packing them up & sending so Early that Wee never had such Lucke before, for by Long Experience I know this to be the most Ticklish seed to bring from your part of the World & pray some Acorns of your Narrow Leafed Okes, Cypress Cones &c.

It is a Detriment to the Cargo of strawberries (there is a pott of Chilli and one of Haut-boye)[1] going so Late. The Captain is very anctious to Carry them safe. I have given Directions to Water them Once or Twice a Week, which if He does & gives them Air, I am in hopes they will come safe. If not Wee will have the other Tryall next year.

I am truly your affectionate friend

P. COLLINSON

A few Days agon I received the Inclos'd Mellon seed from Africa. If it is to Late this year it will keep till Next.

The Oriental Persicary [*Persicaria*] is a Noble Annual, Grows 7 or 8 foot high, makes Glorious show with its bunches of Cherry Color Blossoms. Pray have you Mr. Millers Dictionary which contains a General Systeme of Gardening and the Culture of all sorts of plants. It is a Work of the Greatest use and no Lover ought to be without, all Drawn from the Latest Experience. The Author is Gardner to the Physick Garden att Chelsea and Exceeding well Qualified for the Work. It is in folio, about [blank]. If you are Inclin'd to by it, pray Lett Mee gett it for you, for there is an appendix & some has it not.

There is besides the Culture of the Kitchen Garden after the Newest Methode. Indeed there is everything you can ask & think.

P. COLLINSON

1. Chilean strawberry, (*Fragaria chiloensis*). In 1727 Philip Miller introduced some plants from Amsterdam, whence they had come from Chile by way of France. Hautboye strawberry or Haut- bois, (*Fragaria moschata* Duschesne), grown from the seventeenth century on in England, is native to Europe but not England.

27 🐦 TO SAMUEL EVELEIGH

Draft ALS:LS
London, April 22, 1737

Dear Friend

As I could neither give you profit or much Entertainment by my Writeing, I have deferd troubling you for Some Time, yett the less has not been Regard I paid to your Memory. I have not been a wanting as often as I have happened in the company of your Country men to Inquire after your Welfare. By an accident I was introduced to Mr Hill[1] whose obliging behaviour I shan't forgett. Hee informed Mee of your Recovery from a Dangerous Illness which gave me great pleasure & promised to Convey this to your Hands.

My Good Friend I am persuaded your Active Genius can't be Idle. You will permitt Mee to Inquire what Improvements are going forward.

Have you made any progress in the Makeing Jalap or Opium?[2] Your Soil & Climate is very proper for these productions and what Wee annually pay great Sums to Foreigners.

Pray Does the Rice continue to Imploye all your time & your Hands? It is a Noble & profitable produce and happy for your Colony being so well adapted to your Soil & Climate. Mr. Dubois,[3] Treasurer to the E India Comp, who is yett Living, has Several times told Mee that att the request of Mr. Marsh[4] a Marchant He Procur'd for him a Hundred pound Money bag of Rice to send to Carolina and the Wonderfull Increase is affirmed to Mee.

Is all proceeded from this Small Original? Doubtless there is Some of your Oldest Planters can tell if this is fact, as to its being wholly Raised from so Small a Quantity, first sent from hence, for as to Dubois Relation I have no Doubt, but possibly Rice might be Brought to you from Other Hands. As it was, I should bee Obliged to you if you would Inform Mee what is your Tradition or Knowlidge of its Original.[5]

Pray does Raw Silk make any progress with you, or is the Glory of Raiseing that produce reserved for Georgia? I have Seen Samples of exceeding Good from Carolina worth Eighteen Shillings ye pound. It is a pitty but so profitable a branch of Trade was Encouraged.

I see no way so Effectual to Introduce it by Degrees into a Staple Manufacture, but by makeing It the Good Womans property & that the produce be Solely att their Disposal which would Save the Husband many pounds a year in his pockett for Milinary Wares and a Number of other articles the Ladies are fond off.

Besides as it is a Light, Easie, Indoors work So it Seems calculated the More for their Management, and was the property Secure to them, It is not to be fear'd but all Industrous provident Wives would make the Most on it. And was there Some Bounty given for Every pound of Silk, it would be a great Encouragement to Sett the Worms a Spinning, and that is the Interest of the province in General and of Every One in perticular to encourage. It is very Demonstrable for this Reason that all unprofitable Hands that are a Load on Every Family Such as Old & Young Negroes, Boys & Girles & ancient white Sarvants may be Employed in this Branch of Business to good Purpose and advantage; and be no Interruption to the plantation Business Without Doors.

Thus by Degrees a very profitable Employe will be Introduced into Every Family, and in process of time the Master will find it in his Interest to Turn more of his hands upon it, for if you go on in Increasing in the Rice produce you will over Stock the Marketts, so that it is but common prudence in time to Encourage a branch of trade that will certainly turn to Accot and for its produce Wee pay all Ready Money to Foreigners. I could say much more on this Subject, but that I believe by this Time I have pretty well tired you wch is a Sufficient Reason to conclude by assuring you that I am with much Respect Your affectionate Friend   P. COLLINSON.

PS If Some hints of this kind was thrown Into your Publick papers it might Sett Some Ingenious heads to work to propagate this Scheme which Certainly would prove of the Greatest Consequence to your Colony.

SAMUEL EVELEIGH (1672–1738), merchant of Charleston, South Carolina, an emigrant from Bristol ca. 1698 with close ties to English merchants, the leading exporter of deerskins in the first quarter of the eighteenth century and one of the dominant forces in the Indian trade. He was a member of the Assembly (1707) and the Governor's Council (1725–1727). (Edgar, Walter B. and N. Louise Bailey. *Biographical Directory of the South Carolina House of Representatives*. Columbia: University of South Carolina Press, 1974)

The Colonial Records of South Carolina: The Journal of the Commons House of Assembly, November 10, 1736—June 7, 1739 includes at p. 391 reference to "A Letter to Mr. Eveleigh from his Correspondent in London . . . relating to introducing the Silk Manufacture into this Province so much to be desired by all its well wishers. the 18th January, 1737/8." In 1744 the General Assembly of South Carolina voted "An Act for the further Improvement and Encouraging the Produce of Silk and other Manufactures in this Province. . . ."

While some silk was produced in South Carolina, the quantities and profits never reached commercially satisfactory levels. See Gray, Lewis Cecil. *History of Agriculture in the Southern United States to 1860*. Washington: The Carnegie Institution of Washington, 1933, pp. 184–190.

At the foot of his draft letter, Collinson many years later added this note: "My above Letter was read in the Assembly & a Bounty was voted for the Encouragement of raiseing Silk, but Rice is the prevailing article & Remains to this Time anno 1768. The produce of Silk is reserved for Georgia. The Society of Arts give a Bounty to Encourage it. Some silk has been sent Over."

Collinson regularly urged his colonial correspondents "to pursue improvements, alike beneficial to themselves and to their mother country. How often have I heard him urge to such of them as visited him, the benefit, nay necessity, of cultivating flax, hemp, wine, silk and other products? He would press the Virginians to bethink themselves in time of a more permanent staple, than a plant whose consumption only depends on custom and caprice, and this custom daily declining." [Fothergill, John, *Some Account of the Late Peter Collinson* . . . London, 1770, p. 13.

1. Possibly John Hill, captain of the *Resolution* (See Hamer, Philip M., ed. *The Papers of Henry Laurens*. Columbia: The University of South Carolina Press, Vol I, 1968, p. 61, note 5), or perhaps a cousin of John Fothergill.

2. There is no evidence that South Carolina ever produced commercial quantities of either jalap (a cathartic drug made from the roots of *Ipomoea purga*) or opium [*Papaver somniferia*]. See Gray, *op cit*.

3. Charles DuBois (1656–1740), FRS, lived at Mitcham, Surrey where his garden was full of the newest and exotic plants. His collection of 13,000 dried plant specimens in 74 folio vols. is part of the library of the Oxford Botanic Garden. (DNB) In his introduction to *Catalogus Plantarum . . . London, A Society of Gardeners, 1730*, Philip Miller wrote of DuBois, "To Him . . . we are greatly indebted for many valuable Trees and Plants which enrich this Catalogue. . . ."

4. Thomas Marsh, a South Carolina merchant. In his August 9, 1739 letter to Charles Wager, Collinson reports that according to Dubois it was Marsh who caused "a Hundred pound Bag fill'd with East India Rice" sent over "to try whether it would grow in that province."

5. The Carolina promoters were encouraging rice cultivation by 1677; its cultivation was well under way by 1694, and by 1698 production had reached the point that export was under discussion. Seed stocks probably came from many different sources. According to one account, a ship captain sailing from Madagascar and forced to put in at Charleston in 1694 presented Landgrave Thomas Smith with a bag of seed of "a much fairer and larger Kind." (Catesby, Mark. *Natural History of Carolina, Florida . . .* , II, p. xvii). In 1715 the lower house of the Assembly voted a gratuity to one John Thurber "for bringing the first Madagascar Rice into this Province."

Collinson described the development of the Carolina rice culture, with emphasis on the 1698 Dubois introduction, in the *Gentleman's Magazine* XXXVI (1766): 278, "An Account of the Introduction of Rice and Tea into Our Colonies."

28 ❧ TO JOHN BARTRAM

ALS:HSP

London, December 10, 1737

A little Leisure invites me to peruse thy several Entertaining Letters. I shall proceed in order and begin with thine of feby 27th.

Thy account of the Locusts is very Curious and very Entertaining to Mee & my Friends & shows that nothing escapes thy Notice. Their Surprising method of darting the sticks[1] is admirable. Pray watch as it happens in thy way what shape they take as Soon as they are hatched. Pray have they Wings when they creep out of the Ground? Procure Mee one if thee Canst, in their first state of coming out of the Ground & when the back opens. Is it a Real Grasshopper? for I take it all Grasshoppers are Locusts. Sett me right if I am wrong. Pin some of Each sort in a Box with a number to Each for I am In Some Doubts if they have not three or four Different apearances. First from the Egg they are a worm or Caterpillar, then they go into the Ground and change when they come out of the Ground. Their back opens & produces a Monstrous Large Fly. Then I apprehend they Turn to a Grasshopper or Locust.

As to that Caterpiller that comes in such numbers, Wee have something like it in England. They will eat the Okes & Hedges bare but never kill them which I take to be Owing that, as we have not the Sun's heat so strong with us, so our vegitation is weaker so the Tree by degrees recovers its verdure again but with you the Heat so rarifies the sap or Juices in Trees and puts it in such Vigorous Action and for want of young shoots & Leaves to Divert it by growth & perspiration the Vessels Burst, or the Circulation stop'd for Want of Vent, that the Tree soon Dies. If thee was to observe all these Caterpillars that Spin up Like silk worms produce a Large Moth & all Crysales that thee finds Hanging Naked produce Butter Flies or Day Flies.

If thee was to take the Cluster of Eggs round the Twigs & keep them till time of Hatching & feed them with the Leaves of the Tree they was found on thee might see the whole process, If I could have some sent time Enough with an account of what Tree they was found on, Wee have people would think it worth their while to Hatch them. This would be a pretty amusement for thy Children. They would soon learn, if a Little Instructed.

I have heard frequent accounts of the prodigious Flocks of pigeons by thy Remarks on the wonderful provision made by Our allwise Creator for the support of the Creation is well worth Notice. The ballance kept between the vegitable & Animal productions is really a fine Thought & what I never met with before, but it is more remarkable with you than with us for you have Wild animals & mast in greater plenty than Wee have.

I can't help by being of thy mind with regard to the Rattle Snake, for if Creatures were Bitt by him first, I can't Imagine they could be able to run away. Pray compare notes with Dr. Kearsley,[2] who is of the Contrary opinion & supports it very Ingeniously. I wish it may be thy Lott without harm to Meet with this Creature to observe his Motions, but I am confirmed of his power over men. In the manner thou Mentions, by a very Curious Friend of mine & a great Philosopher Colonel Byrd of Virginia who says you must not think Mee fanciful when I assure you, I have Ogled a Rattle Snake so Long till I have pceived a sickness in my stomach.

Now Dear John I have made some running Remarks on thy Curious Letter, which contained so many fine Remarks, that it Deserved to be read before the Royal Society & thee has their thanks for It, Desiring thee to Continue thy observations & Communicate them. Pray make no apology, thy style is much beyond what one might expect from a Man of thy Education. The Facts are well described & very Intelligible. I am with Love thy sincere friend,

P. Collinson

1. With the sharp end of her ovipositor the female makes a lengthwise cut on a twig and deposits her eggs in the gash.

2. John Kearsley: See headnote to February 7, 1738.

Opposite Page: Magnolia tripetala, *umbrella tree. Georg Dionysius Ehret. Natural History Museum, Botany Library, London.*

ALS: AAS
London, December 24, 1737

Dear Sir

Dont be surprised if a down right plain Country Man, perhaps he may be a Quaker too Into the Bargain & you know they are said to be an odd sort of a People but this makes mee call to mind an old proverbe the Devil is not so Black as painted.

Now if such a Medly Composition should come alltogether, Dont be startled. That you may not Mistake the Man He will bring a Credential From Mee. I so much persuaded my self of such an Interest in your Friendship you'l not Look att the Man but his Mind for my sake. His Conversation I dare say you'l find compensate for his appearance. He is well Vers'd In Nature & Can give a good Acount of her Works. He Comes to Visit your parts in serch of Curiosities In the Vegitable kingdome. Perhaps you'l find him more knowing in that Science then any you Have Mett With.

He is Imployed by a Sett of Noble Men (by my Recommendation) to Collect seeds & specimens of Rare plants, and he has been very successful in this affair which proceeds from His thorough knowledge in these Matters. Be so kind to give him a Little Entertain-m't & Recommend Him to a Friend or Two of yours in the Country, for He does not Value rideing 50 or 100 Miles to see a New plant.

Pray Direct Him to the Umbrella Tree [*Magnolia tripetala*]. This plant or Tree will make Him think his Journey worth Comeing. I have a further Desire in his waeting on you. The Gardens of pensilvania are Well furnish'd with European Rarities possibly He may

assist you with some plants that you Want & you may assist Them for I presume you have Vessills passing too & fro Often from one province to the Other. His name is John Bartram. Your Friendship to Him will be a singular favour to your Affectionate Friend,

P. COLLINSON

Custis wrote Collinson, August 12, 1739: "[Bartram] is the most takeing faceitious man I have ever met with and never was so much delighted with A stranger in all my life. . . ." (Draft AL: AAS)

30 ❧ TO JOSEPH BREINTNALL

ALS: BPL
London, January 31, 1738

Respected Friend,

I have several of thy Obligeing Favours before I recei'd Thine of June 24 with Second Bill, the first being paid. I thank thee besides for the other Curious Matters it Contain'd.

Thy Snake Root so call'd from thy First Imparting It as I have observed is a Sanicle, having all the Charesticks belonging to that Class. But I believe it is not mention'd in Millar because not known when He wrote that Book.

Thee has many Thanks from the R: Society for thy acct of the Aurora Borealis as Mention'd in Thine of Novemr 24.

It gives Mee great pleasure to heare of that Generous proposal of your proprietor[1] to give you a Lott for a Library House, Who In great Gratitude you should Choose President of your Society, which may Encourage him Further. All thy Observations & Schemes re-

Snake Root (with field Fare). Mark Catesby. From Collinson's copy of Natural History of Carolina . . . at Knowsley Hall, *Vol I, plate 29. Courtesy the Earl of Derby, Knowsley*

lateing to It are an Instance of thy Zeal for promoteing the Good of Mankind and Deserves the greatest commendation from all that are Well Wishers to So noble & usefull a Designe.

Your Worthy propritr may be truly said to be a Father to his people when he has the publick Weal So much att Heart. I hope Ways & Means will be found to Carry on that laudable Work. But Really I cannot flater thee with hopes of Benefactions from Hence. The love of Money is too prevalent and Wee have too few Generous, publick Spiritted Men considering our Numbers. However I shall not fail to Impart your Designe to Some Likely persons. If I have any Success in my Solicitations, the Company will be sure to Heare from Mee.

I am with much Respect thy Sincere friend   PC

PS I have here Inclosed the Company's acct which I hope thee will find Right.

The pretty white Ranunculus that Dr Witt sent Mee some Time agon is a Real Delicate Double Flower, but I never knew before it was a Snake Root. It is Described by the Celebrated Plucknett[2] who has most of your Country plants. He names it Ranunculus Nemurosus Aquilegia Foliis Virginianus Asphodelis Radice, Virginia Wood Ranunculas with Collumbine Leaves and an Asphodel or Kings Spear Root.

Please [to give my respects] to Benj Eastbourn.[3] I hope to gett what He wrote for to send by Capt Wright who will be soone after Savage.

Wee had last Decr 5th a very Remarkable and uncommon Bloody Aurora Borealis which was Seen all over Europe. Pray does thee Remember if it Extended to your parts?

Inclosed In the Library Books &c is a Face Glass. I was att a Loss for want of what Size would be Most Suiteable. This is a Middle Size & I think Sufficient for the purposes thou mentions. It Cost Six Shillings.

1. Richard, John and Thomas Penn served as co-proprietors, John as principal until his death (1746) when Thomas became principal. On July 20, 1732 Collinson wrote Thomas Penn congratulating him on his safe arrival in Philadelphia and added, "Only request your encouragement of the Library Company which is a noble-spirited design and will tend very much to improve your province in all usefull branches of science." (ALS:HSP) The proprietors granted the Library Company a charter in 1742, but no lot.

2. Leonard Plukenet (1642–1706), MD, Physician at West-

minster where he had a small botanic garden, Superintendent, Hampton Court Garden and Queen's Botanist. Published *Phytographia,* 1691–96, *Almagestum Botanicum,* 1696, *Almagesti Botanici Mantissa,* 1700, and *Amaltheum Botanicum,* 1705. The quoted description appears in *Almagestum Botanicum* and is cited by Linnaeus as a synonym in naming the plant *Anemone thalictroides.*

3. Benjamin Eastburn, Surveyor General of the Province, an early member of the Library Company.

31 ❦ TO JOHN KEARSLEY

Draft ALS:LS
London, February 7, 1738

I hope you had Mine with the Siberian Rhubarb Seed.[1]

I have to Returne you the thanks of the [Royal] Society for your last Curious Letter. Your paragph Relateing to the Inoculation[2] was very Acceptable. You are Desir'd to Communicate your further Observations and as Exact an Acct as you can Collect of what numbers are Inoculated & the success of that Operation, for some Miscarriages here has abated peoples Inclinations for it.

I have in a perticular manner as well from the Society as from Dr Bradley professor of

Rhubarb. Georg Dionysius Ehret.
Natural History Museum, Botany
Library, London.

Astronomy at Oxford[3] to give their thanks for thy Friends curious Observations on the Transit of the Comet. The Dr said it was a great Help to settle his Calculations. He said he found It more Exact and agreed better with his Observations then any he had from other places.

It is hoped when any Phenomenon happens that Ingenious Gentleman will oblige the Society with it.

Wee had on December 5, 1737 last the most uncommon Bloody Aurora Borealis seen all over Europe, the Northern part of the Hemesphere appear'd all Inflamed with Bloody Fiery Red, but there was no Corruscations or Flashing from the pole to the Zenith as usuall. If any thing of this kind was Seen with you pray give some account of It.

I am with much Respect, Thy Sincere Friend,   P. COLLINSON

JOHN KEARSLEY (1684–1772), physician in Philadelphia, supported inoculation against smallpox and regularly sent Collinson reports on various topics. The report on a comet referred to in this letter, was published in the *Philosophical Transactions*, XL (1741): 119–121 as "Observations upon the Comet seen in . . . Philadelphia. . . ."

1. Rhubarb. *Rheum raponticum.* "In classical times a root or rootstock known to the Greek and Roman herbalists as *rha* or *rheon* was imported from the East, whence its alternative names *rha ponticum* and *rha barbarum*. Its identity and provenance are uncertain. . . .

"From the tenth century onwards dried rootstocks considered the same as classical *rha* or *rheon* and derived from Chinese species of *Rheum* were brought across Central Asia, Iran and Western Asia to Europe from Western China in ever-increasing amount, presumably to relieve ever-increasing constipation in Europe. This material came mostly from *Rheum palmatum*.

"The kind of plant producing these purgatives was unknown until the seventeenth century. Some time before 1608 an Italian medical man, Francisco Crasso, at Ragusa (now Dubrovnik) obtained roots of a species growing in the Rhodope mountains of Thrace (now Rila, Bulgaria) which he recognized as being like the *rha ponticum* of the Ancients. He sent this plant to Prospero Alpino at the medically celebrated Venetian University of Padua. Alpino grew it successfully, distributed seeds to botanic gardens and published a work *De Rhapontico Disputatio* (1612) giving a detailed account of this remarkable discovery. In 1753 Linnaeus named it *Rheum raponticum*. All plants of *Rh. raponticum* in cultivation down to 1913 were descended from this single introduction of about 1608.

"At first this rhubarb, the only Euyropean species, was cultivated simply for medicinal purposes.

"Some time between 1730 and 1768, possibly as a result of increased sugar production by African slaves in the West Indies, the leaf-stalks were used in tarts and ultimately rhubarb came to be grown commercially only for culinary use." [Stearn, W.T. "Rhabarbarologia: *Rheum raponticum* . . ." *Garden History* Vol 2 (2) 1979, p. 75.

2. "Inoculation. C'est la plus belle découverte qui ait été faite en médecine, pour la conservation de la vie des hommes." *Encyclopédie*, t.18 (1782).

There was considerable American interest in inoculation. In Boston, Cotton Mather began to study the procedure in 1706 after his grateful parishioners gave him an inoculated slave. Onesimus, like many of his fellows, had been inoculated in Africa. With the onset of the smallpox epidemic of 1721 Mather began a massive campaign in favor of inoculation. There was great public resistance to

deliberately contracting the disease. "The preoccupation with smallpox on the part of Mather and his contemporaries is understandable when it is realized that smallpox was to the seventeenth and eighteenth centuries what the plague had been to the Middle Ages." Herbert, Eugenia W., "Smallpox Inoculation in Africa," *Journal of African History*, XVI, 4 (1975), pp. 539–559.

No one is sure where the procedure originated. On April 1, 1717, Lady Mary Wortley Montagu wrote to a friend from Adrianople: "A propos of Distempers, I am going to tell you a thing that I am sure will make you wish your selfe here. The Small Pox so fatal and so general amongst us, is here entirely harmless by the invention of engrafting (which is the term they give it). There is a set of old Women who make it their business to perform the Operation. Every Autumn, in the month of September, when the great Heat is abated, people send to one another to know if any of their family has a mind to have the small pox. They make partys for this purpose, and when they are met (commonly fifteen or sixteen together) the old Women comes with a nutshell full of the matter of the best sort of small-pox and asks what veins you please to have open'd. She immediately rips open that you offer to her with a large needle (which gives you no more pain than a common scratch) and puts into the vein as much venom as can lye upon the head of her needle, and after binds up the little wound with a hollow bit of shell, and in this manner opens 4 or 5 veins. The Grecians have commonly the superstition of opening one in the Middle of the forehead, in each arm, and on the breast to mark the sign of the cross. . . ." Lady Mary Wortley Montagu to Sarah Chiswell, April 1, 1717. Halsband, Robert, ed., *The Complete Letters. . .* Oxford, 1965, v 1, pp 338–339.

Lady Mary, a great beauty, had been struck by the pox two years earlier. The disease left her without eyelashes, her face deeply pitted. See Halsband, Robert, *The Life of Mary Wortley Montagu*. Oxford, 1956, p. 51.

Benjamin Franklin always regretted that he did not have his son Franky (Francis) inoculated. The boy died in November, 1736, age four, "a fate that was all the more cruel since Franklin now believed firmly in inoculation." Lopez, Claude Anne and Eugenia Herbert, *The Private Franklin . . .* New York, 1975, p. 37.

3. James Bradley (1693–1762), Astronomer Royal, holder of the Savilian Chair at Oxford, elected FRS in 1718 on the motion of Halley and under the presidential sanction of Newton. (DNB)

In one of Collinson's commonplace books at the Linnean Society there is a brief note from Bradley (October 24, 1743) at the bottom of which Collinson wrote: "Died anno 1762 the greatest astronomer of this age but his Facultys being on a Long Stretch failed Him Some Time before He Died. Of the Greatest Modesty & Humility of any Man I ever knew."

ALS:HSP
London, February 17, 1738

I have sent in a Large Box of Capt Wrights marked EW — No 5 the Goods thou wrote for which I wish safe to hand. I hope thou has the Two pcs of Garlix [fabric] In John Wites parcel. The Bill of parcel, of these Goods are Inclosed with them In the Box with thy Account. As Sewing Silk and all Silk is much advanced I did not Venter to Send the remainder of the Acc't in that Comodity, but I have Sent Two pound for a Tryall. If the price & Silk is Liked more of the same may be had att that price unless there should be an Advance. As I have befored hinted I now request again, Send for no Goods without a price. If thee hast thy Instructions from any Dealer He must know It & According to the price I will Endeavour to Send the Best.

As I know it was with great fatigue & pains that those Laurells was procured from the Mountains, so I would not willingly be behind hand In Making Some Acknowledgment. I have Sent the Drugett for Coat & breeches & 2 lamb cotts Wastcoats & 1 Calico & 1 prunella Gown for thy Wife Linings for thine & woods Cloths with sundry other odd things which I hope will prove acceptable.

As thee designs for Virginia in the Fall I have sent thee Circular Letters to all my friends which letters come to J. Logan to save thee postage. I think it would be better to proceed along the bay of the Western Shore of Maryland first, & so to Williamsburgh & then up into the Country & so back as thou proposed and my Reason Is Little new or Curious is to be met with along the Western Shore or in the Lower settlements of Virginia. The Rare & Valuable things are to be found above, In the unsettled places & then thou will proceed Directly Home with what seeds thou has Gott whereas if thou goes the upper Way first thou will have to bring what thou has Collected down Virginia and over to Maryland, which will be very troublesome and fatiguing, and a Long Way About.

I have sent my Letters open that thou may make Memorandums from some pticular Contants therein mentioned & then seal them up. Of all my Friends In Maryland I know none that are Curious in our branch of knowledge so that unless it is in the Course of Thy Travels it is not worth thy while to go out of thy Way on purpose to see them. I would have thee go if thee can to see Robt. Grover [not identified] to see the place where some surprisingly fashioned angular stones are found. As to the Rest take them as it suits thee. Butt in Virginia there is Colo Custis & Colo Byrd are both Curious Men. Pray take down what I have remarked for thee to Inquire after, the Umbrella Trees at the first & the Ginseng at the last.

Then when thee proceeds Home I know no person will make thee more Welcome than Isham Randolph. He lives 30 or 40 Miles above the falls of James River in Goochland above the other settlements. Now I take his House to be a very suitable place to make a settlement att for to take several Days' Excursion all Round, and to return to his House at Night. I think William Manduet [not identified] Lives in the upper Settlements of Maryland.

One thing I must Desire of thee and do Insist that thee oblige Mee therein that thou make up that Druggett Clothes, to go to Virginia In and not appear to Disgrace thyself of Mee for tho I would not Esteem thee the less to come to Mee in what Dress thou Will, yet

Rhodendron maximum, *Rosebay, Mountain Laurel. Georg Dionysius Ehret. Natural History Museum, Botany Library, London.*

these Virginians are a very gentle, Well Dress'd people, & look phaps More at a Man's Outside than his Inside. For these and other Reasions pray go very Clean, neat & handsomely Dressed to Virginia. Never Mind thy Clothes I will send thee more another year.

I a Little wonder that the Eastern sea shore nor the Island, afforde no shells, that there was none I am persuaded for had they been there they would not have Excap'd thee. Pray observe if there are no Land or River shells different from what thee has sent Mee. I want a fair specimen of your oysters; an uper and an under shell both belonging to one another will be acceptable, but no more Sassafras berries. The Cones of the Swamp Rose bay or Laurell are much wanted, and Acorns of Willow Leafed Oke. Thy last cargo is a fine Collection, & came in fine order. Tulip Poplar or Sweet Gum are not wanting. I thank thee for the Sweet Gum but I want some of the black gum. Pignuts will be acceptable. They are a very small Species of hickery. Send more Acorns & Cones or Seeds of all the Evergreen Tribe will be Acceptable & some more Allspice or Benjamin & any other Forest Trees, Sugar Maple, Birch, Horn Beam, Ash, beach & what thou Canst pick up. Red & White Cedar, pine, firrs & the specimens of the flower of ye Chamaerhododendron was very obligeing. I have much to say to thy Long Entertaining Letter with the Seeds & plants by must Defer till more Leisure. I sent thee a Case of Boxes which are very hard and will save the Trouble of making. Thee may cut down the Rims and accomodate them to thy pockett, pray take one or Two with the fly netts in a bag by thy side & some pins, phaps thee may meet with something Curious & may want Conveniency to Catch & Carry it. If the netts are Torn or worn out send them back to be repaired.

My wishes are for thy Health & Safety. I am truly thine,

P. COLLINSON

Pray give my love to Joseph Breintnall. Hope he had mine by Savage. In thy packett to J. Logan I inclose a Letter to Ben Eastbourne which please Deliver. In the Letter in J. Logans packett I send thee a twig of a pear Tree with an Enamelled Ring of Caterpillars around it. They are not yett Come Out. If not Come out when thee Receives them putt them on a pear or apple & thee will see the produce. More Wild Crabs & Black Haw or Sheep Turds. It is a fine Eating Fruit. The Last specimens of pines was something Like. There was sufficient for myself & to spare a friend a slip. I never saw any thorns to the size thee mentions. Pray send a specimen of your black & white Thorn & a good specimen of Sheep Turds in Flower if this can be done with Conveniency.

As thee mentions the noble stone pine seed was bad I have sent in the Box some Seeds & some More Spanish Chestnutts. The Wasps & Nest are all very Curious & acceptable.

Thy Crysalis that is naked that thee sent Mee is alive as it is not spun up or taken out of the ground. It will prove a Butterfly for all that tribe Change in that manner but they Conceale themselves under the Leaves and against Trees & buildings that it is hard to find them.

Dr Hill [not identified] att London Town in Maryland is the only person that is Curious in Vegitables. He has Sent Some Account of their Vertues to the Royal Society. Pray Call on Him. Thee hast my Letter of Last year. Alter the Date of the Year and it will [serve] Well Enough. Thee need Send no Cock Spur or white thorn. Pray Send Some Seed of your Black thorn. I never heard you had any Except you call the Black Haw or Sheep Turd [*Viburnum prunifolium*].

ALS:BL
August 26, 1738

It is great complaisance in your Lordship to Enter into the pleasures of your friend but I find such is your good nature it is not so much for your own Sake as for Mine but there is much Greater Inducement to Draw Mee to Middleton then the finest Insect that flies.

May your Vigilence be rewarded with the Enamelled Sports of the Great Wood Emperor & May you triumph over the Motled Emperor & Empress of the Rivers, then you'll be as great as Caesar with his Spoils of Cockle Shells.

Above: "Great Wood Emperor." Moses Harris. The Aurelian, *plate III. The Library Company of Philadelphia.*

Right: Mottled Emperor and Empress of the Rivers." Moses Harris. The Aurelian . . . , *plate XXV. The Library Company of Philadelphia.*

Flycatcher in regalia. Moses Harris. Frontispiece to Moses Harris, The Aurelian . . . *London, 1766. Natural History Museum, London, Entomology Library.*

I shall now Conclude with thanking you for the promotion you thought Mee so deserving off, but I expect no popularity. Let them that love Ribbons and Garters take 'em, as for Mee I wou'd willingly slide through Life and be known but too a few and the next Wish I have is to be able to do Some little Services for those few (great ones are out of my Sphere).

This my Dear Lord is the ambition of your sincere & affectionate Friend,　　　PC

WILLIAM VILLIERS, 3rd Earl of Jersey (d. 1769).

This letter is written on the blank side of Jersey's August 20, 1738 note to Collinson: "I read with pleasure in the Gazette of the Fly Catchers erecting themselves into a Society [Aurelian Society], & tho you are yet only a dillitante I think you are so aspiring a one that they would not have made a bad choice in you for their President.... I keep a watchful eye on every fly that passes in hope of meeting with a curious one & should I discover one you shall have timely notice in expectation that, that might procure me another brisk sojourn with you. . . ."

In June, 1744, Collinson read "Some Observations on a Sort of Libella or Ephemeron" to the Royal Society. His paper was printed in *Philosophical Transactions* XLIV pp 329–333) and included a careful account of the insects' "ingendering."

Jersey wrote Collinson on August 20, 1746:

Dear Peter, Having last night read in the Magazine your very learned dissertation upon the libella, I cannot sufficiently admire your infinite pains to be informed of the secret operations of the little Beings. How much more would it be commendable to search into the mysteries of the propagation of our own Species upon which there are so many various opinions among the Virtuosi; the inquiry could not be unpleasing to yourself, & the help of Leuwenhock's microscope might furnish the necessary lights, for I am not quite determined whether all poor Christians don't dart with a Vivacity at least equal to those much admired Insects, & an ascertainment of that fact could not fail to procure you immense Eulogims from that Speculative & learned Body [the Aurelian Society] of which you are so deservedly a member, tho for my part I should wish in the first place to have my curiosity gratified by so observing a Philosopher whether our great Ancestor transgressed with a Cod-Lin (or an edwin) or a pine apple. I shall wait with impatience for your ingenious Answer & am my dear friend, most truly & faithfully yours. Jersey [ALS: LS]

Here is Peter's draft response (written on the back of Jersey's note to him):

September 17. Because an Impudent Fellow Dr Hill[1] had Libelled Mee & putt my Name to It, my Good Lord thinks Mee a Conjurer & a pryer into Natural Secrets, But he's quite Mistaken for I can see no further into a Mill Stone that another Man.

But if I would Improve my knowledge in the Labarinths of Generation, in the deep areas of propagation, I must learn them from your Lordship who is so great a Connoisr in Natural chymestry & if James Says True is now under a Couple of New Experiments, your Great Successes in Applying the Diping Needle to explore the Unfathomable abyss, Besides you travelled into France & Italy and practiced over or under the most Expert Artist of those Countries how to adjust the Motion of the pendulum to Equall Time & how with Infinite Pains & dayly practice acquir'd the art to dart the Ingine with a Surpriseing Velocity. In short, Dame Nature has open'd all her Stores to you and has revealed all her Mysteries. You have penetrated Deep into her most delicate recesses.

So it is only from you my dear Ld I can Expect to be Informed of her most Secret Operations and by what unerring Laws Wee poor individuals take Being.

The Eulogims will be all yours if you will but enlighten your friend with a Ray of yr knowledge, for alas I am a poor Novice & just keep jogging on in the Old Tract—for nice refinements & curious Experiments I must Submit Lave to you for it is a Matter of no Importance to Mee whether Father Adam cracked a Commandment with a pine apple, Cod-Lin or Edwin but that I know he was the first man that tasted the Delicious fruit, his Noble Sons have not lost the Relish but Serve the good thing to this Day. [AL:LS] [Collinson is joking, he wrote the piece he attributes to Hill.]

1. John Hill (1714–1775), Knight of Order of Vasa 1774, apothecary, miscellaneous writer, studied botany and geology, was employed by the Duke of Richmond and Lord Petre in the arrangement of their gardens and collections of dried plants. Beginning in 1751 he contributed a daily gossip letter to the *British Magazine* under the name "the Inspector." Failing to gain the requisite number of names for nomination to the Royal Society he published "A Review of the Works of the Royal Society," holding up to ridicule the *Philosophical Transactions* to which he had himself contributed two papers. On one occasion he abused Christopher Smart who retorted in "The Hilliad: an epic poem" in which he addresses Hill as "Pimp! Poet! Paffer! 'Pothecary! Player!" James Boswell quoted Samuel Johnson in *The Life* as follows: "Dr. Hill was, notwithstanding, a very curious observer; and if he would have been contented to tell the world no more than he knew, he might have been a very considerable man, and needed not to have recourse to . . . mean expedients to raise his reputation." [DNB]

Hill was a prodigious author. Among his titles: *History of Plants* (1751) in which the Linnean system was introduced into England for the first time; *Essays in Natural History* (1752); *Eden: or a complete body of gardening* (1757); *The British Herbal* (1756–57); *Outline of a System of Vegetable Generation* (1758); *Exotic botany* (1759); *Vegetable System* (1759–1775); *Flora britanica* [sic] (1760); *Hortus Kewensis* (1768); *Herbarium britannicum* (1770); and *A Decade of Curious and elegant trees and plants* (1773).

See PC to Trew, Nov. 15, 1752.

See Henrey II, pp. 91–109; and G.S. Rousseau, ed., *The Letters and Papers of Sir John Hill,* New York, AMS Press, 1982.

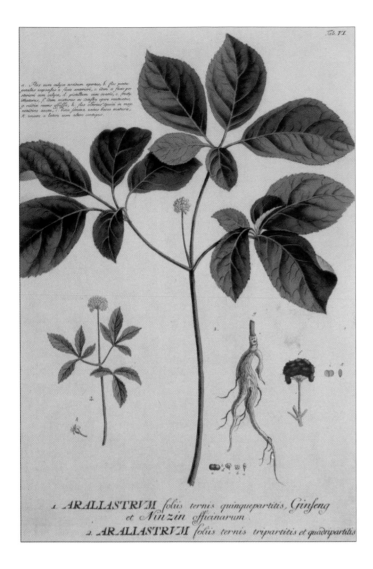

Ginseng. Georg Dionysius Ehret. In Trew, Plantae Selectate, *plate VI. The Linnean Society of London.*

1. ARALLASTRVM *foliis ternis quinquepartitis,* Ginseng *et* Ninzin *officinarum.*
2. ARALLASTRVM *foliis ternis tripartitis et quadripartitis.*

34 ❧ TO HANS SLOANE

Draft AL:LS
November 25, 1738

Sir Hans, would it be amiss to show the Genseng[1] to the Royal Society with this account?

1. "Ginseng is to the Chinese more than [aspirin] or any other drug is to Americans. As its name Panax implies, it is a panacea, being employed for all the ills that flesh is heir to. Though credited with stimulating, aromatic, alterative, carminative and tonic properties, the root is with us seldom used except as a demulcent. The reverence in which it is held, and the high price that it commands in China, led to extensive search for a substitute, which resulted in the discovery in 1716 of American ginseng, *Panax quinquefolium,* near Montreal, Canada. This root was favorably received by the Chinese, and soon became an important article of export." (L.H. Bailey, *The Standard Cyclopedia of Horticulture,* New York. Macmillan 1929, vol II, pp 1338–1339.)

Collinson reported on Ginseng to the Royal Society on December 17, 1738. His account is dated November 25, 1738: "The Ginseng a root so Celebrated for its vertues in China that it is Exchanged for Its weight in Gold is this year discover'd by John Bartram who has sent over these two Specimens of the Roots, Leaves & Seed Vessell of the North American Ginseng.

"It was found growing in the uninhabited parts of the Country on or near the River Susquahanah in the Province of Pennsylvania, in 40 Deg: North Latitude.

"It has been Compared and Agrees with the China Ginseng [*Panax pseudoginseng*] in Its Botanick Likeness, and by those that have Tryed Its Vertues as Efficaceous. Col. Byrd a Membr of the R. Society Gives it great Commendations.

"The Author that I have Mett with that Mentions the Genseng

Botanically is Vaillant[a] who makes it a New Genus which He names Araliastrum Quinquefolii folio Majus in his Treatise, *Sermo de Structura Florum,* page 42, No 1.

"It is mentioned by Kempfer[b] in his History of Japan, folio 819, by the name of Nindsin.

"It is observable that the same Species of plants are found under the Same Degrees of Latitude in Different parts of the world as this plant is a Remarkable Instance, being found in those parts of China & Japon as agrees with the Latitudes of Virginia & Pensilvania." (transcript of AL:RS)

Ginseng fascinated Collinson for years. He first wrote Bartram about it on January 20, 1735, again on June 6, 1736 requesting "a specimen," and on December 20, 1737 (upon receipt of a root), reported back, "The Panax is a choice plant."

Collinson to Bartram on February 24, 1738: "The principal Reason of my writing now is to Desire thee to procure what plants thee canst of Genseng & plant in thy garden & raise what thee Canst from Seed. I am well assured it will prove a very profitable commodity to China who value it above anything.

"I have Compared yours [*Panax quinquefolium*] with the Chinese [*Panax pseudo ginseng*] and find them in all respects the same. Your proprietor was so kind to send me a considerable parcel & I have trusted a particular friend with it to carry to China to see how they approve of it, and to find what price it bears; but my friend is under promise not to Discover that it is *American* for if they know that, they are so fanciful it may not be so good as their own.

"So gett a stock by thee as soon as thee can, & be sure Conceal thy Intention from every one. In 24 months my Friend will be here again from China & then shall give thee notice. Pray send me a root or two in mould for my garden." (ALS:HSP)

Collinson wrote Bartram again on February 1, 1739: "I sent some Ginseng roots to China. If they sell well, a good profitable trade may be Carried on. In the mean time, sow the seed and raise a stock to furnish my friend when he returns. I intend the benefit for thyself. Keep that a secret & raise what thee canst, for I have an opinion it will turn to account if my friend manages it rightly." (ALS:HSP)

The scheme failed because of competition from the French collectors and because cultivation proved difficult, but Collinson's interest in the plant continued. On September 1, 1745 he wrote Linneaus, "The American Ginseng has flowered and fruited with Mee this year. . . ." (ALS:LS), April 1, 1746, "I have the true gensing in my garden. It both flowers and seeds." (ALS:LS)

In 1753 he wrote Christopher Jacob Trew, "The Gensing Flowered First and produced Berries July 1748. I believe it was the first plant on Europe." (ALS:Erlangen)

To Cadwallader Colden, September 7, 1753: "Never was more Impolitick thing done then to Send Such Quantities of Gensing Here. It has so sunk the Market that there must be great losses on it." (ALS:N-YHS)

a. Sebastian Vaillant (1669–1722), French botanist. Published *Sermo de structura florum* . . . London, 1718.

b. Kaempfer, Englebert. *The history of Japan: giving an accounting of* . . . *its metals, minerals, trees, plants, animals* . . . London, 1728.

35 ❧ TO JOHN PENN

ALS:HSP
March 1, 1739

Dear Friend

I have had a Long Conference with Mr Hyde [not identified]. He said he did not Venter to Show your last proposal to Ld Baltimor[1] for He Said, his Lordship Would Say, you now plainly see, What I always told you, that they are not Sincere & never Intend to End this affair amicably. For who can offer Fairer then I have done, and more Effectuall to bring Matters to a Conclusion.

I gave my Reasons for not complying and to be Short told them that I plainly Saw the Drift of his Lordships proposal, which was to Draw in your Title to the Lower Counties[2] to be Disputed, and finally to be Determined by the Umpire, this was In vesting to great a power in a Single Hand who might be Influenced or Byased by Either party. This Scheme I told him was Easily Seen Into and I was assured would never take nor what I could in the Least Advise too, that is to Submitt the 3 Lower Counties into Matter of Debate or Dispute to which his Lordship had not any Shadow of Right, and which had been So often Confirm'd to you both by Charter and Acts of Council in particular the Last, where your authority to appoint a Governr was Confirmed which was Reviting your Title.

That his Lordship must think you very Weake to Subject your Right to be Canvassed by arbitration.

I further told Him that it was In vain for his Lordship to attempt any Concessions Relateing to those 3 counties for you was Determined never to Meet Him or his Council where they was to Made Subject of Debate.

But If any Reasonable Concessions or accomadations could be made on your Side with Relation to the Boundaries, of those Counties or any other parts of the bounds between you I believed for the Sake of peace & amity you would Do every thing that was Reasonable.

Mr Hyde Said the Bounds according to the Late agreement would never Do. Pray Says I Letts know what Will. Here He was att a Loss for a Map, for Sayes he it is to no purpose our talking without Wee Could lay down Some thing.

He Desired to know if you had a Map, In which He would be glad to See you Mark your Limitts, which Should never be out of my Hands and then He would Desire Lord Baltimore to Mark His Limitts of the 2 Counties etc and then He Hopes by Compareing both Maps the Difference between both your Limitts Might be accomadated.

It is too Tedious to Relate Further till I see thee, any time a Saturday till Twelve I shall be att Home, and a Monday till 12.

I am in the Interim thine.

P. COLLINSON

JOHN PENN (1700–1746), eldest son of William Penn, founder of Pennsylvania, trained in the linen trade in Bristol, became a Proprietary (along with his brothers Thomas and Richard) upon Hannah Penn's death in 1733. John Penn lived in Pennsylvania in 1734–35 until called back to London to defend the colony's boundary claims against those asserted by representatives of Lord Baltimore. (Hull, William, *William Penn*. New York: Oxford University Press, 1937). The issue was not settled until Charles Mason and Jeremiah Dixon, under authority of commissioners for Maryland and Pennsylvania, surveyed the disputed boundary and the commissioners signed their report on November 9, 1768. (Cummings, Hubertis M., *The Mason and Dixon Line*. Harrisburg: Department of Internal Affairs, Bureau of Land Records, 1962; Bayliff, William H., *The Maryland-Pennsylvania and the Maryland-Delaware Boundaries*. Annapolis: Maryland Board of Natural Resources, 1959.)

1. Charles Calvert (1699–1751), 5th Lord Baltimore.
2. New Castle, Kent, and Sussex, on the Delaware River, the area that would become the State of Delaware.

36 ❧ TO CARL LINNAEUS

ALS:LS
London, May 13, 1739

Dear Friend,

I could not Omitt so convenient an Oppertunity, by my Worthy Friend Dr. Filenius,[1] to Inquire after your Welfare and give you joy on your Marriage. May much Happiness attend you in that State.

I am glad of this conveyance to Express my Gratitude for the perticular regard shown me in that Curious Elaborate Work the Horts Clifforts.[2] Some thing I think was Due to Mee from the Common Wealth of Botany for the great number of plants & Seeds I have annually procur'd from Abroad, and you have been so good as to pay It, by giving Mee a species of Eternity (Botanically speaking), That is, a name as long as Men and Books Endure. This layes Mee under Great Obligations, which I shall never Forgett.

Carl Linnaeus, age 32, copy by Jean Haagen done in 1906 of the original painting at Hammarby by J.H.
Schefel, 1739. Linnaeus is dressed for his wedding, his arm resting on a copy of the octavo Systema Naturae.
He is holding a sprig of Linnaea borealis. *The Linnean Society of London.*

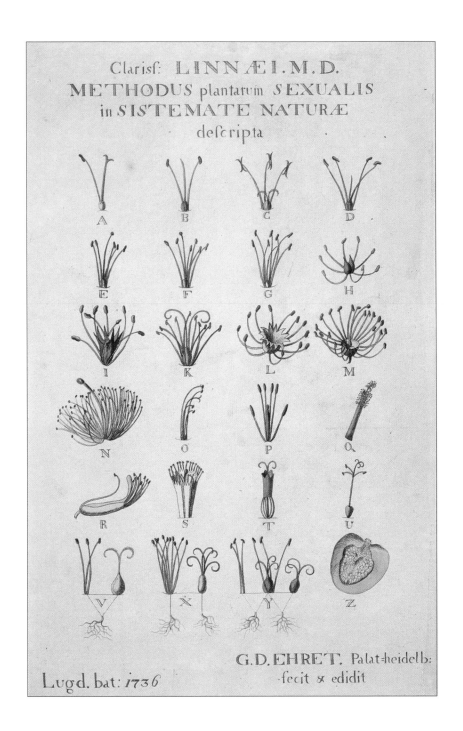

I am concerned I can make no better acknowledgments then by the Small token of Pensilvania Ores [not identified], which the Bearer will Deliver to you.

My Best Wishes attend you, and if I can any ways Serve you Here you may be assured of the Readiness of your Sincere & affectionate Friend,   PETER COLLINSON

As Mr. [James] Logan has had Two Lattin Tracts published in Holland I doubt not but Doctor Gronovius[3] has sent them to you (the one is on generation). When a convenient oppertunity offers, pray let Mee heare from you. Yours   PC

Opposite page: "Clariss. Linnaeai, MD." An illustration of the sexual parts of plants used by Linnaeus to classify them. Georg Dionysius Ehret. From Peter Collinson's commonplace book of prints and drawings, Knowsley Hall. Courtesy of the Earl of Derby, Knowsley.

Right: Collinsonia canadensis. *Georg Dionysius Ehret. The Fitzwilliam Museum, Cambridge.*

COLLINSONIA. *Hort. Cliff.* 14. *Sp.* 1.
a. *Flos magnitudine naturali.* b. *Idem a tergo visus.*
c. *Calyx sub florescentia constitutus.* d. *Idem fructu prægnans.*
e. *Germen.*

G. D. EHRET del.   J. WANDELAAR fecit.

CAROLUS LINNAEUS (Carl von Linné) (1707–1778), Swedish naturalist, discovered at Uppsala by Dr. Anders Celsius (see Note 9 to January 18, 1744) who was so impressed with the impoverished young student's knowledge and botanical collections that he offered him board and lodging.

In 1730 Olaf Rudbeck, professor of Botany at Uppsala, appointed Linnaeus his assistant and allowed him to remodel the academic garden. In 1732 Linnaeus explored Lapland under the auspices of the Academy of Sciences at Uppsala. He left Sweden in 1735 to study medicine in Holland, where he met J. F. Gronovius (see footnote 3 below) and Boerhaave and catalogued Gerard George Clifford's garden at Hartecamp, near Haarlem (*Hortus Cliffortianus . . .* Leyden, 1737).

He visited England in 1736 with letters of introduction from Boerhaave and Gronovius to Sir Hans Sloane. He met (on this his only trip to England) Dr. Thomas Shaw at Oxford, Philip Miller, J. J. Dillenius, Georg Ehret, and Collinson.

At the beginning of the eighteenth century there was little agreement among botanists as to a system of classification. Linnaeus proposed a scheme based on the sexual parts of plants in *Systema naturae,* 1735, and developed it in his subsequent botanical works culminating in *Species plantarum,* 1753, and *Genera plantarum,* 1754. "These two works are internationally accepted as the starting-points of modern botanical nomenclature." (Henrey, Vol II, p. 650) See Koerner, Lisbet, *Linnaeus: Nature and Nation,* Cambridge, MA. 1999.

See Smith, James Edward, *A Selection of the correspondence of Linnaeus . . .* 2 vols, London, 1821.

1. Peter Filenius (1704–1780), Professor of Divinity at Äbo, later Bishop of Lindkoeping.

2. *Hortus Cliffortianus.* Leyden, 1737. In this work Linnaeus designated the common North American horsemint "Collinsonia Canadensis" in honor of his correspondent.

3. John Fredrick Gronovius (1690–1762), Dutch naturalist and friend of Linnaeus, professor of Botany at Leyden, read the *Systema naturae* in manuscript when Linnaeus visited Holland in 1735 (see note 1 to January 31, 1740). Working with plant material supplied by John Clayton, Gronovius published *Flora Virginica,* 1739, the first systematic enumeration of North American plants. Gronovius and Isaac Lawson published the *Systema* at their own expense. See PC to Linnaeus, January 18, 1744, note 8.

Portrait of Sir Charles Wager. John Landseer after Thomas Gibson. National Portrait Gallery, London.

37 🐾 TO CHARLES WAGER

Draft AL:LS

August 9–15, 1739

I can scarcely Justifie my Self to borrow your Attention from the publick Weal to Read my Scrawls, so on the other I can't forgive Myself if I do not Inquire after your & my Good Lady Welfare and lett you know how I employed my Time since I saw you Last.In ComIn In complyance with my Wife I attended Her to pay Her New Married Sister a Visit att Winchester. The Late Rains (tho Heart aching to the Farmers) was pleasant to Us. The Sun was as Indulgent and did not dazel our Eyes with his luster all the Journey.

Within a Mile of Winchester on the Downs something like tents & a Camp made an odd appearance att a Distance but when Wee came Neare it was Long Booths made of Bended Poles 50 and 60 foot long and covered with Silks & Canvas. Within them perhaps is Negotiated one of the greatest Cheese Fairs in England. The Concourse is very Great and it is computed at this *Morlin Hill Fair* not less than 2500 Waggons load with Cheese are sold in 12 Hours Time besides Leather and Wool.

A friend of mine had the Curiosity to toll what pass'd over one bridge & told 1500 hundred.

Wee made no Stay att Winton but proceeded to Southampton, a fine Old Town walled all Round but Time & Weather has Mouldered them away in some places. This was formerly a place of Great Trade while Sweet Wines & French Wine was under Low Duties.

The sudden visit of the [Royal] Duke [one of George II's brothers] putt our Citty in a great agitation. The Mayor puff'd & blow'd with his Alderman in their Furrs att their

Heels to have complemented Him but He was embark'd before they came, but as he lett them know he return'd that Way all things was gott in Order, the old Iron Guns scourd up & Flaggs displayed and Mr Mayor and his Aldermen in their Pontificalibals preceed by Two Large Maces & a Silver Oar conduced the Duke up from the Key. Mr Mayor I will assure you with his Beaver on took the Right hand of the prince who walk'd by his Side to the Town Hall where he had a fine speech made to Him & complemented with his Freedome into the bargain.

Having some Time on my Hands I made an Excursion into New Forest, which after 500 years standing may now with propriety enough have the Epithet of Old. Here in this delightful Wild Nature seems to appear in all Her Virgin Charms. The Hardy Oke & Lofty Beach with Ash & Birch compose the Groves & Border all the Lawns, where Colts & Kine & Herds of Deer mixt with the Grunting Tribe securely graze. Amidst these Delightful Scenes I Dine'd with a Virtuoso Friend whos pleasant Villa opens to the South secur'd on all other Sides from Every Impetuous Blast. From hence I proceed to Limington which is a pretty Town pleasantly situated on a Hill. Att the foot of it there is a Navigable River. The Low Lands between the Town & the Sea makes it very convenient for Salt Works of which there is some Hundreds in this Neighborhood.

Their Methode is to lett in the Sea Water into pools. From Hence they laid it into Shallow Quarters where the Water lies and evaporates by the action of the Wind & Sun till its Saline parts are so contracted that it becomes a perfect Brine capable to bear an Egg. When it is arrived to this pitch then it is convey'd into Large Coppers and with Eight Hours Ebulition is reduced to fine White Salt fitt for use.

4 miles from this place I had a clear & distinct view of Needles,[1] & Hurst Castle[2] to be catch'd threading them. You know the consequences better then I.

A mile East of Limington I call'd to see a Vine yard belonging to Esqr Mettford [Mitford]. It was in very good order but lies high & exposed which is a great Check on the Growth of the Fruite. I tasted a pretty Wine and another that very much resembled Frontigniac.

Cross a tedious open part of the Forest wee came to Bewley, [Beaulieu][3] once an Abby but now the Seat of the Duke of Montague. Never did Monks show their cunning more then in the choice of this House. The Hills cover'd with Woods are an Emphitheater about It. A Fine Brook formes a Little Lake of Fresh Water before It and by an Inlet a course of two Miles the Sea Washes its Walls on the other side. A fine place to keep Lent in, and to grow Fatt with Fasting. From hence through an open part of the Forest I finish'd my Tour much to my satisfaction.

From the key of Hampton the Isle of Wight is in View. This tempted us to make a voyage thither. Wee took Shipping in a Rainey Blustery Day but Wee was not such Fresh Water Sailers to be baulked with a squall or two, so on Board Wee went. We had frequent Turnadoes & hazey thick Weather, Rains & Calms. It seem'd as if Wee was to have Little Smalle Samples of what you experience in Long Voyages. Wee was to have sail'd up to Newport but Want of Water made us cast Anchor at Cowes.

To Divert the Time I went to view the Castle of West Cowes which is in a poor Condition to resist an Enemy or give protection to the Inhabitants. Wee are told Harry 8th built a Castle att East Cowes, but there is no appearance of any that I could perceive. Here is the Custome House. I was told by a Credible Merchant that Forty Sail of Carolina Rice Ships was clear'd att this port for Holland, Hambro etc. There was then there the North Cape, one of the South Sea Companys Green Land Ships which carried 1500 Barrells of Rice bound for Holland. This Rice Trade has been Vastly Improved in the Memory of Man.

In going from Southampton we go to Portsmouth after passing the Ferry.

Att the Entrance of the Common or Moor near a great pound I observed growing near It & on the Right Hand on the Side of a spring Osmond Royall [*Osmunda regalis,* the Royal Fern], a noble plant whose Leaves was five foot long and in the Rill that conveys the Wast Water amongst the Rushes I found the Elephant Caterpillar (August 11th) feeding on Water Ladies bed straw [*Galium,* Marsh Bedstraw], a small tender plant which grew amongst the Rushes. It was near full grown. It went to Capt Salis [not identified] August 15, 1739.

I found Osamond Royall in a Spring in a Wood leading from Hamble or Amble to Nettly Place which is the Ruins of a Stately Church & Religious House. Here I observed a

"The Elephant," Deilephila elpenor. Moses Harris. The Aurelian . . . , *plate VII. The Library Company of Philadelphia.*

Osmunda regalis, *the Royal Fern. Andreas Friedrich Happe. Hunt Institute for Botanical Documentation.*

"Clouded Yellow Butterfly," Colias croceus. Moses Harris. The Aurelian . . . , plate XXIX, The Library Company of Philadelphia.

Vine to grow out of the Stone Work and an Old Vine & Ivy so Interwoven together that it was not very Easie to distinguish the One from the Other.

This seems to be a fine situation for a Vine yard, a little Declining valley being open to the South and protected by Woods & the Old Ruins.

August 13th: In the road to Alsford I saw the Clouded Yellow Butterfly, and on the Chalk Banks covered with Flowers on the Road sides I saw more of the Clouded Yellow.

Since Mr Charles Dubois, Treasurer to the East India Company is now living who att the Request of Mr Marsh, a Merchant, sent over per Richd Diamond [not identified] a Hundred pound Bag fill'd with East India Rice to try whether it would grow in that province and now they make between five and fifty thousand Barrells a year.

From hence takeing the Benefit of the Tide Wee landed att Newport, the Capital of this Island, a real pretty Town laid out in a Regular Manner and is the principall Corn Markett for this Island which produce very Large Quantity for Exportation besides what supplies the inhabitants. I was shown St Katherine's Hill on the South Side of the Island. This and the adjoining Hills command a View all over the Island and on it stands a Tower which is a Sea Mark but now is going to Decay which may be a great Loss to Seafaring Men. Is not these Sea Marks under the care of the Trinity House?

The people of the Island are Very Healthy. I was shown as Wee pass'd by Water a Fisherman a fishing with a Nett that was in his Ninetieth year, and his Wife in her hundredth and but this year was prevailed on to walk with a Stick. I was told also that One of the Aldermen of Newport was in his Ninetieth year, walk'd about and were very Hearty.

CHARLES WAGER (1666–1743), Royal Navy officer who gained great wealth from Spanish prizes (1708–1709), was made admiral in 1734, knighted 1708, and became MP for Westminster 1732–42. He grew exotic plants at Parson's Green, Fulham, where he kept a greenhouse which Collinson managed in his absence. Georg Ehret drew some of Wager's plants. (DNB)

In *Some Account of the Late Peter Collinson . . .* John Fothergill reported that Sir Charles Wager was "a most generous and fortunate contributor to [Sir Hans Sloane's] vast treasure of natural curiosities; omitting nothing, in the course of his many voyages, that could add to its magnificence, and encouraging the commanders under him, who were stationed in different parts of the globe, to procure whatever was rare and valuable in every branch of natural history. To this he was strongly excited by Peter Collinson; for whom and his family Sir Charles had a very singular esteem, and continued it to the last moments of his life." [London, 1770, pp. 3–4]

1. A cluster of tall rocks lying immediately off the western extremity of the Isle of Wight.

2. Hurst Castle, four miles south west of Lymington at the western end of this Solent, erected by Henry VIII. It remained in use as a fortification through WWII.

3. Beaulieu (pronounced Bewley) site of Beaulieu Abbey. The gate house of the abbey was incorporated into Palace House, home of the Montagu family from 1538. At the time it was home to John Montagu, Second Duke of Montagu (1688–1749).

38 ❧ TO MICHAEL AND MARY RUSSELL

Draft AL:LS
August, 1739

Dear Father and Mother Russell

You may with some Reason wonder what Wind has blown Mee hither. My Father says I cant imagine where that Peter is, then runs to the Mapp to find me out and that's no very easy Task for I am here to Day and gone to Morrow, But when my Good Parents you reflect and consider the Rambling Disposition of your Son your Wonder will cease for you pretty well know I am not long in a place. Excited by a Natural Curiosity that haunts Mee everywhere I must be peeping about, tho I don't find that I can see further into a mill stone than another man yett for all that I can't keep prying here & there I am Dayly gratified with some new thing, some Discovery I was not Master off before that affords infinite pleasure and ample gratification and pushes Mee on to Further Pursuits.

I am now gott on the Extreeme Southern border of the New Forest, but I think with 500 year standing it may with propriety be call'd the Old Forest. Here I have rambled all Day. My Father sayes it plainle so by this Letter the Rambling Disposition is not gott out of my head by the Foregoing as I am now gott out of the Forest and in a beaten Tract and having refrest myself with a good Supper being all alone and past nine I thought I could not better Devote my Time and Hour Then by paying my Duty to you Both and inquiring after your Welfare.

After I had made all the Discoverys round South Hampton I could I beg'd leave of my Dear Polly to make an Excursion into New Forest to pay a Visit to a Vertuoso Esq that lives in the Center of this noble & Extensive Wild where Nature appears in all the beautys & Simplicityes of Her Virgin State without the Assistance of Art.

Michael Russell and Mary Russell were Collinson's mother-in-law and father-in-law.

39 ❧ TO JOHN CUSTIS

ALS:AAS
London, January 31, 1740

Dear Friend,

It on the one hand gives Mee pleasure to heare of the kind Reception J. Bartram rece'd under thy Roof. He was much Delighted with thy Garden which is the best Furnish'd & next to John Claytons[1] of any He Mett With in all that Journey.

Butt on the other hand I feel a mixture of passions, concerne for your late Illness and Gladness for your Recovery. Take new Courage, your Temperance has laid solid Foundations that may be shaken but not Easily Overthrown. I take It your late Illness was an Effort of Nature to Discharge & overcome some Malignitys that may have been Latent for some time. Humour Her, take Gentle Exercise Moderate Light, Easie Dyet, Broths &c, Refreshing Drinks, Milk Morn'g & Even It warm from the Cow. If your advances are but slow they will be sure and I doubt not but you'l find a sensible renovation and by Degrees find the happy Effects of your Regular Life which will work wonderfully for your Reliefe.

I have observed Many att or near your years have had almost Bent and then run on a Long Easie Race to above fourscore. My Grandmother was a Remarkable Instance, Sir Charles Wager is another who had so severe Illness att 70 that he had Tenn blisters on Him att one Time, and it is generally allow'd that to the Effects of Temperance His Recovery was principally owing that now He is as Jolly Strong & Hearty as any Man of His years and Continues strictly to Drinking Water and moderate meals.

So my Good Friend you see there is much in your favour. If you find Yourself Hippish or Low Spirited, Endeavour all you can By Gentle Exercise and a constant applycation to something Diverting to Disperse those Mists & Clouds, for the Mind Effects the Body.

I am att times Intolerably afflicted with the head Ach, but a Gentle Vomitt is to Mee an Instant & most Effectuall Cure.

I am very Much Obliged to you for your Care about the Sorrel Trees. I apprehend if they cannot [be] Laid down to take Root, the best way wou'd be to take up a Bush of them and Lett it be planted in your Garden. There it may first take Root, then Cutt it Down to the Stumps which will make it shoot Vigorously, and these Branches may conveniently be laid down.

As you Express'd a Desire for the silver Firr, White Currants, Larch Trees, Yellow Rose, with many other Curious plants, Mr Hanbury[2] happening to heare Mee Read your Letter Desired Mee to procure them for you, and Indeed it was in the nick of Time, for the ship was gone Down to Depford and next tide to Gravesend, but Luckky for us (tho otherwise for the ship) but a Contrary Wind sprung up and kept Her there 2 or 3 Days so had Just Time to gett your Cargo on Board. The plants Look'd Exceeding Well, and Captain Harding had Mr Hanbury strict Charge to Carry them all the Way in the Cabbin.

Being att the Right season I have great Hopes they'l come finely to hand.

Now I shall proceed further to take Notice of yours of the 12 August Last. If Moles are so numerous and troublesome, I should think it would be worth somebodys while to sett up a Mole Catcher in ordinary to your province.

Wee have Variety of Traps for them in England, Butt patience & the spade are Mine, for In the Morning & Evening I wait till I see the Earth Move. Att that Instant I strike in the spade Behind Him & so Turn the Mole out, who then is Easily kill'd. Many a One has Mett with its fate this way.

I am glad to heare the Horse Chesnutts grows. They are great Shooters with us and flower in a few years. To be sure the Hares Eating them has sett them back More then one would think, for they are a Tree that cannot beare the Knife or the Ax & Removeing them is a Check besides.

Perhaps if the soft shell'd Almond was grafted or Buded on some of your Wild plum stocks, may retard their Early Flowering. Here we graft or bud all on plum stocks, and if these Trees was planted Close to the sides of Woods or Groves might protect them from that Quarter where the Wind that Brings the Frosts come. Or if they was planted in Groves or Thicketts of Trees of their own size of Growth may do as Well. There is great Benefits rec'd from these Artificial helps and was I with you I should have Twenty projects.

The nine Little Cluster Cherry Trees are what Wee call the Cornish Cherry. It is a

pretty Flowering Tree and very Different from yours and is a pretty ornament to our Gardens & Wildernesses.

The persian Lilac is a sweet flowering shrub and Flowers Freely with us is but a Low plant so very ornamental in a Flower Garden.

I am glad the strawberry Tree [*Arbutus unedo*] shoots from the Bottome. I think then there is no fear of its growing. It is a Beautifull Evergreen and what makes it the more admired is its Flowering & Ripe Fruite so Late in the Year. That you might not want this fine Tree I sent you another in the Last Cargo. It was full of Blossomes when I saw it on board.

The Yellow Imperial is indeed a Rarity. I hope as that is come up the other Bulbs sent with it will in Time show themselves. There was variety of Martigons yellow & white, Asphodills and other rare flowers, however I hope to remember them over Again.

It Delight Mee Much and I must give you Joye on hearing the Two Trees with the Mulberries are alive. They should be both Double Blossome peaches grafted on plum stocks. These are in my Opinion One of the most Beautifull Flowering Trees in the World and some years bear very Good Fruite.

I take that to happen by some semy-double Blossomes. Graft or Bud this as soone as you can on peach or almond stocks on which they may Thrive better with you then on plum stocks. You'l be Delighted with it when you see it in Blossome against a Wall. I have seen its flowers near as Large as a half Crown but in Common Larger than a shilling. I am glad to heare the Tuberoses thrives so well with you. To be sure your Climate must be very natural to them being Like their own.

My Dear Friend, I heartyly Thank you for the Black Haws [hawthorns]. I wish I had a plant that bears Fruite of this Tree. The Berries are a pretty Fruite to Eat, by some are call'd Indian Sweetmeat, being as I am told a Usuall present from the Indians to their Guests. The seeds was very Fresh and so was the Shomake, which being so fine a Colour must make a beautifull Shew. You take great pains to Oblige Mee with Cucumber seed so much that I am ashamed of It.

I must not forgett to Acknowledge the great Mark of Friendship shown Mee in giving a Consignment to my Worthy Friend J. Hanbury whose Diligence and Industry in His Business is not to be match'd. I doubt not but he will give you satisfaction.

I thank you for the pretty Huming Bird. Now my Dear Friend I come to thank you for yours of August 23rd and For your acceptable present by Captain West. He very Courteously sent it Mee. The seed was very fresh & Good. The Laurell seed was a Choice Cargo and in fine Order. These will Ever be Welcome to yours.

Yours of September 2nd being a further mark of your Favour with the very Valuable present it contained deserves nay requires the Thanks of us all who Love plants & Botany.

Humming bird. George Edwards. Natural History of Birds, *Vol I, plate 38. The Library Company of Philadelphia.*

"Mr Peter Collinson, F.R.S. obliged me with a sight of this curious Pair of Birds and Nest. They are found in Carolina, and as far north as New England in the Summer Season, but retire southward, or disappear in Winter."

The Umbrella is indeed a great Curiosity and the seed was so plump shineing & Fresh that my Heart Jump'd when I saw them haveing Never seen such a Quantity before. I had 1/2 doz seed gave Mee some Years agon and Rais'd Two Fine plants, but very frew Gardens have the Curious Tree. The Ground Cherry is a pretty plant. You are Exceeding kind to think of Everything. This you may be sure, not anything comes amiss to Mee from the Hysop to the Cedar.

I was Really much Concerned for the Box of Autumn Flowers for it is rare to Meet with a ship in the Summer Months to bring them. Butt I am glad to find they are come to hand, but what surprises Mee Extreemly is that you should find no Guernsey Lillies. I trusted no body but myself in this affair. I took them out of the Ground myself, I told them as they Lay & I Immediately putt them into the Box myself. This can Aver Bona Fide. How they should be Houcus pocuss'd away and not the Rest is very Extriordinary.

The Great Roots are not the Narcis of Naples but an Autumn Narciss with a yellow Crocus Like flower, If I remember Right as you'l find from the catalogue. You'l be pleased with it. Its fine shineing Green Leaves makes a pleasant show all Winter.

I hope the spring Acconite will oblige you this spring with its pretty yellow Early Flower. It appears with us in December. Pray Lett Mee heare a particular acco't of the others. If you had not the Cyclamens you must be pleased with them.

I apprehend the Vigorousness of your soil & Climate is the Reason Veriagated plants recover their Native Verdure, for it is a manifest Decay & sicklyness in the Original plant that Occations Veriagations so that it may be recon'd in a Comsumptive state, but your fine Country is a Meare Monpelier to their Natural Complection.

I find you have Extreams of Wett & Dry. Wee have att this Juncture an Extreame of Cold. A sharp Frost began the 26 December and has continued Ever since. Till Last Week Wee had no Relaxation, but it thaw'd pretty much in the Citty but Little in the Country, but now it Continues. The Thames is full of Ice and att sundry Times has been Cross'd by numbers of People & Booths on It, but the spring Tides Frequentyly brakes it Into Islands of Ice & then all Retreat.

This is a Trying Time to Our Gardens & south Country plants. I have been Obliged to keep Constant fires In My stove & Green house by which Means I am in Hopes I shall be but a small sufferer, but those that would not take the pains are quite Demolish'd. The frost was so very sharp & severe. The Like has not been known since the 1715/16 or 1709.

In the Autumn if any Convenient Oppetunity I Intend to try if I cannot send you some Good kitchen garden seeds. But I wish I knew which particular sort would be most Agreeable.

I find you can't well bear Rideing then pray gett a One Horse Chair, and if you can Ride Morning & Evening Once a Day att Least.

Now my Dear friend I must take my Leave of you not knowing when there will be another Oppertunity, for a few Days agon an Embargo was Laid for 3 Months, but nothing shall prevent Mee Assureing you that I am with sincere Wishes for your Health & Welfare Your Affectionate Friend,

P. COLLINSON.

1. John Clayton (1694–1773), English botanist, appointed attorney-general for Virginia by the Crown. Shortly after his arrival in the colony in 1715 he planted a botanical garden at "Windsor" near the Piankatank River in what is now Matthews County. He corresponded with Gronovius, Linnaeus, Alexander Garden (see PC to Cadwallader Colden, May 19, 1756, note 4) and probably sent

seeds to John Bartram. A fine and thoughtful scientist, Clayton collected in Virginia and through Mark Catesby sent his materials to Gronovius for identification. In 1738 he sent "A Catalogue of Plants, Fruits, and Trees Native to Virginia" in which he identified and described the species he had thus far collected.

Gronovius appreciated the value of Clayton's list, extended and revised it and in 1739 published it in Leiden as *Flora Virginica*. He advised his correspondent that the catalogue was too valuable not to be published and that because of distance he'd not had time to consult the author—to whom he gave credit on the title page and in his introduction.

Good-spirited Clayton kept collecting and sending, and in 1743 Gronovius published Part II of the *Flora,* adding 300 species to the 600 catalogued in Part I. Linnaeus relied heavily upon this work. It has been estimated that of eastern North America species perhaps as many as 500 rest for their Linnean typification on the specimens collected by Clayton. When you see the "spring beauty" of Virginia, *Claytonia,* remember him. (Berkeley and Berkeley, *John Clayton, Pioneer of American Botany.* Chapel Hill, 1963).

2. John Hanbury (d. 1758), London merchant and governor of the Hanbury Company. He was interested in the London trade with Virginia and one of the original grantees of the Ohio Company. In his larger commonplace books, PC made this undated memorandum:

> Frd John Hanbury & I went a few Weeks agon to see an Estate of his in Oxfordshire & so of Course to Oxford & Blenheim. Wee found great Entertainment in Citty & Country. All our Sences was most agreeably Satisfied at Some Colleges, our Bellies was most Elegantly feasted, att others Our Eyes. Don't say this too good usage for a Couple of Heretics that won't pay tithes, but I'll tell thee by hook or by Crook they have had a good deal of our Money & we had never any of their Merchandise, never Eat or Drank for it which as the Country Man said was very hard, & I think so too, that it was but a piece of Civil policy to treat us at Our Own Expense, But doth thee think it did not Raise my Spirits with pitty & Concern to find our Friend Barclay Lay'd up in a Corner amongst the Bodleian Worthys as if the Students was afraid to peep & see those truths they had rather have Conceal'd. [LS]

40 ❧ TO HANS SLOANE

ALS:BL
[circa 1740]

Sr Hans

I Send you by Bearer a Male possum. Please to take him out of the Jarr & Keep Him in the Kitchen till the Weather Breaks.

I am yours

P. COLLINSON

Monday

In his January 25, 1739 letter to John Custis, Collinson thanked his Virginia friend "for your Account of the Possum" and adds, "Had I known so much before I doubt not but That Lady Wager had sent might have been alive now Had Wee known its Food, but had yours come alive it would have been a much greater rarity haveing the Young att the Teats." (ALS:AAS)

Possum. William Byrd II. Rawlinson Collection, Bodleian Library.

ALS:BL

[circa 1740]

Dear Sir Hans,

I return'd Saturday from Lord Petres. He gives his Humble Service and is very Much Obliged to you for the plants. I saw them in a growing State before I Left them. The Casada He wants very much. Pray, is the Dumb Cane [*Dieffenbachia*] figured In your History and under what Title? I have the Second part which Sr Charles Wager gave Mee, but I have not your first part.

I Eat part of a fish att Lord Petres. It was called the Kingston Fish. It seem'd akin to the Ray. I should be glad to Know under what Title in Willoughby[1] it is to be found, but these att your Leisure.

I am my Dear Friend much yours,

P. COLLINSON

Below: Diffenbachia sequire, *Dumb Cane (with Phocid) Georg Dionysius Ehret. In Christopher Jacob Trew,* Plantae Selectae, *Vol 1, Knowsley Hall. Courtesy the Earl of Derby, Knowsley.*

Right: Cistus ladanifer. *Georg Dionysius Ehret. Hunt Institute for Botanical Documentation.*

Lord Petre was very much Engaged Elce He would have writt to you, but He will do It Soone and will send you a painting of a Curious plant From China. It has Shining Evergreen Bay Like Leaves and Bears Large Double Crimson Flowers and another that Bears Double White flowers [*Camellia sinensis*]. These are great Rarities, and what is very remarkable they are both very Skillfully Enarched [grafted], but on what Stocks we cant tell. Probably being Double Flowers they bear no Seed, so know no other ways to Increase them.

The flower Budds as you will see by the Inclosed are very much Like the Cistus Ledon, but the Flower when open Is as Large as the aethe a frutex but Double.

Yours

PC

1. Francis Willoughby (1635–1672), *De historia piscum . . .* Oxford, 1686.

Cistus ladanifer. *Georg Dionysius Ehret. Hunt Institute for Botanical Documentation.*

42 ❧ TO HANS SLOANE

ALS:BL

[circa 1740]

Bis Dat Qui Cito Dat[1]

Dear Hans,

For Once I take upon Mee Sr Clemens, and Introduce to you the Great Emperour of China and his Mandarins.[2] I Doubt not but they will meet with a Reception Becomeing their Quallitye.

I am with many thanks for your Last Favours affectonately

Yours   P. COLLINSON

Please to send the Insects I Look'd out to Day By the Bearer.

Please to think on the Shells, for my Hopes are Gone with you.

I have given my Boye a great Charge to Carry them Steady.

Please to keep the Box they are In till you have an oppertunity to Dispose of them. Be Carefull In takeing out the Great Moth, for his Wings are Tender. The Remainder of his Body is under the Cork in the Corner . When they are putt between Glasses, I gum a Small peice of Cork in the Center of the Bottome Glass & then stick the pinn in it (if too Long with a Sharp pair Scissors I Cutt off the Top), for there is no Drawing the pinn without Ruining the Flys.

But this I submitt and am Yours,

P. COLLINSON.

Camellia sinensis—Camellia Japonica "Ts-bekki." Georg Dionysius Ehret. Natural History Museum, Botany Library, London.

If the Box that I have sent will not hold what I Look'd out to Day the Boye shall Come again.

Dr Delenius writes Mee that Ld Petres China Flower [*Camellia*] is Call'd by the Chinese (Swa Tea) and Kempfer[3] has well Discribed and figur'd It in his Aoemetis Exoticas [as Tsabekki, its Japanese name].

1. "He gives twice who gives promptly." (Publius Syrus Proverbs)

2. Possibly the Great Emperor Moth, *Saturnia pavonia.*

3. Engelbert Kaempfer (1651–1716), German physician and traveler, with Dutch East India Company, 1685–1693, and publisher of *Amoenitatum Exoticarum . . . ,* 1712.

ALS:BL
[circa 1740]

Sir Hans,
Dear friend

No doubt but you have heard & know the Species of Maple from whence the Sugar is Made. It is common through the Northern Continent of America, and the Lower Sort of people in the upper Settlements Use the Sugar of the Maple Instead of the Cane Sugar, & if it was refin'd might be Equally as Good. I Send you a Lump of the Sugar & Two Small pieces of White Sugar Candy made from the Same Maple Sugar.

I am with may thanks for Yesterdays Favour

Your affectionate friend   P. COLLINSON

This Sugar Requires to be kept Dry Elce it will Disolve.

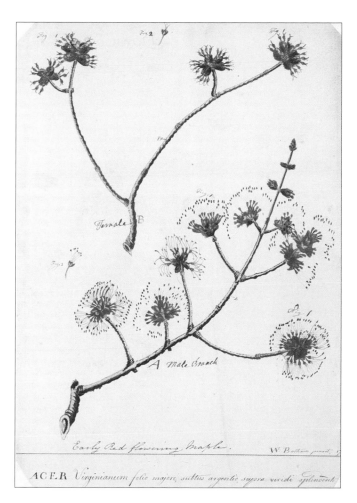

Sugar maple. William Bartram. From Peter Collinson's album of prints and drawings at Knowsley Hall. Courtesy the Earl of Derby, Knowsley

Sugar Maple as it appears when the seeds are fully ripe. William Bartram. From Peter Collinson's album of prints and drawings at Knowsley Hall. Courtesy the Earl of Derby, Knowsley.

Cadwallader Colden. John Wollaston. The Metropolitan Museum of Art, Bequest of Grace Wilkes, 1922.

44 🎋 TO CADWALLADER COLDEN

ALS:N-YHS
London, March 5, 1741

Respd Friend Dr Colden

In returning my thanks for your obligeing present (which I much admire) [not identified], It gives me a pretence to Trouble you with a few Lines & to enclose Mr [George] Grayhams[1] opinion of your Scheme for a Quadrant. His remarks Seeme to mee very Rational but as I am not Skilled in those matters shall Submitt them to your Better Judgment.

Wee are in hopes you will oblige the Curious with the other part of the History of the Five Nations. The first gave such an Idea of the Nature & Constitutions of them which are very informeing & Entertaining the Second no Doubt will Further Illustrate that matter and very possible the reader may reape some Benefit from its Delay by Some Aditions that you may be able to make both as to the Increase & advantages of trade of Further Discoveries & perhaps some more pieces of Natural Histy. Tretises of this kind where they may be rely'd on are much in Request & Demand Here, and if you don't choose to print it yr self there is those In London will Readyly do It and as the First part is quite out of print, what if It Suffer a Revisal or Aditions & Both come out together that would make the Work very compleat.[2]

One thing as an Englishman I beg leave to add that whilst We are most agreeable Informed of the progress & Increase of Trade no hints may be given to the French to our Disadvantage who are Ever on the Watch.

I Rely on your Candor & Goodness to Excuse these Hints. I wish I could otherwise recommend myself to your Esteeme then by offering you my Services. If I can do you any it will be a Real pleasure to your Sincere Friend

P. COLLINSON

I beg your acceptance of a Small Tract on the Yellow Feaver.[3] It has been well Received here. Mr Alexander[4] will send it to you.

PS. If an Ingenious Man and a great teacher unto Nature Named John Bartram of Pensilvania should wait on you please to give him what Information you can on those things he may inquire of You. He has been a Considerable Traveller in your World and is employed by a Sett of Noblemen & others to Colect Seeds & Curiosities for them. Yours

P.C.

CADWALLADER COLDEN (1688–1776), Irish-born physican, botanist, politician, surveyor-general and then lieutenant governor of New York, 1761–1776. He studied medicine in London, then emigrated to Philadelphia in 1710, where he practiced medicine and carried on a mercantile business. He moved to New York in 1718 as surveyor-general of the colony and steadily assumed more important administrative roles. He studied and wrote about history, physics, mathematics, botany, medicine and philosophy. His correspondents included Gronovius, Franklin, Alexander Garden and Linnaeus, whose system he mastered. Linnaeus published in two parts Colden's description of the plants around his estate at Coldingham (on the Hudson near Newburgh) as *Plantae Coldenghamiae* (1749, 1751). Colden also wrote *The History of the Five Nations Depending on the Province of New York,* 1727 and 1747, drew maps and wrote about the properties of light and color, throat distempers, yellow fever, and the medical properties of tar water. He struggled unsuccessfully with what he called an "extension" of Newtonian principles, *An Explication of the First Causes of Action in Matter; and of the Cause of Gravitation.* New York, 1745. (DNB)

See *The Letters and Papers of Cadwallader Colden,* vols 50–56, 67–68 of New-York Historical Society *Collections.* New York 1917–1923; 1934–1935

1. George Graham (1675–1751), FRS, English clockmaker. (DNB)

2. See Collinson to Colden March 7, 1742.

3. Warren, Henry, M.D. *A treatise concerning the malignant fever in Barbados . . . In a letter to Dr. Mead.* London, 1740; Second edition London, 1741.

4. James Alexander (1691–1756), New York merchant. A number of Collinson's commercial letters to Alexander survive. When Thomas Penn gave up mercery and became a Proprietor (about 1733), he turned over to Collinson a number of his customers, including James Alexander. In one letter to Alexander at the N-YHS, Collinson enclosed samples of his stock of ribbons and sundries.

ALS:LS
London, April 3, 1741

Dear Friend,

Mr Biork[1] being so Obligeing to Acquaint Mee of a Convenient Oppertunity of writing to you, I could not forbear indulging myself that pleasure, In the first place to Inquire after Your Health & next to know if you Received Mine with a parcel of american Seeds. I also wrote to you by Dr Filenius (for whom I have an high esteem) which no doubt came to your Hands. But my Dear Friend you have not thought fitt to return Mee an answer, however none is yet come to hand.

I know your Active genius can't be idle. Pray what are you Doing? Some New Work I hope is ready for the press, to Entertain & Informe the Curious part of Mankind.

You know Wee have frequent Varieties by Comixture of the Farina [pollen] of Different Species In Flowers, but not so Rare to be Mett with In Fruits, but I have this Day sent Mee Two Apples, the One a Russett or Brown-Coat Apple, and another a Green Apple. They both was original Fruits of the Green Apple, whose Boughs mix with the Russett, and acquired such Distinguishing Marks of their adulterous Intimacy and too great Familiarity with Each other's Blossoms That One Part of the apple is Russett and the other part Green, the Colors not by Degrees going Into Each other, but a Remarkable Line where One Fruit is divided from the other, Like as In the Hermaphrodite Orange & Lemon.

The Complexion of these Two Sorts of apples being so Different makes the Mixture the more Remarkable. To give you some idea of this Curious Fruite there is a Sketch on the other side.

What is further Remarkable in this Fruite is that tho it is originally from the green apple, and grow on that Tree, yett its Neighbour the Russetting has Impregnated more than Two Thirds of It.

Lord Wilmington[2] has another Instance of this Commixture or Blending of Fruits, for He has a tree that produces Nectarines & peaches without any Art, but Quite Accidental. The Fruite does not Mix together as the apple above but compleat Peaches & Nectarines, both Distinct, are on the Same Tree.

My best wishes attend you. From your affectionate friend,

P. COLLINSON.

Pray my respects to Dr Filenius who I hope is well.

1. Tobias Bjork, Pastor of the Swedish Church, Princess Square, London.

2. Spencer Compton, Earl of Wilmington (1673?–1743), politician and Speaker of the House of Commons. (DNB)

Martin Folkes.
William Hogarth.
Royal Society

46 ❧ TO MARTIN FOLKES

Transcription of ALS:RS
[circa 1741]

Dear Mr Foulkes

    You have been so good as to give me expectation that you and Miss will be so kind to come and take a piece of mutton with me and see my little collection. If either Monday, Tuesday or Wednesday next will be agreeable pleas to let me know which day, and you'll greatly oblige Your affectionate friend,

P. COLLINSON

NB I dine at Two o'clock

May bring a pollypuss with you if not too inconvenient.[1]

MARTIN FOLKES (1690–1754), antiquary and scientist, elected President of the Society of Antiquaries in 1750, and was President of the Royal Society, 1741–52. (DNB)

See Collinson to Colden, March 9, 1744. On March 30, 1745 Collinson wrote Cadwallader Colden: "The surprising Phenomena of the Polypus Entertain'd the Curious for a year or Two past, but Now the Vertuosi of Europe are taken up in Electrical Experiments. . . ." (ALS:N-YHS)

1. Polypus: "In zoology, a species of the [fresh water] hydra, which, although cut in a thousand pieces, and in every direction, still exists, and each section becomes a compleat animal." (*Encyclopedia Brittanica*. Vol III. [Edinburgh, 1771], p. 503)

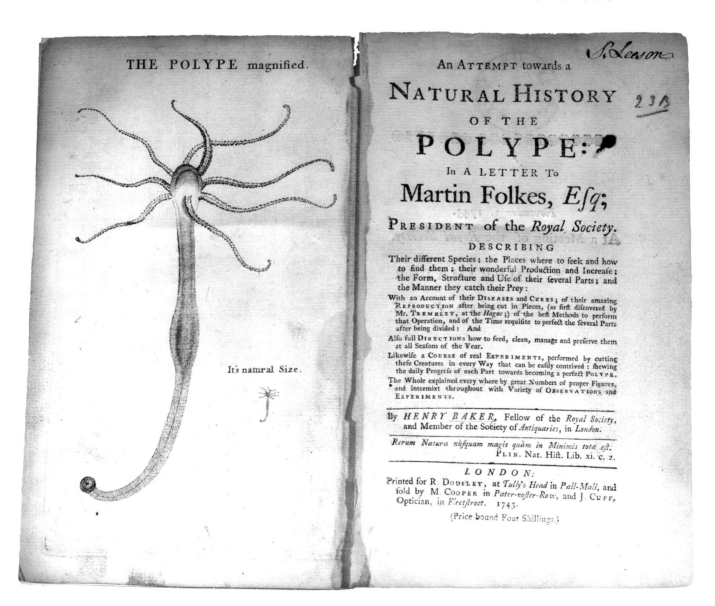

Frontispiece from Henry Baker, Natural History of the Polype. *London, R. Dodsley, 1743. The Linnean Society of London.*

Draft AL:LS
[circa 1742]

Esteemed Friend,

I was greatly Delighted with thy Curious account of the amazing Increase from one Mallow seed, 200,000 may be reproduced. Reflecting on this wonderfull production it led Mee to Consider the great & Wise Ends it was Intended for by the Bountifull Hand of the Great Lord of the Universe whose providential goodness & Regard is always overall His Works for their Continuance & Support. This is Evidently Seen by the provision in thy Calculation which is principally Intended for the Subsistance of the Feathered Tribe & perhaps for the Lesser Animals, mice, Insects, etc.

It is observable that all plants whose Seed is of so great use are very Productive whch is very Requisite not only for the support of numerous Living Creatures but for other purposes. Many Seeds have other Physical uses which occasions are expensive and Require Large Quantities (consumption), So a great Supply is Necessary and then great allowances are to be made for Seeds that may be spoiled by being troden underfoot by Man & beast, and great Quantities are Lost and never Grow through the Inclemency of the Seasons, from great Droughts or by the Tender young seedling plants that are Carried off by Severe Frosts & many more suffer (great nmbers are lost) by their being Exposed for want of protection.

So that if the Bountiful Provider had not given the common Vegitables of the field (that are of such Use and which are Dayly exposed to so many accidents & Hazards) an Abundant Increase, their species might risque being near Lost and the Great and Wise Ends of Providence frustrated.

To an unthinking person the (Wonderfull) great Increase from one Mallow Seed may Seem a Needless Superfluity in what is Reputed a Common Weed, where as a grain of our Corn is not near so fruitfull (productive) on which the life of Man so much Depends. But if it is Consider'd the One is a Spontaneous product (& may be of great use) but Dayly Exposed to the Weeders had to be pluckd up & destroyed besides many other accidents that attends it, so it was Necessary to have an Extraordinary Supply whereas the other being Cultivated by Art, tho less productive from one Grain yett from its Immediate Use to Mankind the Greatest Care is taken of its propagation & Increase, and that proves more than Equivalent to the Greater Increase of the other.

These my Good friend are Some Hints that occurr'd to Mee but as my Time is mostly Ingrosed by my Business I cannot Study regularity or Methode. If my Correspondents are so kind to Consider this they will candidly I hope over Look all omission.

I shall be glad [if] thee will Favour Mee with any future Observations. They will always be very acceptable, and if I can oblige thee any way it will be a pleasure to they sincere Friend   PC

The Beared Mr Plumstead [not identified] is my Perticular friend is informed you want a good ship to carry [obscure] to Jamaica [obliterated].

Joseph Hobson (1709–1765), Quaker, contributed an article to *The Philosophical Transactions* (XLII, p. 320–322) on the seed-bearing properties of "The Upright Mallow," and published *Memoirs of the Life and Convincement of the Worthy Friend, Benjamin Bangs, &c* (1757). Hobson's entry in the *Dictionary of Quaker Biography,* Library of the Religious Society of Friends, London, reports "His death was occasioned by lying in a damp bed."

ALS:N-YHS
London, March 7, 1742

Dear Friend,

You have much obliged Mee with yours of the 22d June and I am glad to find my Little offices were Acceptable to you.

I communicated your Letter & project to Mr Grayham whose answer I inclose. He has also been so good as to gett Mr Sissons[1] proposal to make an Insrmt that will be Suiteable for your purpose.

I also Lent Mr Grayham your History of the five Indian Nations, He was mightyly pleased with It & hoped you would oblige the World with the Second part for that He had not read any that had gave Him that Satisfaction & information that yours Did, because he was perswaded He could depend on your Veracity. You Really Delight Mee In hopes of Seeing the Second Part but pray take your Time and Do it at your Leisure.[2]

Pray have you thought or can you give a Conjecture how America was peopled Or was it a Separate Creation. Most of your Vegetables & many of yr animals are Different from ours, and yett you have some Exactly Like ours of which I have Specimens by Mee for I have a Large Collection considering my years & Station of Natural Rarities & Some Artificial from most parts of the World, which I am Obliged to my Distant Curious friend for Sending Mee. They afford Mee great Entertainmt att my Leisure Hours and In the Country If I may boast my garden can show more of your Vegetables then perhaps any in this Island which I have been Collecting some years from Seed & growing plants Sent Mee by my Friends in your World So that I am no Stranger to America being pretty well acquainted with most of Its productions Wether animal, Vegitable, Mineral & Fossil perhaps beyond which you can Imagine the uses I make of them is to admire them for the sake of the Great & all Wise Creator of them to Enlarge my Ideas of his Almighty power & Goodness to Mankind. In Makeing So many things for his profit & his pleasure I reason on their Natures & properties. So far as I am or Can be Informed I compare them with ours. In short I Esteeme the regard I pay to them as a piece of adoration Due to the Great Author of them.

Thus my Dear Friend you See I open all my mind to you and tell you how I Employe all my Leisure Hours, I may Say Minutes, from Business. I hate to be idle & think all Time Sadly lost that is not usefully Imployed, for which Reason, Clubbs, Taverns, & Coffee Houses, Scarsly know Mee. Home is the most Delightfull place to Mee where I Divide My Houres in Business in Innocent Amusements and in the Dear Society of a Tender Kind Good Woman, A Boye & Girle.

I may now say with Milton I have now brought you to the State Of Earthly Bliss and Sincerely Wish all Mankind as Happy.

I had a Letter from J. Bartram. He much Laments the Disappointment of not Seeing you. I am perswaded you would have been pleased With Him. You would have found a wonderful Natural Genius considering his Education & that He was never out of America but is an Husbandman and Lives on a Little Estate of his own at 5 or 6 miles from Philadelphia on the River Skulkill. He really Surprised Mee with a Beautifull Draught on a Sheet of paper of the falls of Mohocks River which He took when he was there with a perticular account of It [lost] and also a Mapp of His own Makeing of Hudsons River, Dela-

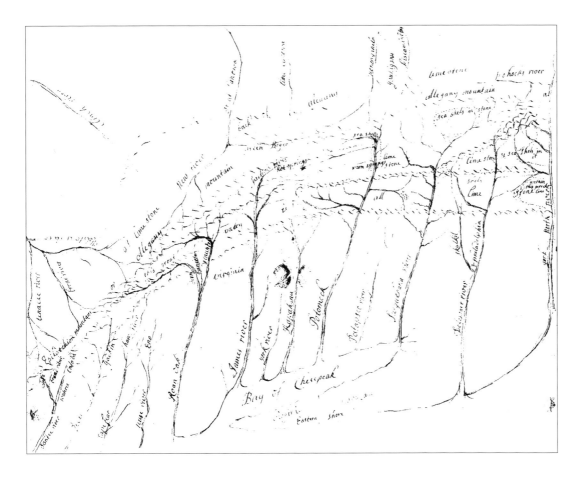

"A map of his [Bartram's] own Making of Hudson's River, Delaware, Katskil, & the bay . . ." John Bartram. American Philosophical Society.

ware, Katskil, & the bay which takes in the provinces of New York, Jerseys, Pensilvania, Maryld & Virginia.[3] For He has travelled all over these Countrys, the Uninhabited parts beyond the Mountains as well as the Inhabited parts along the Bay & the Sea Shores from the Capes to your province. His observations and accounts of all Natural productions that happened in his Way (& I believd few Escape Him) are much Esteem'd Here for their Truth and He wants not terms to Express himself wth Some accuracy and I have procured Him Some assistance from Some Curious Persons Here to Enable Him to make Further Discoveries.

Now my Dear Friend I rely on your Candor to Receive this Rambling Epistle as It is entended in Friendly part From a Man much Engaged in Business. Correctness is not to be Expected for Really I am obliged to write a paragh now & then subject to many Interruptions.

My Best Wishes attends you when leizure offers give a line to your Sincere friend

P. COLLINSON

In May 1742, Colden responded to this letter: "I look upon it as one of the happy incidents in my life that I have had the good fortune to fall into a correspondence with you because I take you to be one much of my own taste such I have often wished for to communicat some thoughts in natural philosophy which have remaind many years with me undigested for we scarcely have a man in this country that takes any pleasure in such kind of Speculations. Your communicating to me your private manner of life is the strongest in-stance of your friendship & in some measure makes up the loss of a personal acquaintance which I cannot hope to obtain. . . ." (ALS:N-YHS; published in *Cadwallader Colden Papers,* vol. II, pp. 257–261.)

1. Jonathan Sisson, a London instrument maker.

2. Collinson saw through the press publication of the second edition of Colden's *History of the Five Nations, Depending on the Province of New York.* London, 1747.

3. This map survives at the APS. See above.

The Whip poor-Will. George Edwards.
Natural History of Birds, *Vol I, plate 63,*
The Library Company of Philadelphia.

49 ❧ TO JOHN BARTRAM

ALS:Haverford
London, April 24, 1742

Friend John,

Mr Catesby Desires that thou wilt Look after a Night Bird call'd Wipper-Will. If this can be Shot & sent in its Feathers being first Boweled & Dry'd in a Slack oven, & then Tied up in Tobacca Leaves or pack'd up in Tobacca Dust. Pray observe if it is cock or Hen. This may be Seen in taking out its gutts, if it has Testicles or no.

What I have further to Desire is to Look after the Horns of that Monstrous Deer or Elk that thou Mentions to be shot by an Indian in a Swamp.

Possibly if thou makes Broad Hints to our Worthy Friend Gover Morris,[1] He may Send Mee His pair, for they are Rare Things Here & I want to Examine them with the Fossil Horns that are Dugg up in Ireland, for they do not Belong to our European Elk, and unless they do with yours the Species of Creatures Seems to be lost.

Wee should be glad to know Something Certain of its Size or to See its Hoof.

I have writt in perticular In J. Breintnall's Lettr & Sent Sundry things in their [the Library Company's] Trunk & a Boxe with Sr Hans Books & a Bundle paper from Dr Delenius all which I hope will Come Safe to hand. I also writt in pticular thy orders for Seeds this year by Capt. Wright & by the Way of New York.

I am in Haste, much Thine

P. COLLINSON

Collinson's interest in fossils continued to the end of his life. See the letter he wrote Emanuel Mendes Da Costa November 15, 1767 about "Elephants Teeth &c Lately found in North America" and the notes to that letter.

1. Lewis Morris (1671–1746), Governor of New Jersey, 1738–1746, and American Agent in London, 1735–1736.

ALS:NHM
London, June 2, 1742

Dear Mr Brewer

I am much much obliged to you for your Kind Lettr by Dr Perkins [not identified]. You have there in Manifested Great Gratitude for Triffles & in Doing what you have been so good to Do, you will have this great Consolation & Satisfaction that a Just Value & Much Care will be taken of Everything of yours and your Memory will not only live with Mee but with my Son Also.

Notwithstanding what you have done, I am perswaded it will not shorten your thred.

Take Courage (This Living Weather) & Chear up, and as much as In you Lies throw off all Gloomy anxious thoughts. You know by Long practice a Little Suffices Nature, but yett I confess it is hard rowing against the Streame. The Cruel Treatmt you have Mett with is Enough to Make a Wise Man Mad.

Butt undoubtedly It is owing to Good providence that you are Able tho with Great Difficulty to surmount all the hard Turns of Fortune.

Oh the peep of a New thing, how it revives the Flagging Spirits. I wish they may prove as Cordials to you & that you may have a Enough of Them to give your mind an Agreeable Turn & if that is made In Some Degree Easie the Body is Sensibly Relieved.

Your Letter I Dispatch'd Last post. I wish I could find any One that could be Confided In, but my Friends all these away are Dead & Gone.

Dr Perkins was so good as to Make my Little Garden a Visit and was pleased to Express much Satisfaction In Doing It. I am sure I was much obliged to Him for the pains, for It was a very Hott Day & I could not stay to attend Him as I could have wish'd.

A few Weeks agon Mr Power[1] Desired his Humble Service to you. Continues tolerably Well Except now & then a Cruel Fitt of the Gout, but his Love of Vegitables does not fail.

Dr Delenius has been Lately In Town. I Communicated to Him what you hinted to Mee in your of the 9 May, & He said as you was an Old Lover you Should have the Two Vols of the Horts Elthamens[2] & his History of Moss, all In Sheets for 2 Guineas. The first binding in pastboard will cost 7:6 & the Mosses about 2s:6d.

I am glad you have been Able to take a Turn to see Mr Knowlton.[3] I doubt not but that you was Well Entertain'd. I know He has a great Respect for you, but none More then your Sincere & Affectionate friend P Collinson

Our Old Gardners are all gone off So that Curious & Rare plants are gott into private hands. Butt Wee have one Lately raised Up, that Is James Gordon[4], a most knowing and Ingenous Man who has had great Experience being Gardner to Mr Sherrard[5] & Ld Petre. He has taken up the Cudggels. I do all I can to assist him. Dr Perkins can give you an account of his present Situation. Who Ever wants Seed for plants may by Sure of being Honestly Served.

SAMUEL BREWER (1670–1743), became a botanist after an unsuccessful career as a woolen manufacturer. He collected for Dilleninus and later became gardener to the Duke of Beaufort at Badminton. He discovered *Helianthemum breweri,* a species of rock rose.

"The loss of £20,000 of his own earnings, and of a large estate

T. 44

Altea Floridana.

Avis Tricolor.
The Painted Finch.

*Loblolly Bay of Carolina. Mark Catesby. From Collinson's
copy of* Natural History of Carolina . . . *Vol I, plate 44,
Knowsley Hall. Courtesy the Earl of Derby, Knowsley.*

left to him by his father, which was taken by his elder brother, gave
a morbid tone to his letters." [DNB]

1. Power gave plants to Collinson. On a loose sheet in his copy
of Miller's *Dictionary,* 7th edition, at the National University of
Wales, Collinson noted receiving plants from "Mr. Power, Dirham
the 4th May 1741."

2. *Hortus Elthamensis* 1732, 2 vols., catalogue of J. Sherard's
garden at Eltham.

3. Thomas Knowlton (1691–1781), gardener to James Sherard
at Eltham until 1725, then to the Earl of Burlington at Londesbor-
ough. See Henrey, Blanche, *No Ordinary Gardener.* London, 1986.

4. James Gordon (1708–1780), gardener to James Sherard at
Eltham and to then Lord Petre at Thorndon. After Petre's death,
Gordon established a nursery at Mile End in 1742, later at Bow, and
maintained a seed shop at the sign of the Thistle and Crown, 25
Fenchurch Street, London. He introduced many exotics, including
the camellia while working for Lord Petre at Thorndon. His general catalogue, 1770, was probably the first nurseryman's list in
botanical form. He supplied Philip Miller with plants and corresponded with Linnaeus. (Desmond) See Harvey, John, *Early Nurs-
erymen.* London, 1974, and Henrey, II, pp. 350–352.

In his copy of Millers *Gardener's Dictionary* (7th ed), Collinson
made this memorandum:

The Skill & Ingenuity of some men is Surprising, I was at
James Gordons Gardner at the last House on the left hand at
Mile End, there he showed Mee a Pott of Seedlings, of the Cactus or Great Melon Thistle p'haps the first ever raised [from]
seed but what shows his great knowledge & Experience in Vegitation is his way of Raising the finest dusty Seeds: I never saw
or heard of any Man before Him that could raise the dusty
Seeds of the Calmias, Rhododendrons, Azaleas. These Charming Hardy Shrubs that Excell all others by His Care, He fur-
nishes every Curious Garden all the Nursery Men and Gardners come to him for them, and this year after more then 20
years Tryal He show'd Mee the Loblolly Bay of Carolina comeing up from Seed in a way not to be expected; this Elegant Ever
Green Shrub, is next in Beauty to the Magnolia Vid Catesby's
Nat History and His Sagacity in Raiseing all sorts of plants
from Cuttings, Roots, & Laying, surpasses all others by which
our Gardens are Enriched with an Infinite Variety and for
many years I have not been a Little assistant to Him, in procuring Seeds and plants from all Countries. This Honourable
Mention of Mr Gordon who is now in his 56 year is an Act of
Gratitude Due to his Memory from his Old Friend Peter
Collinson in my 68 year. Mill: Hill Sept 2: 1763 in Hendon:
Middlesex

In another memorandum, Collinson wrote on 18 July 1764: "From my extensive correspondence I have assisted [him] with plants and seeds . . . who, with a sagacity peculiar to himself, has raised a vast variety of plants from all parts of the world . . ." [quoted in Lambert, A.B. "Notes relating to botany. . . ." *Transactions of the Linnean Society of London* 10, 271–3 (1811)].

5. James Sherard (1666–1738), FRS, apothecary, had garden at Eltham, Kent, noted for rare plants.

51 ❧ TO JOHN BARTRAM

ALS:HSP
London, July 3, 1742

Oh Friend John

I can't Express the Concern of Mind that I am under on so many Accounts. I have lost my Friend, my brother, the man I Loved & was dearer to Mee than all men, is no More. I could fill the Sheet, and many more But oh my anxiety of mind is so great that I can hardly write & yett I must Tell thee that on Friday July 2nd our dear friend Ld Petre was Carried off by the small-pox in the thirtieth year of His age. Hard hard Cruel Hard to be taken from his Friends, His Family, His Country, in the prime of Life when He had so many thousand Things Locked up in Breast for the Benefit of them all, are now Lost in Embrio.

I can go no further but to assure thee that I am thy Friend,

P. COLLINSON

All our Schemes are broke

Send no more Seeds for him nor the Duke of Norfolk[1] for now. He that gave motion is Motionless, all is att an End.

As I know that this will be a great Disappointment to thee, If thee has a mind to Send the Seeds as was ordered for Lord P & Duke of Norfolk on thy own Account & Risque, I will do what I Can to Dispose of them. The Duke of Norfolk shall have the preference, but there is no obliging him to take them, as I had not the Order from Him but from Lord Petre.

Send those for the Duke of Richmond & P. Miller.

Lord Petre was a fine, Tall, comely personage, Handsome, had the Presence of a Prince, yett was so Happily mixt that Love and awe was begot at the same Time, the Affability & Sweetness of his Temper were beyond Expression, without the least mixture of pride or haughtiness. With an Engaging Smile He always met his Friends.

But oh the Indowments of his Mind are not to be Discribed. Few or None could excel Him In the knowledge of the Liberal Arts & Sciences. He was a Great Mechanic as well as a Great Mathematician, ready at Figures and Calculations, Elegant in his Tastes. In his Religious Way, an Example of great piety, and in his Morals of Great Temperance & Sobriety. No Loose Word or Double Entendre did I Ever hear (this is something of the Man).

For his Virtues & has Excellencies and His Endowments I Loved Him & He Mee, more Like a Brother than a friend.

1. Charles Howard, 10th Duke of Norfolk (1720–1786), Lord Petre's cousin. Petre had made plans for the reforestation of Worksop Manor, the Duke's estate.

Transcription of ALS:Oxford

London, August 12, 1742

The Laurus Indica Aldin no where to be sold. The Seeds of it sent to Mr Brewer fresh but not come up.

You are not alone in lamenting the Death of Ld Petre. I never was more affected, not only as my Friend & my Brother, so near he was to me, & I have much reason to believe there was no love lost betwixt us, but for the loss his Family & his Country will sustain. He was the Phoenix of his age who spared no Pains in his Building, Gardening, Farming, Nurserys, Stoves, to add new Improvements & usefull Experiments for the Benefit of his Country. Oh what will now become of his Collections?

I can say no more. I am so dispirited, but it was the will of God & we must submit. But never man dyed more regretted.

How did I pray & carp & care to get every thing for him, because I saw even the least thing taken care of & carried on to perfection. But as Solomon says, I find all things here below are Vanity & vexations of Spirit.

At the Duke of Richmonds [Goodwood, Sussex] there is a great Collection of hardy American Plants & Flowers. The Cetalpha flower wonderfully this year.

Mr Gordon has also had flower Obscoletheca with a red flower. He is the only Gardener now left that has a good Stove. But now Ld P is gone I am affraid all Stove Plants will go down. My hopes are in Mr Blackburn.[1] In your next pray tell me how to direct him.

But I'll tell you a Curiosity that I saw at Capt Goffs, and East India [Company] Director, the true Tea Tree in great Health. It was Brought 2 or 3 years ago, a present from China to his wife. It is an Evergreen. It is housed with the orange Trees, for it grows on the more northerly Parts of China & Japen, about the Latitude of 40 Degg north.

There I saw also in three Ponds in his Paddock the so famous gold & silver Fish & the Scarlet fish & another Sort, which all endure the cold of our Winter without any detriment. There was also fine Spotted Bengal Deer which did not endure the hard Winters Cold so well as the Fish, & two Sorts of beautiful China pheasants, & wee have had a third sort different from them come over last year.

RICHARD RICHARDSON (1708–1781) inherited a famous garden at North Bierley where his father (also Richard, M.D. 1663–1741) had amassed what was reputedly the finest collection of curious plants in the north of England. (DNB)

1. John Blackburne (see headnote to October 20, 1742).

ALS:N-YHS
London, September 3, 1742

Dear Friend

I cannot Enough Acknowledge the favour and Friendship Shown Mee in Sending Mee the Tracts of your Studies & Observations.[1] I shall Treasure them up for the first Leisure to give them a Candid perusal tho I have not the least doubt but the Second Part will be as Informing and as Entertaining as the First. I shall be very Carefull and Tender in this affair & shall not be Rash & Hasty how I expose my Friend to the World & Its Censures. I shall not take my own opinion but that of a Learned friend or Two tho Our Common Friend J. A. [James Alexander] has almost Determin'd Mee to putt it to the press without further Delebration. Butt as you are So good as to place your whole Confidence in Mee I will take such carefull steps as I hope will lead Mee to your approbation.

I must confess to you My Dear Friend that I am not a Little pleased to find myself So much in your Esteeme and yett on the other hand I am ready to blame myself when I reflect How much Trouble I have putt you too. I hope my Good Intentions will Excuse for It.

I am now very much Engaged Shipping Goods for your province which prevents Mee in a perticular Mannr from answering Both your kind Letters. The Contents are Instances of your great Regard & Confidence to Mee. Att my First Leisure shall consider them Fully.

Butt as you have encouraged Mee to be free with you I cannot close these few Lines without Inquireing if you have made Observations on the Wonderfull order that is Shown in regulateing the Increase of Noxious Animals that the Males by much Exceed the Females which proves a check to their Increase Else perhaps by this Time the World would have been overrun with Lions, Tigers &tc Bears Wolve & Foxes. This Last comes within my Knowledge as also polecatts, that they have but one Female to 3 or 4 Males. Pray How is this with you? I have heard you have Some years plenty of Bears and I have been told it is rare to Kill a Female. The party imagin'd by their not being Seen that they had a Stronger Faculty of Sleeping or was better Instructed to provide for themselves than the Males. I shall be obliged to you to know what you have mett with on this Head.

My Dear Friend I rely on your Candor to take these Imperfect Lines & Hint in good part and believe me to be as I really am your Sincere & affectionate Friend   P. COLLINSON

P.S. There was no need of making any apology for your Book for it is very Intelligible.

---

1. On April 9, 1742, Colden wrote Collinson, "I now send you the greatest part the Indian History continued to the peace of Reswick which I presume to put under your tutelage because I may truely say that it is owing to you that ever it had a Birth by you giving me your approbation of the first part & desiring it to be continued...." (ALS:N-YHS)

Collinson's interest in Colden's *The History of the Five Nations* was of a piece with his interest in colonial policy, for the Five Nations of the Iroquois Confederacy were allied with the English, while the Hurons were allied with the French. Collinson saw the revised edition of Colden's *History* through the press in 1747. See PC to Colden, August 3, 1747.

54 ❧ TO BENJAMIN SMITHURST

Draft AL:LS
September 9, 1742

My Dear Friend,

I should have answered your Kind Letter sooner but that I have been so dispirited by the Loss of my Dear Friend Ld Petre that I could not but with great regrett sett penn to paper in which any Vegitable article was Concern'd. Any mention that Way so revived him in my Mind & was so Effecting & so Impressing that it greived Mee dayly and cannot yett totally Disengage myself. He was a man after my own heart Every Way but one (his Religion, & in that He was Sincere). Great was his Vertue and his Temperance, good Learning & a fine understanding. To sum up all as the Duke of Richmond write Mee, I don't know his Equall left behind. I really may say so. His Generous Affable Candid Humane Disposition I shall never forgett. Great is his familys & friends loss, but it is most to his Country. So rich he was in fruitfull & Experimental knowledge, the Remains & Essays that he has left will Evince to future Times what I say to be true.

God know what will become of his Vegitable Treasure which are beyond your thoughts which I am afraid will Lay useless by and Unemployed which for Quantity, Quallity & Variety will not be Equalled soon. If he had Lived, all round Him would have been America in England.

BENJAMIN SMITHURST: not identified.

55 ❧ TO JOHN BLACKBURNE

ALS:Oxford
London, October 20, 1742

Mr Blackburne

I had the pleasure of yours of the 3rd September and have pack'd up the West India Seeds and have added a few Rare Virginia Seeds which will require to be Immediately Sown. One pticular Circumstance I will acquainte you with relateing to Most North American Seeds that they will frequently Lay in the Ground till the Third Summer before they will come up, in pticular the Fringe Tree and what is further very remarkable I have known Some (in pticular the Ceders) come up Every year from the First to the Third or Fourth. This I Esteemed necessary to acquaint you with that no beds may be Disturbed or potts Emptyed till you are Satisfied the Seed is come up. Hard Seeds are not So much to be admired att but even small soft Herbacious seeds will be as Tardy in their appearance, and all this I Imagine to proceed from our want of Heat to Sett their Vegitative powers att work So that With us they require a Long time to Digest & Ferment before they attain to Strength Sufficient Shoot forth and I have found all attempts to assist North American Seeds by art unless the Heat is Moderate Constant & Regular (the Bark is undoubtedly best) [oak tan bark] they Succeed better in a Natural Way; If sown in potts I take care to Shelter them from Severe frosts in the Winter & Sett them under a East Wall or pole or Hedge in summer. The Morning Sun is always best.

As you will Observe there is a great number of Fine Trees, Shrubs & Flowers In North America. There is a very Ingenious man a Native of that Country [John Bartram], for whose Sake being a Poor Man & for the Encouragement of Some Curious people Here (in perticular our Late dear Friend [Lord Petre]) I have taken a pretty deal of Trouble to procure Seeds over and gett them from on board Ship from the Custome House & then to Sort & Divide them. This takes up more of my Time then I can spare, yett for the Motives above Mention'd I did do It, for Except the pleasure of assisting a poor Man, and Obligeing my Friends, I had my Labour for my pains & I am Inclined yett to Continue my Good Offices to a few Deserveing Friends. Lord Petres Subscription is now vacant which was Tenn Guineas a year besides paying Freight & Custome House Charges. Now if you think well to be Two Guineas or Tenn Guineas with a Share of those Charge or any Friend of yours will be the other five please to Lett mee know. You may Discontinue it when you will. If you approve of It any Time beween this & Febuary Give Mee a List of what Seeds you Desire to have them Sent for In Time. I have open'd the whole affair, So do as is most agreeable to you which will be always So to Your Friend   P. COLLINSON.

I presume you have Mr Catesbys Natural History of Florida in which you will See the Trees & Shrubbs Delineated in their Natural Colours.

Inclosed in the Box is some Vertues of the plants produced from the Seeds as they are use in the Country. The Seeds are Sent this Day 2th per T: Tomlinson

percel Seeds ———————	0 : 10 : 0
Box ————————————	: 4
	0 : 10 : 4

JOHN BLACKBURNE (1694–1786), wealthy ship owner engaged in lumber trade with Russia, owned saltworks, maintained a garden at Orford Hall, Warrington, with a large conservatory where he ripened pineapples. In a memorandum in his copy of Philip Miller's *Gardeners Dictionary* (8th edition) Collinson wrote, "John Blackburn Sept 1750. . . . This gentleman spares no expense in building a variety of stoves for all species of exotics. Has by much the largest toda panna or sago palm in England, and has a very great collection of all kinds of plants." (See Edmondson, John and Gordon Rowley. "John Blackburne of Orford Hall and his cultivated succulents." *Bradleya* 16, 1998 pp 14–24.)

56 ❧ TO HANS SLOANE

ALS : BL
[circa 1742]

Sir Hans

Inclosed is the Receipt for the puke [emetic] for Dr Breynius.[1]

If I can do you any Manner of Service you have a Right to Command Mee. I Assure you it gives a Singular pleasure to your affectionate friend

P. COLLINSON

I cannot Express the Trouble I am under for the Loss of our Dear friend Ld Petre. I Lament Most His Countrys Loss, Next His Familys, & then my own. He Loved Mee with a Bros Love. I am Sure you Share in this General Calamity. (I want to See you.)

1. Jean Philipe Breyn (1680–1764), MD, Leyden, wrote on ginseng and fungi.

57 ❦ TO HANS SLOANE

ALS:BL
London, February 4, 1743

Dear Sir Hans,

I here with send you the Remainder of J. Bartram's Cargo and Wish I could have brought them myself, for I long to see you. It is Some pleasure to hear by one & another of your Welfare.

Mr Bevan[1] I think has a great Rarity in my Simple opinion, but I Question if it may be one to you, that is a Maremaid's Hand and arm. Seems more Like Human than it Does what Creature Else it can possibly belong too I cannot Conceive, but very Likely you may. The Gentleman to whome it belongs has give Mr Bevan an Account of It. He Sayes that on the Coast of Brazils the Men being One Night or Evening out in Periagua [dugout canoe] Something like Human came and threw its arm (for so I must call It) over the Gunnel or Side of the Pereagua which Surpised the Men Very much. [illegible] afraid it would oversett It, but one haveing his ax by Him and more Courage then the Rest Struck it off close by the Shoulder. The Arm Drop'd into the Boat & the Creature Sunk Down and was never Seen More.

I Dare Say if you Desire it Mr Bevan will Lett you See It. I am very Desirous to have your opinion off It.

I am with Great Respect your affectionate friend,   P. COLLINSON

I have a bundle of Fossells, a Box of Insects, a Log of Wood. When you Send for these Mr Bevan will Send you the Maremaids arm in a Box which in a Day or Two please to Return with your opinion to yours   PC

1. Silvanus Bevan (1691–1765), FRS, apothecary and physician, proposed Collinson for membership in the Royal Society. (RS)

58 ❦ TO JOHN AMBROSE BEURER

ALS:Erlangen
London, August 5, 1743

My Good Friend,

I had not Leisure to add the Botanical Names to the Specimens, but I believe they will be found in the Flora Virginica pub by Dr Gronovius.

Wee want Seed of the Official Gentian when an oppertunity offers. Pray Send Some.

I am Extremely Obliged to you as well as my Learned & Ingenious Friend Doctor Fothergill[1] for the Curious Specimens of Osteocolla [bone] and Arsnick. I had them not before.

I am with much esteem
Your Sincere Friend   P. COLLINSON
My respects to Dr Trew[2]

It is with Regret that Wee See all our performances fall farr Short of yours. Albin[3] was a poor Man, wanted the Assistance of Ingenious knowing Men in this Branch of Natural

Gypsy Moth (female left, male, right). Bound into the copy of Moses Harris, The Aurelian . . . , *Entomology Library, London, as Appendix II.*

Knowledge who were then very few, So that it is marvellous Considering his abilities. It was, as It is, which was greatly Instrumental to Informe the present Society[4] who keep a Register of all Discoveries & have Lectures Every Month on the Flies & their Natures produced in that Month, but I don't yett hear that their Observations are Likely to be made publick.

Wee have Indeed a Very Curious Gentleman Charles Lockyere Esquire [a member of the Aurelian Society, founded 1740] who Att a very Great Expence has painting in Oyle Colours all the Flies & Moths hitherto Discover'd In England, the Male & Female, the Right Side & Back Too of Each, So that Each Species is four Times Represented. This is performed by a Most Delicate Curious hand that art Seems to vie with Nature. This painter has been kept for this 2 or 3 years past In order to Compleat this Grand Designe which is to Remain a Memorial to the Next Generation of the Progress & Discoveries of Flies.

My Dear Friend, as you are a Philosopher & a Lover & admirer of the Wonderfull Works in Nature and of the Great & almighty author of them I p'swade my Self this Rude Scetch of the present State of this Branch of Natural Knowledge as it Stands with us will be acceptable to you. If it is It will highly gratifie your Affectionate Friend   P. COLLINSON Some Observations on the Curious Book of Insects.[5]

I Should be Glad of the Title page & To know the Ingenious Author & where it is printed & the price, for Some that are Curious in Insects would be Glad to Send for it.

Class: I Tab I pap. Diur..Wee have not discover'd that this Fly is yett in England.

Class: III Tab I pap Noct . . . This Moth is unknown to us.

Class: II Tab II pap Diur . . . This Beautifull Fly is not in England.

Class: III Tab III pap nocr . . . This Moth is a Stranger to Us.

Class: I: Tab VII. pap Diur. This fine Fly Wee call the Silver Wash. Wee was all Greatly Delighted to See that the Caterpiler & Crysalis for Wee have not yett Discovered it in those States, but the Curious Person has ometted to Mention the Day of the Month that He found it on, wch wee Desire much to know, for that will help us to Search after It.

Class: II: Tab X. pap nocr . . . This Beautifull Tiger Moth is a Stranger to Us. We have Three other Sorts of Tiger Moths besides these & Chapt II pap noc. Tab:l. So that now Wee make a Species of this.

Class: II: Tab XII. pap Nocr this beautifull Little Moth was this year found too in England, but not known before.

Class: II: Tab: III. pap nocr. I will tell you a remarkable Story of this Moth. A Friend of Mine was att Osnaburgh [Osnabrück, Germany] and there in an House of Easement as he Sett In Corner He Spied an Insects Nest Spun up in a Silken Tuft. He knew not what it Was but He carefully put it up in a Box & brought to England & Gave it to Mee.

Wee Carefully Watch'd the Time of the Eggs hatching & then Tried them with Several Sorts of Food. They took to the Apple & grew Strong, Copulated & Laid more Eggs & Wee Continue to propagate them Annually, but their numbers Increasing Wee have turn'd them out on the Crabb Hedges, So that now Wee have Naturallized them and Given them the Name of King & Queen of the Gypsies, a Swarthy Ragged Dirty Beggars that Lives in remote places.

I Beg Leave to Mention this only to Show that the Flies that Wee have not may att a proper Season be Sent unto Us Either in their Eggs or in Chrysalis, and if they prove of both Sexes Wee can Easily raise a Stock from them, for Wee Spare no pains.

Perhaps it may not be unacceptable to you to know what progress Wee have made in the Discovery of Insects in England, Where Wee have a Society of Curious Men that Wholely Devote themselves to this part of Natural History and have made very Great Discoveries within these Few years.

The Number of Moths or Night Flies to us are 350 & the Number of Butter Flies or Day Flies are 65. Sorts between Both such as Class III pap noc Tab II & Transparent Wingg'd Flies 7, Total 422.

Of the Flies and Moths that Wee have not & you have Duplicates, Wee Should be Obliged to you for a Specimen or Two of a Sort which may be Easily pinned within Side a Box & Sent when an oppertunity offers, and Wee Shall Gladly Oblige you the Same Way.

JOHN AMBROSE BEURER (1716–1754), apothecary at Nuremberg.

1. John Fothergill (1712–1780), FRS, successful Quaker physician in London, on occasion physician to the Crown, author of medical essays. He cultivated a famous garden at Upton in Essex (described by J. C. Letsom in *Hortus Uptonenesis,* 1783), supported natural history expeditions, contributed to the publication of works on natural history, furnished plants to Kew, and wrote a memorial, *Some account of . . . Peter Collinson . . . in a letter to a friend.* (London, 1770). (Henrey; Fox, R. H. *John Fothergill and his Friends,* 1919; and Corner, B. C. and C. C. Booth. *Chain of Friendship: Selected Letters of Dr. John Fothergill of London, 1735–1780.* Cambridge, Harvard University Press, 1971.)

2. Christopher Jacob Trew: See headnote to March 20, 1746.

3. Eleazar Albin (1713–1742), watercolorist, published *A Natural History of Birds,* 1731–1738, 3 vols. illustrated with 306 copperplate etchings. "William Swainson's stricture that Albin was without much knowlege of natural history and a very indifferent artist is partly true. Albin's birds are recognizable portraits and reasonably true to life, but he knew little about the birds' habits, and the information he gave in the short text concerning each species included nothing new. . . ." Jackson, Christine E. *Bird Etchings: The Illustrators and their Books, 1665–1855.* New York: Cornell, 1985, p. 69.

4. Probably the Aurelian Society, organized in 1740 by a Mr. Whitworth, "a tailor, a great butterfly catcher." Referred to in Collinson's Commonplace Book. (LS)

5. August Johann Roesel von Rosenhof (1705–1759), *Insecten-Belustigung.* Roesel von Rosenhof began publishing his 4 volume work as a monthly entitled *Der monatlich-herausgegebenen Insecten-Belustigung* in 1740. It was published in book form 1746–1761. In the preface he "attempted to define insects as a systematic unity and to divide this unity into classes, orders and families." (DSB)

59 ❧ TO JOHN AMBROSE BEURER

ALS:UBE
London, August 9, 1743

My Dear Friend,

I am no So happy in my attainments In the Lattin & French Languages to write them Well, but I can read them well Enough. My Learned & Ingenious Friend Dr. Fothergill being in the Country who was So obligeing to translate my Letters into Lattin, I am now Obliged to address thee in my Mother Tongue.

I was really att a Loss what returns to make for So many Favours, but I have Collected Some rare plants & Specimens & putt them in a box Directed to the Care of John Fredrick Ernst, Mercht in Amsterdam to be Sent to you by first oppertunity. All Charges I have paid thither & wish I could have done it further.

The Melocactus is the Large Kind. May be Water'd altho Little att first planting. To be Sett in the Warmest place in the Stove & will want no more Water untill next Summer. I shall give a Letter of advice to Mr Ernst by what Vessell the box comes.

I Wish the Specimens was better, but I am much Engaged in Business & my operator that Fixt the Last was gone into the Country, So I hope you will Excuse their Incorrectness. If you admire Shells or Fossills, ores &c I have these Sometimes from abroad & Shall gladly oblige you.

Favour mee with a Line when the Box comes to hand which will greatly oblige your affectionate Friend,   P Collinson

The Box goes In the Sloop Named the Queen of Hungary, John Russell Master. This post I advise Mr. Ernst of it. The Sloop will Sail in a few Days. Vale   PC

60 ❧ TO CADWALLADER COLDEN

ALS:N-YHS
London, September 4, 1743

My Dear Friend

Pray make no apologys about the Length of your Letters. They are very Entertaining. If I have not time to write it is a pleasure to me to Read.

I never See your Indian History, the Fruits of great pains & Industry, but I am sensible of the great favour Shown Mee and of the many obligations I am under for it.

A very Worthy & Ingenious Man Capt Middleton[1] who Went to Hudsons Bay to find out the North west pasage haveing been 14 Voyages into that Bay In the Companys Service, had from time to Time collected Such Observations as gave good reason to hope it was practicable. He Laid them before The Admiralty Board, and he was Sent in the year I think 1741 and Winterd there & made all the Essays practicable but returnd fully convinced there was no passage. As He was a Good Naturallist He had Collected variety of Materials well worth the knowledge of the Curious, I happend to Show Him your History. He was delighted with It & said this will do very Well to publish with mine & you shall Share in the proffits. I thought this a Luckky Incident. Butt Some Malicious people have opposed Capt Middleton and rendred his Journals Suspicious att the admiralty Board, which for the present has obliged the Capt to Lay aside his first Designe and now turns Author to Vindicate Himself.

My Dear Friend as you yett persist in the opinion that your scheme for printing is very practicable as well as advantageous, but as I was no Judge of It, I engaged Mr Strahan a printer to answer yours. He is Esteemed an Ingenious knowing Man So Shall referr you to his Letter here Inclosed.[2]

You can't Imagine how I was surprised to See the great progress you have made in the Linnean Systeme and with what Accuracy you had Drawn up the Two Botanic Enigmas. I profess myself no Botanist neither am I fond of Novelties. The Science of Botany is too much perplex'd already. Our Country Man [John] Ray I like best as my Skill is Slender, and I have not time to make any proficiency in the New Method. You will I hope Excuse Mee if I mistake the Mark. If I say the one Seems to be a plant, that my Botanic friends as a Mark of their Respect have called by my Name, the other Seems to be a Hellebore or Helleborine of which you have variety but the perticular plant I cant say. Pray Send Mee a Specimen Dry'd between two papers that I may have the pleasure to See the Plant that you have So Dextriously Investigated. I have several in my Garden. They are Easily Sent over by takeing them up when the Flower Fades with a Lump of mould about the Roots & putt into a Box of Earth and Nail'd up Close only boreing a few holes for Air & then Sent on board a Ship. My Indefatigable Friend J. Bartram is very knowing & Successfull in these operations.

My Great Delight is in Cultivateing & Nurseing these Rare plants & Seeing them Come to Maturity. This does not Engage the Mind so atentively as Botanic Knowledge Especially If I am to be master of the Several Systems of Tournfort,[3] Ray & Linnaeus. As I have a good Esteem for the Last and personally known Him and annually Correspond with Him I dont know but I may Send Him your 2 Enigmas. I know it will give Him vast pleasure to see the progress of his Science in so remote a Quarter.

My Dear Sir I Salute you with Cordial Respects & am your affectionate friend

P. COLLINSON.

I Send you under the Conveyance of my Worthy friend J. Alexander the History of the Polypus[4] [a species of hydra] for a Winter Evenings Entertainment. You may Depend all is Literally True. Most of the Experiments have been Try'd here & Succeed Exactly.

1. Christopher Middleton (d. 1770), FRS, naval commander and Arctic voyager employed by the Hudson Bay Company (1720), discovered how to tell true time at sea using Hadley's quadrant (1737) and attempted to discover the Northwest Passage. (DNB)

2. William Strahan (1715–1785), Scottish-born printer, admitted to the Stationers' Company of London, 1738, friend of Franklin, and publisher of David Hume, Adam Smith, Samuel Johnson, Edward Gibbon and William Blackstone. (*Franklin* II, 384–385) Colden had proposed printing his *History* from lead plates or thin boards of a smooth grained wood. Strahan's letter does not survive.

3. Joseph Pitton de Tournefort (1656–1708), French botanist, professor of botany at the Jardin des Plantes. His systematic botany, *Institutiones rei herbarie*. 3 vols. Paris, 1700 prepared the way for Linnaeus. (EB)

4. Probably Henry Baker, *Natural History of the Polype*. London, R. Dodsley, 1743.

"Mon. Jussieu proved in his Memoir that certain Substances which many Botanists have taken for Plants, for example, coral, are nothing else but an Assemblage of little Cells, in which lodge a kind of small insect called Polypes, of a length of 3 tenths of an inch . . ." it was reported in the *Gentleman's Magazine* XII (Nov. 1742): 607.

See also John Ellis, *An Essay towards a Natural History of the Corallines*. London, 1755.

ALS:LS
London, January 18, 1744

My Dear Friend Doctor Linnaeus

I almost despaired of a Line from your Hands, for I have not heard from you since the 3d of August, 1739. But att last I had the pleasure of yours of the 25th July ulto. I was much concerned that so Large a Collection of American seeds was lost.[1] I hope Wee shall have better Success for the future. I have now made up a percelle of South American Seeds and hope to add some Northern ones to come by First Shipp. I was Delighted to find the Coreopsis altissima (query if not a Rudbeckia) and the Collinsonia was acceptable to you. I hope John Bartram our Collector will send More this year. For his great pains and industry, pray find out a new genus and name it *Bartramia.*[2]

Your System[3] I can tell you obtains much in America, Mr Clayton & Dr. Colden att Albany on Hudsons River in New York is a Compleat professor as is Dr Mitchell att Urbana on Rapahanock River in Virginia[4]. It is he that has made Many & Great Discoveries in the Vegititable World. I writt to him to know the Reason for his Name Elymus for a Species of Wild Oats & many other New Names.[5] I hope in a years Time you will see his Essays in botany (in Lattin) printed.[6] I have the First part finished but he Intends to Add another, So the printing of the first is Deferr'd.

The Death of the Worthyest of Men, the Right Honorable Lord Petre, has been the greatest loss that Botany or Gardening Ever felt (in this Island). He spared no pains or Expence to procure Seeds & plants from all parts of the World & then was as Ambitious to preserve Them. Such Stoves [hothouses] the World never saw, nor may Never again, for His greatest Stove was Thirty foot High, in proportion long & broad. In it was Beds of Earth in which these plants as under was planted & flourish'd wonderfully.

The Hernandia was 10 feet high, 5 inches round the stem.

The Guajava—13 feet high, 7 inches round, spreads 9 feet.

Male Papaw—17 feet high, 2 foot 3 Ins round the Stem & bears plenty of Fruit every year.

Coreopsis. Buchoz, Pierre-Joseph. Histoire universelle du règne végétal. Paris, 1773–1780.

Annato [illegible] Species 14 foot high 11 Inches round.

Plantain vel Musa, 24 feet high the Leaves 12 feet long, 3 1/2 feet broad, 3 foot 2 inches round the Stem, has abundance of Fruit.

Large Palm 14 feet high, 4 feet round.

Cereus (Cactus), 24 feet high, 1 foot 4 inches round.

A female Papaw, 20 feet high 3 foot 9 Inches round has several branches 7 & 1/2 foot Long.

A Rosa Chinesis or [obscure] 25 feet high, 1 foot four round.

One Sago Palm, Toddapanna of Hort. Mala[7] 8 foot high Two foot round the Stem, a fine plant with a Great Number of very Large plants whose names would be too long to mention here.

The Back of these Stoves had Trellices against which was planted in Beds of Earth, all the Sorts of Flos pasionis, Clematis's of all kinds, that could be procured, & Creaping Cereus, all these mixt together and Run up to the top cover'd the whole Back & Sides of the House, & produced a Multitude of Flowers which had an Effect beyond Imagination. Nothing could be more Beautiful or more surpriseing. There was a Bamboo Cane, in it that was 25 foot high.

Next to this Magnificent Stove there was Two others of Two Degrees Lower but these was Higher and Longer then most are seen. Besides these He had Several others. His Annanas Stove was 60 foot long & 20 foot wide, and his Collections of Trees & Shrubs & Evergreens in his Nurserys att his Death (mostly exotick) I had told over amounted to 219,925 in all.

As this Young Noble Man was the Greatest Man in our Tast that This Age produced, I thought it might not be unacceptable to you to give you some Short Account of the greatness of his Genius. But his skill in all Liberal Arts, in perticular architecture, statuary, Planning and Designing, & planting & Embellishing his large Park & Gardens, Exceeds my talent to sett forth.

Wee have now a wonderful fine Season that makes our Spring Flowers come Forth. I am sure you would be delighted to see my Windows filled with Six potts of Flowers which the Gardener has sent Mee to Town, vizt, great plenty of Acconites, Helleborus albus et Vindis flora, Hepatica flo pleno, Crocus, Polyanthus, Periwinca, Laurustinus, Vernal Cyclamen flo Rubio, single Anemonies flo Simplici, & Narcisso Leucoium [Spring snowflake]. This is my Delight to see Flowers, which makes a Roome look Chearfull & pleasant as well as Sweet. None of these was brought forward by any Art but Intirely owing to the Temperature of the Season, tho' Some years I have known things forwarder then now.

I communicated your Complaints to your English Friends. They promise amendment, in perticular Dr Lawson.[8] From him I doubt not but you have heard, before this comes to hand.

You may remember my Repository in which I have a Collection of all sorts of Natural productions that I can procure from my Distant Friends. Not any thing comes amiss that furthers the knowledge of Natural History. One sort of seed I will Mention to send Mee of the Pulsatilla flore albo et Rubro [Anemone *pulsatilla*], if you have it, & pray send Mee your Systema Natura in Octo or Quarto, for the Large Sheets are not so convenient for common perusal.

Now, my dear friend, I shall Tire you no Longer then to assure you I am your Sincere Friend

P COLLINSON

Pray make my complements to Messrs Fillenius & Celsius.[9]

Dr Cadwallader Colden beggs his Complements and Desired Mee to send you the inclosed Specimen of his proficiency in your Systeme.[10] Perhaps when you have examined It you will find Reason to make the Actea & Christophoriana of Different Genus's.

I herewith send you a box of Cranberries or Oxycoccus. Perhaps if sown on your Mossy Boggs the Seeds may Grow. They came from Pensilvania. Ours in England are very small, not bigger than Red Garden Currants.

1. Collinson had written Linnaeus on April 10, 1740: "I now come to make good my promise to send you some North American seeds." (ALS:LS)

2. Collinson worked doggedly to have Bartram honored with a genus name. See Collinson to Linnaeus, August 5, 1746. Linnaeus finally named a genus of tropical burr weed *Bartramia* L. (in *Flora Zeylanica,* 1747), but that genus was later renamed *Triumfetta* L. John Bartram is now honored by a genus of moss, *Bartramia* Hedwig.

3. *Systema Naturae.* Leyden, 1735. See Note 3 to May 13, 1739.

4. John Mitchell (1711–1768), FRS, American physician, botanist, author and map-maker. Studied medicine at Edinburgh and settled in Urbanna, Virginia in the 1720s, where he practiced medicine and collected plants until 1746 when ill health forced his return to England. In 1741 he sent Collinson a list of Virginia plants, "Nova Genera Plantarum," which Collinson forwarded to Trew who published it in *Nuremburg Transactions* of 1748. Mitchell is credited with discovering twenty-one genera. He wrote on such varied topics as the opossum, potash, electricity, and race and color. On his way back to England in 1746 he was captured by the French and lost all his papers.

From the records of the Board of Trade he prepared an authoritative *Map of the British and French Dominions in North America,* 1755. The map (in eight panels) is huge—135x194.6 cm.—and was frequently reproduced. It was used in the peace negotiations of 1782–83 and in many controversies regarding boundaries and grants. It has been reckoned the most important map in American history. Its cartouche is large and handsome. (DAB; Berkeley and Berkeley, *John Mitchell: The Man Who Made the Map.* Chapel Hill: The University of North Carolina Press, 1974; Hindle, Brooke. *The Pursuit of Science in Revolutionary America.* Chapel Hill, 1956, p. 58;

Bell, Whitfield J. "John Mitchell" in *Patriot-Improvers.* American Philosophical Society. Philadelphia, 1997. Vol. 1, p. 138.)

5. *Elymus* Mitchell became *Zizania* Gronov, ex L., wild rice. Mitchell's *Elymus* was not accepted as a name.

6. "Dissertatio Brevis de Principiis Botanicorum" in *Acta Physico-Medica Academiae Caesare Leopoldino-Carolinae.* Frankfurt, 1748.

7. *Metroxylon* Rottb. The reference is to H. A. van Rheede tot Draakenstein, *Hortus Indicus Malabaricus.* Amsterdam, 1678–1703.

Dr. John Edmondson, Curator of Botany, Liverpool Museum suggests that the plant was actually *Sabal blackburniana,* obtained by Lord Petre from Sir Charles Wager in the West Indies. See note to Letter #55.

8. Isaac Lawson (fl.1747), MD, physician to the British Army, friend of Linnaeus and Gronovius. He and Gronovius caused to be published Linnaeus's *Systema Naturae.* (Desmond)

9. Anders Celsius (1701–1744), Swedish astronomer chiefly remembered for the centigrade thermometric scale ("the Celsius scale") presented in a memoir read before the Swedish Academy of Sciences in 1742. From 1730 until his death Celsius was Professor of Astronomy at Uppsala. He published some of the first systematic observations of the aurora borealis and observations on the relative brightness of stars. See headnote to Collinson to Linnaeus, May 13, 1739.

10. Inspired by Linnaeus's *Genera Plantarum,* Colden classified the flora in the neighborhood of his country estate, Coldengham. He sent his report to Gronovius who in turn forwarded it to Linnaeus. Linnaeus published it as *Plantae Coldenghamiae* in *Acta Societatis Regiae Scientarum Upsaliensis* for 1743 (1749–1751).

62 ❧ TO CADWALLADER COLDEN

ALS:N-YHS
London, March 9, 1744

Dear Mr Colden

You cannot be more Surprised att the progress of Botany in Dr Linnaeus than I am to See what a proficient you are in his Scheme. I could not have Imagind It had reach'd in so Short a Time to the remote parts of North America for I hear He has made Several proselites in Different places on your Continent. But your Fame reach'd Mee Long before your Letter. My Valuable Friend Dr Gronovius Lett Mee know what a fine present you have made Him.[1] The Good Man is in Raptures. I doubt not butt Dr Linnaeus has heard of it Long before this. It is a remarkable Instance what Leisure & Application assisted with a Great Genius can attain too.

I shall Soone Send your Curious Observations to Dr Linnaeus. Your Criticisms are perfectly just. You have done Mee a Pleasure in Circulateing It Through my Hands because it Setts Mee Right who have not Leisure for Such Nice observations & to the Dr I know it will give him the greatest Delight. Any omissions in Him is not owing to his Judgement but want of Growing Subjects whose Minute parts are more Distinct, which are Lost in Dry'd Specimens. So that att the Same Time that you are Improving your own knowledge you are Greatly obligeing your Friend and if all his Pupils was Equally as Communicative as you are His Works would be more perfect & Compleat.

It is no Little Disadvantage to Him to be Setled as in the fagg End of the World. In His Letter to Mee he Envies Our Happyness who have a free & frequent Intercourse with your World and our Gardens abound with its productions and then Wee have Annually Seeds & Specimens which produces Something New & proper to exercise the Talents of So Learned & Curious a Botanist.

But a Gentlemen of Your Benevolent Disposition may in Some Degree Soften the Severities of the North and Flora may in Some Little Disguise by your Assistance for once appear amidst Ice & Snow. A few Specimens preserved & Dry'd in paper, & a few Seeds, Sent him as oppertunity offers, with your Curious Remarks, would be to Him all that I have allegorically Hinted and I will take care they shall be Safely convey'd to Him.

I am Glad to find the Polypus gave you Some Entertainmt. The Searching after this has been a Means of Makeing New Discoveries in the Minute Creation. One is called the Bell animal and is found under the Lenticula palustris. It takes its Name from its Figure being Like a Bell of the Size of a Silver Penny and from its Center it putts forth Fibrils from Ten to fifteen in Number which on any Motion or Touch Shrinks in & then project out and are presumed to be as so many Hands to Collect its Nourishment. To give you a Little Idea of It I here inclose a Scetch [not found].

Another Strange Surprising animal I saw by the help of a microscope very Distinct Like a Small Smooth Caterpiller which is called the Wheel animal from haveing in its Snout or Head Two Wheels one att Each Corner Exactly Like the wheel of a Watch, these seeme to Turn on pivets on a Center with Such a Velocity that one can Scarsly See their Teeth, both Wheels going together is one of the Wonderful pretty Phenomenas I ever Saw. It is an acquatic animal & this Motion in the Water is Wee apprehend Intended to Draw all the Little animalcule for its Support within its reach.

Poor Capt [Christopher] Middleton meets with Renew'd attacks on his Character so your Curious Treatise [*History of the Five Nations . . .*] for the present Lies Dormant. It is att this Juncture under Cap Rutherfords perusal who Seems a very obligeing agreeable Gentm.[2]

I am entirely of your mind that It Deserves the perusal of the Legislature but att this Juncture Wee are greatly Embarressed with an Intended Invasion from Dunkirk with the pretenders Son ["Bonny Prince Charlie"] att the Head. And there is Reason to Suspect Some ploting att Home from whome the French hoped to Reap great advantage. Butt Wee have confidence in the Good hand of providence to Frustrate all their Designs by the Vigilance of the Government att Home & Our Fleet in the Channel.

The Rear Admiral Mathews after 3 Days Terrible Hott Engagements has obtain'd a Compleat Victory over the French & Spanish Fleet that saild from Toulon. The French Scheme by the Great Bluster that they make to Invade us is to Distress our Alliance with the Queen of Hungary. By preventing the Kings going abroad & Obligeing us to Recall Our Troops from thence.

In a Boxe of Instruments to Mr Alexander I refer you to an anser to your Letter to Mr. Sissons.

I am with much Respect Your Affectionate Friend   P. COLLINSON
Mr [William] Strahan Intends you a favour Soone.

1. See note 10 to Collinson to Linnaeus, January 18, 1744.
2. Possibly Capt. John Rutherford, British Army officer, who retired to Albany, NY.

63 ❧ TO JOHN CUSTIS

ALS:AAS
London, April 2, 1744

My Dear Friend

I have scrawled 2 or 3 Letters which I sent to Mr Hanburys with a Box of Garden Seeds & some Flower Seeds which by his Care I hope will come safe to hand. Tho I sent them In January, I wish they Come time Enough to sow this year, so many Accidents have happened, and now we have a French Warr in Reallity I am afraid our Intercourse will be [remainder of this passage torn away]

A Little Leisure now offers which gives Mee [illegible] of a more perticular Answer to your kind Letter of the 15th of september Last. I am greatly Delighted to hear that you have some tolerable Enjoym't in Life. I hope with Gentle Exercise & proper Regimen it will Increase.

I take an Almond to be a Tree of Quick Growth but of no Long Duration but so soone a Decay of yours may be owing to the Roots penetrating into a Cold poor Bottom. This I have Observed Here in many Instances, & Wee find no Remedy but new planting & Trying some other Spott. I have sent Some more for that purpose if they yett in season, with my project to sow some of them & some of the Pistacio Nutts in your Island.[1]

It is a common Observation that Our Tast & that of animals is very Different, for they will feed on that which is poisonous to Mankind so the [illegible] of the Mice is not to be Admired in prefering the pelitory seed to all others.

That your Good House Wives may be no Longer puzzled I hear send you my Wives Receipt. It is a pudding that pleases Mee & all that have Tasted It, & another pudding made of West India production I have often Eat & is much admird and Loved by all that Tast it, and that is a Cassada [Cassava] pudden made of the Poisonous Roots of a plant of that Name in all the West Indies, but when the Pernitious Quallity is press'd out it Makes a pretty sort of Bread which no doubt you have Tasted. Perhaps may have been Brought as a Curiosity by sloops Tradeing too & fro from the Islands to you.

Arum maculatum, *Cuckoo pint. Gilbert Thomas Burnet. The Wellcome Trust Library, London*

I am Glad to hear that some of the plants are alive. Neither Firr nor pine will bear Cutting in shapes, but They Naturally grow in Conic Figures which looks Ornamental in a Garden. I hope the Buckthorn will grow, being of Great Use. They may be Increased by Layers as well as by seed.

[torn] have the Oriental [illegible], you may say that [torn] one of the plants of Paradice for the most authers [torn] that this was Found by [illegible] in or near the spott where Eden was situated. But I presume Wee must Esteem this as only one of the Weeds of Paradice which is suffer'd to remain and is the king of its Tribe. But all the most Elegant & Charming Flowers & Fruites of Paradice are Removed or Disperssed through all the fine Countries and Climates of the World, which were they all Again Collected in one spott would Raise our Admiration beyond Expression.

I am well Acquainted with the Bunch of Scarlet Berries tho it has happen'd to Escape your Curious Discernment. I have 3 sorts of this species in my Garden.[2] It is an Arum or Cuckow point when in Flower. From its pretty Ellegant figure our Children Call them Lords & Ladys.

My three sorts are very Different in Leafe. One was sent Mee by the Name of Skunk Weed or skunk Wort, the Others by the Name of Indian Turnips. They thrive in the shade in a Rich moist soil, but I am much Obliged to you for the seed to pleasure my Curious Friends, for it seldome Ripens Here.

But writing of this Brings to my Mind Two very Curious & Rare plants which if they have not found a place in your fine Garden may Deserve it. The one is a new species of Magnolia [*Magnolia tripetala,* Umbrella tree, cucumber tree] growing in Nicholas Smiths Esquire[3] plantation in Essex County, which Doctor Mitchell Informes Mee is the only One in all Virginia, and the Other is an Arbor Vitee of a very Rare sort [*Thuja occidentalis*] and the Only Tree of the Kind Ever found, only one Tree on or near the plantation of Isham Randolph Esq Deceased,[4] but the Tree is so remarkable that all know it as I am told a fine Evergreen. This Ellegant Tree was Discover'd by John Bartram. It will take off Cuttings planted in a shady place in October. Sprigs of 4, 5 or 6 Inches Long are best for that purpose and may be raised from seed sown as soone as Ripe.

It is very Likely the swallows whose pretty Nest is Cemented together may gather the Persimon Gum to use for that purpose. But then they dont use it as they gather it, but Digest it & then Disgorge it for that purpose, for if you do but burn it in the fire or a Candle [torn] the smell Fetid Like burnt bone or Flesh and nothing Like a Vegitable production.

Wee are not Hott Enough for the Chinquapin to produce seed Here. A Trial att a proper season of a Quarter of the Quantity of the Last may be sufficient.

It is a Thousand pitties but that such Curious Gentlemen as you, Colonel Byrd, Mr Clayton & Dr Mitchell should annually sow seeds of the Umbrella Tree to preserve it from being Intirely Lost. Can any Tree from the particularity of its Growth & Flower Deserve better place in a fine Garden then the New Early flowering Magnolia at Esquire Smiths?

I thank you for the papaw seed. This is also one of Your Rarities from the singular structure of its Fruite. Please to send some more seed.

I shall now Relieve you & Conclude with my best Wishes, Your sincere & Affectionate Friend,

P. COLLINSON

I herewith send some kernells of stone pine. They are pretty sweet Eating, and it is an Elegant fine Tree. As it will be too Late this year they will keep till Next. I have sent this sort before, but with what success I know not. They thrive & bear well in England.

I am greatly obliged to you for the Huming Bird & Nest. It is a Charming pretty Contrivance and so neatly Cover'd with Moss that it so much Resembles the bark on the Branch that it is hardly to be discover'd from it which makes it so Difficult to find. The Eggs in proportion must be very small.

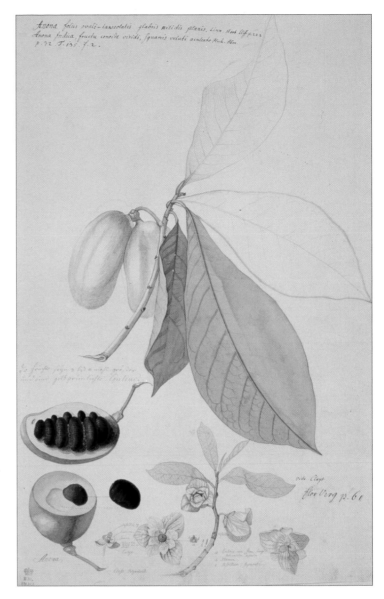

Papaw. Georg Dionysius Ehret. Natural History Museum, Botany Library, London.

Some time agon I Inclosed a Letter for Doctor Mitchell which I hope is come to hand. I doubt not [illegible] care off it. As your summer is Longer then Ours [illegible] the pine kernells this year.

Pray send some pelitory seed, some Yoppon seed and any other sort you fancey.

1. Mockkhorn or Smith's Island.
2. Collinson seems to be describing three plants: *Asimina triloba,* jack-in-the-pulpit or indian turnip; *Arum maculatum,* Lords & Ladys or Cuckoo pint; and *Symplocarpus foetidus,* skunk weed.

3. Nicholas Smith of South Farnham parish in Essex County, Virginia, a justice between 1720 and 1730. The plantation was on the Piscataway in upper Essex.
4. Brother of Sir John Randolph.

ALS:N-YHS
London, August 23, 1744

My Dear Friend

I was glad to find you had made such proficiency in Botanic Inquiries. You have a Large Field before you which will afford you a Lasting fund of Amusemt. I Intended you no complements because your skill in that Science was Self Evident. I again felicitate you on It for you Tast a pleasure but few know & have it. Where Ever you go, the Wasts & Wilds which to Others appear Dismal to one of your Tast efford a Delightful Entertainmt. You have a Secret to beguile a Lonesome Way and Shorten a Long Journey which only Botanists know. Every Step as it were Introduces new objects. By these the Mind is highly Delighted, Its Ideas Inlarged, the Great Creator admir'd & adored. These are Sensations better felt than Express'd and the more you Gratifie your self in these Inquiries, the higher will be your Sensations.

This year my Ingenious Friend J. Bartram Sent Mee Two Curiosities, a Lychnidea [Phlox] which produces a wonderful Spike of flowers, but the Greatest is a Species of

Martagon in its appearance untill it flower'd & then its flowers did not reflex like the Martagons but hung down Like the Crown Imperial. They was of a deep Gold Colour on the Out Side & finely Spotted with purple within [*Lilium canadense*].

I can't enough commend the Authors & promoters of a Society for Improvemt of Natural knowledge Because it will be a Means of uniteing Ingenious Men of all Societies together and a Mutual Harmony be got which will be Dayly produceing Acts of Love & Friendship and will ware away by Degrees any Harsh opinions, parties may have Conceived of Each other.[1] The Fruits of Wisdome & knowledge are Excellent, besides the Mind being Enlarged the Understanding Improved, the Wonders in the Creation Explored, and Ingenious & Good people will know one another & Rejoice in the Friendship of those Like minded as themselves, and as there will be a Laudable Emulation to Excell in the Several Branches of Science, the Same good Desposition will Influence them to Benevolence & Good will to Each other in Every Capacity.

Lychnidea, *phlox. Artist unknown. From Collinson's album of prints and drawings at Knowsley Hall. Courtesy the Earl of Derby, Knowsley.*

I Shall wait with Some Impatience for their Memoirs. I expect Something New from your New World, our Old World as it were Exhausted tho I really Mett with the other Day a very Singular odd Phenomenon in its Kind which I will briefly relate.

This year I took a Tour with my family to See a Relation In the Isle of Wight [Benjamin Cook]. I happend to go to a place Calld Crab Nighton famous for the Breeding of this animal. Inquireing of the Fishermen into the Nature of this Creature, I was told that if its Leggs was broke or Bruised and it could not (through weakness voluntaryly) throw or break it off, it would bleed to Death. I wanted Faith like St Thomas to Convince Mee. A Large Crab was brought & Laid it on its back & then with a pair of Iron pinchers Wee Crack the shell on the thickest & Fleshyest part of its Legg. It bleed much, but in Less than a Minute it cast off its legg and there was Seen a thick Gelly like Substance which Stop'd the Bleeding which is wonderfully provided for that purpose. All Its Leggs Suffer'd the Same Operation, thus in a few Minutes the Creature was Legless. Now it is wonderfull to Consider by what Innate power It can crack & Break the Solid Shell (not in a Joynt) but in the Smooth pt Its Flesh and Muscells, and all the Blood Vessells, as if Cut wth a Knife. I never was more astonish'd att so amazeing a Sight & to reflect how the operation was performed. But as these Creatures are very Quarrelsome and what ever they catch hold off with their Great Claws they will break it, & hold it fast a Long while, So to Save their Lives & gett Clear of their Adversary they break off a Legg & Leave it as a Trophy of Victory.

"Great Martigon . . . From Pennsylvania." Georg Dionysius Ehret. Bound into Collinson's copy of Mark Catesby, Natural History of Carolina *. . . at Knowsley Hall. Courtesy the Earl of Derby, Knowsley.*

Collinson wrote on this plate,

This Noble Martigon was Sent from Pennsylvania by John Bartram in Spring 1736. It is named by Him the Great Marsh Martigon It being found in moist ground. The Flowers are much larger and it grows Taller than the common American sort. It flowered in the Garden of P. Collinson att Peckham in September, 1736, which is Much Later than the other Sort Commonly known by the name of the Virginia Martigon and called by the Duch [Dutch] Catalogues Canada Martigon. Both sorts are described by Mr Catesby in his Natural History of Carolina *&c. In the years 1739 & 1740 It produced a Stem 6 feet 2 inches High with a Pyramid of 30 Flowers which was a most Delightfull Sight."*

You will reasonably Expect to hear Some News of your Manuscript [*The History of the Five Nations Depending on the Province of New York*]. I have Lent it to Mr Scroop [not identified] who is pretty well Acquainted att the Helm & has not yett Return'd it.

I am my Dear Friend very much yours.

P. COLLINSON

1. In June, 1744, Colden reported word from John Bartram about "a Philosophicall Society now forming at Philadelphia. They have given an invitation to several in the neighbouring Colonies to join with them & have done me the honour to take me into their Society. . . ." (*Cadwallader Colden Papers,* Vol. III, 1919, p. 60) This was the American Philosophical Society, founded in 1743.

John Bartram was an original member of the American Philosophical Society and perhaps the first in Philadelphia to suggest that a scientific society be formed. (Bell, Whitfield J., *Patriot-Improvers.* American Philosophical Society, Philadelphia, 1997, Vol. 1, p. 48.)

65 🐾 TO JOHN FREDERICK GRONOVIUS

ALS:LC
Xmas Day, December 25, 1744

My Dear Friend

I have Two things in perticular to Mention to you the First is that in all your Letters this year you take not the least Notice of your receiving the Box with the Jarr of Cranberries that I sent you, the Next is that I have no Cataloge or Names to the last Quire of plants you was So Good to fix for Mee on paper. I desir'd acquainting you with It because I was in hopes to receive it by Mr Chappal [not identified], but there was none came by Him. By some accident it is left behind for I have over & over again Examined Every Leafe & Every Letter & percell & none can be found. Under this Misfortune I must beg your advice & assistance what to do, & how I must contrive to gett them Named. My hopes Is that you keep a Coppy by you of them, then you can Easily Help Mee for I can give no account of them to our Friend J. Bartram untill I know their Names.

The Next thing to take Notice off to you is the Receipt of your Curious Letter to J. Bartram of July Last. This was kept so Long with the Books by the accident of Mr Chapples Leaving part of his things behind, that the oppertunity was Lost off Sending them this year, but I shall take Care in about a Month to Send them.

Pray when are Wee to Expect the Remainder of Ramphius?[1] In yours of March the 6, you mention our friend Dr Lierthon [not identified]; I am heartyly Glad to find him in Favour again.

I am much oblig'd to you for your perticular account of the Salmon. It is Strange it should not be taken notice of be-

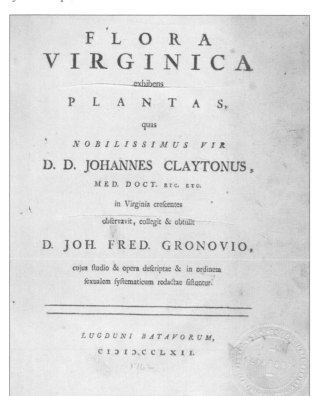

Cover, Gronovius, Flora Virginica. The Library of Company of Philadelphia

FLORA
VIRGINICA
exhibens
PLANTAS,
quas
NOBILISSIMUS VIR
D. D. JOHANNES CLAYTONUS,
MED. DOCT. ETC. ETC.
in Virginia crescentes
observavit, collegit & obtulit
D. JOH. FRED. GRONOVIO,
cujus studio & opera descriptae & in ordinem sexualem systematicum redactae sistuntur.

LUGDUNI BATAVORUM,
CIƆIƆ.CCLXII.

fore. I am glad to hear you have Such Success with the Seeds. Pray Lett Mee See the Specimens of them as they come in flower.

Dr Canwan [Peter Canvane][2] & Dr [Patrick] Brown[3] both Called on Mee but where they are now I know not. I wish proper Care is taken of Dr Coldens Pacquet. It was a pitty it was not sent to me.

I take your Letters in Course but those that I should have came first came Last per Mr Chapple. In yours of July 30th, pray is the Gilder & gift Received of van Royan?[4] I had not Sent Dr [John] Mitchells papers but that I thought Such Curious Matters would have been readly printed in the Miscellaneous Observationes Critum Nova.[5] I am greatly concern'd our Learned & Ingenious friend will be Disappointed seeing his Works publish'd. Is there not an oppertunity of doing it att Leipsic? They are to Large for our [Royal Society] Transactions, & no one Cares to print Lattin books in England.

I never mett with the Musk Ratt Described but in Mr Ray. If you Desire it Mr Bartram will Send you the Skin of one Stuffed. It has two baggs with musk, distinct from its Testes.

I am greatly obliged to you for procureing the [illegible]. I hope the Cranberries are good & acceptable. Wee had Some of them Same a few Days agon as good as when they first came over.

Mr Scharblen [not identified] is very obliging & a very Worthy Man. For your Sake Shall do all I can to Serve Him. He very Kindly brought Mee all the things you Sent Mee. Your Letter was Delivered to Mr Husseys [not identified] for Dr Brown. It would be the greatest pleasure to Mee to Ramble the Sea Coast with you. I shall be obliged to you for Some of your Marine plants. Your being So good to Name them will very much Increase my knowledge in those Matters.

So much for yours of Septr 7th. I next by Mr Scharblen had yours of the 15th Instant. Am glad to find mine per Mr. Hamilton[6] is come to hand. I cannot yett recollect what the Mineral was I sent you by Him.

I have had lately Sent Mee from Russia a Large Smooth Bezoar Stone.[7] It has a Nucleus in its Center found in the Beluga Fish on the Volga also another Oblong Stone found

Belluga stone. Illustrations to Collinson's essay, "Observations on the Belluga Stone" Phil Trans 44, 1747, p451. American Philosophical Society.

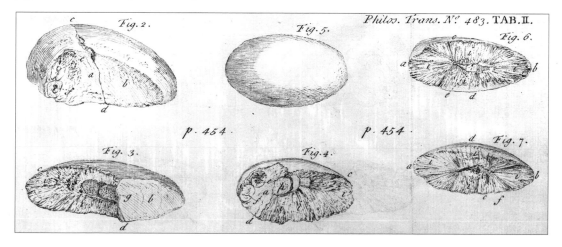

in the Sturgeon or Cibrina. I don't find these in A. Seba's pompous Work,[8] neither has Sr. Hans Sloane them in his Collection. Pray have you Seen any of this Nature.

I have not yett reced the 2d part of a Curious Work on Insects from Mr. Beurer & other things, but I understand by Mr. [Georg] Ehret[9] they will come to a Merchant in London.

It has been Long known that Iron or Steel will acquire by Several Means a Magnetic power, but Dr Knight[10] has found a way to do it in a wonderfull Degree for he Showed before the R. Society that half pound Weight of Magnetic Steel Lifted Twenty pound Weight with many other Experiments. It operates or Communicate a Magnetic Power to the Needle for the Sea Compass, and to Knives etc. The Load Stone is in Disgrace by this powerfull Magnetic Steel.

This Gentleman has also the Secret to Invigorate a Load Stone & can almost give Instantaneously a New Strength to It. Our president give him a Load Stone that would at-

Georg Dionysius Ehret. George James. Ehret is painting Cestrum diurnum. *The Linnean Society of London.*

tract but Two ounces, but takeing it away a Minute or Two, he made it take up Four Ounces, & Next Day it took up Six Ounces. This puzzles our Philosophers more than giving So Strong power to Steel.

It has been found by repeated Experiments, that 16 Grains of Musk, 16 Grains of Cinaber & 16 ounces of Vermillion is an Infalible Remedy for the bite of a Mad Dog, & the Like Ingredients Increased from 16 Grains to 20 & to 24 Grains has Cured Many Distracted people & the Most Malignant Spotted Fevers Such as Wee call Jail or prison Fevers [typhus] has never failed tho in the Worst Symptoms. This has been Successfully Try'd on our Condemned prisoners from 12 to 16 & to 20 Grains of Each, Musk, Cinabar, & Vermillion. This putts the patient in an Immoderate Sweat for 30 or 40 Hours and what (is wonderfull) are not Weakened by It.

This Recipe was procured from Tongueen [Tonkin] in China for the Bite of a Mad Dog but has been found most Successfull in the other Disorders.

I shall give Your Memorandum to Mr Catesby.

This year I found the Hermitt Crab in Several Large Welk Shells in the Isle of Wight in the Sea Near it, & Differs Little from that Described by Mr. Catesby.

Wee have wonderfull fine Spring Weather. Our Fields are as Green as in May & our Gardens Show the Spring Flowers.

Now my Dear Friend I shall conclude with my best Wishes that the New Year may prove Happy & auspicious to you & your good family.

I am affectionately yours

P. COLLINSON

JOHN FREDERICK GRONOVIUS (1690–1762). See Note 3 to May 13, 1739.

1. George Eberhard Rumphius (1628–1702), German-born Dutch naturalist with Dutch East India Company, chiefly in Amboina, Indonesia, wrote *Herbarium Amboinense*. . . . Utrecht, 1741. First published in Amsterdam, 1705. (See also note 1, PC to Gronovius, March 24, 1753.)

2. Peter Canvane (1720–1786), Physician. Elected to Royal College of Physicians, London, 1744.

3. Patrick Browne (1720–1790), MD, lived in Antigua in 1737 and Jamaica 1746–55, published *Civil and Natural History of Jamaica,* 1756.

4. David van Royen (1727–1799), professor of Botany at Leyden and director of its Botanic Garden.

5. *Miscellaneae Observationes Criticae Novae.* Amsterdam, 1732–1739.

6. Possibly the Hon. Charles Hamilton of Painshill, Surrey, who was a customer of Bartram's through Collinson.

7. "In natural history, is a stony concretion found in the stomach of several animals of the goat kind. It is composed of concentrical coats surrounding each other, with a small cavity in the middle, containing a bit of wood, straw, hair, or the like substances. . . . (B)ezoar, on account of its high price, if it serves no other purpose, is of an excellent use in the apothecaries bill." (EB, I, 541)

Collinson published his "Observations on the Belluga stone" in the Royal Society's *Philosophical Transactions* XLIV (1747): 451.

8. Albert Seba (1665–1736), Amsterdam apothecary and collector of natural curiosities, published *Thesaurus of natural history* in three volumes, 1734–1758.

9. Georg Dionysius Ehret (1708–1770), botanical artist, born in Heidelberg. He began his working life as a gardener for the Margrave of Baden and others, drawing in his spare time. Christopher Jacob Trew saw some of his drawings and asked Ehret to paint as many plants as he could "on large fine paper." Ehret sent him eighty drawings in 1732, followed by many more over a number of years. Trew published Ehret's drawings in his *Plantae Selectae,* Nuremberg, 1750–1753.

In 1735 Ehret visited England where he met Sir Hans Sloane and Philip Miller and made drawings of new plants for Trew. He then went to Holland where he met Gerard George Clifford, the owner of a noted garden near Haarlem where Carl Linnaeus was employed compiling the *Hortus Cliffortianus.* Ehret showed Linnaeus and Clifford some of his drawings, which Clifford bought. He then employed Ehret for a month to make drawings for the *Hortus Cliffortianus.*

When Ehret returned to England in 1736 he secured the patronage of Dr. Richard Mead, the Duchess of Portland, and Dr. John Fothergill. He gave instructions in botanical illustration, prepared engravings for various publications including Philip Miller's *Figures of . . . plants,* published in parts from 1755 until 1760, and the later editions of the *Gardeners Dictionary.* A number of his illustrations were made from plants in Collinson's garden. See Henrey, Vol. II, pp. 62–64, and Calmann, G. *Ehret, Flower Painter Extraordinary.* Boston, New York Graphic Society, 1977.

10. Gowin Knight (1713–1772), FRS, studied the effects of lightning on the ship's compass for which he received the Royal Society's Copley Medal in 1747. His account of the experiment is in *Philosophical Transactions* XLIII, (1745): 161–6.

ALS:N-YHS
London, March 30, 1745

My Dear Friend

It gives Mee Concern that I am Deprived the pleasure of yours by the Unfortunate Loss of Capt Bryant. I commend your prudence in Directing your Seeds for the Paris Garden. The proffesors are Messrs Jussieu.[1] Without that precaution a hundred to one but that they had been thrown into the Sea. But if you had Improved that precaution & Divided the Seeds into Two parcells & Sent by Two ships, then in all probability I should have had the Delight of shareing in the pains that you had taken to oblige Your Friends. Whilst these perilous Times Last I recommend it to you for the future.

As this may I think very Justly be Stiled an age of Wonders, It may not perhaps be Disagreeable to Just hint them to you.

The Surpriseing Phenomena of the Polypus Entertain'd the Curious for a year or Two past but Now the Vertuosi of Europe are taken up In Electrical Experiments, and what can be more Astonishing than that the Base rubing of a Glass Tube Should Investigate a person with Electric Fire. He is not Touched by the Tube, but the Subtile Effluvia that Flies from it pervades Every pore and renders him what Wee call Electrified, for then Lett him touch Spirits of Wine & the Spark of fire that flies from his finger on the touch will Sett the Spirits In flame. This is a Common Experiment, but I have Seen oyle of Sevil-oriangs & Camphire Sett on fire & Gun powder mixt with oyl of Lemmons will take Fire. But What would you say to see Fire come out of a Piece of thick Ice & Sett the Spirits In flame or Electrical Fire drawn though Water & performe the Same? These are some few of a great Number of Surpriseing things that are formed by the Electrical power which you will find Difficult to Comprehend but are all facts.

Electricity Seems to furnish an Inexhaustable fund for Enquiry, & Sure & Certain Phenomenas so Various and So wonderfull that can only arise from Causes very General & Extensive and Such as must have been designed by the Almighty Author of Nature for the production of very great Effects & Such as are of very Great Moment no Doubt to the System of the Universe, which by Degrees may lead to Higher Truths, in perticular to Discover the Nature of that Subtile Elastic & Etherial Medium which Sr Isaac Newton Queries on, at the End of His opticks. Had these Discoveries happened in that Great Mans Time, His Illuminated Mind would have apply'd them to wonderfull purposes.

The Walcans [Walachians — Rumanians] have discover'd Some very unaccountable properties in unealed or untempered Glass. You must know that Glass Immediately after it is Blown in what Fashion you please and Exposed to the air to Cool, is called unnealed, whereas all the Glass in use is by Degrees Harden'd or Temperd, but take a Cruit of this uneal'd Glass that is made of the Size of an Oyle or Vinegar Cruit but thicker and Stronger to Appearance, Take a Wooden Mallet and beat it, on its Bottome as hard as one could drive a Nail & it will not break. Drop a musket Bullet or an Ivory ball into It, it has the Same effect. But take a Shiver or a small piece of Flint that weights no more than three Grains & Drop it into the Cruit as gently as you Can & in a Moment it flies into a Thousand peices. This I saw tryed over & over & it never Fails, nay I Saw a Grain & half of flint Drop'd into a Cruit & it did not Instantly break, but laying it aside & in about 2 or

3 Minutes it flew all to peices. These are Notorious Facts. No one pretends to offer any account for them but had they been Shown in the Dark Ages of the 7th & 8th Century nothing could have saved the operator from the flames. The Devil or his Imps must have been concerned in Both operations to produce Such Surpriseing Effects beyond Human Comprehension.

But I verily think the next wonderfull operation could not in the Deadest times be apply'd to such a Satenical power.

Wee have Large Sea Crabs that Weigh 3 & 4 to 7 or 8 pound. This Creature by a Wonderful faculty has a power in it self voluntarily to Crack & Break of his Great & Small Leggs, notwithstanding his flesh is cover'd with so hard a Shell, it breaks readily & the Fleshy Muscles & Ligaments Divide and the Limb Drops off. I have seen in a few minutes Two Large Crabbs Leggless. I fancy you may try the Experiment, which is no more than Laying a Crab on its back then take a pair of Iron Pincers and break the Extremities of its Leggs & bruise its Flesh, that it may feel pain. And if it is of the Same Nature with ours it will presently cast off its Legg off in the Middle of the Second Joynt from its Body.

As it is too Long & I have not Leisure to assigne the cause the fact is Certain you will now Dismiss Mee & with Candor Excuse the Innacuracy of these hints. Such as they are you may thank the Leisure of Easter Day Evening for them.

I am with much Respect your affectionate friend,

P. COLLINSON

1. The brothers Antoine (1686–1758) and Bernard de Jussieu (1699–1777), were respectively director and sub-demonstrator at the Jardin des Plantes in Paris.

67 ❧ TO CADWALLADER COLDEN

ALS:N-YHS
London, April 26, 1745

My Dear Friend

I did not Expect that I should have found any Leisure to answer your kind Letter of the 8th Dec Last but I will find time to thank you for the perusal of your papers to Dr Gronovius which I read over & over & was much pleased with. Your Reasons & Objections are of Such Weight as must Effect the Linnean System & prevent its being universally Received. Tournfort & Ray in my Judgment are much perferrable. Take this in general. I wish I could be more particular. I really wonder att your proficiency in so Short a Time. I transmitted those papers by a safe hand to Dr. Gronovius who writes directed to J. Bartram by (Hargrave) a many Curious Remarks on the things sent by J. Bartram in Distinct pages. Could you see them they would I am sure give you Entertainmt and putt you in a Regular methode for future Inquiries. In some matters I really don't know such a knowing Indefatigable Man as Dr Gronovius.

Your Brother sent Mee a Letter for you complaining He had not heard from you which I inclosed Early in the Spring to J. Bartram by Cap Bream, whi I Desir'd to forward It to you.

I am glad to hear of the Philadelphia Society.[1] I certainly think cannot Labour Long when Such wonders are all round them Ready brought forth to their hands and to Which Wee are great Strangers, Butt because you see them Every Day they are thought Common & not worth Notice.

Hither to I have wrote only to blot paper, but now I tell you Some thing new. Dr Knoght [Gowin Knight] Physition has found the Art of Giveing Such a magnetic power to Steel that the poor old Loadstone is putt quite out of Countenance. His Steel Magnets act on the Needle & transmit their power to Knives &c as the Loadstone. Butt He has also shown a Secret on the Loadstone not Known before by Increasing its attractive power to a great Degree & can att pleasure Change the poles how he pleases. Take these examples. A Loadstone of a parelle pipeid[2] Form he made the opposite Ends south poles & at the Middle quite round all North poles. In another flat Stone he made the opposite Ends North poles & the opposite Sides South poles. In another load Stone of an Irregular flat Shape he made half of Each of the flat Surfaces a North pole & the other half a South Pole, So as that the Two half Surfaces opposite Each other Sould be of a Contrary Denomination with many other Changes & Varieties Showing. He had the power to Impress the faculty of Either pole in any part of the Load Stone with as much ease as Load stone will Influence a Needle.

I am Yours

P. COLLINSON

Dr Gronovius hope you'l continue your Remarks & send him seeds of any of your Vegitable production.

1. The American Philosophical Society; John Bartram proposed such a society in 1739, but nothing came of it. Franklin took up the idea in 1743, drafted a prospectus, sent copies to friends in Philadelphia and in the other Colonies, organized meetings and collected papers. The APS as we know it today was organized in 1744. In 1745 Franklin announced that the first number of his "American Philosophical Miscellany" would appear within six weeks, but it never did.

68 🐄 TO GEORGE PARKER, 2ND EARL MACCLESFIELD

Draft AL:LS

[circa 1745]

On Friday last as I was with Mr Hanbury to be Introduced to your Lordship on Mr Colden's affair,[1] I happened on the Capt that Brought the Head & Horns of the Great Elk or Moose Deer from New England as a present to your Lordship, which I presume is the largest of the Specie in the known World, & what is believed to be the very animal that belongs to that Species of Deer [*Megaloceros*] whose horns are found Dugg in Ireland, Which no doubt your Lordship (may have seen Each) had Seen at Lord Pembrokes[2] at Wilton.

Sir Hans Sloane and the Royal Society amongst Naturalists there is a doubt whether the Great American Moose Deer is the same with the Irish & that can not bee Determined any other wise then by comparing the Horns, which now can easily be done as you have the horns, and I doubt not of your Lordship's condesension to favour the Royal Society with a sight of them which now can be safely Done as you have the Horns.

It is Received Opinion that no Species of animal was annihilated at the Deluge & as

"Megaloceros, Great Elk or Moose Deer from New England." Artist unknown. The Wellcome Trust Library, London

God's providence is over all His Work to preserve Every Species as Evidences of his Almighty Power, yett if these Horns Do not Match with the Irish, there is some foundation to think that this creature does not now Exist unless in the undiscover'd Countries on the South Side of the Globe.

The Great Elk or American Moose Deer I am informed is only found in that Great Track of land (covered with Immense Woods & Swamps) that lies between Nova Scotia and Quebec. Mr Jocelyn in his Little Tract Intitled New England Rarities[3] I think gives a Description of It. La Hontain[4] Mentions it much about, but He is an author of Little Credit. Catesby in his Nat History Describes from others for He never Saw It, & tho I have been all my Life time Acquainted with American people I never Mett with any that Ever Saw this Great Animal Alive, said to be 14 or 15 Hands High.

An apology is necessare for takeing up so much of your Lordship's time (which would have) so much better Imployed in promoting the publick Welfare for which your Country is under the Greatest Obligations.

I submit my Self [torn].

GEORGE PARKER, 2nd Earl Macclesfield (1697–1764), astronomer, President of the Royal Society, 1752–1764.

1. Colden corresponded with Parker through Collinson, sending him a copy of *Principles of Action in Matter* followed by a series of clarifications.

2. Henry Herbert, 9th Earl of Pembroke (1693–1751).

3. John Josselyn (1638–1675), published *New England Rarities Discovered*. London, 1672 and *An Account of Two Voyages To New England,* 1674 and 1675.

4. Louis Armand de Lom d'Arce, baron de Lahontan (1666–1715?), published *Nouveaux Voyages . . .* the Hague, 1703.

Above: Christopher Jacob Trew. Artist unknown. A copy of a painting at Erlangen, given by Trew to Collinson in 1752. The Linnean Society of London.

Opposite page: Lilio Narcissus. *Georg Dionysius Ehret. In Trew,* Plantae Selectae, *plate XIII. The Linnean Society of London.*

ALS:Erlangen
London, March 20, 1746

My Dear Friend

I could not Suffer the Box [of roots] to go without a Token of the Respect I bear you whose Endeavours to Cultivate Natural Knowledge & Improve Mankind Justly Intitles you to the Love & Respect of Every Man.

As I hear you have a Stove I was willing to Try again & I hope in a better Season to Send you Some Curious Bulbs which may Deserve your Care and in return I hope they will Oblige you with their Flowers. I am doubtfull in none but N 4, their being no Green Leaves; and I could not go into the Country for them So was obliged to take them as the Gardner Sent them, but I know them all by their Green Leaves being Children of my own procureing and Raiseing up (all but the China Narciss [not identified]) for I had the Sole Management of Sr Charles Wagers Stoves, who Delighted to See those things, but His Engagemt in publick affairs prevented his particular Care of them. A great many rare plants was in his Collection, who Spared no Expence, but now the Worthy Man is Dead, they are given away & Scater'd.

I Secured what I could & these I now Send are Some of Them & I wish you Success with Them. They are good natur'd plants & Easily Cultivated. If they flower in the Summer Months they Like Water whilst in Flower. If they Flower in Winter give them less Water, then in Summer, after Flowering give them but very Little or none att all for Some Time untill you See the Root to begin to putt out new green Leaves.

I am with much Respect Your Sincere Friend
P. COLLINSON

I Recommend Dr Mitchells Tracts[1] to your protection & Patronage. Beg the Favour that you will give them Suiteable Title pages. You may Insert the Dedication to Sr Hans Sloane, or Leave it quite out, as you Like best. This Dr Mitchell Desired Mee to Tell you. Mr. Beurer will Deliver the Tracts to you. vale
PC

A Catalogue of Lilio Narcessus
No 1 Lilio Narcissus wth White Flower from Jamaica Tolabo dicta
No 2 Ditto From Bahama Islands

Tab. XIII.

LILIO-NARCISSVS *Africanus scillæ foli is, flore niveo linea purpurea striato Mill.*

No 3 Ditto From Island of St Christophers
No 4 Ditto from Barbadoes

When these Roots are in full perfection with their fine Green Leaves & Charming Flowers all White & Fragrant and they Happen to flower in the Summer Months, I bring them out of the Stove and Sett Them in the Parlor Chimney on the Hearth & they perfume the whole Roome, & So they will keep flowering a Long While.

As I keep a Coppy of the above Numbers & Sorts I shall be greatly obliged to you to favor Mee, with the Author, that Describes Each Species. Sr Hans Sloane mentions but one with a White Flower in Jamaica. Pray tell Mee which plant of the Four you take to be His.

Dr Martin in his 3d Decade Mentions one from Barbadoes which I take to be No 4 but your Nicer Distinction will Determine that. Perhaps some of these may be found in the 2 Vol. of the Hortus Amstelodamus[2] When they flower you will Judge.

5 Roots of the Red Mexica Lilie (vulgo). But they are found in all Our Islands and are undoubtedly what Sr Hans Sloans mentions in his History of Jamaica.

6 Roots of Red Flowering Narcissus from China [not identified]. This was procured from Thence with Other Bulbs, by that Great Lover & propagator of Rare plants John Blackburn Esqr att Orford near Warrington (He has now the true Cinamon & Sago palm). As this Charming Flower is a nondiscript I hope to See it appear in the Commercium Litterarium.[3]

7 Root of Redish purple & white Lilio Narcissus From Cape Coast Castle in Guinea was Sent to the Right Honble Sr Charles Wager First Lord of the Admiralty in the year 1734 and Flowerd in his Stove with Surpresing Beauty anno 1736. I am perswaded Mr. Erhet has sent you a painting of this fine Flower, which I cannot find describd by any Author, So I hope you will oblige the World with It.

CHRISTOPHER JACOB TREW (1695–1769), F.R.S. physician, scholar, collector of natural curiosities and botanist at Nuremberg. Collinson called him "the Linnaeus of Germany" (PC to Trew, June 30, 1767). Trew was an early patron of Ehret's botanical illustration. His works include *Hortus Nitidissimus*. Nuremberg, 1758–92 and *Plantae Selectae*. Nuremberg, 1750–53, both with plates after Ehret's drawings.

Collinson's friendship with Trew suffered when Trew proved a dilatory correspondent. On August 3, 1763 Collinson wrote,

For what purpose did Doctor Trew Send Mee His picture, unless it was Dayly to remind Mee of His Ingratitude.

When I look on your Portrait, it Seems to Smile on Mee. Can I forebear Saying those Smiles aggravate the Guilt of an ungratefull Man, who can So Easily forget his Friend, that Loved Him.

Can any Thing be More Ungenerous, More impolite, More unbecoming a Gentleman than not to give Mee the common Civility of a Letter of Thanks for the Box of Things I sent Him.

Unless I hear from Him very Soone I must Hang a Curtain before his Picture that I may no longer See Doctor Trew who has not been True to Old Friendship.

So adieu,

P. COLLINSON

Pray My respects to Mr De Murr

[ALS: Erlangen]

Trew at last replied. Here is Collinson's answer:

London, February 7, 1765

It really Surprised Mee after So long Silence To receive a Letter Dated 26 January 1764 Signed with the Name of my Honoured Friend Doctor Trew. I am Glad He is in the Land of the Living and Hope for the Future a more Punctual Correspondent.

As I am a Lover of Natural History I read with pleasure the Catalogue of So many Curious Works, but Such Long Delays Cools the Ardour of the Mind Tired out with Expectation. It makes Mee repeat often when I look at your Picture, Bis Dat que Cito Dat.

You was so Obliging to Send Mee Eleven Plates of finely Coloured Shells on Large folio paper. I wish you my Good Friend could Send Mee the Twelth plate, N 12, to compleat the Sett.

I hope you will favour Mee Soon with Advice that the Chest with your Generous presents is Sett forward.

I am with much Respect and Esteem your Sincere Friend, P. COLLINSON.

my Respects to Mr. Meurs

[ALS: Erlangen]

1. In 1738 Mitchell sent Collinson a paper, addressed to Sir Hans Sloane, titled "Dissertatio Brevis de Principiis Botanicum et Zoologorum" in which he struggled with classification. In 1741 he sent a list of Virginia plants, "Nova Genera Plantarum." Collinson forwarded both to Trew who published them in the *Nuremburg Transactions* of 1748.

2. Cornelius, Hermann. *Catalogus plantaeum horti publici Amslelg damonsis.* Amsterdam, 1661.

3. Published 1731–1745 in 15 volumes, Nuremberg, *Sumtibus Societatis Litteris Adeibulneransis.* Trew published in it often.

70 🎋 TO CARL LINNAEUS

ALS:LS
London, April 1, 1746

My Dear Friend

I am obliged to you for your favour of Dec. 31 ult. and am glad to find the seeds I sent last year were acceptable. I have added another parcel this year with those from Dr Dillenius, but he complains that you send no seeds to him, which he says is very discouraging.

The Hermanus Para Bots[1] cost 8:6.

Mr Ehret desires your acceptance of a coloured print of a new Cereus that flowered at Chelsea [Physic Garden].

Our valuable friend Dr Lawson is daily expected over from Flanders. He was taken prisoner by the French, but was afterwards exchanged.

There is variety of American plants to be bought, but there is a great deal of trouble and expense to get them on board a ship, and then unless some careful person was to look after them they might not be good for much when they come to you.

Dr Mitchell lives in Virginia and has described several nova genera not yet printed.

I have the true gensing in my garden. It both flowers and seeds.

I will endeavour to remember to speak to Dr Dilenius to save you some seed of the St Timothy's or lady finger grass.

Your letter was carefully sent to Dr Dilenius which I conclude he has answered.

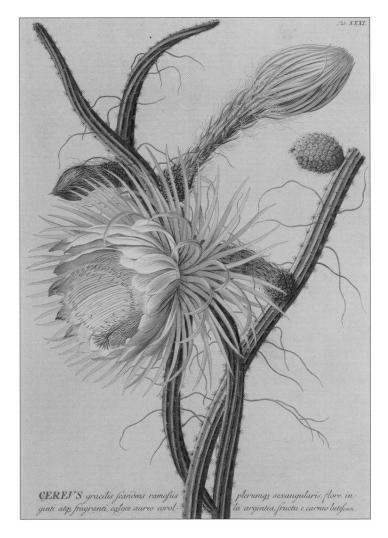

Cereus. Georg Dionysius Ehret. In Trew, Plantae Selectae, *plate XXX. The Linnean Society of London*

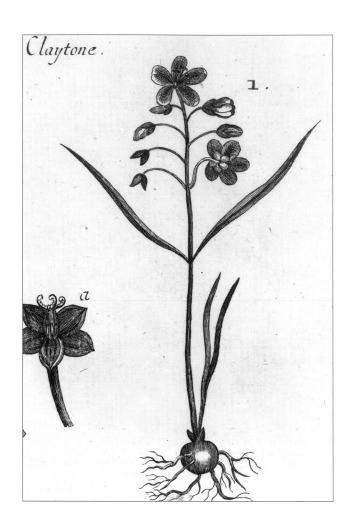

Claytonia virginica, *Spring beauty. Jean Baptiste Pierre Antoine Monet de Lamarck. Hunt Institute for Botanical Documentation.*

I love all books of natural history and every production God has made. Pray what sorts of land, river, and sea shells are found in your country, any thing peculiar observed in their natures? What sorts of fossils are found in Sweden? Your animals, rein-deer excepted, are near the same as ours. Any perticular species of fish that are found in no other parts of the world? Any insects peculiar to Sweden or Lapland? Send me specimens of them, or any other natural production, as mineral etc.

The Claytonia [*Claytonia virginica,* Spring beauty] is now near in flower, and the Echium or blew mountain cowslip flo vera and a pretty Ranunculus with a yellow flower, and a Fumaria bulbosa of Plukenet. These four species are the first flowers from Virginia.

Now I must take my leave, wishing you health and happiness.

P. COLLINSON

Our dear friend Dr Beck[2] was so good to send me your Systema Naturae in octovo edition which I am mightily pleased with. Pray is Dr Beck returned to Sweden?

1. Paul Hermann (1646–1695), German-born Dutch botanist and explorer traveled in Africa, India and Ceylon, was professor of botany at Leyden, and published *Paradisus Batavus.* Leyden, 1698. The work was edited by William Sherard.

2. Abraham Bäck (1713–1795), Swedish physician, President of the College of Medicine at Stockholm, Physician in Ordinary to the King, often addressed by Linnaeus as "My dearest Brother." (Blunt, Wilfred. *The Compleat Naturalist: A Life of Linnaeus.* London, 1971, pp. 204–205)

ALS:Oxford
Thorndon, April 4, 1746

My Dear Friend,

I was agreeably surprised with yours. It seem'd to Mee as if one spoake to Mee that was risen from the Dead, for I really thought you So. All Letters from my Friends told Mee it was Impossible you could hold out, but since I find It otherwise, accept of Such Intelligences that I can Give you.

As I am on a Visit to Lady Petres, I there had Leisure to answer yours. Since Our Dear Lords Death My Lady is so respectfull to his Memory that the Stoves & Nursery are Kept in Good Order. But as there was great Numbers of a Sort, so Abundance has been sold & Disposed off & yett there is not Such a Collection in England except Oxford or Chelsea, but yet Here is a great many plants that they have Not.

The Great Stove is the most Extraordinary Sight in the World. All the plants are of Such Magnitude & the Novelty of the appearance strikes every one with pleasure.

The Trellices all round cover'd with all Species of Passion Flowers which run up near 30 feet high, the Creeping great Flowering Cerus Blows annually with Such Quantities of Flowers that surprises every one with their Beauty & at the Same Time perfumes the House with their Scent.

There is variety of Cerus that have Carried up their perpendicular Heads to the Very Top, Papaws both Male & Female, Guavas, Plaintains, Several Sorts of Palms, Dragon Trees, Ficus Malabaricus, Rosa Chinesis, Acacias, Bambo's, besides a Great Variety of Species raised from New Spain Seeds that I don't know. Many Have flowerd & fruited. The papaws hang Now full of fruit & Blossome & there is a Most Delightfull Show of Several Sorts of White Lillio Narcis now in Flower.

The Lesser Stove 60 feet Long & 20 Wide is full of a Vast Variety of all Species of Tender Exotics, and the Nurserys abound with rare Hard Exoticks, a great Variety of Pines from North America not found in our Gardens, Red Cedars & White Cedars, great Magnolia & the Small Magnolia flowers every year in Great plenty. Sarsifrax, Sweet gum or Liquid amber Trees, yew Leafed Firr, Balm Gilead and Spruce Firrs from New England and New found Land, with a great Variety of all other Hardy America Trees & Shrubs in plenty.

To see his plantations now arrived to Such perfection, the Variety is So great that one would think ones Self Transported to Some other Country, American & European Productions are So Blended together.

The Only Man that Makes a Figure in Raiseing plants for Sale is Mr Gordon at Mile End in the Essex Road. He has a peculiar Skill & fortune in Raiseing a great Variety of Rare hardy Exotic Seeds both from america & Europe. I have not spared to assist Him. His great Love & Care gives Mee pleasure of Mind in Doing it because I dont see what I have procured with Some pains & Success thrown away.

If please God I Live & He Lives our Gardens will have more Curious plants in Them then Ever.

I know my Dear Friend that this must rejoice you & give you Some Comfort to find your Favorite amusement not Deserted.

I will accept of your Kind offer of Helianthemums [Sun rose or rock rose] &c.

I wish you Comfort in your Bodyly Weakness & a Serene Mind. I am with much Respect yours,

P. Collinson

My Son gives his respect, is a very hopefull youth and will make a great Naturalist.

72 ❧ TO JOSEPH BREINTNALL

ALS: Staatsbibliothek Preussischer Kulturbesitz, Berlin

London, May 20, 1746

Respd friend

As the Account of Electrical Experiments was not publish when I sent the other Books & Pamphlets, I have sent one under Cover to my Worthy & Learned Friend James Logan from whome no doubt you'l receive It, which will give you some Hints in that Phenomena & how to proceed in Experiments, if the Glass Tube[1] in the Trunk of Books come safe to your Hands.

I am much thine

P. Collinson

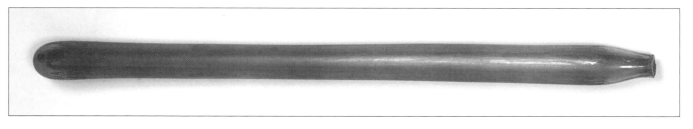

Glass electrical tube, 18″ long, 3 1/2 inches circumference. The Library Company of Philadelphia

On behalf of the Library Company Franklin wrote Collinson on March 28, 1747 acknowledging the gift: "Your kind present . . . has put several of us on making electrical experiments, in which we have observed some particular phaenomena that we look upon to be new. I shall, therefore communicate them to you in my next. . . ." (*Franklin* III, 115–119) In his next twelve letters to Collinson, Franklin described the discoveries which made his reputation as a scientist. Collinson showed the letters to his friends, read some of them to the Royal Society, and in 1750 published them under the title *Experiments and Observations on Electricity, Made at Philadelphia in America, by Mr. Benjamin Franklin, and Communicated in several Letters to Mr. P. Collinson, of London, F.R.S.* Several editions of this work, enlarged and supplemented, appeared during Franklin's lifetime. (See Cohen, I. Bernard. *Benjamin Franklin's Experiments.* Cambridge, Mass., 1941)

1. The "Glass Tube" is on display at The Library Company of Philadelphia, sea-green, 18″ long, open at one end, 3 1/2″ in circumference, worn from rubbing.

Dodecatheon meadia, *shooting star. Georg Dionysius Ehret. In Trew,* Plantae Selectae, *plate XII. The Linnean Society of London*

73 ❧ TO CARL LINNAEUS

ALS:LS
August 5, 1746

Dear Doctor

I hope you have the Seeds I sent you in the Spring under the care of our good Mr. Biork.

I now send you a Specimen of a New & Rare plant,[1] not yett Discribed that I know off, Except in Pluckenett.[2] I forgot to gather the First Blown Flowers, which are four Times as Large as the Specimens I now Send you. The Leaves are so much Like the First Leaves of Coss Lettice in Shape & Colour, so that for 2 years before ye 8 Flowers appear'd I took it for a Lettice. You have now the Leaves, Flowers & Seed Vessell, so I hope you'l find out what Class to give it.

Perhaps you may, (if a New Genus) call it Bartramnia, for John Bartram found It Growing behind the First Ridge of Mountains in Virginia. It is a Most Elegant Beautifull plant, the Petals being a Violet Colour.

Sow the Seed Immediately & you may hope to see it in 2 years. It is perrennial and very Hardy. Next year I may send you a better Specimen of the Flowers.

Sir Hans Sloane continues Hearty & well.

Pray is Dr Beck return'd from his Travels?

I am much yours,   P. COLLINSON

This Leonurus Canadensis[3] is a charming flower is very finely blown in my garden.

1. The "new and rare plant" seems from the description to be the *Dodecatheon meadia,* or shooting star, originally discovered and drawn by John Banister, then rediscovered by John Bartram.

2. Plukenet, Leonard. *Almagestum botanicum.* London, 1696.

3. *Monarda didyma,* Oswego tea, beebalm, or bergamot, discovered by John Bartram in Oswego, New York, 1743.

Monarda didyma, bergamot, beebalm, horsemint. Georg Dionysius Ehret. In Trew, Plantae Selectae, *Plate LXIV. The Linnean Society of London.*

Benjamin Franklin.
Charles Willson
Peale. American
Philosophical Society.

74 🐾 TO BENJAMIN FRANKLIN

ALS:N-YHS
London, April 12, 1747

My Dear Friend

The Inclosed Account [not found] came from a very Ingenious Friend of Mine [1], & being the first that I have heard, In which Electricity has proved of Benefit to mankind. I believe it would be Entertaining to you. But before Wee can rely on the Experiment It must be confirm'd by many successively.

It is amazing to what a pitch the Electrical power is carried. I am well Informed that In Germany they knock'd down an Ox. Several Men have been struck down at London, one was an Irish Bishop, a Lusty strong Man & yett could not surmount the Shock.

I presume by this Time the aparatus is got into the Colonies, for there is no discribeing the Electical power unless a person feels it himself.

You will Expect to hear Some thing of Doctor Coldens Ingenious performance.[2] It is much admired by Some, and those of most abilities have told mee that it was no trifleing affair but required great Consideration, but one was so meane Spirited as to say He did not believe it was Doctor Coldens Work but that the Ship wrack papers of Some Ingenious European had fell into his hands. As this was so very Meane I would not Hint it to Doctor Colden & indeed I am much ashamed for the person that wrote it.[3]

Several have promised mee some observations on his Scheme but none is yett Come to hand, but I have sent his Books to my Correspondents in Sweden, Russia, Paris, Holland, Nurenbergh, Scotland &c.

So no doubt but wee shall hear from some of them & our curious people In England have been supplyed. The Demand was so great It was reprinted Here before his Bundles Came.

This comes from behind the Counter. You know what a shop Is to write under no Interruption, but I am used to It & my friends are so good to Excuse all my Blunders.

I am Truly yours,

P. COLLINSON

BENJAMIN FRANKLIN (1701–1790), American author, printer, businessman, government official, and scientist.

See Collinson to Breintnall, May 20, 1746, and Collinson to Franklin, April 12, 1748.

1. Probably William Watson who published *Experiments and Observations Tending to illustrate the Nature and Properties of Electricity*. London, 1746 and *A Sequel to Experiments . . .* London, 1746. Franklin acknowledges receipt of these in his letter to PC May 25, 1747. (*Franklin* III, 134)

2. *An Explication of the First Causes of Action in Matter; and of the Cause of Gravitation*. New York, 1745. (See Collinson to Colden, August 3, 1747) Franklin disagreed with certain of Colden's fundamental assumptions. See Franklin to Colden, April 12, 1753, *Franklin* IV, 463–465.

3. Probably William Whiston. See PC to Colden, August 3, 1747.

75 ❧ TO CARL LINNAEUS

ALS:LS
[circa April 1747]

My Dear Friend

As Wee have lost our Worthy Friend Doctor Dellenius [Johann Jacob Dillenius] before your Letter came to hand, I then gave his Letter to our Ingenious Learned Friend Doctor Mitchell who was so good as to return the answer on the Other Side.

It is to no purpose to send Seeds if you do not contrive a better and safer way of Conveyance.

No doubt but you have heard of dear [Isaac] Lawson's death, who is greatly regreted. Catesby's Noble Work is finished.[1]

I drank Tea a few Days agon with Sr Hans Sloane & he continues to admiration in

George Edwards. Self portrait.
Frontispiece to Gleanings of Natural
History. *The Linnean Society of London.*

Good Spirits & Hearty. Wee often Talk of you. Mr. Edwards[2] has lately publish'd 2 very curious volumes in 4to of Rare & non-described birds & animals all Colours after the Life price 4.4:0.

Dr Martin[3] & Mr Miller are both very well. His Dictionary has passed Several Editions.

I should be glad to see the Itinerary[4] you mention. I doubt not but they will be Translated into English, for Wee are very fond of all Branches of Natural History. They Sell the best of any books in England.

Dr Sibthorpe M.D.[5] is chosen Professor att Oxford in the Roome of Dr Dilenius.

When you see Dr Beck, pray thank Him from Mee for the many Curious Books & Seeds that He sent Mee.

My best Wishes attend you.

I am your sincere friend,

P. COLLINSON

This letter is written on the back of John Mitchell to Linnaeus, April 16, 1747.

1. Mark Catesby's *Natural History of Carolina* . . . appeared in 2 volumes, 1730–1747.

2. George Edwards (1694–1773), FRS, artist, ornithologist, Librarian, Royal College of Physicians. He published *The History of Birds* in 4 vols (1743–1751) and *Gleanings of Natural History* in 3 additional volumes (1758–1764). "Nearly six hundred subjects in natural history not before delineated are here engraved." [DNB]

3. John Martyn (1699–1768), Professor of Botany at Cambridge 1732–1762, prepared for the use of students attending his first course of botany lectures *Methodus Plantarum circa Cantabri-*giam Nascentium, 1727, and published *Historia Plantarum Rariorum,* 1728–37; *A Natural History of Uncommon Birds.* London, 1743; translated de Tournefort's *History of Plants,* 1732 and Virgil's *Georgicks,* 1746.

4. Probably *Olandska och Gothlandska Resa* . . . Stockholm and Uppsala, 1745.

5. Humphrey Sibthorp (1713–1797), M.D. Magdalen College 1745, in 1747 succeeded John James Dillenius as Sherardian professor of botany at Oxford. During his thirty-six years' occupancy of the chair he is said to have delivered only one lecture and that a poor one. (DNB)

ALS: BL
July 23, 1747

Friend Da Costa

I believe you are the Only Man living that can write in raptures from the Bottome of a Cole pitt, but pray Take pitty on the Rest of Mankind. Dont Soar out of their reach. I am glad our Friend Tissington [not identified] is with you to temper your Fire or else what might Wee not fear from One so deeply impregnated with the Steams of Nitre & Sulphur when he revissits the Regions of Light.

But a Terrible Explosion out bursts a New Hypothesis. The Theory of the Earth Shakes, down Tumbles poor Woodward,[1] Wilkins,[2] Derham[3] Barnet [Burnet],[4] and all.

But now to be Serious. I wish it was my Lott to make a Day or Two's Excursion in such good Company. Have you been at Bakewell to Mr [blank] the Masons to see the variety of marble thats found in Derbyshire.

The alter piece in the Chapple at Chatsworth deserves your seeing as it exhibits the collection of Curious Marbles, & when you are there pray visit Matlock. I never passed Time so agreeably as there.

I am much obliged to you for the Kind Concern you expressed to gratifie my Vegetable Curiosiity. The Vitis Idea Semper Virens is the plant I want. [*Vaccinium vitis-idea*] The other plant is the black berry bearing Heath [illegible] Erica baccefera of Parkenson 1485 & the Erica Bac procumbens nigra C.B. Pin 48 [illegible] vulgo [*Bearberry?*]. Crowberries, or Crakeberries in [illegible] Derbienscbus vid Synopsis p 444 [*Empetum nigrum, Crowberry*].

As you are not Botanicall Enough to know this plant if you see it, so pray don't give yourself any further Trouble or Thought about It. I shall communicate your kind notice to all yr friends.

My best wishes attends you & your Worthy friend Mr. Tissington. I am yours very sincerely,

P. COLLINSON

The cranberry I know very well [*Vaccinium oxycoccos*] & have found in mossey boggs on the Mountains, but Berry bearing Heath is another plant very different. Crow berries may be the very plant, & I believe it is.

EMANUEL MENDES DA COSTA (1717–1791), FRS, Notary, conchologist, published *The Elements of Conchology,* 1776. Imprisoned for debt in 1754, he became clerk of the Royal Society in 1763, but was dismissed in December 1767 for embezzlement of £266–4–0 and sent to prison where he completed his treatise on shells. (See *Franklin* XIV, 341–342) The Royal Society's Record Book reports, "His life was a long struggle." No portrait is known.

Da Costa's letter to Collinson was written "From the bottom of a Coal pit at Sanwich, Derbyshire 135 feet deep, 17th July 1747."

1. John Woodward (1665–1728), published *Attempt towards a Natural History of the Fossils of England.* London, 1729 (recognized the existance of strata, but thought fossils got mixed in the flood).

2. John Wilkins (1614–1672), Bishop of Chester, friend of John Evelyn and Samuel Pepys, helped found The Royal Society, wrote *A discourse concerning a new Planet . . .* 1640.

3. William Derham (1657–1735), wrote *Physico-Theology, or A Demonstration of the Being and Attributes of God, from His Works of Creation.* London, 1715.

4. Thomas Burnet (1635?–1715), Master of Charterhouse, wrote *The Sacred Theory of the Earth,* 1681, many subsequent editions.

ALS:N-YHS
London, August 3, 1747

My Dear Friend

I have taken the first opportunity to send you a Sample of your Indian History. The Dedication [to James Edward Oglethorpe[1]] was made without my Leave or consent, which makes mee uneasie. I was out of Town, & Mr Osbourn[2] was in hast to publish, & so it happen'd or Else the person I should have Choosen would have been Lord Lonsdale.[3]

Pray does Mr Barclay[4] continue amongst the Indians? Would he not be a proper person to give us some account of Their notions of the Diety & Futurity? Who can enough admire his Christian Resolution, the Almighty power that has Kindled such a Noble Ardour on his Soul, no doubt will Bless his Pious Endeavours. Some Hints of his proceedings & Success of his Mission will be very Acceptable to Mee. The progress of Piety & Vertue fills my Mind with Joye unspeakable.

I was agreeably delighted with thine of May the 11th, & I hope Bryants arrival will Establish my Credit. I am not yett able to send any remarks on Thy Cause of Gravitation. In Short I find the more it is Examined the more they are at a Loss what too offer & so in Short say nothing. But tho Wee are silent yett the oppertunities I have Lately had of sending it to most of the Capital places & universities in Europe, I perswade my Self Some or other will at Last saye Something for it or against It. I communicated thy Last Scheme to our Principle People in that Branch of Science & from one of them I Receed the Enclosed, but it is now with Mr Jones [not identified]. What I hear further I will report with Candour.

Butt I omitted giveing a hint of the Maleovolent Temper of a Certain great Mathemat'n amongst us on Reading thy Tract on Gravitation. He says, "I am amazed how this Book got to New York, for I am satisfied it came originally from Hence and was once under a Cover with other things, & the pacquet has been Gutted."[5]

This poor Man is a Little touched in his pericranium, So That I hope will Excuse Him.

Our people at the Helm are so taken up with Raiseing Supplies for the Warr & Choosing a New Parliamt that they haven't time to Think of you.

As I told you before, your Govrs [George Clinton] recommending you to his Majesties Favour I take to be Meer Amusement. When any place becomes Vacant in your Governt or any other Government or in the Customes, that is fitt for you or your Son, then Try your Great Man & see the Effect of his promise. He finds He cannot do without you & now he carresses you with Fair Speeches, but pray remember his first behaviour, then you was not worthy his Least Notice. This you may Excuse but cannot forget, So you will keep in with Him as He does with you for Interest, & this is the faith that is to be Kept with Courtiers, untill they appear of a Different Cast of Mind, & then Wee will receive them into our Bossoms.

Your Good Brothr [James] has two Sons, Hopefull men now in Town. He reserves a Little Money in my Hands to supply them if they Want. As I had a very Safe oppertunity as I thought by Governr Balcher[6] in his pacquet, I sent you your Brothers Discharge, which I hope will come Safe.

If you write by bitts & starts so must I or Else not write at all. As Such you have the Sincere Endeavours of your Affectionate friend,

P. Collinson.

Mr. Jones sends mee this Short Observation: "Colden is Mistaken in every part of his Conjectures. He mistakes Dr Bradley as to the principle."

From another Person I receiv'd this: "I am thankfull for Mr Coldens Paper, but to consider it thro' out will take more Time than I can conveniently spare. I shall only observe to you that I think he has mistaken Doctor Bradley, and therefore charged him with an Error in the first Foundation of his Theory, and which it appears to me that Mr Colden has fallen into, from his not considering that the Parallax is either insensible or very inconsiderable in different Parts of the Earths Orbit. His whole Objection and which he calls Doctor Bradlelys Slip is entirely founded on this."

October 20th 1747

I reced your Last with the Queries which I shall answer in Due Time. I have yours of July 24th under Consideration. I wish you could carry the point you Wish, but the Secretarys of State are so taken up with the Embarasments of our present uncertain Situation that Little notice can be taken of Colony affairs.

1. James Edward Oglethorpe (1696–1785), general, philanthropist and colonist of Georgia, encouraged friendly relations with the Indians in his colony and relied on their aid in defeating Spanish incursions from St. Augustine, Florida 1736–1743. (DNB)

2. Thomas Osborne (1738–1767), London bookseller and publisher. See "Thomas Osborne" in Nichols, John, *Literary Anecdotes of the Eighteenth Century,* edited by Colin Clair. Carbondale, 1967, pp. 264–267.

3. Henry Lowther, 3rd Viscount Lonsdale, (1713–1751).

4. Possibly Henry Barclay (1715–1764), Missionary of the Society for the Propagation of the Gospel and Minister of Trinity Church in New York City.

5. Probably William Whiston (1667–1752), wrote many theological and mathematical works. Was known to fall into trances. "A man of very acute, but ill-balanced intellect." (DNB)

6. Jonathan Belcher (1682–1757), Governor of Massachussets and New Hampshire 1730–1741 and of New Jersey 1746–1757. (DNB)

78 ❧ TO CARL LINNAEUS

ALS:LS

London, October 26, 1747

I had the pleasure of my Dear Friend Doctor Linnaeus Kind Letter by the hands of your good Theologus [not identified]. I shall gladly do him all the service in my power.

I am under great Obligations both to your Learned Royal Society & to you, for the Honour of your Nomination for a Member. But I think my Self no ways deserving that Favour, yett I shall submit my Self to your Disposal, and shall always retain a gratefull sence of your Friendship & good Intentions towards Mee.

I have sent you Mr Logans Dessertation on the Operation of the Farina on the Maize. As it is in Lattin, I recommend it to be read at a Meeting of your Learned Society.

The Treatise on Gravitation, by our Friend Doctor Colden of New York is a New System which He desires may be thoroughly Examined. I wish it had been wrote in Lattin to have been more universelly Read but as a great many of your Learned Men read English I hope it will be acceptable to some of them. Be so good as to present one of each of these

Books to the Royal Society in my name & I will send you more by first oppertunity. Our good Friend Mr Biork sayes he gave them to a Captain who sail'd about a Week agon.

I thank you for the several Curious Tracts you have sent me. I am greatly delighted with the Hortus Upsals.[1] I hope to send you some seeds, but pray contrive that they may come soone to your Hands and not lay a whole year undelivered. I shall with pleasure send you a pott with a Root of Collinsonia in it, by First Ship in the Spring.

I am pleased to see your Nov. Plant Genera.[2] I wish you had sent 2 books one for John Bartram & the other for Doctor Colden. I know they would be acceptable to them. I thank you for the Flora Zeylandica.[3] The seeds are not yet delivered to Mee. Now, my dear friend, farewell; and be assured that

I am truly yours   P. COLLINSON

I thank you for the Seeds. There is several Curious plants which will deserve a place in my Garden.

Doctor Dellenius was prosecuting, or Working att, the Pinax, when he Died. What will be its fate now I know not, for the present Professor [Humphrey Sibthorp] I don't think of Skill sufficient to under take it.

The North American Ursus I have often eat of it in England & think it is the most agreeable tast of all Flesh. My friend a Merchant had large young Bears brought over every year & fatted them with Dumplings & Sugar. It is really fine Eating & the Fatt is whiter & finer than the Fatt of Lambs.

Dr Mitchells System will be published under the Direction of Dr Trew at Nurembergh in a New Work called or intitled Ephemeridum Caesar.[4]

Have you seen Rudigers curious prints of Beasts published at Nurembergh?[5]

N:B. please to remember that one Letter enclosed in another & a Letter with a Cover pays here double postage. But 2 Letters wrote on the same sheet of paper pays but single postage.

My Garden is in great Beauty, for Wee have had no Frosts, a long dry, warm Summer & Autumn, grapes very ripe. The Vine yards turn to good profit, much Wine made this year in England. Sir Hans Sloane is Hearty, Miller is well, and so adieu.

This letter is written on one open side and around the margins of the sheet containing John Mitchell's 25 October 1747 letter (in Latin) to Linnaeus.

1. Hortus Upsaliensis . . . in *Theses and Orations,* 1745, published in book form at Stockholm, 1748.

2. *Nova Plantarum Genera.* Stockholm, 1747.

3. *Flora Zeylanica.* Stockholm, 1747.

4. *Acta Nat. Cur. Ephemerides* 8 (app) 187–224, 1748.

5. Ridinger or Riedinger, Johann Elias (1698–1767), published collections of copperplate engravings depicting horses, field sports, hunting scenes, birds with prey, and wild animals.

ALS : LS
London, March 27, 1748

My Dear Friend

I herewith send you Some of the Early Ripe Indian Corn.[1] I expect better Seed another year, but this may be Sufficient to make the Experiment. As it grows, draw the Earth up round its Lower Joints, from whence it makes New Roots. It loves a Rich Soil & Warm Situation.

The author Mr Blackstone[2] sends you this Book which you wanted Some Time agon. Sir Hans Sloane Continues Hearty & Well.

You promised Mee Some Books, but none are yett come to my Hands. Pray send Mee Corallia Baltica Iter Oelandicum et Gothlandicum,[3] Animalia Svecicae,[4] and any other Book of Natural History.

I am your sincere friend.

I have your Botanic Works & also your Flora Laponica,[5] which Sir Hans Sloane says the best Book of all your works.

I shall be obliged to you for specimens of the Various Species of Cochla Terres et fluviatiles et Nautilus testa recta & in Mare Balthica Concha N1330, 1331, 1332, 1335, 1336, 1337, 1347.

My good friend, I must tell you freely, though my Love is universal In Natural history, you have been in my Museum & seen my Little Collection & yet you have not sent Mee the Least Specimen of Either Fossil, Animal, or Vegetable. The Seeds & Specimens I have sent you from year to year, but not the least Returns. It is a General Complaint that Dr Linnaeus Receives all & Returns nothing. This I tell you as a Friend, and as Such I hope you'l receive It in Great Friendship. As I love & Admire you, I must tell you Honestly what the World sayes.

I am yours,

P. COLLINSON

I Desire your acceptance of Two Tracts from your Botanic Friend & admirer Dr Colden at New York. This work has mett with a very Good Reception & is much Esteemed by Many Curious Mathematicall People Here. Vale   PC

---

1. *Zea mays.* Linnaeus may have wanted to duplicate James Logan's experiment.

2. John Blackstone (1712–1753), a London apothecary and botanist. Wrote *Fasciculus Plantarum circa Harefield sponte Nascentium.* London, 1737 and *Specimen Botanicum,* 1746, which is probably the work referred to.

3. *Dissertatio, Corallia Baltica . . .* Uppsala, 1745.

4. *Animalia per Sveciam observata,* published in *Acta Literaria et Scientarvon svecial.* Uppsala, 1742.

5. *Flora Lapponica.* Amsterdam, 1737.

ALS: West Sussex Record Office
March 29, 1748

Tuesday Night

My Dear Lord

This day was sent to Bennett at Kingshead in the Borough 2 Basketts & 5 Bundles of Trees as by Inclosed Acct. Which I heartyly Wish you a pleasant Time of planting, but as for Mee I must be So unhappy as to Stay behind, but wether I catch'd Cold in coming to see you being my first going abroad from a tedious painfull Disorder. I was taken Ill on Tuesday & So continued with the return of a Gouty Humor which seizes both my Jaws & Teeth with Intolerable pain & Defluction that I can neither Eat or Sleep & then I believe it was Increased by A terrible fire so Near Us, that I was Obliged to gett & Call our people to send them to the relife of our Friends and indeed had the Wind sett our Way Wee Should have been in Eminent Danger.

But Thank God the Fitt att the heighth Sunday Noon [abated], my Salivation Left Mee & the Gout now has posession of my Foot. My Doctor [tells me] nothing is so Good as at this Juncture to Turn soft & gett fudl'd [on] Negus made with Old Crab Strong Hock to Drive this Terrible Invader from the [head] to the Heel. This is to Mee almost makeing the Remedy as bad as the Disease, but what can I do. I have born Two Strong Attacks in so short a Time. The Necessity has no Law, so my good Lord if you'l kindly contribute to the fud'ling your Friend perhaps in Some Secret corner of your Vault a Bottle or Two of this Old Stuff may be found, however such as will soon do my business I hope will answer the End.

I am with much pain your Affectionate friend,

P. COLLINSON

Apparently the Duke sent help, for a few days later Collinson wrote:

Fryday

ALS: West Sussex Record Office

I am very Glad my Dear Lord is return'd safe from Goodwood & had so good a Season for planting. I am Concern'd that the pines are so badly Rooted. However it happens I cannot say, but I am perswaded they have been Twice if not Thrice Removed. I will write to J. Miller for your Acct.

I am greatly Obliged for the Old Hock. I tryd the Experiment, & in a few Minutes drove with a Jehu the pain into my great Toe where it Exercised Mee smartly for 4 or 5 hours & then went off on a Sudden, & I am now as well as Ever.

Hope nothing will prevent a May Expedition, for I Long to See Goodwood.

I am under great obligations.

Truly yours,

P. COLLINSON

81 ❧ TO BENJAMIN FRANKLIN

ALS:LCP
London, April 12, 1748

Respected Friend

I was very fortunate to receive both thy Curious Experiments on Electricity. I have Imparted them to the Royal Society to whome they are very acceptable and they are now in the hands of our Ingenious Friend Mr Watson[1] Who has promised as soone as his accounts are printed to send them to Thee with a Letter and hopes for thy further Favours.

My Letters and Books for the Library Company by Mesnard Last fall was luckkly saved[2] and are in the hands of E. Bland to Come by this ship, which I Wish Safe to hand, and am thy Sincere friend

P. Collinson

Great Numbers of Ingenious Men are very Earnestly Engaged in Electrical Experiment in applying them to various purposes. I have lately seen a Letter from a Doctor of Physick att Turin[3] who gives 3 Instances of the Electrical power on Human Bodies By filling the Electrical Phyal with a purgative Portion and Transferring it into a Patient and it had all the Effects as if taken into the Stomach. The like account has been communicated from another Hand.[4]

I am much Obliged to thee for thine of Novr 28, 1747 with the pamphlets Inclosed[5] of which in my Next.

Doctor Mitchell has been out of Order himself this Winter, for His Wife was so very Ill he had near Lost Her. He desires his Kind Respects and Intends to Write by this Ship.

I am much Concern'd for the State of the Colonies Northward of you and for our friend Colden. As Mesnard was taken I conclude thine to Doctor Mitchell and Fothergill never came to hand [line missing].

Aprill 25 Wee have a Strong Report of a Peace. I wish it may prove True. Our Stocks are advanced 3 per Cent on it.

1. William Watson (1715–1787), FRS, physician, naturalist, and electrician. In 1745 he was awarded the Copley medal for his electrical research. His report on Franklin's papers was read to the Royal Society on January 11, 1750.
2. Capt. Stephen Mesnard's vessel was captured by the French.
3. Probably Giovanni Battista Bianchi (1681–1761), director of hospitals and professor of anatomy at Turin.

4. A letter in Latin on the subject from Johann Heinrich Winkler of Leipzig to Cromwell Mortimer, secretary of the Royal Society, was read in the Society, March 31, 1748, and printed in *Philosophical Transactions* XLV (1748): 262–70.
5. Franklin, Benjamin. *Plain Truth or serious considerations on the present state of the city of Philadelphia*. Philadelphia, 1747.

82 ❧ TO BENJAMIN FRANKLIN

ALS:UPa
London, June 14, 1748

Friend Franklin

The Bearer Mr Kalm[1] is an Ingenious Man and comes over on purpose to Improve himself in all Natural Inquiries. He is a Sweed per Nation and is as I am informed Im-

ployed by the Academy of Upsal to make Observations on your Parts of the World. I recommend Him to thy Favour and Notice.

By Him I send the first Vol. of the Voyage to Discover NorWest passage.[2] I hope the pacquett &c. sent under the Care of Hunt & Greenlease [not identified] is come safe to Hand.

I am thy sincere friend

P. COLLINSON

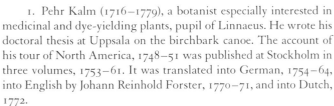

1. Pehr Kalm (1716–1779), a botanist especially interested in medicinal and dye-yielding plants, pupil of Linnaeus. He wrote his doctoral thesis at Uppsala on the birchbark canoe. The account of his tour of North America, 1748–51 was published at Stockholm in three volumes, 1753–61. It was translated into German, 1754–64, into English by Johann Reinhold Forster, 1770–71, and into Dutch, 1772.

To finance his expedition, Kalm applied for a travel grant from the Royal Academy of Sciences in Stockholm. He proposed to collect:

"1. Eight different kinds of oaks, which are very useful for building ships and other things;

2. Mulberry trees, which are useful for silkworms;

3. Vine trees or vines, which have good-tasting grapes, useful for making good wine;

4. Several kinds of chestnut and hazelnut trees with beautiful fruit;

5. Wild growing hemp, which the inhabitants use for making clothes for themselves;

6. A type of corn called fol. Avoine which grows wild in the moorlands; all say it is better than rice; the inhabitants use it; it grows in regions where the winter frost is hard . . . ;

7. An endless number of peas, which grow in the poorest soils;

8. Quite a number of medicinal plants . . . ;

9. Cedars and cypresses, sassafras;

10. Various kinds of roots, which the Indians use for bread and nourishment;

11. Maples, which in spring produce a sap with the Canadians use for making sugar;

12. A kind of bog myrtle . . . the green wax of which can be cooked, which is used to make green candles;

13. Several kinds of dyers' plants;

14. Not to speak of many other plants, of different kinds of grasses, which would be useful to the betterment of our meadows."

[Quoted in Ruoff, Eeva, "Plant trials of Pehr Kalm in Turku, 1751–1779," *Museol. sci. IX,* 1992 (1993): 249–263.] And see Koerner, Lisbet, *Linneaus: Nature and Nation.* Cambridge, MA, Harvard University Press, 1999, pp. 117.

2. Probably the first volume of Charles Swaine's *An Account of a Voyage For the Discovery of a North-West Passage by Hudson's Streights,* which was published in May 1748. (*Gentleman's Magazine* XVIII [1748]: 240).

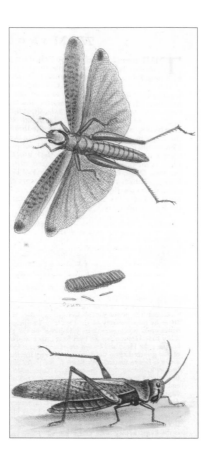

"The Great Brown Locust." George Edwards. Natural History of Birds, Vol II, plate 208.
"On the Fourth day of August, 1748, vast numbers of the great brownish Spotted Locusts settled in all parts of the City of London. . . ." The Library Company of Philadelphia

83 🐛 TO CADWALLADER COLDEN

ALS: N-YHS
London, August 25, 1748

I have very Little more to say to my Dear friend then to Inquire after his Welfare and Acquaint Him with Mine and to felicitate Him on the peace. The finishing Stroke Wee expect very Soone, but so many contending Interests have a multitude of Clothing [Closing?] articles to Settle. Wee have, thanks to the Bountifull Giver, a year of great plenty of all Sorts & Grain & fruits & a fine Harvest.

But a remarkable thing has happen'd, a Long Series of Easterly Winds the begining of this Month has brought a Swarm of Locusts amongst us. They fell very much in and about the Citty. Doctor Shaw[1] who resided many years in Africa Sayes they are some Species that come in such prodegious Swarms to infect that Country & where they Lite they devour all before them.

I wish they Lay not their Eggs & become a future pest Here.

As you make Little Excusions next year about the Country, pray think of your Botanic friends with a few Seeds of particular plants.

This is the Time of the Long Vacation. Every one is retreated to their Country Abodes so that Wee have Little Stirring of any thing thats Curious.

My Dear friend farewell. I am yours affectionately

P. COLLINSON

1. Thomas Shaw (1694–1751), "African traveler," FRS, wrote *Travels and Observations Relating to Several Parts of Barbery and Lev-* *ant.* Oxford, 1738, which described plants, mammals, insects, and "especially the Locust swarms." (DNB)

ALS:N-YHS
August 17, 1749

By Last ship I took Some Notice of my Dear Friends Letter of may 31st and by him sent in my Letter Mr [blank] proposals for fire Engines, for I did not think it prudent to buy one before you had some Intelligence about them.

Next I must tell you I am Confounded between Grasshopper, cicada & Locust. These Two last you tell Mee are very different. I always thought them the Same. Pray give orders to your people in the Country to Catch 2 or 3 of Each Species & pin them within side a Little Box, but first drown them in Spirits of Wine or Else they'l Live a Long while in pain with the pinn through them. Pray amidst your Numerous affairs don't forget this for I am Impatient to know the Difference.

I had the pleasure of yours of July 7th with the pacquet for Doctor Mitchell which I shall Deliver when He returns from Scotland with the Duke of Argyle.

I wish poor Kalm may get safe to Canada & back again. I wish He is not picked up [by] Some Straggling French Indians.

The Books you Desired I have procured and the Clover Seed as per accot. I gave Strict orders in writing that the Barrel of Clover Seed Should not be putt in the Hold of the Ship, for the Heat of that place very much Impairs if not totally Kills the Seed, the reasons I am perswaded you'll easily suggest without my Sentiments being straigtened for Time can only Add that I am your affectionate Friend

P. COLLINSON

1749 Aug 17: parcell books as by Bill	10: 2:0	
Clover Seed &c	3: 1:6	
Shipping Charges, bills Loadg & primage	9: 9	
	£ 13:13: 3	

85 ❧ TO BENJAMIN FRANKLIN

ALS:APS
London, February 5, 1750

I have so many Obligations to my kind Friend, that I dedicated a time to Visit all the Booksellers in London to search for foreign Electrical Books and could only find Two in French. One I take to be the same I sent for thy perusal but could not be certain which Elce [I] had not bought both for I sent it away just as I received it from France.

I have many Things to say but am att present so Engaged I cannot Collect my Thoughts together, but shall do it I hope by Next, for this is our busiest time a year shiping Goods to the plantations.

I have sent a parcell of books to Elias Blands[1] and thine with them.

The Guinea came safe. I wish I could have laid it all out to thy satisfaction. Pray what must I do with the remainder?

Your very Curious pieces relateing to Electricity and Thundergusts have been read before the [Royal] Society and have been Deservedly Admired not only for the Clear Intelligent Stile but also for the Novelty of the Subjects. I am collecting all these Tracts together: your first Account with the Drawings and your Two Letters in 1747 and your Two last Accounts with Intention to putt them into some printers Hand to be communicated to the publick.

The Almanack had many Things very Acceptable.

On the Books and Scheme of Education[2] more in my Next. It is much Approved. If some prizes was given annually to the greatest proficients on a publick Day in presence of the Magistrates, Governors, &c. it stimulats greatly and begets a Laudable ambition to Excel which produces surprising Effects. In short my Dear Friend I scrawl any thing. Thy Candor will excuse and thy Ingenuity will find out my Meaning.

Your American Electrical Operator seems to putt ours out of Countenance by his Novelty and Variety. Certainly something very usefull to Mankind will be found out by and by.

Douglasses and Elliots Essays[3] are productive of many pretty Entertaining Articles which I read with pleasure and the Elephant by [blank] [not located] has its Admirers.

I shall be glad to hear the Books come safe and print of London &c. I am now out of Town to shake off the Citty Dust so have not my Memorandums with Mee so my Dear friend fare well. Its Late and I am Tired. Thine   P. COLLINSON.

But I must add that on Thursday the Fifth Day of the Week on the 8 Instant at about 20 Minutes past 12 at Noone, Wee felt a very Surpriseing Shock of an Earthquake. It was more sensible and Violent in some places than others. To Mee and many others it seem'd as if a Bale of Heavy Goods had fell down by Accident at my Next Neighbours and shook my House which sometimes Happens. But a Friend of Mine whose House is near the Thames, hear'd (as did others) a Loud rumbling sound like cannon at a distance and then so Terrible a shock ensued that he instantly ran out of Doors, thinking his new House was tumbled about his Ears. There is an Endless Variety of Relations about its Effects but its certain Extent and Direction is not yet known, but accounts came that Day that it was felt from Twickenham on the Thames to Greenwich. I dont find any people that was rideing or Walking was sensible of It. At my House in the Country 10 Miles North of London near Barnet it was not felt nor in our Neighbourhood.[4]

1. Elias Bland, London Quaker merchant who apprenticed under John Reynall of Philadelphia before 1743. Dealt often with Benjamin Franklin.

2. Franklin's *Proposals Relating to the Education of Youth in Pensilvania.* Philadelphia, 1749.

3. Douglass, William. *A Summary, Historical and Political, of the first Planting, Progressive Improvements, and Present State of the British Settlements in North-America,* first published at Boston in separate numbers, 1747–48. The first bound volume appeared in 1749, the second in 1751. The first two parts of Jared Eliot's, *Essays upon Field-Husbandry* appeared in 1748 and 1749 respectively.

4. Reports of this earthquake fill the whole of No. 497 of *Philosophical Transactions* XLVI (1749–50): 601–750.

86 ❧ TO PIETER CAMPER

ALS: University of Amsterdam Library
February 23, 1750

My Dear Friend Dr Kemper

I was unwilling to send you a bare Letter of Thanks & Complements with out Some Thing to Entertain you. I think my Friends accot of the Pholas[1] is more Satisfactory than any I have Mett with. I wish it may prove so to you. I had not time to Transcribe it fair so hope you will Excuse It with all its Blots.

The Honour you have confer'd on Mee in your Dedication[2] Deserves my Most Gratefull ackonwledgemt.

I am Conscious that through an Excess of Politeness & friendship you have bestowed too much on your Friend, but it may have this good Effect on Mee, that for the future I may Endeavour to Deserve It. I thank you for your Kind Letter which Was very Obligeing.

My Family Joyns With Mee in our Sincere Respects; It is with much pleasure I Cherish the Hopes of Seeing you again Here. To None you will be More Wellcome than to your affectionate Friend   P. COLLINSON

I presume you heard of the smart Shock of an Earthquake the 8 Instant, a Rare Phenomea in England. You may depend on all my Interest at the [Royal] Society. Such as it is, you will Command It.

Poor Catesby is dead. I advised our Worthy Learned Friend Dr Gronovius Last post.

We have had the Mildest Warmest Weather from Xmas to this Time. Our Elm Hedges are Green, our Gardens full of Flowers of Aprill. I am very Busie removeing my old Garden to my New Garden 10 Miles from London. Vale   PC

I don't know how to send you any Seeds for your garden.

PIETER CAMPER (1722–1789), Dutch anatomist and naturalist. He spent a year in England, 1748, and visited a second time in 1752.

1. Collinson's letter follows a transcription of John Payne's August 8, 1749 description "on the Shell Fish you call Phola's, but I think agreeable to Its Nature it may be Named the Piscis Terebellum or Wimble Fish, from its Boreing into such Masses of Chalk & Hard Stone as I have seen . . ."

2. Linnaeus, Carl "*Amoenitates Academicae, seu Dissertationes variae Physicae* . . . V. Lugduni Batavorum . . . 1749. Edited by Pieter Camper and dedicated to "Petro Collinson."

87 ❧ TO ARTHUR DOBBS

ALS: Public Record Office of Northern Ireland
London, March 10, 1750

I have been long in expectation of seeing my Good Friend Here as Usual. I have had a packet from Pennsilvania has lain by mee Some Months for your Comeing, but as you dont intend Us that Pleasure I will Send it to Mr. Smiths [not identified] & Come [word incomplete] to be Sent by their Conveyance.

I was Glad at the Sight of yours, for now all my Doubts & fears are dessipated. It is very fortunate for our friend Bartram that all his Cargoes in Ireland & Engld came Safe. I have I think a dozen Boxes more ordered this year, all new people, so you may see how the Laudable Spirit of planting prevails Here.

The Cargo of living plants are Curious Sorts, the great Chamoe Rhododendron may be Easily known by its thick Laurel like Leaves. It grows in their Mountains in a Cold Region where there is frequent Rains & Springs. The Rose Laurel is remarkable for its Leaves being of a Laurel figure but Less and of a Blewish Cast on their back Sides [*Kalmia angustifolia*]. The Sweet Service is a pretty forward Tree with Small oval Leaves & white Blossoms is now in flower in my Garden.

I have the Same Account from others that above Ten Thousd Germans came to

Pennsilvania besides what went to the other Colonies. Certainly the Germans Princes are blind to Suffer the Riches of their Country to go out by thousands, but the oppresssion of the Last Warr & their princes & preists drives these poor wretches at any rate to gett from under Such Tyranny.

Wee have had as Well as you No Winter Except a few frosty Mornings at Xmas. All has been Mild & Warm Since to Surprising Degree & Wee have had the least Rain fell Since June Last that Ever was remembered & No Snow. The Barges could not come down the Rivers, Wells was Empty, & our ponds wants filling, but our fields have had all this Winter the most Deleghtfull Verdure as in May & the Grass in our Rich Grounds is higher then I have known Some years in April & May. The Corn [wheat] of all kinds is very prosperous. Wether God Intends this for a Blessing or a Scourge time well Shew, for if Late Frosts & Blasts Should Ensue all our Hopes will Vanish. We had a Specimen the Last Day of Feby, So Smart a Frost happen that it is Said there was not So thick Ice any Time this Winter. A Second Night would have demolishd, but delightfull Weather has been ever Since.

No Doubt but you heard of our Earth quake. The Shock was Very Violent. Multitudes ran out of their Houses thinking them falling. It was preceded with Distant rumbling Noise. Some Slight Damages happen'd to Old Houses & Chimnies. Before & Since has been auroras, one to the South & Two to the North. Its Extent from West to East was from Twickenham to Greenwich and about 4 Miles North & South of the Citty, but that Seem'd to be the Center of its Effects.

The Ohio Company [1] goes on briskley. A great Quantity of Goods & fine Cloths for presents are gone to Engage our New Allies to be firm to our Interest. The French have Sent threatening Letters to all our Governs not to suffer our people to come Near their

Bounds, which they have taken Care to make Large Enough. It is an old Observation they have gett more by Treaties then by Warr. So it may be most politick for our Commissars to Evade Comeing to the point but Invent Delays untill Wee have gott sufficiently Secured in our New Settlements & then Lett [missing].

Our Friend Hanbury has been So engaged in Marrying his Daugh & many other Ways that it is possible he may forget to answer yours however I will Endeavor to remind Him.

At our [Royal] Society Wee have had Little of Moment Except Electrical Experiments & some curious Mathematical papers.

I am glad to hear Some Germans are gone to your Estate in No Carolina & other Colonies, for Pensilvania will be over done by them. There has been with Mee Two Agents who are gone over to procure a party for Maryland, for Lord Baltimore is very desirous of them & gives them great Encouragement, for he plainly Sees by the Neighboring Colony of what consequeance they are to a proprietor.

I never was within Scots stove [hothouse] So Cannot answer for their Contrivance.

Pines [pineapples] are in great demand Here, so many Gentlemn build Stoves, and Indeed of all the foreign fruits Wee have yett tasted this only deserves the Expense & preference. Year old plants are to be had from Sixpence to half a Crown according to their Sizes. Two year old Fruiting plants from 5:6 to 6:6. The best Way of Transporting them is to pack them in Very Dry Moss heads & tails in a Box bored with Small Holes on all sides. Thus I had them come from Barbadoes in fine order.

Wee had again the Same Day Month the 8th Instant at half past Five in the Morning another Astounding Shock of an Earth Quake which Shook Violently the Citty & the Country all Round Longer & Smarter than before. God only knows the Event of these Shocking Phenomena.

I am my Dear Friend much Yours   P. COLLINSON

As you have had a great deal of Stormy Weather the Sea may have thrown up much of its hidden Treasure. Pray order Somebody to pick up what Ever they can find and in your Digging and Delving what Fossells are thrown up Lay them by for Mee.

When any oppertunity offers pray Send an Accot how your protestant Schools goes on & what premium are Given by the Dublin Society for Improvmt & Arts & Sciences.[2] I am much Delighted with Sr Coxs[3] Letter to Prior. I have Sent Some to america to Encourage New Beginers in any branch of Improvement.

ARTHUR DOBBS (1689–1765), born at Castle-Dobbs, County Antrim, Ireland, died at Town Creek, North Carolina, Governor of North Carolina 1754–65. He investigated insect pollination of flowers and published in *Philosophical Transactions,* "Concerning Bees and their Method of Gathering Wax and Honey, 1750." Long interested in Arctic exploration, Dobbs was convinced that there was a Northwest Passage and in the 1740s persuaded the Admiralty to organize an expedition of discovery. (DNB; and see Clarke, Desmond. *Arthur Dobbs, Esquire, 1689–1765.* Chapel Hill, N.C., 1957, and Rankin, D. H. and E. C. Nelson, editors *Curious in Everything: The Career of Arthur Dobbs of Carrickfergus, 1689–1765.* Carrickfergus, 1990).

Collinson wrote John Bartram (June 30, 1764), "I hear my Friend Dobbs at 73 has gott a Colts Tooth in his Head & has married a young lady of 22. It is now in vain to write to Him for seeds or plants of Tipitiwichet [*Dionaea muscipula,* L., Venus's fly trap] now He has gott one of his Own to play with." (ALS:HSP)

1. Ohio Company: organized in 1749 upon a grant sanctioned (but never made) by George II of 500,000 acres generally N.W. of the Ohio and to the eastward between the Monongahela and the Kanawah Rivers. The Company had two purposes, to secure English control of the Ohio Valley, then in dispute between England and France, and as a commercial project for trade with the Indians. Its members included Virginians and English, among them Thomas Lee, two of George Washington's brothers, and John Hanbury.

2. Dublin Society for the Promotion of Agriculture, Manufactures, Arts, and Sciences, founded in 1731 by Thomas Prior (1682?–1751).

3. On May 15, 1749 Sir Richard Cox, proprietor of a linen manufactury at Dunnanway, Co. Cork, wrote Thomas Prior "shewing from experience a sure method to establish the linen manufacture, and the beneficial effects it will immediately produce." (DNB)

ALS: APS

London, April 25, 1750

I wish I have before this advised my Worthy Friend that his pacquet per Cap. Clark came at last to my Hands, with the Electrical Papers, which are now on the Press under the Inspection and Correction of our Learned and Ingenious Friend Doctor Fothergill, for Wee thought it a great Pitty that the Publick should be deprived the benefit of so many Curious Experiments.[1]

Great Doctors will differ as may be seen by the Inclosed Paper from Mr. Watson Which was read some Time after thy papers had been communicated to the Society, who was greatly pleased with them and Desired their Thanks for so kind a Communication.

Abbe Nolet[2] has been at the pains to Travel on purpose to Turin, to Venice and Bologna to see those Experiments Verified of Giveing Purges, Transfusion of Odours and Cureing the Gout &c. but to his great Surprise found very Little or no Satisfaction. The Ingenious Men in those Cities had been too premature in publishing for Facts, Experiments [which] if they did once succeed, could not be depended on for Certainty to do again, to the no small Disappointment of Abbe Nolet, Who Indeed could never make them do, but thought they might have a Knack in performing those Operations that He was Ignorant Off.

I am Obliged to thee for the Constitutions.[3] They are very Rational and well Calculated for the Purposes Intended. I am glad to find so Laudable an Institution Meets with such Encouragement.

Wee have had Heithertoo the Warmest and Mildest Winter and Spring that Ever was known. Our Apricots and Peaches are sett Like ropes of Onions, and the Face of plenty smiles Every Where. But our Neighbours complain Spain, Portugal and South of France by this Long Warm Dry Season are like to Loose their Crops of Corn unless suddenly retrieved by Rain. Our Wheat is risen on this News.

I have seen no Snow and Scarsly any Ice, and Winter has been Insensibly Lost in a very Early Spring, but yett as the Season has been so agreeable on one Hand, yett on the other it may have furnish'd Materials or putt them in Action to the Great Surprise of all that Felt four Earthquakes, the 8th feby and March at London and then at Portsmouth and the Isle of Wight, and Since at Chester and Liverpool.

Divers Hypotheses's are advanced to solve these Phenomena, Hales I send.[4] Others have been read before the Society wholy Accounting for it on the principle of Electricity. Others presume as Wee have had a very Long Dry Time for 6 months past, the Caverns are Exhausted of the Water, Air has Supplyed its Roome. This had putt the Beds of pyri[tes] in a Ferment. Such unusuall Warmth has Rarified it, an Explosion Ensued. Thus in short Hints my good friend take it as I can give, and be assured I am thine.

P COLLINSON

1. *Experiments and Observations on Electricity, Made at Philadelphia in America* . . . London, 1750.

2. Jean Antoine Nollet, Abbé, "An Examination of Certain Phenomena in Electricity, published in Italy." *Philosophical Transactions* XLVI (1749–1750): 370–97, was read in the Royal Society, March 29, 1750.

3. *Constitutions of the Academy of Philadelphia.* See *Franklin* III, 421–8.

4. Stephen Hales (1677–1761), wrote *Some Considerations on the Causes of Earthquakes.* London, 1750, read in the Royal Society, April 5, 1750, and printed in *Philosophical Transactions* XLVI (1749–50): 669–81.

ALS:Erlangen
London, April 5, 1751

To My Dear & Esteemed Friend Dr Trew

It was with great pleasure I received your Favour of the 10th Novembr ulto.

You Do Mee great Honour by the Several Rare & Curious presents you have sent Mee, all which Demonstrate that you are the great Patron of Learning and Curiosity. I hope on my part I shall never be ungratefull and forget the Liberality of the Donor.

It is with admiration I see the pains you have taken, and with what critical Exactness, you have settled, the Class of the fine Lillio Narcissus with a Red Flower. I believe that with a purple & white Flower is a nondescript, but your great knowledge in Botanic Learning will soone settle that point.

The curious Here very deservedly admire the Elegance & Beauty of the Flowers and Fossills etc in this New Methode of Colouring them so Exactly after the Life, but it is with regret wee see the Shells so mixed together, as if intended for Pictures for Ornament for Ladies Clossetts. Had they been intended for the improvement of Natural History, every Genus & Species should have been Classed by themselves, then at one view, what Additions & Improvements, had been made to this New Work would have been readly seen, but now Great Trouble & perplexity will attend consulting the Index & then what Difficulty to bring, & (comprehend) the variety of Species of one Genus Scater'd through Every page.

It is with great Delight I see the fine Portrait of my Dear Friend, a man to whome the Learned World are Indebted for the Great pains He has taken to Instruct & Improve Mankind.

Long May you live to Enjoye the Best Wishes of your affectionate Friend

P. COLLINSON.

Lilio Narcissis. *Georg Dionysius Ehret. Natural History Museum, Botany Library, London.*

Last year I sent you a present of Roots of the Famous Gensing, but I never heard if you received them.

The Index to the Commerciam Litterarium and the Title page is much wanted. It is a great pitty so Capital a Work should be left so imperfect. Can it be an Honour to the Editors.

All the parcells for you and Mr Beurer sent by Mr Ehret and a Token from my Self with parcells & Letter for Mr Beurer, are all this Day inclosed in a Box directed for you & sent to the care of Messrs Kruger & Grote to come by first Ship. Vale my Dear Friend London Aprill 18th, 1751.

Mr Ehret is well and is now settled at Oxford.

It a little surprises Mee that your The Curious Works of Flowers, Plants & Shells & Fossills in their Natural Colours & Mr Rosels Work of Insects,[1] are so little known att Paris, for Mr Buffons at the Head of the vurtuosi writes Mee word by last post that He had not so much as heard of them. It may be of great advantage if the Editors & authors of those Elegant Works was to send their proposals & have them Inserted in the publick Gazetts at Paris.

1. AUGUST JOHANN ROESEL VON ROSENHOF (1705–1759), published *Insecten-Belustigung.* Nuremburg, 4 vols, 1746–1761.

90 ❧ TO JOHN FREDERICK GRONOVIUS

ALS: Hunt
[1751]

My Dear Friend, I can learn very little certain of the Cortex Peruvianus for Wee have nothing certain printed about It. This is certain that the Quina Quina which was the first febrifuge of the Jesuits is quite a different plant from the Cortex now in use.[1] By the Specimens I have seen It is a species of Lilac and may be named Lilac Peruvianus flore Coccineo.

Dr Mortimer our Secretary[2] has collected Materials for a History of this curious plant and made Variety of Drawings of Its Leafe flowers & Seed Vessell &c but is in hopes of more accurate Accounts & then He will communicate them to the R. Society.

Condemine[3] is the last that has mentioned it in print that Wee know off. I have made all the Inquiry I can but to Very Little purpose. Its place of Growth & its effects wee know but there is a many other particulars required to give a general History of It.

Pray give my Respects to Dr Breyne & his Grandson. I sent you Bartrams Journal per Mr. Slawter [Schlatter] which I hope is come safe to hand. I am with sincere Respects Truly yours

P. COLLINSON.

Pray if an oppertunity offers Buy the plants as under for Mee & send by any Friend:

4 Roots of Geele Franse Roos Narcissus
4 Roots of Narcis campanelle flo Luteo Reflexo
4 Do—of—Camp—flo Albo reflexo

Cortex Peruvianus, *"Cinchona." "Drawn by Santisteban" and sent to Linnaeus, according to Collinson. The Linnean Society of London.*

1 D—of Moly purpureo Major
2 Narcisus Nana Minor—2 Stvven Stuck
2 Ranunculus fol plantagines
12 Duc Vanloe Tulips

This I had formerly from Van Hassen [Jacob van Huysum?][4] but in removing my garden lost them. All the Charges I will repay with thanks.

1. Quinine, an alkaloid contained in cinchona bark. It is a specific antidote to malaria, against which it also possesses a powerful prophylactic action.

The earliest authenticated instance of the medicinal use of cinchona bark is found in the year 1638 when the countess of Chinchon, the wife of the governor of Peru, was cured of an attack of fever by an infusion made from the bark. The medicine was recommended in her case by the corregidor of Loxa who had experienced its virtues eight years earlier.

Knowledge of the bark was disseminated throughout Europe by members of the Jesuit brotherhood, whence it became generally known as Jesuits' bark. According to one account the name arose when its value was discovered by a Jesuit missionary prostrate with fever who was cured when an Indian gave him a drink prepared from the bark. In each of those cases the fever was probably malaria.

Until 1867 English manufacturers of quinine were entirely dependent upon South America for their supplies of cinchona bark, which were obtained from uncultivated trees growing chiefly in Bolivia, Peru, and Ecuador. Subsequently, cultivation of the trees was commenced in Indonesia, India, and Jamaica. Chemical synthesis was achieved in 1944. [EB]

2. Cromwell Mortimer (d. 1752), physician, secretary to the Royal Society 1730–1752. (DNB)

3. M. de la Condamine, "Sur L'Arbre du Quinquina," 226 *Mémoires de l'Academie Royale.* Paris, 1738.

4. Jacob Van Huysum (1687?–1746), flower painter, brother of the celebrated Amsterdam flower painter Jan Van Huysum. Jacob came to England in 1721 and was patronized by Robert Walpole. He did illustrations—among the first to be printed in color—for the Society of Gardeners' *Catalogus plantarum: a catalog of trees, shrubs, plants and flowers . . . which are propagated for sale in the gardens near London.* London, 1730.

ALS:MdHS

February 20, 1752

I am greatly obliged to Mrs. Golsborough for her kind Present of the Pretty Huming bird. The Singularity of the Red Feathers has not been Observed before in the hen. Does not your little Negro Boyes Some times mett with their Nest & Eggs which must certainly be very Curious.

I had a friend in Pensilvania that brought up a nest of young Huming Birds in order to send to Mee by Giving them Honey & Water untill they could feed themselves and on my friends holding a Tea Spoon with Honey & Water in her Mouth the Birds would Come on the Wing & with their long tongues dipped up the Liquor & this they'd do at a Call. I only relate this as a Curiosity. My friends Intention was good, but it was Impossible to send them here Alive.

Now you'l want to know what became of the Birds, why they Continued in this Pretty manner untill autumn and then comes an Old Huming Bird & flutters at the Window of

Humming Bird—"the Least Humming Bird," George Edwards. Natural History of Birds, Vol II, plate 105. The Library Company of Philadelphia.

"The Bird . . . weighed not over twenty Grains when just killed. Mr Benjamin Cowel obliged me with this Bird, and Mr. P. Collinson with the Egg; they were brought from Jamaica."

the Roome (where they was Kept for Several Days) & in a Language they understood told them its certain "you have been well Entertain'd where you are, but if you have a Mind to go with your Father & Mother & your Friends the Time is come, give your Kind Nurse the Slip the first time She opens the Door to feed you."

They took the Hint & flew out & perch'd on a Tree Near Here but all Her temptations was in vain. Instinct got the Prevalence & away they Flew.

These Seeds Loves a rich Deep Soil.

But the Angelica Loves a Moist one. It always grows on the Sides of Running Water. If it is sown on a Bed in the Garden & Water'd in an Evening & when the Plants are Strong plant them out in Moist Places.

I will remember to send you Some Polyanthos Seed, but anemonys & Ranunculas must be had from Roots sent in the Autumn.

I hear your Son is Well.

I am with respects to you and Mr Goldsborough your Sincere & Obliged friend,

P. COLLINSON, in hast.

HENRIETTA MARIA (TILGHMAN) ROBINS GOLDS-BOROUGH (1707–1771), of Peach Blossom, Talbot County, Maryland. Married in 1731 to Collinson's friend George Robins, she was widowed and subsequently married Judge William Goldsborough.

(Bevan, Edith Rossiter. "Gardens and Gardening in Early Maryland." *Maryland Historical Magazine* XLV No. 4 (December 1950): 27)

Draft ALS:LS
October 9, 1752

This Gentleman's General plan of a Rural Garden [not found] is most agreeable to Nature & what is so will always please.

It is a pity He had not decended to perticulars & given us Hints how We are to Embellish Nature by plantations where they are wanting to conect the whole of his Scheme together.

Who can without pleasure survey the Rising Groves & Clustering Thickets that adorn our Chaces & Forests but without reflecting from whence does this Delight arise, Either from their Situation or the Different Gradations of Growth with the Mixture of Trees etc. with their Various Shades of Green, perhaps all compounded objects.

Every one that would Beautifully imitate Nature should Well Consider the Diversity of growth of Trees and think the Sizes & Shapes of their Leaves & their many Shades of Greens to know how properly to Dispose and Mix them in planting which is another means of painting with Living Pencils, for Greens properly Disposed throw in a Mixture & Contrast of Lights and Shades which wonderfully Enliven the Picture and these which insensibly strike the Sences with wonder & Delight.

The Effect must be Charming to see the Dark Green Elm with the Lighter Shades of the Lime & Beach, or the yellowish Green planes with the Silver Leafed Abele, the Chestnut, the oak and ash & the poplar, the Acacia & Horse Chestnut, *cum multis aliis,* (these blended Greens Plantation) when Fann'd by a Gentle Breeze then how Beautifully the Contrast, how Delightfully the Light & Shades fall In to Diversifie the Sylvan Scene.

This Mixture of Trees is no Trifleing affectation but arises from the Spontaneous acts of Nature. No one that has a Tast in planting but in his Travels must have been struck with admiration at seeing a Variety of Trees in Consort Blended together in our Chases and Forests.

These observations lead the late Noble Lord Petre at Thorndon in Essex to Coppy Beautifull Nature in his beautiful plantations on Each side, enriched with the Trees of America from the Lodge in the Great Avenue up to the Esplanade at the Head of the Park. These was his first Essays or I may call them, but Lines of the Grand Picture. Had he Lived, the Vast Variety of Materials that He had collected together would have shown with what a Masterly & Skillful hand he would have given the finishing Strokes to his Extensive plans.

This Blending of Shades has the Like good Effect on the Ever Greens, the Pines and Firrs, the Yew and the Varegated Holley & Philerea &c &c. How beautifull the Scene when suffer'd to grow unconfined in Groves & Thickets.

All Flowering Shrubs may be thus Diversified with Tast & Elegance as they now Enter so much into Rural Plantations.

These are Hints Borrowed from Nature so cannot fail of their Desired good Effect and may be so much improved when Executed by a Skillful Ingenious hand.

A gent [Duke of Richmond] that has a Villa [Goodwood, Sussex] planted on Every Side with Exoticks collected by a person [John Bartram] sent by mee into America [obscure] black & white Spruce, Firrs, Clump Scotch pines, Silver Balm Gilead Spruce & Cornish Firrs, Cedars, Junipers & Cypresses, this painting in planting to show the contrast of Lights & Shadow.

As I rode through the Park with what Pleasure I surveyed the Rising Groves and Clustering thickets & reflected from whence does this Delight arise, Either from their Situation, different gradations of Growths or the Mixture of Trees & their Various Shades of Greens. This delightfull Confusion of objects so blended by Nature is the Great plan & original from whence wee are to Copy, & the nearer Wee approach to Her, Wee shall be sure always to please.

Every one that would in the most Elegant Manner forme his Design of Planting from Nature should be well Experienced in the diversity of growths of Trees & shrubs & their Different shades of Greens etc. etc.

PHILIP SOUTHCOTE (1698–1758), bought Woburn Farm, near Weybridge Surrey, in 1735 and created a landscape garden there in the "Ferme Ornée" style which he helped develop. (Desmond)

"Painting with Living Pencils" long interested Collinson. In 1741, he wrote Bartram:

Last yr Ld. Petri planted out about Tenn thousand Americans which being at the Same Time mixed with about Twenty Thousand Europeans, and some Asians make a very beautiful appearance, great Art & skill being shown in consulting Every one's particular growth and the well blending the Variety of Greens, Dark green being a great Foil to Lighter ones and Bluish green to yellow ones and those Trees that have their Bark and back of their Leaves of white or silver make a beautifull contrast with the others. The whole is planted in thickets & Clumps and with these Mixtures are perfectly picturesque and have a Delightfull Effect. (September 1, 1741; ALS:HSP)

93 🦤 TO CHRISTOPHER JACOB TREW

ALS:Erlangen
London, November 15, 1752

Honored Friend Dr Trew

I am obliged to you for your favour of the 30th September. It really gives me concerne that I should forget the Title of the papers I sent you, for I really thought it was the Vires plantarum.[1] I went & carried your letter to Dr Mitchell & requested Him to lett Mee have the Vires plantarum to compleat your 50 exemplairs. His answer was that he intended to make great aditions to that Work his first leisure. I know he is full of Employe and I have little or no hopes of his compleating It, so I pressed Him then the more to lett Mee have It as it was. He then putt Mee off, untill next Spring.

My Dear Friend, I am sorry it happens so. Unfortunately (at Present) it is not in my power to help It, but this I will assure you, I will not forget to remind Dr Mitchell when your Next Box goes in the New year, to trye if I can prevail with Him to send the Veres plantarum in it.

The next Thing that troubles Mee Is the Damage Hills Work[2] sustained, but Wee had a Long Wett summer which spoilt many sorts of Goods after they was taken out of the ship. For the time to come I will have the bottome of the Boxes stoped with Pitch or Rosin to keep out the Water. This would have been (very probably) prevented If you had thought to have asked my Opinion of Hills Botanic Work before you sent for It, for really It is such a wretched performance that I believe you never would have bestowed so much Money on the Printed Book that has so little in it to Deserve Illumination.

On the 5th of September Mr Osborn bookseller sent mee a Box of books directed for you. I sent it directly to Messrs Kruger & Groot to be sent by the First ships.

Next time what Books or Goods you want, send your Orders directly to Mee that I may Buy them & Pack them up my self in the Box, for I may have Little things to send you or Mr Beurer. Mr Osborns Box I was Obliged to open to putt in the seed etc.

For the Things you Desire give Mee an Order for the Money on Kruger & Groot.

I do assure you my Dear Friend I shall think it no Trouble but a pleasure to serve you who, your self, take so much pains to serve the publick.

Soon will be delivered the First book of the Philosophical transactions, published by the Order & under the Direction of the Royal Society. Before it was the Act of the Secretaries, for which the Society is no ways answerable for any Faults.

Our president Mr Folks[3] continues so Weak by a paralytick disorder that he will resign, and the Right Honorable the Earl of Macclesfield will be choosen in his Roome, a very Learned Man.[4]

Our Worthy Friend Sir Hans Sloane is very Hearty & Well, for his great age.

You see by the French Papers how farr the French have verified Mr. Franklins doctrine of Points, to unload a Thunder Cloud, of all Its combustable Matter, for they have Erected Iron Rods Pointed on their Churches, Towers & Magazines, for that purpose.

As I said before Wee had a very Wet summer but for Two Months past have had the finest Warm, dry Weather ever known, our Harvest good & great plenty of Every Thing.

I shall add a list of Curious books Lately printed on Medicine, Natural History, &c. If you approve of any of them they may be sent in your Next Order, Inclosed to Mee.

Now my Dear Friend I shall conclude with my sincere Wishes for your preservation & am your Affectionate Friend,   P. COLLINSON

Dr Parsons Observations, a very Curious book	8vo[5]
Dr Huxhams Epidemicks 2 vls	8vo[6]
Dr Pringle on Camp Diseases	8vo[7]
Dr Simpson on Vital Motion	8vo[8]
Capt Ellis Voyage to Hudsons Bay Curious	8vo[9]
Mr Coldens New principles of Action on Matter (with great additions & Emendations)	4o[10]
Dr Whytt on Vital Motion	8vo[11]
Dr Huxham on Fevers	8vo[12]
Dr Meads Monita	8vo[13]
Mr Armstrongs Natural History of Minorca	8vo[14]
The Life of Dr Swift by Lord Orrey	8vo[15]

A Monthly book price Sixpence Intitled the Gentlemans Magazine contains Variety of Miscellanious subjects in Physick or Medicine, Natural History, Mechanicks & Mathematicks &c which I believe will prove an Entertainment to you & is much in Request Here.

I went to Mr Manby & He told Mee that the ship was in the River that had your Box on Board and that as soon as He gott it Delivered He would write you a Letter.

I believe Mr Ehret is Well but he lives at the Court-End of our great Citty, above 3 Miles from Mee. He is fully Employed in teaching Painting & drawing.

I very much desire seed of White, Red & yellow Flowers Pulsatilla. The Blew Flower grows spontaneously Here in England, but Wee have no other Colours.

I beg this favour you will please to Give my Love & Respects to my Good Friend Mr Burer.

1. Probably referring to John Mitchell's *Nova Plantarum Genera,* 1741.

2. This was probably Sir John Hill's *A History of Plants,* 1751.

3. Martin Folkes (1690–1754), elected President of the Royal Society in 1741.

4. George Parker, 2nd Earl of Macclesfield (1697–1764).

5. Parsons, James (1705–1770). *Philosophical Observations on the Analogy between the Propagation of Animals and that of Vegetables.* London, 1752.

6. Huxham, John (1692–1768). *Observationes de Aere et Morbis Epidemicis.* 2 vols 1st edition 1731; 2nd edition 1752.

7. Pringle, Sir John (1707–1782). *Observations on the Diseases of the Army.* London, 1752.

8. Simson, Thomas (1696–1764). *Enquiry on the Vital and Animal Actions.* London, 1752.

9. Ellis, Henry (1721–1806). *Voyage to Hudson's Bay . . . for Discovering a Northwest Passage.* London, 1748.

10. Colden, Cadwallader. *The Principles of Action in Matter.* London, 1751.

11. Whytt, Robert. *On the Vital and other Involuntary Motions of Animals.* London, 1751.

12. Huxham, John. *An Essay on Fevers and Their Various Kinds.* London, 1750.

13. Mead, Richard. *Monita et Praecepta Medica.* London, 1751.

14. Armstrong, John. *The History of the Island of Minorca.* London, 1752.

15. Boyle, John, 5th Earl of Orrery (1707–1762). *Remarks on the Life and Writings of Jonathan Swift.* London, 1751.

94 ❦ TO CHRISTOPHER JACOB TREW

ALS:Erlangen
London, January 18, 1753

To my Honored Friend Dr Trew

To whome I am under Infinite Obligations, for His many Favours & Noble Presents, Especially for the Lively Portrait of my Dear Friend [Trew], which will perpetually Smile on Mee, and remind Mee of our Friendship, as well as reproach Mee, If I am [or] can be guilty of Ingratitude to so Generous a Benefactor.

Your Favour of Sepr 30th was very acceptable. It will give Mee pleasure if I can do you any Services, my proffessions are few, but sincere, so I will next proceed to give what answers I can to your several Queries but first I must give you my sincere Thanks, for your Kind presents, the Continuation of the Select & Rare plants & for the Elegant Flowers from 7 to 20 etc, the Title page etc & Life of the Celebrated Gesner.[1] I have seen his Botanic Work, which is finely Executed & all True Lovers of Botany are under great Obligations to you for it.

But my Dear Friend Wee are all surprised, considering your great Practice as a Physician, and the many other Works, that are under your Hands, & require so much of your Time, That you could find Leisure, or think it worth your Notice, (unless you Intend it as a complement to the Fair Sex) to bestow so much time & pains to republish Mrs Blackwells Herbal,[2] a Work without Order or Methode, & of no Esteem Here and only Encouraged as an act of Charity to the Poor Woman.

Dr [Cromwell] Mortimar had he Lived, intended to publish an account of the Cortex Peruvianus, exhibited by Hawkins, he was a relation of the Doctors & collected his Materials from Dryed Specimens sent the Dr. I dont remember that an acount is in the Trans-

Sisyrinchium. *John Parkinson,* Paradisus Terrestris, *folio 169, fig 6. The Linnean Society of London.*

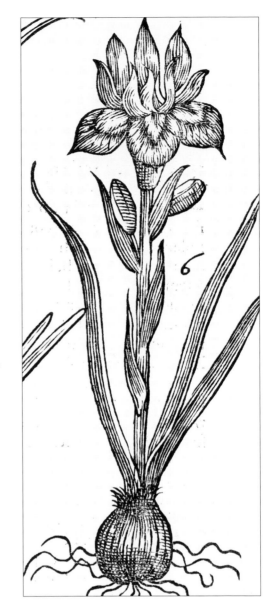

actions or that It was ever Coloured in their Natural Colours, the Letters on it refer'd, I believe was to what the Dr intended to saye about It, but since His Death his Son & Family are retired into the Country so wee are like to be deprived of that performance, but I think it is in your Transaction.

If I live I will send you the seed Visell & Seed of the Pulmonara it was first made a Symphytum, it has 4 Naked black seeds in the Seed Vessell, but I hope if a good Oppertunity offers to send you a Root for your Garden, for it thrives well with Mee and is very beautifull Early in the Spring. I had it first over anno 1747.

I am at a loss to give you any satisfaction about the Chenmolia of Seville [*Annona cherimoya*]. It is not now in our Gardens, that I can hear off, but I shall endeavour to informe my self. Unless I knew what name it is known by in the Islands that's inhabited by English, I cannot write for it, as it is a West India production (grown in Stoves) Fruit is very Rarely produced. I never saw any of the Anonas or Guarambanus's [tropical custard apples] produce fruit in our Stoves for they are to tender to live in the open air, but I have seen them Blossome & that is Rare & Seldome.

Mr Ehret promises Mee to send you the analosis of the Monarda [Bee Balm] it is a great pitty the Seed does not ripen in our Climate, & there is no sending the Roots, it is plenty in some of the Gardens in holland, att Van hassean [Van Huysum] perhaps. From thence in the Winter Months I should think it not difficult to send it to you growing in a pott, the Earth on the Topp of the pott, being well cover'd with Wett Moss, would keep it moist a Long While. It is very hardy & grows in all sorts of soils and makes a Glorious Show in flower, it increases prodegiously att Root. I had the Seed first Over & Raised it anno 1745.

The Penguin [*Bromelia piguin*] is 2 Species, one with a long & one with a short pod, but as they produce no Seed in our Stoves, it is hard to say whether Mr Ehrets Figure was from a Long or Short Pod. I gave Ehret the Long pod to send you, you may add it, to his Figure for you have Equal reason to believe that it came from a Long pod, as a Short Pod.

As the Sysinnuchium [*Sisyrinchium*] grow with Mee I will send you a Root by First oppertunity, which will be better then any discription. My flower was the same, as you will see in folio 169 fig:6 of Parkinsons Paradisus Trerrentris.[3] Was sent Mee from Spain. Parkinsons discription is very good, for it is but a flower of a few Hours or a Day but Parkinsons flower is made to Large.

I will send you some Fresh Seed & the Seed Vessell of the Coroladendron Carolineanum & besides, as the plant is rare & scarse & in very few Gardens. I will send you a painting, done by Van Haysens [Van Huysum] Brother that you may compare with Ehrets &

Catesbys. Possibly that may answer your wants, & then please to return it to Mee agin when an oppertunity offers. I wish I could Tenn Thousand Times more to serve you, who spares no pains or Expence to Improve Natural History.

The Arbor Coral Affinis you will receive Information from Mr Ehret and also the Cestus Virginiana and also the Red Wood vulgo.

I shall endeavour to think of the Lychnidea. I have 5 Species of Lychnideas in my Garden. All the Lychnideas that are in our Gardens came from my Garden where they first Flower'd.

Now my Dear Friend I think I have taken Notice of all your Queries I wish any, may prove to your Satisfaction if not, I will Endeavour to do it.

The Gensing I sent you was gather'd on [illegible] Mountains off Pensilvania, and is also found in [torn] Mountains of Virginia & Maryland. vid: Bartrams Journal.

I am not skillful enough to enter into the Nice botanical distinctions of the Lilio Narciss purple & its Flowers but I will give you the history of It, for I had the first direction of its culture & gave it first to Chelsea Garden & to Lord Petres Garden & others. I take it to be a plant unknown before Miller mention'd it in his Dictionary.

As I was this year of the Council of the Royal Society I moved in consideration of your many Benefactions that you might have the Transactions to the Time of Dr. Mortimars Death, which was readly Granted you with the Thanks of the Society for your last presents. Our new Secretary Mr Birch[4] will give you an account what parts is wanting to make the Com Littm [*Commericum Litterarium*] compleat.

January 18 I am this Day returned from the Funeral of our Dear & Worthy Friend Sr Hans Sloane Baronett. I was one of the Few Friends, that by His Will was desired to attend Obsequies, which was very Grand, & Magnificent. But 2 or 3 days before his Death He Sent to Mee for you Petivers Works.[5] He was sensible to the last which was the Eleventh Day of January aged Ninety Two Years.

I raised the Medea from Seed gather'd behind the blew Mountains in Virginia it flowerd First May the Eleventh 1745. The Genseng Flowerd First & produced Berries July 1748. I believe it was the first plant on Europe.

I here inclose some Fresh Seed of the True Scammony from Aleppo. Sow it soone don't keep it to Warm, but harden it to the open air by Degrees (sow it in a pott).

Pray my Respects to my Esteemed Friend Mr Beurer & my thanks for his last favours.

Mr Osbourn has sent a pacquet for you, Sir Hans a Packquet, Mr Miller at Chelsea a Pacquet and the Transactions of the R Society and Mr Ehret will send something. These Pacquets I shall keep untill I have your orders how & which way to send them to you.

I am with my best wishes for your preservation your Sincere & affectionate Friend

P. COLLINSON

1. Konrad Gessner (1516–1565), botanist. Trew rediscovered and published Gessner's manuscript as *Opera Botanica*. Nuremberg, 1753–9. Almost two hundred years before Linnaeus, Gessner used floral parts as a means of classifying plants.

2. Elizabeth Blackwell (1700–1758), published *A Curious Herbal*. London, 1737–9. Trew edited an enlarged and improved version as *Herbarium Blackwellianum*. Nuremberg, 1750–73. She drew plants at the Chelsea Physic Garden to raise money to free her husband from debtor's prison.

3. Parkinson, John. *Paradisi in sole paradisus terrestris*. London, 1629.

4. Thomas Birch (1705–1766), DD, FRS, historian and biographer, was Royal Society secretary 1752–1765.

5. James Petiver (1663–1718), see note 6, PC to Gronovius March 24, 1753.

ALS:MdHS
London, January 18, 1753

It gives mee great delight to find the son of my Dear Deceased Friend inherit his good Fathers Vertues & Curious disposition, but at the same time that I lament his loss it revivies in my mind the many Entertaining Rides & Walks Wee have had together In our pleasant Country round London & the agreeable Conversation wee entered into on the great variety of Objects found with you, all so Different from what He observed Here, which displays the almighty Power & Infinite Wisdome of the Great Creator so to Enrich every Part of his Creation.

You are struck with admiration att the Bettle you sent Mee and very deservedly, but consider every Creature apart, those that Glasses must assist us & those that the Naked Eye can discover, & you find every one Wonderfull & deserves our Particular Notice & Examination. In your fine Climate what numerous Insects abound both Volatile & Reptile, for the Warmer the sun the more numerous the Progeny, the Richer the Colours & the Larger the species. See how the Little Huming Bird glows with Brilliant Fire, the Butterflies Wings shine with burnished silver blended with livid spotts shaded with all the Colours of the Bow, the Great Flocks of Beautifull Birds, Wandring Beasts, Lovely Flowers, stately Trees, & if Wee dive into the Waters what Wonders There, what a Glorious scene Opens to Imploye all our senses in contemplating these Wonders which well Inflame the Head with a Pious Ardour to Adore the Beneficient Hand that made all these Things for the Entertainment, Comfort & Preservation of Mankind.

I just in hast give General Hints to excite your Curiosity, to stimulate your Industry. Its Plain you have talents for Natural Inquiries by your Pertinent observations on the Bettle which I read with Pleasure & attention, tho it was not New to Mee, yett coming from so Promising a Genius, who I would not discourage, I wish I had not had it before but yett if you look round you & Consider all your Productions are Peculair to your World, then what an ample Field opens to gratifie your Curiosity & Mine.

Notwithstanding my Time is wholey Engaged in Business I have stole a few Minutes to assure you how much I am your Obliged Friend,   PETER COLLINSON

HENRY HOLLYDAY (1725–1789), Ratcliff Manor, Tred Avon River, Talbot County, Maryland, well-to-do farmer, minor office-holder, and second son of James Hollyday (whom Collinson described as one of his "particular friends," writing John Bartram on March 22, 1737). Henry Hollyday married Anna Maria Robins, the daughter of George Robins and his wife, Henrietta Maria Tilghman, both of whom corresponded with Collinson. Hollyday wrote Collinson September 10, 1752 enclosing a "Beetle of such a Size, Colour & form as I nor any of the Curious to whom I have Shewn it have ever Seen before." (ALS:LS)

ALS: Museum of the History of Science, Oxford
London, March 24, 1753

It really gave Mee inexpressible pleasure to receive my Dear Friend Dr Gronovius Letter of the [blank], for my last Letter was dated July 5, 1752, which is now a Long Time in which I congratulated my Dear Friend on the Increase of his Estate. But haveing no answer in so long Time, I was very [concerned] the Report of your great Legacy was not true, and I had given you offence in giveing you Joye on a Fact that was not True. This made Mee very uneasie, & your Long Silence Made Mee more So. I was ashamed to write, for I fear I had done wrong. But as you have confirmed the Truth of your good Fortune I now write with Courage. But I was come to that resolution to write to your Good Son in a post or Two, but your kind Letter has luckkyly prevented Mee & Dissipated all my Fears.

Good providence has been as kind to Mee as to you. My Wives Father has Left Us a Comfortable Old Dwelling & Lands & Gardens [at Mill Hill]. Here I am now retreated from the Hurries of the Town to Indulge My Favourite amusement. I am sowing Seeds & Transplanting all Day & In Long Evening I am makeing a Cataloge of my Garden which will amount to above a Thousand plants, without takeing Notice of Common plants & Flowers & annuall Flowers.

I hope now my Dear Friend you will have leisure to give us another part to your Flora Virginica and also to gett the remaining part of Rumphias[1] for my Self & Lord Petre. If the booksellers are so unjust as not to Lett us have the Books att the abated price that they now offer them att, As Wee can not help our Selves, Wee must be forced to give our Subscription price if they will not abate It, but I shall leave it to you & Do as you Do. But it is high time the affair was brought to some Conclusion, for the parts Wee have are worth Little unless the Work was Compleat.

Wee long have had a Chamber Horse[2] but not under such command of Motion as you Mention. It certainly must be very Curious.

It is the opinion of all our Philosophers that Snakes only Change their Skin but once a year & that in the Spring of the year.

It is really unpardonable in Dr Hempe [not identified] to use the Widow so Ill. I see him frequently, He looks very poor & not able to pay Her.

It is certain the Pinax of Dr Sherrard is at an End and as you well observe with concern Botany is in a Low Way at Oxford & I know not when it will Revive.

I am obliged to you for another Species of the Collinsonia. It rejoices Mee to Hear your Good Son applies himself to Natural History.[3] I hope I shall have the pleasure of seeing him in England. I am pleased to hear Seba's 3 Vols[4] to come out at Last.

The Faba Egyptica was found by Dr Kalm a Sweed in New Jersey. The same Species described by professor Alpinal[5] & what you see so frequent in Chinese pictures.

Our Honourable friend Sir Hans Died on the Eleventh of January Last aged 93, retain'd his sences to the last, was Buried the 18 at Chelsea with great Funeral Magnificence.

I was by his Order, & by his Will, one of his perticular Friends that attended his Funeral, & made Trustee to his Will. He has Left all His Curiosities, Books &c & his House at Chelsea where they are Deposited, to the publick for 20,000 pounds Sterling. Our King had the first offer and he refer'd it to the Parliament, who are about the Purchase, the money to be raised by Lottery.

347 Vols Drawings & Illuminated Books the whole Library 50,000 Vols

3516 Vol Manuscripts & books of prints 38 Vol in Folio being the Catalogue of His Cabinet

8 Quarto

Medals, Coins &c	32,000
Antiquacties	1,125
Seals &c	268
Cameos, Intaglios	700
Precious Stones & Agates & [obscure]	2,225
Vessells of agates & Jaspers	542
Chrystalls & Sparrs	1,864
Fossells, flints & Stones	1,275
Mettals, Minerals, Ores	2,725
Earths, Loads & Salts	1,035
Bitumens, Sulphurs, ambers &c	399
Talcs, Mica &c	388
Testacea or Shells [obscure]	5,843
Corals, Sponges	1,421
Echine, Echinites [obscure]	695
Assena, Troche, Eabroche &c [obscure]	245
Crustacia, or Crabs	363
Stella Marine [illegible] [sea stars]	273
Fishes & their parts	1,555
Birds, Eggs, Nests &c	1,172
Vipers & Serpents	521
Quadrupedes	1,886
Insects	5439
Humana	756
Vegitable, Seeds, Grains, Roots &c	12,506
Hortus Siccus	334
Miscellaneas Natural things	2,098
In frames pictures, Drawings Framed	365

I thought these general Heads of his Noble Collection might prove some entertainment. I presume Petivers Works & His History of Jamaica are included in the purchase.[6]

I am with Cordial Respect & Esteem, your affectionate Friend   P. COLLINSON

1. Georg Eberhard Rumpf or Rumphius (1628–1702), German botanist in the service of the Dutch East India Company, sent to Amboina in 1653 where he remained for the rest of his life. Called "the Indian Pliny," under the greatest difficulty (he lost his sight in 1670, in 1674 his wife and a daughter were killed in an earthquake, and about 1686 his manuscript of thirty years' work was lost at sea), he wrote twelve volumes of natural history but died before their publication. Johannes Burmann edited and published the whole in

1741 in which more than seventeen hundred plants were described and 1,060 illustrated. (See Coats, Alice. *The Plant Hunters.* New York, 1969, p. 201)

2. Collinson was probably referring to a piston and cylinder steam engine called the Newcomen engine developed "to raise water from great depths of mines." (Martin, Benjamin. *Philosophia Britannica.* Reading and London, 1747. See also Hindle, Brooke. "The American Industrial Revolution." in *Science and Society.* Philadelphia: APS, 1986, p. 278–9)

3. Laurens Theodore Gronovius (1730–1777), edited the second edition of the *Flora Virginica* (1762) for his father, published *Museum Ichthyologicum sistens piscium indegenorum* . . . Leyden, 1754.

4. Seba, Albert. *Locupletissima rerum naturalium thesauri,* 4 vols. Amsterdam, 1734–1745.

5. Prosper Alpino (1553–1617), published *De Plantis Aegypti liber etc.* in 1592.

6. James Petiver (1663–1718), FRS, botanist and entomologist, demonstrator of plants for the Society of Apothecaries. Contributed twenty-one papers to the *Philosophical Transactions* between 1697 and 1717. Sir Hans Sloane purchased his collections as well as his books and manuscripts after Petiver's death and they became part of the British Museum. His herbarium, consisting of plants from all countries, is now part of the Sloane Collection at the Natural History Museum at South Kensington. (DNB) See Slearnes, Raymond Phineas: "James Petiver, Promoter of Natural Science . . ." *Proceedings of the American Antiquarian Society,* 62, 1952, p 243–365.

The "History of Jamaica" refers to Sloane's work.

97 ❧ TO ALBRECHT VON HALLER

ALS: Burgerbibliothek, Bern

London, May 1, 1753

I hope this will find my Dear Friend Safe return'd from his Expedition to Switzerland Loaded with Vegetable Spoils. I herewith Send you Some American Seeds.

Mr. Best [not identified] acquaints Mee you have Sent Mee a paquet which He will Send Mee Soone.

I hope Mr. Barrese[1] will Send Some of his Works to the [Royal] Society & then I doubt not of his being Chosen.

But the Society is very Cautious of admitting Strangers, because they have been greatly Imposed on by the French, for their Great people in an Excess of Complacsance have Sing'd their names to recommend people of Slender abilities, and our Society in the Like Compacsance have taken their Great Names as a Sufficient Voucher & have Inquir'd no further. But Since they have been better Informed they have putt a Negative on Some which will putt a Stop to Such politeness for the future.

Pray Lett mee hear from you & what Discoveries you have made in your Journey.

I am my Dear Friend affectionately yours,

P. COLLINSON

ALBRECHT VON HALLER (1708–1777), anatomist, botanist, administrator and poet, he made an extensive collection of Swiss plants and published *Historia stirpium indigenarum Helvetiae inchoata,* 1768 and *Bibliotheca botanica,* in two volumes, 1771–1772.

1. Pierre Barrere (1690?–1755), naturalist who practiced medicine in Cayenne, French Guiana. After returning to France he was named Professor of Botany at Perpignan and published works on the role of plants in medicine.

ALS:RS

July 12, 1753

I have the pleasure to Lay before the Royal Society a Wonderful Fossil for its Size & Weight being between 70 lb and 80 lb. Probably it may be three Vertebra of an Elephant or Hippopotamus, &c. It was found Incorporated with Stone in a Quarry near a Little Town called Stone Field Three Miles behind Woodstock in Oxfordshire. It was discover'd Whole & Intire, but in dislodging It from its Stoney Bed, It broke into Three joynts. Each is about 5 Inches long and nearly that Diameter. The Bone is very porus, of a Chesnut Colour, & the Out Side is of a fine polish, the Canal for the Spinal Marrow is very plain to be Seen. There Is besides three other Pieces of Leg or Thigh Bones, probably belonging to the Same Animal.

P COLLINSON

ROYAL SOCIETY, the oldest scientific society in Great Britain and one of the oldest in Europe. It is usually considered to have been founded in 1660, but a nucleus had in fact been in existence for some years before that date. When King Charles II offered to be entered one of the society, in October 1661 the society was incorporated under its present title. (EB)

"If one were asked to choose a date for the beginning of the modern world, probably July 15, 1662, would be the best to fix upon. For on that day the Royal Society was founded, and the place of Science in civilization became a definite and recognized thing. The sun had risen above the horizon; and yet, before that, there had been streaks of light in the sky. The great age of Newton [Royal Society president 1703–1727] was preceded by a curious twilight period—a period of gestation and preparation, confused and only dimly conscious of the end toward which it was moving. It might be called, perhaps, the age of Hobbes, whose half-mediaeval, half-modern mind was the dominating influence over intellects which came to maturity in the middle years of the century." [Lytton Strachey, "John Aubrey" in *Portraits in Miniature*. London, 1931.]

The Royal Society Premises at Crane Court, Fleet Street, London. C.J. Smith. The Royal Society.

99 ❧ TO CASPAR WETTSTEIN

ALS:BL

August 12, 1753

Benn Franklin Esq Observations of the present State of the Germans in the province of Pensilvania In a Letter to R. J. Esq, Philadelphia [Richard Jackson], May 5, 1753 [the extract of Franklin's letter which follows in Collinson's is not quoted here. In it Franklin expressed concern about the concentration of German immigrants, the need to distribute them more equally to prevent their assuming control of local governments, and to "mix them with English, establish English Schools where they are now too thick settled." *Franklin* IV, 477–486]

Thus my Dear Friend I have transcribed what Relates to the Germans. It seems very Necessary that Some Immediate Steps be Soone taken to Disperse them more in the Colonies & to Incorporate them more & more with the English. If they could be Induced to Intermarry more with the English & the English with them by granting them some priviledges for so doing might be a great Means to break the Connection they have one with another. Undoubtedly the Erecting English Schools will be of Great Service, and what would Induce them to Learn English if an Act of parliament passed Here, that no German should be Capable to take & Enjoye any post in the Government Even so Low as a Conestable unless He & his Family could Speak English.

I am with much respect, your Sincere Friend,   P. COLLINSON

CASPAR WETTSTEIN (1695–1760), FRS, born and educated in Switzerland, became a private tutor and chaplain. Sent to view the 17-year old Augusta of Saxe-Colburg and report on her suitability as a wife for Frederick, Prince of Wales, he became her librarian. He was active in the Society for the Relief and Instruction of Poor Germans and their Descendants, in Pennsylvania. (*Franklin* IV, 478, note 6)

100 ❧ TO BENJAMIN FRANKLIN

ALS:APS

August 12, 1753

I have much to say but am on the Eve of marrying My Daughter[1] and many Orders in hast from Abroad that I can only add a few Lines to Informe you tht your bill of 60 pound is Accepted, and I Intend to pay Osbourn £ 50. The remainder is for your Disposal when I can find time to Lett you know the Ballance.

Your Impartial Account of the state of the Germans[2] came very Seasonably to awaken the Legislature to take some Measures to Check the Increase of their Power. A Coppy was Desir'd by 2 of the Members for the German Affairs to show Mr Pelham [and] Lord Halifax.[3] With my Thoughts How to remedy or redress Impending Evils I have Drawn up 7 Proposals which you shall see—but alas, I am no ways Equal to that Task but was obliged to Do It but that Province is Yours, Who is so well Versed in your Constitution and the Nature of the People that possibly what I propose may be Impracticable in the Reason of things which I cannot be thought to know or understand. I am much concerned for the

French Expedition to Ohio. I gave that Paragraph to the Minister but Alas what can He do without the Concurrence of many More. I am with Cordial Esteem thy Sincere Friend

P. COLLINSON

How your Proprietors are taken up cannot say but it highly becomes them to bestirr themselves for I think its plain their Estate is In Danger. Pray Tell John Bartram I have so many affairs on the Anvil that I think I cannot write to Him.

I expect by first Vessell thy thoughts on the Means most practicable to Secure your Constitution. I wish I had leisure to take more Notice of thine of June 1: Aprill 17 and May the 9. I am much obliged for the Various Papers.

Mr Smith's a Very Ingenious Man.[4] Its a Pitty but He was more Solid, and Less flighty.

The Books Mapps &c I hope is safely arrived per Capt.Shirly.

Our Connoiseurs are greatly Disappointd for the bad Luck that Attended the View of the transit of Mercury but your Zeal to promote that Observation is not Enough to be Commended. Is it 5 degrees, or 25 degrees west of London. I wonder I heare nothing from Mr Alexander or Mr Colden on this Transit. I don't yett hear of any Account of It, from any of our Colonies. Doc Kersley [John Kearsley] and his Friends used it formerly to be sending their Observations on Coelestial Phenomena.

I writt to you both by the Sarah Cap. Mitchell July 20th.

Monsr. Dalibards[5] Letter Came Just in Time. It ought to have good things in it for its very Dear postage, 5s. I have paid Osborn fifty pounds this Day Augt 16.

[Enclosure]

Hints Humbly proposed to Incorporate the Germans more with the English and Check the Increase of their Power

1st To Establish More English Schools amongst the Germans.

2dly To Encourage them to Learn English Lett an Act of Parliament pass in Great Britain to disquallifie every German from accepting any Place of Trust or Profit Civil or Military Unless both He and His Children can speake English inteligibly.

3d To prohibit any Deeds, Bonds, or writeings &c to be Made in the German Language.

4 To suppress all German Printing Houses that print only German. Half German half English in a Page of Books or publick News papers To be Tolerated.

5th To prohibit all Importation of German books.

6 To Encourage the Marriages of Germans with English and Contra by some Priviledge or Donation from the Publick.

7ly To Discourage the sending More Germans to the Province of Pensilvania When Inhabitans are so much Wanted in Georgia, North Carolina and Nova Scotia &c.

1. Mary Collinson married John Cator, a businessman, later justice of the peace, Sheriff of Kent, and M.P. for Ipswich, 1784.

2. On May 9, 1753 Franklin wrote Collinson a "rambling letter" about "the German Labourers; They retain the habitual Industry and Frugality they bring with them, and now receiving much higher Wages an accumulation arises that makes them all rich." (*Franklin* IV, 477–486)

3. Henry Pelham (1695–1754), First Lord of the Treasury and Chancellor of the Exchequer, Prime Minister, 1743–54, and George Dunk, 2nd Earl of Halifax (1716–1771), President of the Board of Trade, 1748–61. The Board of Trade was interested in settling foreign Protestants—German and Swiss—in Nova Scotia.

4. Rev. William Smith (1727–1803), wrote and published, *A General Idea of the College of Mirania,* 1753 and was invited by Franklin and Richard Peters to come to Philadelphia. He was named provost of the Academy and College of Philadelphia in 1755.

5. Thomas François D'Alibard (1703–1779), French botanist. Published *Flora Parisiensis.* Paris, 1749.

ALS:N-YHS
London, September 1, 1753

My Dear Friend,

I have the pleasure to tell you that all the Suckers of the prickly ash thrive very Well. It is by your Characters a Zanthonton [*Zanthoxylum americanum,* toothache tree]. Probably your plant may be a Male or Hermophradite as it bears no Seed. The Face of your plant is apparently different from the Virginia one, but so farr as you have Examined their Characters Agree. It is very different from the Azalea Arborea. I have all in my Garden before I had yours, but a store is no sore of Such rare plants. The Canada Tree called by the French the Bonduc is a New Tree. There is Two in England that grow Well, but wether it will Agree with Linneus Characters I cannot say, for I never Saw the fruite.

Never certainly was a more Impolitick thing done then to Send Such Quantitys of Genseng Here. It has so Sunk the Markett that there must be great Losses on it.

Zanthoxylum Clava-Herculis, *Toothache tree.* *Mark Catesby. From Collinson's copy of* Natural History of Carolina . . . *Vol I, page 26, Knowsley Hall. Courtesy the Earl of Derby, Knowsley.*

My Lord Macclesfield as I believed I before told you Buried his Wife & Married his Son who now Stands Member for the County of Oxford, which has so Engaged his Lordship in politicks schemes all his Time is Engrossed, to the surprise of Every One that his Lordship could be prevailed on to Sacrifice his Serene Life to Noise & Party. Untill all the Hurry is over it will be to no purpose to show the professors remarks & your answer.

I wish for Some plants of your Small opuntia or prickly pear. I apprehend this is the most northern Situation it is found growing in. If the Leaves are putt on a small Box wrap'd up in Dry Moss & naild up or Tied up will come very well by the Spring Ship.

Wee are vastly alarmed with an account of the French Marching with some Hundred Men to build Forts & fix a possession on the Ohio River or Country thereabouts. This occasions the Hurrying away your New Governor [Sir Danvers Osborn],[1] whose particular Character I cannot Learn, but his General One is that He is a very Good Sort of a Man.

I have no Letter Since yours of Feby 16. Pray did you make any observations on the Transit of Mercury?

Dr Mitchell has laid aside all his pretension to post Master, for they Insist on a Certain Income from Him before he is Certain what His Income will be. He is complaining and cannot gett a Good state of Health.

Perhaps you now may have leisure to Indulge some natural Inquiries which I doubt not but you will Impart to your Sincere friend   P. COLLINSON.

Wee have had a most Delightfull Spring & Summer that Ever was Remembered. Wee have a great plenty of Wheat & a fine Harvest. There was new Corn at Market about a Month agoe & our Trade is very forward. Ripe Grapes in the Mid-August & now Sold about the streets.

Our Ingenious Friend Mr Franklin Has obliged us with 3 curious papers

>   On the Increase of Mankind
>
>   On the properties & Phenomena of the Air
>
>   On the present state of the Germans in America

My Dear friend, since my writeing the Letter I received your favour of July 7 with the answer to Eulers remarks which shall be inserted in the Magazine [*Phil. Trans.*] but as [Professor Leonhard] Eulers[2] remarks was read before the Royal Society, In Justice yours ought also to be read first before them before it is printed.

The use application of your principles to other parts of nature, is the very thing Wee Wish to See So you will certainly do a very acceptable piece of Service to all Ingenious Men. I have told you of Lord Macclesfields Engagements. I cannot find fault with your tartness. If I had not soften'd his state you would had more Cause for so Doing. I think first to Send your answer to Ld Macclesfield for his perusal and afterwards take his advice in the affair.

I am pleased to hear your Daughters Likeing to Botany. It is a Delightfull amusement & a pretty accomplishment for a young Lady, for after the knowledge of plants, it may Lead her to Discover their Virtues & uses.[3]

1. Sir Danvers Osborn (1715–1753), was appointed to replace George Clinton in August 1753. He arrived in New York in early October and committed suicide October 12, 1753.

2. Leonhard Euler (1707–1783), prolific mathemetician, left his native Switzerland in 1727 and moved to St. Petersburg to become a member of the Academy. He published 560 books and articles during his liftime. (DSB)

3. Jane Colden (1724–1766), Cadwallader's daughter, learned the Linnaean system of plant classification and produced an album of several hundred flower illustrations with descriptions. Her manuscript is in the Botany Department, Natural History Museum, London. It was published as *Botanic Manuscript of Jane Colden, 1724–1766.* New York, Garden Club of Orange and Dutchess Counties, 1963.

*Jared Eliot. Artist unknown. Connecticut Historical Society.*

102 ❧ TO JARED ELIOT

ALS:Yale
March 1, 1754

My Dear Friend

Having so conventient an Opportunity by Our Learned Friend Mr [William] Smith[1] I will again revise your 3 kind Letters of Aprill 24, July 20, Sept 24. Tho I may repeat the same thing over again your Candor will excuse It & may in part supply what was lost in Capt Davis of Novem 23, but before 8–25 [August 25th] I took Some Notice of the Above Letters under Cover to your Friend Franklin which I hope is come to your Hand.

In the first place I must beg the favour of a More particular Account of that Surprising Disorder that attended the Man, Woman & Child in breding anemalculas that came through the Pores of the Skin. What is Singular that 3 persons should have it, it seeming to be Catching like the Itch. If the Surgeon, apothecary or Doctor of p'haps all 3 center in one Ingenious Man if he will be So Good as to Draw up the case with the Symptoms attending the parties before the Animals appeared, and which under Cure & when they went off, & pray send those you have in the box, but if they was putt in a Little Vial of Rum they would keep plumper & better. Pray Lett the account be signed by the Doctor, the Minister

& Church Wardens, for it is a very Extraordinary Case and requires to be Well attested. The Physitians belonging to the Royal Society & Others will be extremely Obliged to you for this wonderfull Disorder & Method of Cure.

By Capt Budden who left London the begining of this Month in a Box to our Friend Franklin sent 2 fulls of Black Oats from different Counties & Some More Cole Seed that Some Other fair Tryals may be made, for I cannot comprehend the reason of its not producing Seed with you, but supposeing it does Not, is the Herbage hardy Enough to Insure your Winters, to make an Early Food for Sheep in the Spring, for I presume Turnips (on which is our great dependence) are kill'd by your Severe Frosts.

Perky Wheat I never heard of, but Cone Wheat sells best to Portugal & Spain being more Like Sicily Wheat. By our Friend Smith I send you some in a Box to sow in the Autumn which is generally allow'd to be the best Season but yett it is very commendable for other seaons, & by Him I send the St Foin. I don't wonder that it may miscarrie for it Takes Two Voyages & So its Vegitative quality may be hurt by them, for Wee sow foreign Seed because it is more perfectly ripened than ours.

You'll Lett Mee know the Success of your New Machine [seed drill]. I am afraid it is to do too many things which makes it more Complex and will be Liable to be Often out of Order So will never become of General Use Like Tulls Husbandry[2] which I never yett saw practiced anywhere. Some Gentlemen & yoeman may do It, but the Common Farmers or Husbandmen would not come into It, tho its Advantages was So conspicuous.

I can tell you good News of the Thessaly Wheat. I sent Some to John Clayton Esq in Gloucester County in Virginia who has had Success & is Delighted with It as you will see by the paragraph from his Letter. In a Little While He will be able to supply you with seed. So you see my Dear Friend it is not good to have but one String to ones Bow, and He had as bad Success with the Barley So you may make an Exchange.

It gives both Mee & our good Friend Mr [Richard] Jackson[3] no Little Pleasure to Hear you will be able to produce a Fifth Essay.[4] I trust good providence will be with you & Inspire you with Usefull knowledge as well as Heavenly Knowledge, which by your Example, your publick Teaching, & your Useful & Beneficial Experiments all so conducive to the Future as well as the present Interest of Mankind which you So freely undertake for the public Good, & springing from Such Motives cannot fail of the Desired End.

I am with Cordial Respect & Esteem your Sincere Friend,

P COLLINSON

I thank you for the fourth Essay.

JARED ELIOT (1685–1763), congregational minister, and physician, was interested in natural sciences. Eliot discovered that the local black beach sand in Connecticut was a rich source of iron ore. He published *Essay on the invention, or Art of making very good . . . Iron from black Sea Sand,* 1762 which received the gold medal from the Society of Arts. His *Essay on Field Husbandry in New England* was published in six parts (1748–1759). Eliot made the earliest bequest for a permanent endowment for the Library at Yale University and with Ezra Stiles introduced silk culture to Connecticut. See Carman, H.J. and Rexford G. Tugwell, eds, *Essays Upon Field Husbandry . . . Columbia University Studies in the History of American Agriculture.* New York, 1934.

1. Rev. William Smith returned to England for ordination in December of 1753. He came back to America in the spring of 1754 and was elected rector of the Academy and College of Philadelphia.

2. Jethro Tull (1674–1740), English farmer and influential writer, advocate of drill sowing and frequent hoeing. Wrote *Horse-Hoeing Husbandry,* 1731 and *An Essay on the Principal of Vegetation and Tillage . . .* London, 1733.

3. Richard Jackson, Pennsylvania agent in London, corresponded extensively with Franklin. (see *Letters and Papers of Benjamin Franklin and Richard Jackson, 1753–1785.* edited by Carl van Doren. Philadelphia, 1947)

4. Eliot's *Fifth Essay on Husbandry* was published in 1754.

ALS:N-YHS
London, March 6, 1754

Dear Mr Alexander

I am pleased that the Mapps was acceptable. In the Trunk I send you some others. When I know the price of these last may add it to Your account.

We are much Obliged to You for Your account of Bonneau In Yours of October 25.

No Doubt But you have heard, our Ingenious friend Mr. Franklin is presented by the Royal Society with a gold Medal for his Curious Electrical Discoverys.

We have no Other account But from Antigua, of the Transitt of Mercury.[1] That of Venus We may hope to see, But God knows How we shall Be disposed of Before that Time Comes. As we have a very Good understanding with Royal Academy at Paris that Point no doubt will Be settled Between us, for Recriprocal Observations on that Planet.

You have my Dear friend the thanks of our Astronomical members for the pains you took, and Your friend Mr Dice and Your son Mr. Stevens. It is with great Concern they read In Yours of the 21 May Last, how Curiously you was accomodated for the Observation, Indeed it was a great disappointment To You, but more to us, for we had fixed our attention On You. But since it Could not be Prevented. We will hope for Better Success. If Please God You live till Venus make her Transit.

I am with Sincere respects Your Affectionate friend,   P. COLLINSON

We are all here greatly unhinged on the death of Mr. Pelham Who was Walking in the Park seeming very well recovered. On fryday March 1 Came home and Eat a hearty dinner of Oysters, & Beef Stakes, soon after felt a Shivering Cold went to Bed, a stronger Shivering fitt took him in the night, Indigestion Brought on a fever which carried him off Wednesday Morning March 6 to the great Loss of the King and his Country who was a worthy man & Generally Beloved.

We all are Greatly Concerned for the King, at his years to be so Embarrassed for before the administration was settled, and all went on Smoothly, so that he hoped to have Gently Slide on to his Period. But now a new Minister, and New Parliament is to Be Chosen for the first there is none thought Equall To the Old One, Expect Mr. Fox and for the Parliament no Scheme can Yet be formed, it may be happy If the new Minister falls in with the Old. But that's uncertain He having Schemes & friends of His own. I hope good Providence will direct the King for the Best in his Choice for his own Peace and the Nations Good.

1. The transit of Mercury afforded astronomers a means of checking longitude and an opportunity to refine astronomical calculations in preparation for the 1761 and 1769 transits of Venus.

The transits of Venus across the sun's face offered astronomers opportunities to calculate the solar parallax—the angle subtended at the sun by the earth's radius—and thus provided a basis for computing the actual distance from the earth and other planets to the sun. (4 *Franklin*, 415)

AL:LS
London, April 20, 1754

Viro Candido et Amico D:Car. Linnaeus, F.R.S.

I hope before this comes to your Hands that you are full Satisfied that you have had the Honour to be Elected a Fellow of the R:Society. I very Industriously promoted your Election and Engaged my Friends to Support It, Because I knew that you Meritted that aditional Mark of the Esteem of the English Literati.

I have had the pleasure of reading your Species plantarum, a very usefull & Laborious Work, But my Dear Friend Wee that admire you are much concern'd that you should perplex the Delightfull Science of Botany with Changeing Names that have ben well received and adding New Names quite unknown to us. Thus Botany, which was a pleasant Study, and attainable by Most Men, is now become by alterations & New Names the Study of a Mans Life, & none now but real Professors can pretend to attain it. As I love you, I tell you our Sentiments.[1]

I am glad to hear the Collinsonia Thrives so Well.

Wee are greatly Obliged to you for the account of the Curious & Learned Works printing in Sweden. It is really very wonderfull, How it is possible for you to carry on so many Great Works.

I am glad to Hear our Worthy Friend Professor Kalms Voyage is printed. I hope Some Ingenious Man will translate it into Either Lattin, English or French. All books of Voyages & travels printed in English sell the most of any books in England.[2]

I must not forget to tell you that I have received the Two Guineas, so now all accounts are adjusted between Us.

By the last Ships I sent you a Letter & Specimen of what Wee thought a climbing Apocinon, but when it came to Flower we found it a New Genus. Mr. Ehret discovered It, so it should be named Ehretiana.

I am makeing a Catalogue of my Garden in which I have great Variety of Rare Plants, but whether I shall find Time to finish it I cannot saye.[3]

[The remainder of this letter is lost.]

---

1. *Species plantarum,* Stockholm, 1753. See PC to Linnaeus December 20, 1754.

Collinson long complained about the systemization of botany. In 1737 he wrote Bartram, "His [Linnaeus's] coining a set of new names for plants tends but to Embarress & Perplex the study of Botany as to his system on which they are founded, Botanists are not agree about It. Very few like it . . . : (ALS:HSP)

See PC to Linnaeus, December 10, 1754 and April 10, 1755.

2. The English translation of Kalm's work did not appear until 1770–1771. This reference is to either the 1753 Swedish edition, *En Resa Til Norra America.* Stockholm, 1753–1761, or the 1754 German edition, *Reise nach dem Norlichen America.* Leipzig, 1754.

3. In 1752 Collinson arranged for David Sigismund August Butner [1724–1768], later Professor of Botany at Göttingen, to prepare a catalog of his garden. Lewis W. Dillwyn's *Hortus Collinsonianus* (Swansea, 1843, not published) was prepared from Butner's work. On September 2, 1762 Collinson wrote Linnaeus that Daniel Solander was "methodizing" his hortus siccus of sea plants.

105 ❧ TO JOHN CANTON

Transcription of ALS:RS
September 11, 1754

My good friend,

A noble Russian[1] is desirous of knowing your method of impregnating [magnetising] steel bars.

I shall be greatly obliged to you if you'd send me an abstract or what would be better if some of your young folks would write me a copy of your memoirs on that subject and the favour will be acknowledged per your sincere friend,

Peter Collinson

JOHN CANTON (1718–1772), FRS, London schoolmaster and electrical experimenter, awarded the Royal Society's Copley Medal in 1751 and again in 1765. (DNB)

1. Possibly Paul Gregorivitch Demidoff. See PC to Demidoff, March 5, 1760.

106 ❧ TO CARL LINNEAUS

ALS:LS
December 20, 1754

A celebrated Botanist [probably John Stuart, 3rd Earl of Bute] Desired Mee to Lend Him your Species Plantarum. He returned Mee the Books with the following Observation —

"I have very Carefully examined Dr. Linnaeus's Species Plantarum, and do find this to be the most careless of his performances. And through the Whole Work He seems so Vain as to imagine he can prescribe to all the World."

"The Strange Confusion of Synonims shews his want of Knowledge, and his applying of them in many Instances to various Plants is a proof of his want of Attention."

P. COLLINSON

See PC to Linnaeus, April 20, 1754 and April 10, 1755, and Note 4 thereto.

107 ❧ TO CADWALLADER COLDEN

ALS:N-YHS
London, March 13, 1755

My Dear friend

I cannot acquit my Self without Just giveing you a hint how your Affairs Stands,[1] I am So hurryed & Straight'd for Time that I cannot have recourse to your Letters.

The Alarum of an approaching Warr Quickens our Merchnts in dispatching their

Cargo's in which I am much concernd & the Capt is Eager to gett away for fear of an Embargo. All this putt together you see my Situation.

However I will tell you I have been Twice with Ld Halifax who was very Gracious—you had Quallified Mee to Enter into the Merits of your Solicitation—His Lordship allowed what ever I could urge in your behalf but, the Result was that He Meet Mr Horace Walpole[2] on purpose & Carefully examined if there was any Room to gratifie your Requests and the Incomes did but just answer their appropriations of your province, so concluded with some fine speeches courtier Like but was concern'd that He could not Serve you.

So my Dear friend I See no hopes of prevailing. If [Governor George] Clinton[3] had been a Man of Gratitude & had Interests Something might have been done, but tho' he is greatly allied his conduct abroad has lost him all Interest at Home.

I Recevd your Revisal of your principles. It is now under the Inspection of Dr Bevis,[4] for really its Bulk, and the attention it requir'd to Enter thoroughly into your System would take more time then I could find any would please to Dedicate for that purpose. The state of the Case seems to be this, that every one is so Satsfied with Sr Isaacs [Newton's *Principles*] that they have no Curiosity to Examine yours.

Was it in Lattin, in Germany or France it would not want for perusal.

I wish the same Indifference may not attend your Tables, but the first time I See Dr Bradley [the Astronomer Royal] I will acquaint him with them.

Your Lettr was delivered to Ld Macclesfield but he has been so Ill of the Gout I have not Seen him Since & indeed I don't expect much from Him for He for his Son is so deeply Engaged in a very Long & Expensive contested Election for Oxford, I fancy he has not much roome to think of any thing Else. How ever the first time I see him I hope to ask Him.

I have in the first place my thanks & next to tell you that the Saracena [*Sarracenia*, pitcher plant] came with the Ferns as fresh & fine as if just taken from the Bogg where it grew & a flower was Sprung up 2 or 3 Inches high.

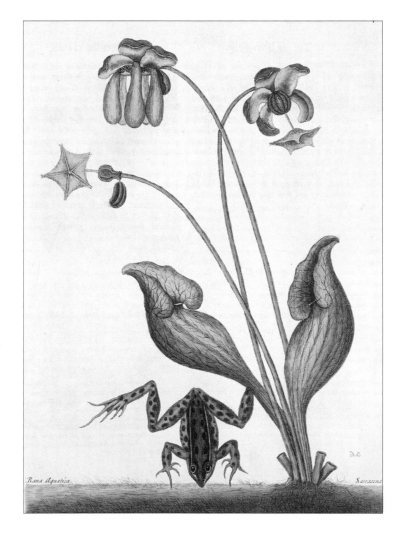

Sarracenia, *pitcher plant. Mark Catesby. From Collinson's copy of* Natural History of Carolina, *Vol II, plate 70, Knowsley Hall. Courtesy the Earl of Derby, Knowsley.*

As now I see no hopes of applying your Money in my hands for the purpose you intended it is now, as it always was, at your Disposal. If I can find Leisure I will answer your letters more fully by next ships.

I am with Respects truly yours   P Collinson

We are now drawing near to a very great Crissis for Ld Halifax told Mee in about 2 Weeks it would be known peace or Warr. Wee are takeing very vigorous Measure to be ready to oppose the French.

1. Colden's petition for additional income.
2. Horace Walpole, 4th Earl of Orford (1717–1797), wit, dilettante, author and gardener.
3. George Clinton (1739–1812), first governor of New York.
4. John Bevis (or Bevans) (1693–1771), FRS, astronomer, and medical doctor. "Newton's 'Optics' was his inseparable companion. . . ." (DNB)

On May 15, 1755 Bevis wrote Collinson, "After I had attentively read Mr Colden's Work I had difficulties that I could not well reconcile, and the like upon a second perusal. . . ." (ALS:N-YHS)

108 🦋 TO JOHN FREDERICK GRONOVIUS

ALS:LS
London, March 14, 1755

I have long denied my Self the pleasure of Writing to My Dear Friend Dr Gronovius. Untill I could Beg His Acceptance of Mr Ellis's Essay on Corals & Corallines[1] as an Acknowledgement for his many Favors confer'd on Mee. This Book is given to the Care of Dr [John Albert Schlosser—blank in original] Jr, Son of a Physitian at Utrecht, Directed for you & packed in his Box which will go in a few Days. I know this Curious Work will give you great Entertainment, for there is many New Discoveries in those Delicate productions.

It was with great Concern that I hear'd of your late severe Illness. I most Heartily congratulate both you my Dear Friend & your Family on your Recovery. I doubt not but your prudence will suggest to you proper Cautions to prevent such terrible Effects for the Future. At your years, I am afraid your Drink & Food was too Low. So great an alteration in your Usual Regimen might not agree with your Constitution.

I hope it will please God to prolong a Life so very Usefully spent, for the sake of your Family & Friends and give you a Share of Health to Finish your Flora Virginica. So Curious a Work & so much Wanted as will for Ever Doe Honour to your Memory.

I must not forget to thank you for the Care you had to Send Mee the Remainder of Rumphius (which is very Curious) per Mr Lamberg [not identified] to whom I showed all the Civilities in my power.

Is there any Thing come of Genete's Machine?[2]

My Dear Friend, that the Spirit of Elija should rest on Elisha. Must give you the Greatest Consolation to see your Learned Vertuous Son tred in your footsteps and really for a young Gentleman of his Rank & Fortune to Dedicate his Youth to such Noble Studies, in first place is an Excellent Example & next will give Him an Eminent Reputation and will transfer his Name with Honour to latest posterity. I am greatly obliged to him for a Specimen of his Fishes. It is Elegantly Executed & the Subject very Accurately Described. I shall be obliged to him for the Sequel.[3]

At Paris they are on the Natural History of Beast.[4] My Worthy Friend, Mr Buffons[5] sends Mee them as they are publish'd.

Don't remember any Fish amongst Dr Meads Curiosities.[6] Butt every Thing of his has been sold at a very High price as His Pictures, Books, Rarities, Coins, Medals, Antiquities are now selling of which I may give you some particulars for my next.

I thank you for informing Mee of Valentyn History of E. Inds in 5 Volume. I wish it was abridged & Confined only to Natural History.[7]

I am afraid I never thank'd you for the Information of another Species of Collinsonia. I wish I could have some Sort of Drawing of It.

By what I have read of Rawolphs Travels by Mr Ray & his Catalogues He must have made a Large Collection of Rare Plants, but certainly it was a Work of too much Labour to Methodize them.[8] Cannot Dr Haselequests[9] papers be procured? They would be a great Help.

You see Gessner[10] is publish'd by Dr. Trew. Your account is very Right. I shall pay the Guinea to Mr Catesby's Heirs. His Work is republished at 15 Guineas & very well executed from his original painting.

Your last favor is June 30, 1754.

Mr Slawter [Schlatter][11] is gott well to Pensilvania.

J. Bartram writes Mee he has putt in a Box a Choice Collection of Okes & some Drawings of his Sons[12] which you may Expect Soon with Many Curious Remarks. This will Enrich your Flora Virginica. The last Edition was Deficient in this article. The acorns are on the Specimens which will be a great assistance for the Species.

Mr. Miller is publishing in Copper plates Engraved & Colour'd the Genera & Some Species of plants that are described in his History.[13] It is well done. His proposals I will send in Bartrams Box.

Now my Dear Friend to Tire you no longer having done Honour to all your Late Kind Letters I shall Conclude with much Respect & Esteem.

Yours & your Sons affectionate Friend,   P. COLLINSON

Dr. Fothergill gives his respects & begs [illegible] favour you will buy Rumphius for Him & send it when an oppertunity offers, & will also pay for its being Collated and Examin'd, that it is a perfect Work, & Desires that you will Draw a bill directly on Mee for the Value in our Money.

Pray in what Language is Valentine History publish In & what is the price in Sheets?

1. John Ellis (1714–1776), FRS, Irish-born linen merchant, agent for West Florida, 1764, and for Dominica, 1770. Imported many seeds and was particularly interested in transportation of live plants and seeds. Published *An Essay towards a Natural History of the Corallines.* London, 1755. *Directions for bringing over Seeds and Plants from the East Indies and other countries.* London, 1770. *A Catalogue of such FOREIGN PLANTS, as are worthy of being encouraged in our American Colonies, for the purposes of Medicine, Agriculture, and Commerce.* From a pamphlet by John Ellis presented by the Honorable Thomas Penn, Esq., to the American Philosophical Society. Transactions of the American Philosophical Society, Vol. 1 (January 1, 1769–January 1, 1771), 255–271.

2. M. DeGennes, "an officer belonging to the Sea," published in the *Philosophical Transactions* for 1678, "A new engine to make

linen cloth without the help of an Artificier" (XII, 1007): "This Engine is no other than a mill, to which are apply'd the parts of a Weavers ordinary Loom...."

3. Laurens T. Gronovius (1730–1777) published *Museum Ichthyologicum sistens pisciuim indegenorum . . .* Leyden, 1754 and edited the second edition of the *Flora Virginica,* 1762 for his father.

4. Georges Louis Leclerc, Comte de Buffon. *Discours sur la Nature des Animaux* in *Historie Naturelle,* IV. 1753.

5. Georges Louis Leclerc, Comte de Buffon (1707–1788). No correspondence between Collinson and Buffon is known to the editor or noted in the calendar of Buffon's correspondence.

6. Richard Mead (1673–1754), FRS, M.D., successful physician and collector, experimented with viper venom and the influence of stellar bodies on humans, mastered Newton, and formed the

largest collection of books in his time. (DNB) At his "large and spacious house in Great Ormond Street" he maintained a collection of 10,000 volumes including many works on botany both English and foreign which he made available "to the inspection and use of others." He was Georg Ehret's first major patron in England. (Henrey, quoting M. Maty, *Authentic memoirs of the life of Richard Mead, M. D.*, 1755.) See Collinson to Gronovius, June 5, 1755.

7. Francois Valentijn (1666–1725). Published *Oud en nieuw Oosr-Indien . . .*, 1724–26.

8. *A collection of curious travels and voyages in two tomes: The first containing Dr. Leonhart Rauwolff's Itinerary into the Eastern countries . . .* London, 1693. Edited by John Ray.

9. Fredrik Hasselquist (1722–1752), Swedish explorer of the Levant and pupil of Linnaeus. Linnaeus published his *Iter palestinum*. Stockholm, 1757.

10. Gessner, Konrad (1516–1575). Published *Opera Botanica . . . Omnia ex Bibliotheca D. C. J. Trew.* Nuremberg, 1751–1771. See Collinson to Trew, January 18, 1753.

11. Reverend Michael Schlatter (1716–1790), sent to Pennsylvania in 1746 to organize the German Reformed Churches, visited Europe 1751–1753, and returned to Pennsylvania as superintendent of the German Charity Schools. (*Franklin* V, 203–4n)

12. On December 16, 1754 John Bartram wrote Gronovius in care of Collinson: "I have received thy kind letter of January 10, 1754 which was indeed very acceptable & more so being I thought thee had forgotten me. I am very glad thee approves my notions about several of my observations.

"I have a little son [William] about fifteen years of age that has travelled with me now three years & ready he knows most of the plants that grows in our four governments. He hath drawn most of our oaks & birches with a draught of the drownded lands & several of the adjacent mountains & rivers as they appeared to him in his journey by them. This is his first essay in drawing plants & a map. He hath drawn several birds before when he could find a little time from school whre he learns Lattin. I now send these draughts to our friend Peter Collinson whom I shall desire to send them as soon as convenient oportunity offers to thee with our discription of the birches their general & particular characters and wherein one species really differs one from another in any soil or situation. These I send to thee to have thy opinion of the method I have fallen into, and if thee can inform me of a better I shall readily embrace it and whether it would not be better to have it published in Lattin. I design next spring to set my son to draw some of our flowereing trees & shrubs in their flourishing state. Our friend Slater [Schlatter] tells me that thy son is like to be a great Curioso. If he will write to me and let me know what will be acceptable I can furnish him with several Curiosities. I have some thoughts of traveling to Carolina next spring, however pray write to me as soon as possible which will oblige much thy friend John Bartram."

On the back of this letter Collinson wrote Gronovius: "His sons Drawings are very fine. I wish they could be published. If that could be done there is some natural history, belonging to each species, which you shall have besides very fine specimens of all the oaks & acorns and another Quire of all the evergreens of north America, but it is to be hoped your new edition of the Fl. Virga. will take in all." (ALS:LS)

William Bartram's early oak drawings are now in Lord Derby's collection at Knowsley Hall. (See Ewan, Joseph. *William Bartram Botanical and Zoologial Drawings, 1756–1788.* Philadelphia, 1968)

13. Miller, Philip. *Figures of most Beautiful, Useful and Uncommon Plants.* London, 1755–1760, 2 Vols.

109 ❧ TO CHRISTOPHER JACOB TREW

ALS:Erlangen
London, April 5, 1755

For more than a year past, I have expected with Impatience a letter from my Dear & Honoured Friend Dr Trew, but as that favour has not yett come to my Hands, I Entertaine Many Doubts wether you are Well or what can be the reason of so long Silence.

Your Dear Picture smiles on mee Dayly & reproaches Mee Why don't you write. This I can bear no longer but I immediately putt Penn to paper to Inquire after your Welfare.

Pray my Dear Friend give some Intelligence what has prevented you from renewing Old Friendship.

I Humbly Lament the Loss of that Worthy Man Mr Beurer. He never failed once or Twice a year to Lett Mee know how Arts & Sciences flourished with you at Nuremberg, Frankfort &c &c &c.

Butt now I live as out of the World & know nothing [of] the Learn'd & Ingenous Men of your City which is the Fountain of Ingenuity & Art, which flows on Every Side through your neighbouring Countries. But its Circulation is Stop'd to poor remote England, unless you my Dear Friend will direct the Currant of Inteligence Heither We shall Quite Sink into Oblivion.

If wee had not heard of Poor Beurers Death He had been Elected a Member of the Royal Society in Two Weeks More.

I sent Him a Box of very Rare Fossills, being as Wee apprehended Impressions of some of the Large Capiliary plants on Slate which Mr Knorr was to have published in his Curious Work[1] & then Mr Beurer was to returne Mee the Box of Slates again. Pray tell Mee if Mr Knorr did Engrave these Slates and if I am like to have the Box of the Figured Slates again, for none in England had the like, and being very Rare was the Reason I sent them to you (that is to Beurer) to be published. Mr Beurer had a fine Collection of Rare things. Pray what is become of Them?

Does Regenfusius continue his Shell[2]

Does Rosel continue his Insects

Does Haid continue Ehrets plants[3]

Does Seligmann continue His Curious Work?[4]

I hear Catesby Nat Hist Florida is publishing Some where in Germany.[5] His work is now republishing in London very Well executed, for Fourteen Guineas.

Wee have lately had a very Curious Desertation on Corallines, Corals &c by Mr Ellis F R S with a great Number of Copper plates in 4to in which there's Many Wonderfull Discoveries in the formation of those and other Marine Bodies, which is submitted to the Opinion & Decision of the Learned.

This New & Ingenious performance I would Willingly, If I could tell How, send to you, my Dear Friend, as a Token of my Respect, for I am sure it would give you both pleasure & Information, for Mr Ellis has taken Infinite Pains to Oblige the World with his discoveries.

Some years Agon all Our Young Profficients in Physick & Surgery Resorted to Paris, to Improve themselves in Midwifery, but that Art is carried to such perfection in England under Dr Smelin[6] & others that now Great Numbers from Abroad & all our Natives that intend to practice Midwifery attend his Lectures with great advantage, & the Dr Haveing sett up a Lying-In-Hospital where the Poor are Deliver'd & Maintained a Month Gratis, He Has always Living Subjects ready for the Improvement & Immediate operations of His pupils.

Inoculatin is also practiced Here with great Success, not one in an Hundred Fails, which saves a Multitude of Lives, for you know very Well In the Natural Way how many Dies to one that Recovers. Wee recon Two out of Three Dies in the Natural Way. Inoculation is also practiced in our Northern Colonies in America with greater Success.

Master Ehret gives his Humble Service. He has More Business than He can do in Teaching the Young Nobility to Draw & paint Flowers &c which is now a Great Fashion with us.

Do all I can I cannot yett prevail on Dr Mitchell to send you His *Vires plantarum.*

Now my Dear Friend I will Tire you no Longer than to assure you that I am your Sincere and affectionate Friend Peter Collinson.

I find my Dear Friend your last Letter bears Date the 30 Sept 1752. Since then I find none from you, a very Long Silence Indeed. This I answered January 18, 1753 & sent the 23 Transactions, but I do not find you have in so Long Time Taken the Least Notice of them. If you Ever received them, or my Letter, which is not Friendly.

The Symphytum, Pulmonaria non Maculosa [illegible] [*Symphytum,* comfey] has 4 naked Seeds.

You know, if you want any thing Here that I can procure you, it is always a pleasure to Mee to serve you.

I heartily Wish you Health of Body & Strength of Mind that you may Long Continue the Patron of Natural History.

I am with much Respect & Esteem your Sincere Friend   P. COLLINSON.

1. Georg Wolfgang Knorr (1705–1761), German botanical painter and engraver of Nuremberg, author (with P. F. Gmelin and G. R. Bohm) *Thesarus re: herbariae hortensisque universalis*, 1771–72.

2. Regenfuss, Franz Michael. *Auserlesne Schnecken, Muscheln und Andere Schaalthiere*. Copenhagen, 1758.

3. Johann Jakob Haid (1704–1767), engraver, produced plates of Ehret's paintings for Trew's *Plantae Selectae*.

4. Johann Michael Seligmann. Probably a work translated by Seligmann—*Sammlung verschiedener ausländischer und seltener Vögel . . .*, which included portions of the text and some illustrations from Catesby and G. Edward's *A Natural History of Uncommon Birds*, published in Nuremburg, 1749–70.

5. *Die Beschriebung von Carolina . . .* Nuremberg, 1744.

6. William Smellie (1697–1763), MD, male-midwife, practiced and taught midwifery in London, 1741–1759.

110 🐾 TO CARL LINNAEUS

ALS:LS

London, April 10, 1755

I am greatly obliged to my Worthy Friend Dr Linnaeus for his Letter of the 20 June Last.

I did all in my Power to Oblige & serve Your Friend [not identified] by recommending Him to our Mathematicians.

I Thank you for so many pretty Desertations. I am mightyly pleased with them, in perticular with the Herbarium Amboinense[1] (for I have the 6 Vols) but it is a great Defect not to publish an Index, but Dr Stickman has in part supplyed that to very Good purpose.

It is a Curious Performance of Dr Barck [Bäck?] to show how the Spring advances in the several Provinces.

And I must not forget to thank the Ingenious Authors of the Flora Anglica & Herb: Upsalienses.[2]

You will See by Mr Ellis Title Page to his Curious Desertation on Coralines, Corals & Polyp that Wee are not Idle whilst your pupil [not identified] is very Busie makeing Discoveries in Italy.

It gives all Botanists a True Concern to See the Pinax[3] sink into Oblivion & Lost for Ever. It is only you my Dear Friend can restore It. You have Began by your Species Plantarum. Butt if you will be for Ever Makeing New Names & altering Old & Good Names — for Such Hard Names that convey no Idea of the plant — It will be Impossible to attain to a Perfect Knowledge in the Science of Botany.

You Desire to Know our Botanical People. The First in Rank is the Right Honourable the Earl of Bute.[4] He is a perfect Master of your Methode. By His Letter to Mee you will see his Sentiments & that of Another Learned Botanist on your Sys Plantarum.

Then there is Mr Watson, Mr Ellis, Mr Ehret, Mr Miller, Dr Willmer,[5] Dr Mitchel, Dr Martyn. These all are well skill'd in your Plan & there is others.

But Wee have great Numbers of Nobility and Gentry that know plants very well but yett don't Make Botanic Science their Peculiar Study.

John Stuart, 3rd Earl of Bute. Sir Joshua Reynolds. The National Portrait Gallery, London.

"A Map of the British and French Dominions in North America. London, 1755." John Mitchell. Cartouche. American Philosophical Society.

Dr Mitchel has left Botany for some Time & has wholy Imployed Himself in makeing a Mapp or Chart off all North America which is now publish'd in 8 Large Sheets for a Guinea & Coloured a Guinea & half.[6] It is the most perfect of any before Publish'd which is universally approved & by which He will gett a good sum of Money which He deserves for the Immense Labour & pains he has taken to perfect It.

I am glad Dr Back is well. I hope to write to Him soon.

The Next thing I have to do is to thank you for yours of 23d Novembr. I am glad the packett came safe. Your Letter I deliver'd to Mr Miller, and He promised Mee He would give you all the Information in his power relateing to Rivinam, Dusapium, Liquotroidum. Miller will no doubt tell you what He is now publishing. If I don't forget I will putt in one of his proposals.

In a great Hurry I have pack'd up some Seeds for you & gave the pacquett to Dr Schuk [not identified].

It is to You my Dear Friend that the Learned & Curious Naturalist is so amply Gratified, from Every part of the World with new & Rare Discoveries. Your Agents Bring you Tribute from Every Quarter. Wee are to thank them for their Observations on the Nile & at Brasil. I am greatly Obliged to you for those Informations. The New Fish must be very acceptable to young Gronovius, who I much Admire for dedicateing His Youth to Usefull Knowledge.

Your last Letter with Dr Askanius[7] came Safe & was Deliver'd to Him.

Now Accept of my best wishes for your Health & preservation.

I am yours,

P. COLLINSON

[illegible] not Discribed is in Flo. Virg.

I have 2 plants of the Mediola fol. Stela tis Lanceolatis [*Medeola virginiana,* Indian cucumber root], is now beginning to putt forth its Long Spike of Flowers. This I believe is the first Time this rare plant has Flower'd in Europe. I hope to gett Mr Ehret to paint It. Its first appearance is Like a Small Cone in the Center of the Leaves.

Vitis Idea Americana Longiori mucronata folio Flo Verg [*Vaccinium macroparpon*] is now in full flower.

Convolvulus Scammoniaca Syriaca [*Convovulus Scammonia,* bindweed] Stands in the Open Ground all our Winter & is now above 8 feet High in Full Flower.

I thank you for your Kind Letter of June the Sixth which I shall answer my First Leisure.

1. *Herbarium Amboinense,* a commentary on the *Herbarium Amboinense* of Georg Eberhard Rumphius (1628–1702), one of the botanic treatises prepared by Linnaeus and his student Olavus Stickman, published at Amsterdam, 1741–55 and at Uppsala, 1754.

2. Linnaeus and his student Isaac Olai Grufberg published *Flora Anglica . . .* Uppsala, 1754. With the help of another student, A. N. Fornander, Linnaeus published *Herbationes Upsalienses . . .* Uppsala, 1753.

3. *Pinax Theatri Botanici, seu Index in Theophrasti, Dioscoridis, Plinii, et botanicorum qui a seculo scripserunt opera,* 1596, an encyclopedia of plants compiled by Caspar Bauhin (1560–1624), Swiss botanist. William Sherard (1659–1728), set out to continue the *Pinax* by incorporating subsequent discoveries. Dillenius worked to complete Sherard's work but died in 1747 with his manuscript incomplete.

4. John Stuart, 3rd Earl of Bute (1713–1792).

In an undated letter to Collinson commenting on the *Species Plantarum,* Bute said, "I return the book . . . Dr Linneus has immensely Changed his names and genera in this book, so that till he publishes a new Edition of his Genera it will be of small use. I cannot forgive him the number of barbarous Swedish names, for the sake of which he flings away all those fabricated in this country. . . .

I own I am surprized to see all Europe suffer these Impertinences. In a few years more the Linnaean Botany will be a good Dictionary of Swedish proper names. . . . There are also many bold Coalitions of Genera. . . . [B]y degrees we shall have more confusion with order, Than was had formerly with disorder. . . ." (ALS:LS) See Collinson to Linnaeus, December 20, 1754.

5. John Wilmer (1697–1769), apothecary and "Demonstrator" at Chelsea Physic Garden, 1748–64.

6. John Mitchell (d. 1768). *A Map of the British and French Dominions in North America.* London, 1755. Said to have marked an era in the geography of North America. (DNB) See Note 4 to January 18, 1744.

7. Peter Ascanius (1723–1803), Danish zoologist and mineralogist, superintendent of mines in Northern Norway.

111 ❧ TO JOHN FREDERICK GRONOVIUS

ALS:LS
London, June 5, 1755

My dear Friend

It is long since I have the favour of a Line. I shall be glad to Hear Mr Ellis Work on Coralines & Sea Mosses is come safe to thy Hands. I sent them under the Care of Dr Schlosser's Son att Utrech who is Here. He promised Mee he would take care of the Book.

I should be well pleased to have your Sentiments on it. His Discoveries I have been Witness to Most of them & they are Wonderfull.

Dr Schlosser tells Mee the Book was sent in a Box to his Brother a Merchant in Amsterdam.

Wee have now Catesbys Accaca Flo Rubro [*Robinia hispida,* rose acacia] (Last in his Appendix) now in flower. It is a Charming Sight.

Last week I committed those papers of J Bartrams & Drawings of Oakes to the care of your Cousn Demetrias to be forwarded by first ship. Besides you will find on a sheet of papr writt on all

Robinia hispida, Rose Acacia. Mark Catesby. From Collinson's copy of Natural History of Carolina . . . *Vol II, plate 120, Knowsley Hall. Courtesy the Earl of Derby, Knowsley.*

Catesby in his annotation, "What with the bright verdure of the leaves, and the beauty of its flowers, few trees make a more elegant appearance. . . . I never saw any of these trees but at one place near the Appalachian mountains, where the Buffellos had left their dung."

sides, Mr Bartram's System.[1] When you have perused it, take an oppertunity and return it to Mee by any Friend coming Hither.

His Sons Drawings are very fine. I wish they could be publish'd. If that could be Done there is some Natural History belonging to Each Species which you shall Have besides very fine Specimens of all the Oakes & acorns and another Quire of all the Ever greens of North america, but it is to be hoped your new Edition of the Flo Virg will take in all.

Dr Linnaeus has sent Mee a sort of Index to Rumphius made by one of his pupils, which I was glad off.

I have now the Sarracena [*Sarracenia,* pitcher plant] most finely in flower. I take a large pott & fill it full of Moss & there in plant the Sarracena, Leaving holes open at the bottome. Then I sett this pott in a Larger pott, or Tub of water. This water is drawn up through the Holes & so makes an artificial Bogg, thus Oxococus [cranberry] thrives well & bears fruit.

Your last favor was by Dr Ascanius September 27th, Since which I have not heard from you. If you do but Enjoye Health, the Long Silence I can bear. Dr Ascanius has taken great pains to Informe himself of all English Improvements & Setts out for Paris next Week.

Montague House a Noble Palace is purchased and Fitting up with all Expedition for the Reception of our Worthy Friend Sir Hans Sloane Museaum, so that we hope all will be Lodged there in before Christmas next.[2]

A very fine Mine of Cobalt has been Lately discovered in Cornwal which has as I am told all the good properties of that Wee have [page torn] from abroad viz Germany or Saxony.

I hope in my Next to give you the perticular Value of Dr Mead's Sale of all his Books and other Curiosities of Medal & Antiquities &c &c.

The Sale of our Late President Mr Folks[3] Consisting of his Library will be Sold Next Winter. His fine Collection of Mathematical Instruments was Sold Some time agon.

I am with much Respect & Esteem yours and your worthy sons Sincere friend,

P. COLLINSON

1. "Descriptions of native trees," Oct. 1753 (MS:HSP): a detailed description of evergreens, oaks and ten deciduous genera.
2. The British Museum opened to the public in 1759.
3. Martin Folkes (1690–1754), FRS, antiquary and man of science, president of the Royal Society, 1741. "Under Folkes the meetings were literary rather than scientific. Stukeley describes them at that time as 'a most elegant and agreeable entertainment for a contemplative person.'" (DNB)

112 ❧ TO CADWALLADER COLDEN

ALS:N-YHS
London, June 9, 1755

I cannot Lett this Ship Sail without asking you how it fares this Troublesome Time.[1] Your situation makes Mee anxious for you & your Family. Crown Point[2] I may call in your Neighborhood if Wee are So fortunate to take it. It will be Well, but unless Wee can Maintain It, & Support The Country round It, its probable the French Indians as well as Troops may come to Distress and the Country Round It in Revenge.

John Bartram's Ingenious Son William has Sent a very pretty Map of the Drown'd

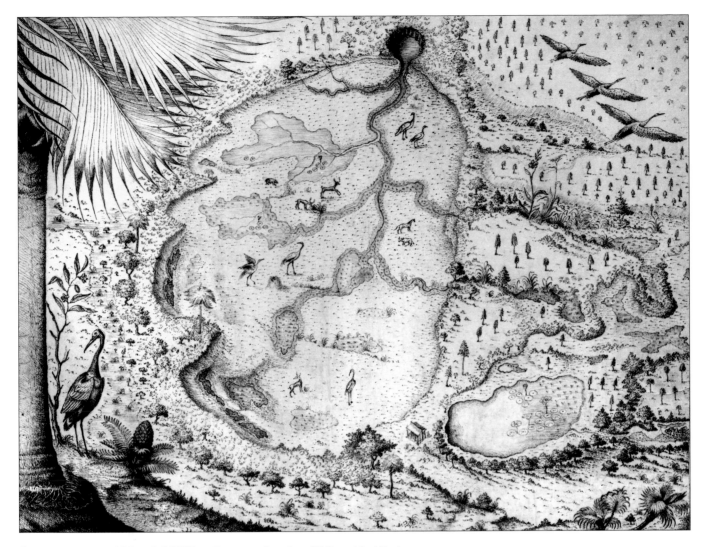

"Map of the Drown'd Lands." William Bartram. American Philosophical Society.

Lands[3] Including the Mountains & a Branch of Deleware on One Side, & North River & the Wall Kill on the Other, near which between Two Rivers you are pleasantly as well as Securely Setled, which may Preserve you from Sudden Incursions. As Inhabitants Increase the Drown'd Lands will by degrees be Drein'd and become a most fertil Spott.

J.B. has made many curious observations on all the Country Round, & the Course of the Rivers &c. He says the Lime Stone in the Vale near the Last Run in the Wall Kill that is between the Blew Mountains & Katkill Mountains is Composed of Sea Shells, Cockles, Clams &c but the most remarkable is below Gosion, where the Lime Stone has the most perfect Cockle Shells that Ever he saw. If any of these happens in thy way I should like one or Two Specimens as confirmations of the Universality of ye Deluge, and Seemingly not a great way from thy House are found the Oddest Kind of Scollop Shell in Stone that Ever He Saw. A Sample of these will be acceptable.

I have the pleasure to tell you that the Sarrcenas are now in flower by planting them in Moss in Artificial Boggs. I had your Cranberries fruited last year by the same method.

The Catskil Mountains have a very Singular appearance & very different from ours.

As the Intent of Sending Mee thy Alterations on thy Principles was to have the opinion of our Connoisseurs Here, I Sent them to Dr Bevis & He has Sent them to Some Curious friend of His in the Country. But I had lately a Letter from Him in which He tells Mee I shall soone have them Safely return'd. The Result shall be Known in my next.

As Pensilvania, Maryland & So Carolina have made delays in Supporting the Common Cause,[4] the finding of Wayes & Meanes to resist the common Enemy, I think nothing can Contribute to facilitate that Business for the future but the comeing into the plan for the Union of the Colonies which Lord Halifax has prepar'd to have laid before the parliamt this year, but the King's going abroad So Soone prevented.

Att thy Leisure a Line will be acceptable of what progress is made in Driveing the French from our frontiers. Our Principal Dependence is on your Native Troops. Cape Britton is a Specimen what they can do. I hope our people here will not fail to give the Encouragement.

I am my Dear friend Truly Yours

P COLLINSON

1. In 1753 the French drove the English traders out of the Ohio and Monongahela valleys and erected Fort Duquesne at present-day Pittsburgh to prevent their return. Two years later the British sent out General Braddock's expedition to re-establish English rights. In July 1755, the expeditionary force was destroyed by French and Indian attackers and Braddock was killed. See Collinson to Thomas Pelham-Holles, 1st Duke of Newcastle, February 25, 1756.

2. Crown Point on Lake Champlain. The French realized its strategic importance on the route from New York to Canada, and in 1731 began building Fort St. Frederic. It was demolished in 1759 by British troops under command of Jeffrey Amherst.

3. William Bartram (1739–1823). The map is at the APS.

4. "The English Colonies, except Massachusetts, were unwilling to strike in defense of their own interests and seemed incapable of uniting in a common policy. Physical communications between the English settlements were difficult, and concerted action was prevented by the rivalries between Colony and Colony, between Assembly and Governor, and by the intense individualism of a raw new world that had never been under feudal or royal discipline." (Trevelyan, G. M. *History of England,* III. Garden City: Doubleday Anchor Books, 1952. pp. 56–57)

113 ❧ TO CADWALLADER COLDEN

ALS:N-YHS
London, September 26, 1755

My Dear Friend,

Since our Scandelous defeat near fort Duquene the French haveing nothing to fear from that Quarter can spare Supplies to reinforce Niagra whilst I hope Troops destin'd for that place via Quebec are now order'd to strengthen Crown Point, which is now become a very serous affair Here & Wee are doubtfull of Success. On this Account I am sensibly effected for your Preservation, as I am well acquainted with your Situation, But good providence that has been with you all your Life will I doubt not Suggest to you the most prudent measures to be taken on that Occasion.

I never had any dependance on our Troops. I often said some Ambush or some French

Trick or other would Embarrass the Expedition. It is from your people who are acquainted with the Country & the manner of Bush fighting that Wee expect Success on Such Excursions. Under providence I can See no Improbability of their Succeeding unless they are over power'd with Numbers. Cape Britton is an Instance & the Same spirit & Resolution (wee have the Same reason to believe) animates them now, as then. Butt if they should not be able to Carry Crown point that will render it a place of such importance. It must not remain in the possession of our Enemies, it must be carried another Time, Cost what it will, for the future Safety of your Colony depends on its being in our Hands.

Since the defeat of Bradock Wee have had no News from your Parts, neither by the Way of Virg. M'd, Pensv or New York &c, which makes our people very uneasie.

October 5th

Every Parent is to be Comended for Advanceing & providing for his Family, but the Channel of all promotion is through the Duke of Newcastle.[1] If any Regard would be paid to your late Governor's recommendation to his Nephew Lord Lincoln[2] from Him to the Duke, then Some thing might be done, for it is all in his Breast.

You Desire to know who Dr Bevis is, a gentleman well skill'd in all mathematical Learning, So I lent Him your principals with their Amendmts, for I could gett nobody Else to Peruse It, Dr Bradley so much Engaged he could not do it.

Inclose you have a short remark by Dr Bevis. He has now your Tables under Examination.

Pray favour Mee with a Line how affairs stand with you, for your Situation is so exposed I can't help Fearing for you.

I am Truly Yours,

P. COLLINSON

1. Thomas Pelham-Holles, 1st Duke of Newcastle (1693–1768).
2. Henry Clinton, 9th Earl of Lincoln (1720–1794). His uncle was George Clinton (1686–1761), governor of New York, 1743–1753.

114 ❧ TO JOHN FREDERICK GRONOVIUS

ALS:HSP
London, October 14, 1755

My Dear Friend

I have very short Notice by my Ingenious Friend Doctor Schossher [Schlosser], yett I cannot forbear to Inquire after your Welfare & your Good Sons.

Some months (June 5th) agone I delivered into the care of your Cozn Demetrius some Curious Drawings from Mr Bartrams Son with Mr Ellis Book.

You have not yett favour'd Mee with an Acount that you have received them.

I here Inclose a Supplement to Mr Ellis's Work, which please to gett bound with the Other. There is no other reading to It but what is contained in the Sheet at Bottome.

We have long lived in hopes of seeing a New Edition of the Flora Virginica which would be a Work of Real Use. I look upon Ramphius as Done for your Amusement. I am much obliged for the 2 first Sheets.

I am my Dear Friend with my best wishes for your Health & preservation.

Your sincere Friend

P. COLLINSON

verte

Pray my Dear Friend tell Mee if Mr Jerastrum [not identified] has discovered the Rhubarbum Chinense [*Rheum palmatum*]

There has been but one Voyage or Journey printed of John Bartrams.[1]

If I remember right all his other Journeys was Little Expeditions contained in one Sheet of paper. If you much Desire them I will try to gett them coppyed.

1. *Observations on the Inhabitants, Climate, Soil, Rivers, Productions, Animals and other matters worthy of Notice. Made by Mr. John Bartram in his Travels from Pensilvania to Onondago, Oswego and the Lake Ontario, in Canada* . . . London, 1751. Republished as *A Journey From Pennsylvania to Onondaga in 1743* . . . Whitfield J. Bell, ed. Barre, MA, Imprint Society. 1973.

115 ❧ TO EDWARD WRIGHT

Draft AL:LS

December 5, 1755

I have with pleasure perused Mr. Ed: Wright's Ingenious Conceptions on the Cause of Thunder which carry an air of great probability in them, but as there is no End of Hypotheses, the most that can be expected is its being read before the R.S. and that I cannot promise, for our Motto is Nullis in Verba & (but yett) I think it should be printed, for as you well observe it may Excite others to Verifye your Conjectures in some degree by Experiment. I could wish our Incomparable B. Franklin to see them, Who is obliged to you for the Honorable Way in which you Mention Him.

EDWARD WRIGHT, Not identified. This letter on Thunder was apparently never published in the *Philosophical Transactions.* There is no mention of Wright in Franklin's letters.

ALS: Yale
December 15, 1755

The 10th of last Augt I wrote to my Dear Friend very full with some little hints. Oakes 5th Essay[1] inclosed to our Friend Franklin per Cap Lyon which I believe takes in yours of Jany 8, April 10, May 24 & July 7th, but now I come to thank you for your last Favor with the Sermon & those bound up which shall have my perusal. But the unkind people that took charge of it putt it into the Bagg or Box of Letters so I was charged Seven Shillings & 6 d Postage, but I gott some abatem't but for the Time to come send no Little parcell or pacquet but when you can do it by some trusty Friend, for there is no trusting to Captains or Seamen, to save them a little trouble they putt all into the Letter Bagg.

But one principal reason of My now writing is to express my concern to that Worthy Man & Patron of Science Mr Clap[2] for the Delaye of the Air Pump. All the Care has been taken under the Solemn promise of the Operator that it Should be ready to go by the latter Ships. I told him if it went not by them it might be 6 months before it could arrive. Well I had repeated promises, but all too no purpose, which hurts Me very Much because it is a check to the Improvement of Natural Knowledge. Pray lett Mr Clapp know how much I am concern'd for this Delaye. I have this Day wrote a thundering letter to the Operator. I hope you will not fail of it by the first Ship Early in the Spring.

All your letters in course have been Deliver'd to our Good Friend Mr [Richard] Jackson. J. Bartram writes Mee he has been to make you a visit, was well pleased with his reception.

Bad news flies apace So no doubt but you will have heard of the Totall overthrow of the Great City of Lisbon by an Earthquake Novembr 1 in the Morning on which Day was to have been their Cruel auto de Fae, but it pleased God to shake the Strong hold of Satan & Bury those Workers of Iniquity in its Ruins, not only Lisbon but all the Cittys of Portugal & Sevil & many other Cittys in Spain have felt the Tremendous power of Almighty God in overturning the Cittys & Destroying many thousands of the Inhabitants.

It is now Late & Ship goes tomorrow so must Conclude with my best Wishes for your preservaton.

Your Sincere & affectionate Friend,   PC

We Long to hear News from Crown Point & General Shirly.[3]

---

1. Possibly Oakes, Abraham. *A Short Essay on the Creation, Fall and Redemption of Man.* London, 1750.

2. Thomas Clap (1703–1767), Congregational clergyman, astronomer, rector and then president of Yale College for twenty-six years. "He was a calm, still, judicious, great man." DAB.

3. William Shirley (1694–1771), colonial official and lawyer. In 1755 Shirley was appointed supreme commander of the British forces in America. Served as Governor of Massachusetts and later the Bahamas.

Draft ALS:LS
[circa 1755]

Mr Urban

Some Observations on the Use of the White Pine [*Pinus strobus*] commonly known in our Nurseries by the Weymouth Pine.

It has been frequently Said (to the Discouragement of planting) what are Wee doing in raiseing so many useless Foreign Trees. If so many Oakes stood in their places, in process of Time they would be of Real Benefit to the Nation.

Not considering that Ships must have Masts (& other Trees then oaks) or perhaps not Knowing that the present Nobility & Gentry are cultivating the Mast Tree with as much ardour as if they foresaw its future Use under the Name of The Weymouth Pine or Five Leaved or New England Pine. This Is known There by the name of the White Pine or Masting Pine. Dr Douglas[1] in his accot of New Hampshire Describes it: Pinus Excelsior cortice Laevi, foliis Quinis angustis perpetuis exodem exortu Conis longioribus.

As this Stately Tree exceeds all others in heighth, it may be Justly Stiled King of the Woods, for its Towering Head is Seen from afarr overlooking all other Trees, arriving to near 150 foot in heighth, and from 3 to 7 feet Diameter.

As the Doctors Book may be but In few Hands, the further account he gives of this Useful Tree may not be unacceptable to those of your Readers who do or would promote Its Cultivation in this Island.

In the Article of New Hampshire, page 53, Vol 2 "Anno 1736, near Merrimack River a Little above Dunstable was cutt a White Pine or Masting Pine Streight & Sound Seven feet Eight Inches Diameter at the Butt End."

The Commissioners of the Navy Seldome Contract for any exceeding 36 inches Diameter at the Butt, and those to be so many yards in Length as they are Inches in Diameter at the Butt End.

Besides the Use of the White Pine for Masts, It is much employed in frameing Houses & in Joiners Work. Scarce any of this Tree is found South of New England but from thence along that Coast, & it also grows in Newfound Land.

Pinus strobus, *white pine. Georg Dionysius Ehret. Natural History Museum, Botany Library, London.*

In Joiners Work it is of a Good Grain, soft & easily wrought.

The best White Pine is from the upland. Those from Swamps & Marsh Lands are apt to Shake & Shiver on the Least Violence.

From its Northern place of Growth it is very Hardy & Endures all Weathers but [if] it is planted in exposed places it should be in Large Clumps or Else Surrounded with plantation of Scotch Pines or Firrs to Break the Violence of the Winds which may Check their Growth with us. For in their Native Country they Grow in Great Woods where they Naturally Screen Each Other, which, with the fertility of the Soil, is the principal Means of their attaining to so Vast an Height.

If this Little Essay to encourage planting by Showing the use of the Exotic Trees now cultivated is Acceptable, some further remarks may be Imparted for your Next.[2]

Friend Henry, if this meets with your approbation, Insert it in your next Gentleman Magazine, Else return it to yours. P. COLLINSON

You forgett to Send Mee Mr Franklins Last Electrical pieces, which you had to Coppy. I want to Show them to the R. Society.

EDWARD CAVE (1691–1754), printer. In 1731 he purchased a printing office at St. John's Gate, Clerkenwell, and began publishing the *Gentleman's Magazine* as Sylvanus Urban, Gent. See "Edward Cave" in Nichols, John, *Literary Anecdotes of the Eighteenth Century,* Colin Clair, ed. Carbondale, 1967, pp. 76–89.

1. William Douglass (1691–1752), native of Scotland, practiced medicine in Boston, published *A Summary, Historical and Political, of the First Planting . . . and Present State of the British Settlements of North America,* 1749–52.

2. This essay was published in *Gentleman's Magazine* XXV (1755): 503–504.

The Admiralty had long regarded the great white pines of New England as an important naval store for masts, bowsprits, yards, and spars. These "sticks" as they were called were often a yard in diameter at the butt and thirty yards long. By 1729 restrictions were imposed on cutting and surveyors were appointed to identify mast pines in the forest and mark them with the "Broad Arrow" on the trunk—the old sign of naval property, shaped like a crow's track and made with three blows of a marking hatchet.

With the Revolution those pines were denied the Royal Navy and it suffered keenly from the lack. "It is futile, of course, to stress a single factor as the sole cause for victory or defeat in a contest so complex as the American Revolution, but certainly the lack of masts deserves more of a place than it has yet received among the various reasons for England's temporary decline in sea power." Albion, Robert Greenhalgh, *Forests and Sea Power: The Timber Problem of the Royal Navy,* 1652–1862. Cambridge, Harvard University Press, 1926. p. 282. And see Gipson, Lawrence Henry, *The British Isles and the American Colonies: The Northern Plantations, 1748–1754.* New York, Alfred A. Knopf, 1936. Chapter II is of particular interest, "In the White-Pine Belt."

118 ❧ TO THOMAS PELHAM-HOLLES, 1ST DUKE OF NEWCASTLE

LS: BL

February 25, 1756

Some thoughts on the French Schemes and the importance of the country on the River Ohio to Great Britain.

The Preservation and Enlargement of our Northern Colonies is of the highest importance as they are sources of the greatest part of our wealth and trades. And if the French are suffered to keep their encroachments on our possessions on the River Ohio and its branches, they will soon be in a condition by the nature of that situation to seize on either Pennsylvania, Maryland, Virginia or the Carolinas, or drive us from the whole.

They have already forced us from our settlement on the River Monanungaley [Monongahela], a branch of the Ohio, which has brought them within about eighty miles of Wills Creek on the R. Potomack. This opens them a free passage down to Chesapeak Bay, by which they have an easy access to the first mentioned colonies, and at the same time opens to them a ready communication from the great ocean with their own settlements on the Lakes and the Mississippi.

The French know they cannot establish colonies of their own for want of those supplies of people from Germany, that has greatly increased ours; therefore it is presumed to have long been their original plan, and is now undoubtedly their view, to put themselves in such a tract to seize on ours, which seems near a completion unless timely and vigorous measures are taken to prevent them.

The French in pursuance of this plan are fortifying themselves on or near our settlements on Greenbriar River, a branch of Kanhawna, that runs into the Ohio, by which they will have a near communication with the southernmost parts of Virginia and North Carolina, and by other forts on the Ohio, they have an intercourse by water with flat-bottomed vessels for 400 or 500 miles North and South of our western bounds, by which they can and will entirely cut off our Alliance, as well as our most valuable trade for skins and furs, with the Western Indians.

And then on the other side the French being suffered to raise forts build and fortify Crown Point, and other works. They extend their encroachments on the back of New York & New England, to Nova Scotia; thus it is evident, unless they can be confined to the River St Lawrence and the North Side of the Lakes, which are their natural and proper boundaries, they will in a very few years overrun and subdue all our colonies.

I must not forget to hint another very material part of the French scheme: it may be remembered in the late war when a prohibition was laid on Irish beef etc their Islands [1] were starving and their fleets distressed and retarded for want of provisions, they had recourse to Denmark and Sweden for supplies, but to very little purpose. Can then a better plan be formed to remedy so great a defect, and to enable them at all times to victual their Navy and supply their islands which in times of peace are chiefly supported from Ireland or our colonies.

This is effected if they distress, or drive us from those rich lands on the Ohio, and its branches, being 4 or 500 miles in extent, which are so productive in pasturages that part of it is called the long green meadows; indeed I have had it from many that have been there, that no country in all America is so fertile, so [obscure], so proper for our enemies to settle farms, to raise great stocks of black cattle for dairies, &c.

This will not appear chimmerical but a very practical scheme if examined by a map— an easy communication is opened to the sea, as I observed before, if the French get but possession of the River Potomomack, it shortens the conveyance without going an immense way about by Quebec, which is not navigable for 4 or 5 months, whereas Potomac's course is from 40 to 38°. So the River is open almost all the year.

The foregoing Article if well considered, I hope will have great influence with the Legislature to dislodge the French from their near and unjust encroachment.

Those that know the situation of this fertile country, and its rivers that lay between our colonies are agreed, that whosoever keeps possession of the Ohio lands will be undoubtedly master of all the settlements. If the french are, they will eat us up by piecemeal, witness their encroachments in Europe on the Low Countries, the Rhine, Lorraine and Germany, and in the East Indies &c.

Your Grace who knows so well their usurpations may easily see the consequences of such a restless implacable, ambitious neighbor to our colonies.

It is computed by very good judges that our foreign trade brings in three millions per annum; and they think that it can be clearly proved that two millions are the produce of our colonies which is besides an improving trade.

This gives our merchants and trading people great concern for their preservation, which is only alleviated in the reflection of your Grace's perserverence and unwearied application as well to encourage every branch of our commerce as to support in every shape the honor and real interest of this Kingdom.

THOMAS PELHAM–HOLLES, 1st Duke of Newcastle (1693–1768), a zealous Whig, became First Lord of the Treasury in 1754.

Although signed by Collinson, this letter was written in another hand, perhaps by his son Michael.

1. The French supplied their North American forces from Louisburg on Cape Breton.

119 ❧ TO CARL LINNAEUS

ALS:LS
London, May 12, 1756

My Dear Friend,

Without further Ceremony I must tell you I was highly pleas'd with your Friendly Epistles of Aug 10th and Oct 17th ulto.

Dr Martyn is in good Health has lately publish'd an Abridgment of the [Royal Society] Transactions to the year 1753 in 2 vols 4 to.[1]

Mr Ehret is fully Employed with teaching the Noble Ladys to paint Flowers, has no time to Spare has only published the Beveria being what at Paris is named Butneria [*Calycanthus*, sweet shrub]. It is a Charming subfrutex (little shrub) & grows in my Garden in the Open Air or en plein Terre as the French call it, & bears flowers abundantly every year.

Mr Miller has published to No XIV[2], But Dr [John] Hill is publishing a Histy of plants of which I Send you a Specimen. As he proceeds through the Genus's he Criticises on your Methode, but not like the foul-mouth'd Germans. He treats you like an English Man with Decency & Good Man-

Calycanthus, *sweet shrub. Pierre-Joseph Buchoz. Hunt Institute for Botanical Documentation.*

ners & although Wee cannot agree in all points, for no System can be perfect, yett Wee Honour and esteem you for Spreading of Arts & Science & Increasing Knowledge.

I can tell my Dear Friend With great pleasure that I have the Rubus arcticus Now in flower. It increases with Mee but as you have a readier Methode of doing it pray tell Mee.

Dr [Patrick] Browne has publish'd his History of Jamaica, the plants Drawn by Mr Ehret. Dr Russell,[3] a very Learned Man & master of all the Eastern Languages spoke about Aleppo [N.Syria, on the Quweig River] has Lately published the Natural History of that Citty & Country about it, the Nondescript plants all drawn by Mr Ehret in large 4to, price bound 17 Shillings.

I hear you have published your Somnus Plantarum.[4] I have for Many Years observed these Sleeping plants of which there is great Variety.

Pray what progress has my learned friend Kalm made in his Travels to N. America? How many vols is publish'd?

I but lately Heard from Mr Colden. He is well, but what is Marvelous, his Daughter is perhaps the First Lady that has so perfectly Studied your system. She Deserves to be Celebrated.

Your friend John Bartram is also very Well. His Son is an admirable painter of plants. He will Soone be another Ehret, His performances are So Elegant.

You must remember I am a Merchant, a Man of great Business & many Affairs in my Head & on my Hands. I can never pretend to publish a Catalogue of my Garden unless I had one of your Ingenious Pupils to Digest and Methodize it for Mee. It only serves now for my own private use.

Now, my Dear Friend, Live Happy & Contented as you have so much the Love of Mankind & believe Mee to be as I really am Your Sincere Friend

P. COLLINSON

1. This work was published in five volumes between 1734–1756 covering the *Transactions* from 1719–1750.

2. Possibly refers to Philip Miller's *Figures of the . . . plants described in the Gardeners Dictionary.* London 1755–1760.

3. Alexander Russell (1715–1768), Scottish physician and naturalist, British consul in Aleppo, published *The Natural History of Aleppo.* London, 1756.

4. *Somnus plantarum.* Uppsala, [1755].

120 ❧ TO CADWALLADER COLDEN

ALS:N-YHS
London, May 19, 1756

My Dear Friend

I am now to thank you for yours of January 3d & February 12th, which was very acceptable, for News from your part of the World on your Authority will be always valuable as well as very Interesting, for your Prosperity & ours is united in one Link and if that Breaks we shall Equally Suffer.

If the London Medical Essays[1] was publish'd no doubt But Dr Fothergill will Send you a Coppy. When it comes to my Hands, I will take Care you shall have it.

I am Extreamly obliged to you for the Fossils. They came Safe & are remarkable Evidences that the Deluge reachd your World. The Large Stone contains a different Species of Bivalve Shell than I have Seen before, & my Collection is said to be Excelled by few. I presume this is the stone that J. Bartram Mention'd. The Two Small ones are very Singular, being a Species of Histerolithos, Sent Mee also from Germany. You know the Meaning of the Word.[2] But the prettyest Specimen I ever Saw was that what Wee call Sprig-Iron-Ore, exceeding Rich. This is call'd So because it Seems to be an Incrustation of fine Iron round a Sprig of a Tree. If more of this happens in your Way it will be Acceptable. You have my Hearty Thanks for them all.

I commend your [illegible] Prudence in retreating from Such perfidious Infidels [Indians]. I had a Different notion of them where they entr'd into friendships & of Such Long Standing that they was Sacred. It is a Sad reflection, that the Christian Religion after So many years being near them should have made So little progress amongst them. I am afraid the Bad Examples of those under that Name has prejudiced them against it.[3]

I have had a Letter from Dr Garden.[4] He Seems an Ingenious Man. I recommended Mr. Clayton to him. I find they correspond together.

It is true what the Dr Says of a Society newly Establish'd for the Encouragmt of Arts &c, [The Society for the Encouragement of Arts, Manufactures and Commerce Arts (Royal Charter, 1847), London, was founded in 1754] but I think he must be misinformed about the Rhubarb Seed, for the Country where the True Sort grows Lyes so remote between China & Tartary that to procure it is almost Impossible, because no Europeans that I can learn trade thither. It is brought by the natives to the Russians who lay nearest & have engrossed that Trade, but then the Russ are a people of No Curiosity & are Easily Imposed on, for I have had Seed through their Means & through the Jesuits in China. I have raised plants from all these & have had them many years in my Garden. They thrive well but never produced ripe Seed, & the Roots has been tryed by our Doctrs but want the Efficacy of the Eastern—well that was Imputed to our Want of Heat—then to remedy that defect it was Sent to Mr Clayton in Glocester County in Virginia. He expected to do great Matters with It, but still it does not come up to the Virtues of the Eastern. This makes us Suspect that Wee have not yett the Right Sort but Some Bastard Species.

I wish you would write to Mr Clayton who is a very Learned Friendly Obligeing Gentleman & has made Physick Some of his Study but only for his own & Familys Use. He will I doubt not send you his observations on the Rhubarb & I dare Saye it bears Seed with Him So he can furnish you.

Dr Fothergill tells Mee he has wrote to you. I hope the Goods, Books &c ship'd in the Irene are Safe arrived to your Satisfaction. The following Numbers of Dr Hills Herbal[5] to No XVII Inclusive I now Send In Mr Alexanders Box.

I also Send Him Dr Russell Hist of Aleppo in 4to price 17s. You may borrow a Sight of It & if you Choose it, give orders in your next. There is also an Abridgemt of the Transactions lately publish'd by Dr Martin in 2 Vol 4to about 25s, bound &c.

The Bookseller had Over Charged. When I paid his Bill, He Deducted Eight Shillings, with which I have Credited your Accot. Your kind Donation to your Sister is paid. Charge of Insurance as under.

On the 18 was a publick Declaration of Warr against France.[6] They have amused us with an Invasion the better to carry on their Expedition against Minorca & keep our Fleets at Home to guard our own Coasts. But the Steed is Stole, they are Landed at Minorca, &

now Wee are shutting the stable Door & sending a Fleet after them. Our Delays are Intolerable, but a Day or Two ago Ld Louden[7] Embark'd for your Colony. This is the old English Way. My pen is Tired, So Adieu my Dear friend.

Yours

P. COLLINSON.

Insurance on £45 : 8s: at 7 Guineas per Ct	3:6:7
It is customary to Insure the Insurance &	
a Little more to make the payment Sterling	
in Case of Loss	
half of the policy	2:3
	£3:9:10
Hills Histry Plants from X to XVII Inclusive . . .	3:6

1. Probably *Medical Observations and Inquiries*, 6 vols. 1757–84, published by "A Society of Physicians in London."

2. "Hysterolithos" 18th C Hysterolite, a fossil shell hystero = of the womb; Lithos=stone; refers to "fancied appearance." (OED)

3. Referring to Indian raids on frontier settlements in Ulster County, western New York.

4. Alexander Garden (1730–1791), FRS, physician and botanist at Charles Town, South Carolina, friend and correspondent of Franklin, John and William Bartram, Colden, Collinson, Gronovius, Linnaeus, Dr. John Huxham, Henry Baker and John Ellis. He was interested in the work of the Society of Arts and was elected that society's first colonial correspondent (March 19, 1755). He took an interest in silk culture, viniculture and in the cultivation of indigo in South Carolina. (Stearns; Berkeley and Berkeley, *Dr. Alexander Garden of Charles Town*. Chapel Hill, 1969.)

5. Dr. John Hill's *British Herbal* was originally issued as a serial publication in fifty-two consecutive sixpeny numbers between 24 January 1756 and 28 January 1757. Hill explained and used Linnaeus's system in the *Herbal* at a time when the fame of Linnaeus and the novelty of his sexual system of botany were creating interest throughout Europe. (Henrey)

6. The start of the Seven Years' War in Europe. It had been going on in America for two years. In 1756 there was fear of a French invasion. See Anderson, Fred, *Crucible of War: The Seven Years' War and the Fate of Empire in British North America, 1754–1766.* New York, 2000.

7. John Campbell, 4th Earl of Loudoun, (1705–1782), Governor of Virginia and Commander-in-Chief of armed forces in America.

121 ❧ TO HENRY CLINTON, 9TH EARL OF LINCOLN

Draft LS:LS

London, June 22, 1756

I am obliged to my Dear Lord Lincoln for the kind reception He gave my Nephew [Thomas Collinson] yesterday, Who Intimated pleasure I shall meet you on the Terrace at Oatlands, where your great Works are always Subjects of my Admiration. If I could rekindle my Juvenal Fire I should soon be with you. But alas I find my Inclination to run much faster than my feet can follow. Yett when ever your Lordship will add wings to them, by sending a brace of Pegasuses, with a conveniency [carriage] at their Heels, on 2 or 3 Days Notice I shall be your Humble Servant.

PC

HENRY CLINTON, 9th Earl of Lincoln (1720–1794), succeeded his uncle as the 2nd Duke of Newcastle and became Henry Pelham-Clinton.

ALS:LS
London, September 17, 1756

I had Long before this Time thanked my Dear Friend Dr Gronovius for his Favour if I could have communicated any Thing worth the Postage. Butt I could no longer Delay Testifieing my Respect, having so agreeable an oppertunity by the Bearer, Professor Ramspeck from Basil.[1]

I am exceedingly Delighted that any production from Hence could Tempt your Good Son to learn our Language. I hope he will find such encouragement & Entertainment in our English Books of Natural History as to perswade Him to perfect himself in It. But I am concern'd Wee have so few in that Branch of Study which He has so successfully Adopted.

At the same Time Wee commend the Son Wee Lament his good Fathers detaining from the Press his New Edition of the Flora Virginica, a Work so much Wanted & so much Desired & no one is so well Quallified as Himself for so Usefull a Work. Therefore Wee all flatter our Selves with Hopes it will be no Longer Detained from the Publick.

I ask Pardon if I did not before Now acknowledge the favour of your kind present of the Flora Orentalis Rau[2] which Mr Hoke [not identified] Carefully Delivered & those Copies for Mr Clayton and for John Bartram was forwarded to them.

Our Ingenous friend Mr Ellis has published another Dissertation &c on Coralines in our Magazine which I here with send you. The plates & Description you may take out and paste in at the End of his Work, which will make it Compleat.[3]

Wee have had a very Rainey Summer which if it had continued would have spoiled all our Corn, but it pleased God most graciously at the Very Critical Time when our Harvest begins to send us Three Weeks continued Fine Weather, so now Wee have all Cause to be very Thankfull. The Harvest is over in the South parts of England and Hay in such plenty & the Grass so Strong that for 3 Weeks past Wee are mowing a Second Crop almost as good as the First Crop of Haye.

This moist year our American Trees & plants grow wonderfully. I had the Giant Pensilvania Martigon [*Lilium Superbum*] figur'd by Mr Ehret that grew Eight foot five Inches high with 12 Flowers on it which made a Glorious Show.

The Magnolias Major & Minor flowered this year. The Umbrella Magnolia has shot five Feet high & Continues growing & the accatia flo rubro [*Robinia hispida,* Rose Acacia]. flowered finely, a Charming plant.

I am extreamly Obliged to my Dear Friend for so many Curious Articles of Literari News.

It is a pitty Mr Valentyn had publish'd his History in Dutch, yet Dr Fothergill would be glad of that Volm which contains his account of Shells, if it can be had by it Self only.

I am glad your Learned Son goes on with his History of Fishes & that He has Verified Mr Valentines account of Such wonderfull Fish as he has described, for really & Truly, I much doubted some very wonderfull Fish that I have Seen publish'd.

It is a Long Time that Genete has been at Work. If the Nobility did not See a probability in His Machine, they would not encourage Him to go on, but when it is finished I could never learn what it was to Do that other Mills did not Do.

I am glad you have alter'd your Regimen and Travel about. It certainly must be very good for your Health. I hope you well Continue It as your Occasions & Weather permits.

I am Surprised how the Hernhatters[4] Support their Scheme of Living. They are much on the Decline Here, & the Count has privately Left his fine House at Chelsea on which it is said that He has Laid out Six or Seven Thousand pounds.

I must Beg the Favour of you to Send Mee the appendix to Rumphius & the Index, & the Money it Costs I will repay to your Order.

I am my Dear Friend with much respect, Yours and your Sons affectionate Friend,

P. COLLINSON

1. Jakob Christoph Ramspeck, physician in Basel, published *Selectarum Observationum anatomico-physiologicarum atque botanicarum specimen Basel,* 1751–52.

2. *Flora Orientalis, sive reconsio plantarum quas L. Rauwolffus annis 1753, 1754 et 1757 in Syria, Arabia . . . collegit.* Leyden, 1755.

3. Ellis, John. "An Account of a Curious, fleshy, coral-like Substance." *Philosophical Transactions* XLIX (1756): 449–452.

4. Moravian Brethren. Count Zinzendorf of Saxony gave refuge on his estate at Berthelsdorf to a persecuted band who there established the town of Herrnhut (1722–1727). In the face of further persecutions, the Count sent a band on to Georgia and another to Bethlehem, Pennsylvania.

123 ❦ TO WILLIAM PITT

ALS: Public Record Office, London
Grace Church Street, January 11, 1757

My Worthy Friend Mr Pitt is very Sensible of the Melancholy Situation of our Publick affairs in many respects, none of the least is the Aprehension of the Dearness of Bread Corn.[1] Some prudent measures have been taken to prevent its Exportation.

But a further Step is Submitted to your Consideration, & that is, that a Temporary Act pass Immediately to prevent the Use of Wheat in the Distillery & in Starch-Making. These Two articles make a vast consumption of that Grain, the Staff of Life.

A Sack of Flower is on a sudden advanced Four Shillings. What does this presage, in Eight Months, before next harvest Especiall as the last Crop was Short & bad, & very little old Corn in store, and this severe weather may kill the Green Wheat & then a Famine will ensue.

I am with much Respect & Esteem, Yours,   PETER COLLINSON

PS   In times of plenty it is of Great Service to the Landed Interest for the distillers to use Black, Smutty or ordinary Wheat.

But when Famine begins to show her Meagre Face in the Midland & Northern Counties, it is time to take Measures to prevent her future depradations.

For if the Distillers was prohibitted using any species of Wheat, that sort of corn would remain in the country, but for its indifference would be sold at a lower price & mixd with Barley Meal, will make a very wholesome Cheap food for the Common People.

This will indeed abate the Revenue in the Excise; better that suffer, than the People Perish. That may be feard as our future Supply depends so much on the prosperity of the present Crop, & the next harvest.

I hope & Wee all Hope that a Strong Reinforcement will be sent to America, that we may act vigorously on the offensive and that it may be with Expedition for Hitherto Delays have been our undoing.

A word to the Wise is Sufficient

WILLIAM PITT, First Earl of Chatham (1708–1778), popular statesman ("the Great Commoner" and "the first Englishman of his time"), a noted orator famous for his "spirited declamations for liberty" (Horace Walpole). A vigorous opponent of the Stamp Act, he implored the ministers "to adopt a more gentle mode of governing America." He was succeeded upon his resignation from the ministry by another of Collinson's correspondents, Lord Bute.

Collinson was not sorry when Pitt resigned. See Collinson to Colden, April 6 and June 5 1757.

1. The price of wheat had risen from 30s 1 d per qr in 1755 to 40s 1 d in 1756 as reported in *Records of the Seasons, Prices of Agricultural Produce, and Phenomena Observed in The British Isles.* Collected by T. H. Baker, Fellow of the Meteorological Society, London, n.d. p. 199. In 1757 wheat rose to 53s 4d per qr, and Baker quotes one authority as describing it, "A famine year." The price fell to 44s 5d per qr in 1758, 35s 3d per qr in 1759.

124 ❧ TO THE SOCIETY FOR THE ENCOURAGEMENT OF ARTS, MANUFACTURES AND COMMERCE

LS:RSA
Grace Church Street, March 23, 1757

Mr Secretary

I am very sensible of the Honour the society does Mee in inviting Mee to their committee. Their laudable Designs deserves the assistance of Every one that Loves his Country. I wish my situation in public Business would allow me to persue my Inclinations, then any little assistance in my Power would be at your service.

Safflowers & Avignon Berries will prosper well in all the Colonies from Pensilvania to Georgia. I apprehend the Difficulty will be to gett the true ripe berries from Avignion. Mon Du Hamel at Paris sent Some of these Berries to the Late Duke of Richmond, just at his Death. They was by his Family sent to Mee to Raise them.

I doubted my own Skill & gave part to Mr Gordon, a very sensible practical Gardener at Mile End. Wee both raised Them & He has plenty for Sale. It was but yesterday I was with Him & looking at these very Trees that was raised from the Dukes Seed, & yett He doubted if they was the True Tree that produces the Avignon Berries, so it becomes you to consider how to procure the True Sort of Seeds.

As to Logwood, it will grow no where but between the Tropics & Wee have nowhere any uncultivated Lands fitt for to Raise this valuable Wood but in Jamaica that I can remember. I sent Seed to South Carolina. It came up & grew freely, but their Cold, (Short as it is) Kill'd It.

I am with my best Wishes for the prosperity of the Society, Your Friend,

PETER COLLINSON

The Society for the Encouragement of Arts, Manufactures and Commerce (Royal Charter granted in 1847) was founded in 1754 to improve "the polite, useful, and commercial arts, in all their various branches, by exciting industry an emulation among all who can be stimulated by honorary or pecuniary rewards." One early project encouraged the planting of dye madder.

On March 16, 1757, the Society entered the following Minute:

"Order'd, That it has referred to the same Committee [of Premiums] to consider of the different Species of Trees proper to be propagated, and that Mr Collinson, Mr Ellis and Mr Miller be wrote to, to desire them to attend the said Committee."

The Society's archives include three letters from Collinson; two are reproduced here. See also November 10, 1763.

ALS:N-YHS
London, April 6, 1757

In February last I had the pleasure to Acquaint My Dear Friend that your second part was so fortunate as to Escape our Too successfull Enemies who of Late have made sad Havock with our Homeward bound ships. I sent it Immediately to Dr Bevis & He gives his Humble service & Expects your answer to some observations He made, or his Friend, on the other part, which I hope is come to hand but by what conveyance it went I cannot charge my Memory.

October 10th I wrote you by Capt House who I am concer'd to hear is Taken, for Mrs. Alexander had Goods on Her but they was Insured & I fancy some of Hills Herbal was in the Trunk. So you must see when the London Capt Finglass Arrives, for by him comes the last Numbers in Mrs. Alexander's Trunk what is Wanting that they may be supplyed.

I have att last been so luckky to gett you a fine Tournforts Herbal & his History of Plants [by] Martin [1] in Excellent preservation to which have added the 2 Vol. of Edinburgh Essays [2] for the sake of the Curious Botanic Desertation of your Ingenious Daughter. Being the Only Lady that I have yett heard off that is a proffessor [of] the Linnaean system of which He is not a Little proud—these books are putt in Mrs. Alexander's Trunk.

I have no Letter from you Later then June 30 except that short one with your second part. The Reviews I had absolutely forgot, but they shall Come in the Next Trunk per Capt Jacobson who is safe arrived.

The London Medical Essays [3] are very Tedious, not yett publish; however, they are soone Expected. Dr. Fothergill is Well & Gives his Love.

Our Hopes & Confidence Is that Good Providence will Favour your Expeditions against the French. Butt Here Wee have had the most untoward season Ever Remembered. 3 parts of March has been (& part of february) a Continued range of Impetuous Contrary Winds Even at Times to Hurricans, which has Given the Vast Uneasiness on your Accounts that supplies was so Delay'd & the Course of Trade so Interrupted & what I may as well as others think Worse in its consequences the Instability & Weakness of our New Ministry, att the Helm Mr. Orator Pitt & his Family who I believe are by this time fully satisfied it is Easier to Arraigne, Declaime & find Fault, than to Mend. Their plan has not answer'd & their New schemes for Raising Money by a Lottery & Annuitys was so Injuditiously Calculated that they will not succeed unless putt on a better footing by a New Ministry.

The Admiralty is totally Changed & Ld Winchelsea again the Head of that Board, supported by Boscawen, Forbes & Rowley & 3 Land Men.

Mr Fox its thought will have the Chief Direction of the Finances &c &c & be made pay Master of the Army, D. Bedford & Ld Sandwich Secretarys of State, but These last is Newspaper view so can't be Depended on. [4]

Mr Girle a very Eminent Surgeon [5] has read in the History of N. England perhaps by Cotton Mather to the Royal Society that an Herb by the Indians Nam'd Tautrittipang was a Sovereign Rememdy for the French [venereal] Disease. Desires some Intelligence about It.

I am afraid by the Loss of Two of your ships I have been Deprived of thine & thy sons obligeing Correspondence. I hope you will not be discouraged but renew It. I have received no Letter from Him since July the 9th.

I am with much Esteem Thy affectionate Friend   P. COLLINSON.

Tournfort. 2 Vol	18
Ditto Hist. of plants. 2 Vol	6
Edinburg Essays	6
	1 : 10 :

As I heard nothing for 8 months [from] your province relating to its Civil & Military state I hope you have been preserved from the Molestations of your Enemys & that you are preposeing to attack them.

1. Joseph Pitton de Tournefort (1656–1708). John Martyn translated his *Elemens de Botanique* as *Tournefort's History of Plants Growing About Paris*. London, 1732.

2. *Essays and Observations, Physical and Literary*. vol. 1 (1754), vol. 2 (1756).

3. The first volume of *Medical Observations and Inquiries* was published in 1757.

4. Edward Boscawen (1711–1761) admiral; John Forbes (1714–1796) admiral; Sir William Rowley (1690–1768); John Rus-sell, 4th Duke of Bedford; John Montagu, 4th Earl of Sandwich (1718–1792).

On April 5, 1757, Richard Temple Grenville was dismissed as head of the Admiralty, the following day William Pitt was re-lieved. Henry Fox had resigned his post as Secretary of State in 1756. A shake-up of appointments followed. See PC to Cadwallader Colden, June 5, 1757.

5. John Girle, a surgeon at St. Thomas' Hospital, London.

126 ❧ TO JOHN FREDERICK GRONOVIUS

ALS:LS

April 29, 1757

My Dear Friend Doctor Gronovius may very well wonder at my Long Silence. The Reason was that I Delayed from Time to Time in hopes of receiving the Pacquet. Indeed it was so Long Since your Letter of December advised Mee of it, that I gave it over for lost.

Butt the 24th of this Month Aprill it was Deliver'd Mee in good order & the percells for Ld Bute & Dr Russell Deliver'd. I am extreamly Obliged to you & your Learned Son for his Curious Work. Great pains is taken to settle their Genus & to arrange them in Such a Manner as to be Well understood of all Naturalists.

You my Dear Friend requested some Seeds, and I have endeavor'd to oblige you. They was all Collected by our friend J. Bartram but their comeing so late is occasioned by this Cruel Warr which Interrupts all Sorts of Commerce. They are putt in a Small Box cover'd with White Paper and on It I Directed for you to Mr. Leonard van den Hock en Basch [not identified] & Comes in The Prince of Wales Capt. Reynolds. As such Small Packets are li-able to Miscarry I took Boat & Carried it on Ship Board and Deliver'd to the Capt with my Own Hands which I heartyly wish Safe to yours. The Ship will Sail with 3 or 4 Ships more in a few Days with Convoys.

I am with much Respect and Esteem your affectionate friend,   P. COLLINSON

Da Costa's Book is near Finished.[1]

Mr. Edwards 5 Vol of Birds & Rare animals is finish'd & will Soon be publish'd.

Doctor Patrick Brown is sailed to St. Croix, but how long he will stay there he did not Informe Mee

It takes up a great Deal of Time to regulate Sir Hans Sloans Museum & make New Catalogues. It is Question'd if it will be open'd before Next Year.

I am much Obliged to you for the account of the Hamhutters (Wee call them Moravians). They are on very Singular people but are grown in Discredit Here & are on the Decline, and I am told the Count has left his fine House att Chelcea for Debt on which he has laid out near Seven Thousand pounds.

You will please to remember that many of the Seeds will not come up untill the Second Summer.

1. Emanuel Mendez Da Costa published *The Elements of Conchology* (1776). See Headnote to July 23, 1747.

127 🌾 TO CADWALLADER COLDEN

ALS:N-YHS
London, June 5, 1757

It is with great Concern that I see this Cruel Warr amongst innumerable other Calamities it is to Mee a great Loss that our Correspondence is so Interrupted & Difficult, for I have received No Kind Token from my Dear Friend since you sent the Second part of your principles which fortunately came safe to my Hands & Feby 6. I sent it to Dr Bevis, but my answer to yours April 23 & June 25th By Capt House was not so fortunate for he was taken.

Your Good Son was so Obligeing to send Mee some News in his of June & July 1756 but since that Time no other has come to hand. I hope He does not take amiss any thing that may have happen'd undesignedly on my side. I Writt Him a Civil Letter of thanks, but I conclude that never come to his hands or Else he had not so suddenly drop'd a Correspondence so agreeable to Mee.

By a former Ship in Mr Alexander's Trunk I sent the Review & the Remainder of Hills Herbal, but I have some Notion a parcel went in Capt House that was taken, so must Desire you in order to Compleat your sett to send Mee what Numbers are Wanting & I also sent you Tournforts Herbal & his Essays & 2 Vol Edinburgh Essays. I have Divided these books & sent by Two ship the London & the Chippenham in Mr Alexr Trunks and I know send by the Irene from Dr Fothergill the four Vol of London Essays.

I also wrote to you by the Chippenham, so I have nothing More to Add Butt the sincere Respects of your affectionate Friend   P. COLLINSON

Wee presume Lord Loudon has Laid an Embargo on the Pacquets which is a great Check to Merchantile affairs & Keeps Us in great susspence how our affairs both publick & private stands with you.

Mr Pitt & His Faction is Turn'd out for they could not support his administration. His Brother Lord Temple is Turned out & his Friends, from the Admiralty to the Ministry [except] the Admiralty is unsettled. Its said Duke New Castle is again made First Lord of the Treasury but a First Minister & Secretary of State is not determined. Some saye Mr Fox stands fair for the First, or else to be pay Master of the Army. He is a very able Worthy Man & has Cutt Pitts, Comb, & His party Greviously, & yett our Citty & other Towns by the Violence of the Tory party are Intoxicated with Opposition to the King & his Friends & Vote Gold Boxes to Pitt & Legg for doing nothing to the purpose.[1]

 Yours in haste,   PC

 Mr Girle an Eminent Surgeon Desired Mee to ask if you knew an Herb by the Name of Taututtipang mentioned by Cotton Mather as a sovereign remedy for the Pox.

 Pray did you ever Hear if this terrible Disorder was amongst the Northern Indians?

 Wee are Credibly Informed & I have read that the Florida Indians, who are said to be very Lascivious gave that Distemper to the French & they first Imported that fatal Distemper into Europe. I think some of them that returned after they was beat off by the Spaniards & Indians carried it with them into Naples & there it first began to Communmicate its fylthie Effects from thence all over Europe.

 I dayly expect our Friend Franklin who comes Here to have it Determined if the proprietors Lands are to be Taxed with the peoples, for his Governor putt a Negative on Bill to raise Money for publick Service in which the proprietors Lands are Taxd with all others

---

1. Lord Temple, Richard Temple Grenville (1711–1779) and Henry Fox, 1st Baron Holland (1705–1774). Temple Grenville and William Pitt were dismissed from their posts on April 5 and 6, 1757. After an eleven-week ministerial interregnum, Pitt was appointed Secretary of State, Temple Grenville as Lord of the Privy Seal and Fox as Paymaster General of the Army as Collinson predicted in his earlier letter to Colden. (DNB)

128 ❦ TO THOMAS BIRCH

ALS:BL
Grace Church Street, August 16, 1757

Dear Doctor

 I have lately received a Letter from Dr Trew in which He begs the favour of the Society accepting of the Several Curious articles I presented to Them, & by the Next opportunity He will Send to the R. Society the First Vol of the New transactions of the Academy Nat Car Lately published.[1]

 He beggs the favour of the Continuance of the Transactions which has been Sent Him in Sheets to the year 1752.

 I hope there will be a Council before the Society Meets or Else I am afraid Wee Shall loose the Sending of them this year which will be a great Disappointmt. When you see Mr Watson I wish you'd confer with Him about & See if for Once one could not Strain a point & Gett them from the Booksellers & gett an Order of Council afterwards. But this I Submitt.

 I conclude you have heard our Friend Franklin is come. He Lodges as on the other Side.* A Visit from you will be acceptable. I believe it will be better not to mention any thing about printing his papers, for he is So very Modest & Deffident, perhaps he may put a Check to their appearing with his knowledge.

 I am perswaded He will like it better to be my Act & Deed & He knew nothing of the

Matter. But this is my Surmise, So Shall Leave it & assure you that I am your Sincere Friend,

P. COLLINSON

* Mr Franklin at Mrs Stevensons in Craven Street.

1. Academia Caesarea Naturae Curiosorum. The transactions, *Nova acta Leopoldina,* began publication in 1757.

129 ❧ TO MR. LEIGH AT TOTRIDGE

Draft AL:LS
September, 1757

It was a pleasure to Every one that Loves Planting & Improvements to see with what Skill the young Elms was planted on the Walk & properly, staked & Fenced.

But alas about Two weeks ago I passed that Way I was surprised to see the Fence gone & the young Trees pulled about by the Cattle, some Laying on the Ground.

It really grieved Mee to Heart to see so fine a plantation for want of a lettle Care all comeing to Nothing all your Labour, pleasure & Love thrown away.

Certainly Sir your Steward or Gardener must be very unworthy Careless people to suffer such Depredation in your Absence.

Young Trees are like young Children, they require frequent Looking after untill taken Sufficient Root.

Mr. Leigh has not been identified.

130 ❧ TO JOHN ELLIS

ALS:LS
London, November 24, 1757

Dear Friend,

I have on the other side copied an account of a wonderfull E India plant named Amapacherie[1] but it was so surpriseing I doubted its veracity untill it was confirmed to Mee by a very Worthy Family some of whome had seen it tryed in India.

To try if it would have the like Effects in England some Seed was sent from Fort St George [Madras] & plants raised. Several persons of that Family made the experiment & it had the same Effects. For a small pebble being wrap'd in its Leaves & held in the mouth for a Small Time it brake into Sand.

This surpriseing operation led Mee to think that the Juice of this plant injected into the bladder wherein there is a Stone may prove a powerful dissolvent.

I presume you have acquaintance with some of the gentln of the E Ind. Comp. I wish you will desire their assistance to procure Seeds of this plant from Fort St George or Maddrass where it grows about or near the Walls & High Ways &c to Make that experiment to desolve the stone in the Bladder.

I am with much respect yours,

P. COLLINSON

Captain Stevens In his translation of Anthony Teixeira[2] in fol 157 has this remarkable observation on the Amapacherie or breakstone of Madrass. I remember sayes Teixeira there is a Sort of Herb along the Coast of Coromandel & at Malacca. It is so common it grows about the Streets & pathways, but being Small is little regarded. But if the small tender Roots of it (others say the Leaves) be chewed so that the teeth or Mouth remain full of its Juice & then any Stone or pebble be taken into the Mouth & turned about or chewed it will dissolve into dust, or Sand, so easily as neither to hurt the Teeth nor give the least trouble, which says Teixeira, I have often tryed my Self & seen done by others. A Quallity Wee ought to admire.

JOHN ELLIS (c.1714–1776), FRS, Irish-born linen merchant in London, naturalist termed by Linnaeus "a bright star of natural history" (DNB), appointed King's Agent to West Florida in 1764 and King's Agent for Dominica in 1770. Published *An essay towards a natural history of the Corallines . . .* (1755), *Directions for bringing over Seeds and Plants from the East Indies and other distant countries in a State of Vegitation . . .* (1770). (See Savage, S. *Calendar of Ellis Manuscripts (The Correspondence and Miscellaneous papers of John Ellis, F.R.S.)* The Linnean Society of London. London, 1948; "John Ellis, FRS, Eighteenth Century Naturalist and Royal Agent to West Florida." *Notes and Records of The Royal Society of London* Vol. 32, No. 2 (March 1978): 149–164.)

1. Possibly "Amumpatchay—arissi," *Euphorbias pilulifera* L. (Watt, Sir George. *The Economic Products of India.* Calcutta, 1896, vol. 3, p. 298). According to Watt, "Indian writers have very little to say as to the properties of this plant." He goes on to speak of its use for "the afflictions of childhood, in worms, bowel complaints, and cough. Sometimes prescribed also in gonorrhoea."

2. John Stevens or Stephens (d. 1726). In 1715 Stevens translated Anthony Texeira's Spanish version of Mirkhand's *History of Persia.* (DNB)

131 ❧ TO CARL LINNAEUS

ALS:LS

Ridge Way House, December 25, 1757

To my Honour'd & Learned Friend Sir C. Linnaeus

Some Time Since a most magnificent Book[1] was sent Mee without a Letter or any Information who I am to Thank for It.

But when I consider the Royal Museum It describes, and who it is presides therein, I no Longer doubt but reasonably conclude it must be the Noble Present of my dear Friend Linnaeus.

This Curious Performance doth both Him & his Country Honour.

The Engravings are Fine, and the Descriptions show the Learning & great Knowledge of the Compiler of that Pompous Work. All that I have shown it to deservedly admire it.

The ingenious Mr Edwards has now finish'd his Fifth Vol of New & Rare Birds & Beasts & is ready to be Deliver'd.[2]

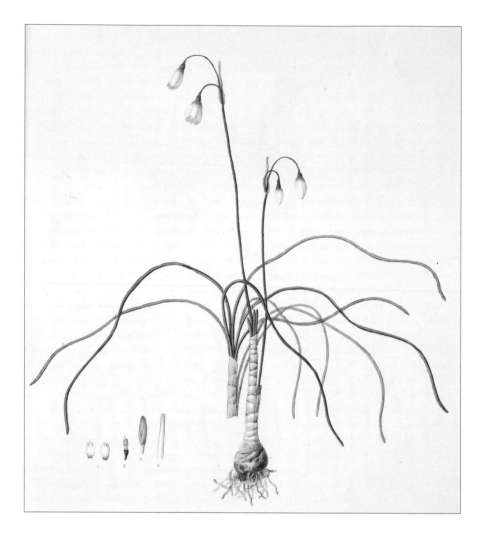

Mr Ellis continues to add new Illustrations to his Corals & Corallines to prove they are the Work of Polyps &c which I will send you by first Ships, But I have not heard if you received those I sent you in Last May committed to the care of Mr Brander [not identified].

The Extraordinary Heat of our Summer Has ripened all Sorts of Fruits to perfection & Wee had plenty.

In two Gardens I saw (this year) Pomegranates against South Walls without any Art ripened beyond what can be imagined in so Northern a Climate. They look extreamly Beautifull and of the size of some that is brought from abroad.

Our Autumn has been Long, Dry & Warm & so continues, for a few Slight Frosts has not strip'd the Garden of Flowers. At Christmas Day Wee have 4 sorts of Aster & Virga aurea in Flower & plenty of Leucojums [*Leucojum autumnale,* Autumn snowflake], double and single, Chrysanthemums, &c.

The Winter Scene is not closed before Spring Flowers begin, for there are plenty of Narcissus polyanthus Viola, Pansies and sweet Violets, Primula veris, Polyanthus, Aconite, Hepatica, Anemonies both double and single, and Laurustinus.

My dear friend, you would have been Delighted & surprized to see the Large Nosegays that was all Flowers gathered out of the open Garden without any Art, December 27, 1757.

Now the old year is makeing its Exit. May the New Year prove Healthfull & Happy is the Sincere wish of your affectionate friend,   P. Collinson.

Virginia, Sept 7, 1757, Mr Clayton writes to Mee that at Last I have compleated a New Edition of the Flora Virginica. But when or where or how it is to be printed He Sayes not a Word.[3]

1. Probably *Museum Regis a dolphi Friderici.* Stockholm, 1754.

2. Edwards, George (1694–1773). *History of Birds.* 1743–1764. The fifth volume, under the new title *Gleanings of Natural History* was published in 1758.

3. The second edition was edited by Laurens Theodore Gronovius and published in Leyden in 1762.

ALS:LS
London, March 6, 1758

I do not know which to Admire Most in my Dear Friend Klein, His Learning or his Judgment, in compileing so many Ingenious and Instructive Books in Natural History.

But I must beg Leave to dissent from my Learned Friend. In an Article He takes great Pains to Establish, In his Historiae Avium Prodromus, Which Is that Swallows are not Birds of Passage, but at the Time of their going away They retire under Water and Live There in all Winter.

This is Not to be comprehended, being so contrary to Nature & Reason, for as they cannot live in that State without some degree of Breathing, this requires the Circulation of the Blood, however weak & languid. Now as respiration is absolutely necessary for Circulation, how is it possible to be carried On, for so many Months, under water, without the Risque of Suffocation.

Besides, if so Remarkable a Change was Intended, the Great Wisdome of the Almighty Creator would undoubtedly be Seen in Some perticular contrivance in the Structure of the Organs of the Heart of this Bird to enable It to undergo so very remarkable a Change of Elements, and My Learned Friend Klein has not attempted to show any Thing of this Nature in order to confirme his System.

An Easie experiment may throw some light on this doubtfull affair. At the time of their going away, take a Swallow & confine it in a Tub under Water. If it remains There for a Week or Two without any remarkable Inconvenience, then there may be Some probability for its continuing so many Months in that State.

The conclusions that are drawn from Some of the Tribe of Insects subsisting under water are farr from being conclusions to found an analogy upon as insects differs from other animals in so many Particularities that very little or nothing can be concluded or inferred of the one from what wee observe in the other.

Towards the end of September the Swallows assemble on the Reeds (arundo) in the Islands in our River Thames, and have, no doubt so done for ages passed, and yett I never heard or Read of any fisher man or other Person that has ever found in the Winter Months a Swallow under water in a Torpid Living State, for if such a very Marvelous Thing had ever happened it would have been soon communicated to the Nation. Besides, as these Islands of Reeds and willows (salix) are annually cut down for several uses and yett not a Swallow has been discover'd in his Aquatic Aboad, and considering the multitudes I have seen on these Reeds & Willows in the Autumn, if they took their Winters residence under Water it is most reasonable to think in a River so frequented, and in so long a Course of years, some Swallows would have been found in that Situation.

Another circumstance I must add. In great towns remote from Water, where Rivers & Reeds are not near, I have frequently observed a little time before the Swallows depart they every morning Early gather together in Large Flocks on the Roofs of Houses exposed to the Morning Sun. This they dayly do for Some Time to collect Themselves before they take Their flight.

Next, to confirme my Opinion that the migration of Some Species of swallows is certain, I think I have Some Proofs. I have often heard Sir Charles Wager (first Lord of the

Admiralty) relate in one of his voyages Home to England, in the Spring of the year, as He came into Soundings in our Channel, a great flock of Swallows came and Settled on all his rigging. Every Rope was covered. They hung on one another like a Swarm of Bees. The Decks & carving about the Ship was filled with them. They seemed almost Spent and famished, was only feathers and Bones, but being recruited with a Nights Rest they took their Flight in the Morning.

Capt Wright a very Honest Man who I could depend on Told Mee the Like Happened to Him in a Voyage from Philadelphia to London.

But a yett stronger confirmation of the Swallows being Birds of Passage is Mr Adansons Observation in his History of Senegal[1] lately published vizt "The Sixth of October, at half an hour past Six in the evening, being about 50 Leagues from the Coast between the Island of Goree & Senegal four Swallows came to take up their nights Lodging on the Ship and alighted on the Shrouds. I easily caught all four and knew them to be true European Swallows. This lucky accident confirmed Mee in the Opinion I had formed that these Birds pass the Seas to gett into the Countries of the Torrid Zone at the approach of winter in Europe, and to that purpose I have Since remarked that they do not appear at Senegal but in that season. A circumstance no less worthy of remark is that at Senegal the Swallows do not build Nests as in Europe but lie every night in the Sands upon the Sea Shore." Hist de Senegal page 67.

This Observation as it comes from a professed Naturalist and One who went into those Countries on purpose to collect what was Curious certainly puts the Question out of doubt, that Swallows are Birds of Passage, and the Hear Say stories of Ignorant Peasants & Credulous People are by no means to be putt in competition with It.

I have for many years been very watchfull in takeing notice of the Times when the Swallows Leave Us, and have Twice seen Them undoubtedly taking their Flight at two Different years on the 27 & 29th of September. Walking in my Garden about Noone on a Bright Clear Day looking up to the Sky at a very great Heigth I distinctly saw Innumerable numbers of Swallows soaring round & round, higher & higher, until my Eyes was pained with Looking, I could no Longer Discern them.

But as my Learned Friend Klein seems to be so positive that the Hirundo Riparia at the approach of Winter retires into the Holes (in which they bred up their young & made their summer residence) and there Pass that Cold Season in a dormant state, as Snakes, lizards &c and some other animals do, I have been the More Solicitous to come at the Truth. But as these Sandy precipices in which these Birds Build their Nests are mostly inaccessible, Some years have passed before I could find a situation where the experiment could be fairly made without difficulty or Danger.

Such a Sand Hill I found at Byfleet in Surry. The Clergyman or Pastor being my Friend [not identified] & well Quallified to make the Tryal, at my Request he was so Obliging to undertake it.

I shall give his Letter to Mee in his own words.

Byfleet, October 22, 1757

Dear Sir

I took a Square of about Twelve Feet over that part of the Cliff where the holes was thickest, which in going down from the Surface would Take in 40 Holes. I Sett to work and came to the Holes but found No Birds, nothing but Old Nests at the end of the Holes, which were from 18 Inches to 30 inches deep from the Entrance.

"Wee carefully Searched Forty holes but found no Birds but at least Thirty of them had Nests. The passage to them was very Near in a Streight Horisontal Line. The Nests was Sunk about an Inch and 1/2 below the Level of the passage. The Materials next the Bottome was Straws, then Course of fine Grasses, the whole Structure of no great Elegance. The few Eggs that was left behind were of a Clear unspotted White, the Size of a Robin redbreasts."

This Carefull examination being made by a gentleman of Veracity & Ability is very Satisfactory & conclusive. For it certainly & clearly proves that the Hirundo riparia does not take up their winter abode in their Summer Habitations. Therefore there is Sufficient reason to Believe from all the before recited Observations that the swallows are Birds of Passage.

P. Collinson

JACOB THEODORE KLEIN (1685–1759), FRS, Zoologist, studied law at University of Königsberg and served as court secretary in Danzig from 1714. Studied sea urchins; founded botanical garden and naturalists society in Danzig; based his taxonomy purely on external characteristics and opposed the Linnaean system for that reason. Member of St. Petersburg Academy of Science and Royal Society and was a frequent contributor to *Philosophical Transactions,* 1730–1748. (DSB) His *Historicae Avium Prodromus* was published in Libecc, Germany in 1750.

This letter was read to the Royal Society on March 9, 1758 and filed in the Society's *Letters and Papers,* III, 300. A few days before Collinson had written Thomas Birch, the Society's Secretary, "Dear Dr, I see there is to be a Committee on papers. Pray bring Mine on the Migration of Swallows. I think it hard it should be postponed for Others who you see have done Nothing in So Long a Time. If It had been publish'd its probably by this Time Some other Discoveries might have come to Light." (ALS:BL)

On August 22, 1758 Collinson sent Linnaeus a copy of his letter to Klein with this note: "I wish the foregoing Dissertation was translated into Swedish and read before your R Society, of which I am a Member. Possibly it may excite some Person of Probity to give Matters of Fact of his own Knowledge relateing to the Migration of Swallows, for there is no depending on the reports of Ignorant Country People." (ALS:LS)

The letter was not published in the *Transactions* until 1760. See PC to Thomas Birch May 23, 1760.

Collinson long complained that Linnaeus did not refute the notion that swallows hibernated. See his May 20, 1762, September 15, 1763, September 25, 1766 and March 16, 1767 letters to Linnaeus.

The notion that swallows hibernated rather than migrated in the winter went back to Medieval times. Since European swallows migrated to North Africa and little was known of this area, it was thought that the swallows hibernated like frogs in the marshes. Naturalists investigating supposed "hibernating" swallows often found dead birds killed by starvation or cold. The belief that swallows hibernated persisted into the nineteenth century.

1. Michel Adanson (1727–1806), botanist and explorer, published *Histoire naturelle du Senegal.* Paris, 1757.

133 ❧ TO JOHN FREDERIC GRONOVIUS

ALS:APS
London, September 10, 1758

I had great pleasure in my Dear Friend Dr Gronovius Letter by Dr Seepin [not identified]. I am concern'd his Stay is so short In England. By Him I send you some fresh Seeds Just now arrived from the Coast of Malabar. Where there is Enough of a Sort, Sow half Directly & the other half next February.

I am pleased to hear the Gleditsia flowers in your Garden, but pray tell Mee what can be the Reason it has flower'd but once in England that I ever heard of it. I have a very Large Tree in my Garden but it never offers to Flower.

You have heard of the [obliterated]. This Gleditsea contradicts that System, for Take a young Tree in a Pott & Carry it into your Chamber or your Study which [passage missing] most convenient for the Observation. Att one a Clock at Night it begins to unfold its Leaves. At four a Clock in the Morning they are Quite expanded & so Continues untill twelve or One a Clock at Noone. From that time it continues gently Closing its Leaves untill one at Night.

I am glad to Hear Sebas 3 Vol is near publishing. In your next pray Mention the price.

Wee have had a very Rainey Summer, yett there was Some intervals of Dry Weather to gett in the Corn, of which there is plenty.

The Great Magnolia is now in Flower in Mr Grays[1] Garden, a Large Tree that Stands in the Open Air.

I am with much Respect your Affectionate Friend,   P COLLINSON

I had almost forgot to tell you that Mr Clayton has revised his Flo Virg & made great aditions and amendments. I am about getting it translated into English & so print the Lattin on one Side of the page and the English on the other Side. For you must know that very few of the Common People & also of the Gentry who have had University Education understand Botanic Lattin for no Dictionary gives the Synonims & Technical Terms, so it is very Difficult for an English Man to understand Description of plants unless he makes it his whole Study. When printed will send you a Coppy but that cannot be before next Christmas.

1. Christopher Gray (1694–1764) nurseryman on Fulham Road, London. He was known for his North American exotics. About 1737 he published *A catalogue of American trees and shrubs that* *will endure the climate of England,* illustrated with Mark Catesby's etching of *Magnolia grandiflora* (Henrey, p. 348).

134 ❧ TO JOHN FREDERICK GRONOVIUS

ALS: Library, Musée National D'Histoire Naturelle, Paris
London, December 26, 1758

In September last I had the pleasure to write to my Dear Friend Dr Gronovius by Dr Seepin [not identified] who made Leyden in his Way to Paris. By Him I sent a Box with Seeds & Fossells which I hope he delivered safe to your Hands.

I Doubt not but it will be very acceptable to you to see the Bearer Dr [Thomas] Clayton[1], in consideration of the Respect and Friendship & Long Correspondence you have had with his Father, John Clayton Esq of Virginia.

He has revised the Flora Virginica & made many aditions & amendments. Wee only wait for an English Translation, to print with the Lattin, and then it will be published.

The young Gentleman studies Physick, Has taken his Degrees of Doctor at Edinburgh. He comes over to go through a Course of your Coledges if they will not detain Him too long, for He Intends going to Virginia in the Spring Ships.

As He is Quite a Stranger, beg the favour you will recommend Him to the professor & where He may Lodge & Diet.

I beg your acceptance of a Curious Print of all the Botanic that are come to our Notice [not located].

I am with much Respect, your affectionate Friend,

P. COLLINSON

As you have more frequent oppertunities of Sending to Paris, beg Leave to trouble you with Small percell for Mr Bufons.

When Dr Clayton returns if any Books are come to your hands from Dr Haller or Mr Buffons, they may be sent by Him to your friend,   P C

And pray write Mee what New Works & Discoveries have been made since your last Letter of June 1758.

No Seeds are yett arrived but these Inclosed from Mr Clayton.

1. Thomas Clayton, see headnote to PC to Thomas Clayton, March 25, 1768.

135 ❧ TO CADWALLADER COLDEN

ALS:N-YHS
London, March 6, 1759

I had the pleasure to receive my Dear Friends Letter of November 14 & your Good Sons of December 14th, the 19th of January. I Joyn with you in the Common Joye in our success at Fort Duquene. No Doubt but Crown point had been in our Hands if your General Officer had been Equal to the Trust reposed in him, Intrenchments without artilery. I that understand so Little of the Matter was surprised. When I read the Account I cry'd out where was Our Great Ordinance to Batter down the Entrenchments, and then to med the Matter to trust to a single Letter to Gen Amharst.[1] The least He could have Done was to have sent Messenger after Messenger for fear of Mistakes, & Delays. Such a poor Fool has Deservedly the resentment of the principal people Here.

I instantly had recourse to your Dedication and find your prediction verifyed by the Conduct of the Indian [in] this Warr. The Remedy is in our Own Power, but who is their Equall to It? Where is the Man of Integrity & Probity to be found to undertake this reformation. Wee may Lament want of Publick Spirit & the Situation of our Colonies under a Sett of Governors who has their own private Interest most at Heart.

I am now reading Father Henepin[2] & although Some of his Accounts are rendering Suspicious by a Sett of Crafty Jesuits, who envied his successfull discoveries, yett in his Accounts of the Natives I think he may be Credited as He was the first European that Vissited many Indian Nations, yett it is his General observation that He found no sort of Worship amongst them by some very Imperrfect Ideas of a Bad Spirit & Sometimes of a Good One & to the Sun they made some compliment on some Occasions.

It may be very True that your Nephew may not mention the Receiving your papers with Considerable Corrections from Mee, yett by the Tenour of my Letters which metion those papers being Deliver'd to Dr Bevis Implies as Much, & now Wee are requesting their return, & I have writt & your Nephew has been with Dr Bevis in some Men that I cannot Account For—they neither Will, nor Will Not but make promises—because Easiest done.

The Reasons you assin may be very Just for the Leaving Niagra unattempted. As Fort Duquene is so Luckyly fell into Our hands that I hope will come next in Course on that side the Country.

Pray give Mr. Ellis's & my Respects to Miss Jenny. All that Wee have done, & said, is Due to Her. Wee hope to see more of her Works.

I wrot you by the last pacquet the 19th January and acquainted you Wee was so happy as to receive your Ingenious Sone Davids Electrical Experiments which I sent Directly to your Nephew & Next to Mr Franklin [who] is to have them for his Examination. It happens very suiteable for Him for he has Just finish'd an Electrical Machine on his own place which is remarkly Different from any I have seen. This answers yours of November 14 as farr as my Leisure will allow Mee at present.

Now I come to Consider yours of November 25th. When Wee gett your papers from Dr Bevis, I shall be glad of your more particular Order and Directions about printing them. Mr Dodesly[3] told Mee he lost so much by the first Impression, that He will not undertake a Second. If it is printed it must be at your own expense.

The correcting the press is another Article of the greatest consequence in Calculations. The Least Error will make Sad Work. Your Nephews Time is so much Engross'd as He is now I take it principal Clerk in a Vast extensive Business, I don't see how He can do it, if he had ever so great an Inclination.

This my Dear Friend is the State of the Case as it appears to Mee at this Juncture.

I shall be rejoiced to hear your Amiable Daughter is well over Innoculatin that her person may be as fair, as Her mind.

Now my Dear Friend Farewell   P. COLLINSON

Fail not to make my Thanks & Respects acceptable to your Son Alexander.[4] His obligeing Letter & the News paper Inclosed was very Acceptable. I hope he will not Insist to write home a particular answer. If I had Leisure I should Certainly do, but really I am so press'd for Time that this Letter if it may be Called So has had 2 or 3 Essays before I could patch it up as it is.

The 14 February our Fleets saild for your World. Wee hope it will please God to give a Blessing to arms, the War may Drive the Enemy from all their strong Hold.

Our African Expedition you'l see Succeeded by the publick papers & Wee hear our Troops was Landed safe at Martinico [Martinique?]. For all that they will have hard Work to Conquer the Inhabitants. I wrote Last Month by the Packquett which I hope you received.

You formerly sent Mee the Saracena which thrives and flowers every year. In the Moss with it came Little Spruce, Firr, & a Larch. They are Now grown pretty Trees, & this year I transplanted them out of the Nurssery where they may grow & make a figure & be Memorials of our Friendship.

The Books all that I could gett will be putt in Mrs Alexander's Trunk to come by first Ships. Possibly May not have Leisure to Advise you of them.

1. Jeffrey Amherst (1717–1797), British soldier sent to America in 1758 after several successful campaigns on the Continent. Led the capture of Louisburg, the first British victory in the Seven Years War.

2. Father Louis Hennepin (1626–1705), Franciscan Recollect, missionary and explorer in North America. He went to Canada in 1675 with La Salle, who made him chaplain of his proposed Western expedition in 1678. After some time at Fort Frontenac, Hennepin's party sailed in the first ship on the Great Lakes to Green Bay. He then crossed to the Mississippi by the Illinois River route. His party became the first to explore the upper Mississippi Valley, ascending the River to Minnesota where he was captured by the Sioux.

He was rescued by Duluth. In 1681 he returned to France where he wrote an account of his travels in *Description de la Louisiane* (1683–84). (*Dictionary of Canadian Biography,* II: 277–281)

3. Robert Dodsley, London bookseller and publisher. See

Nichols, John. *Minor Lives.* Edward L. Hart ed. Cambridge MA, 1971

4. Alexander Colden (1716–1774). Postmaster of New York.

136 ❧ TO JOHN RUSSELL, 4TH DUKE OF BEDFORD

Draft LS:LS
April 12, 1759

I cannot forget the Duke of Bedfords Extensive plantation of Evergreens when it is in my power to Add to it, which I now hope to Do, by this present of Siberia White firr seed & Russian Larex.

It gives Mee real pleasure to hear of its prosperity, because with your Grace's leave I think my Self in Some Small Degree interested in It, by procuring that Variety of North American Pines, firrs & Cedars &c &c of which it is composed.

For Mr Miller knowing I had correspondence abroad in our Colonies desired Mee to send for a Collection of Seeds from thence for your Grace. Accordingly I brought Over in the years 1742, 1743 & 1744, each year, a Large Chest of Seeds of Trees & Shrubs from Pensilvania. From these I have hear'd Sprang up the principal Materials for raiseing this Noble Plantation which I am informed excels all others in this kingdom.

Yours,   P. COLLINSON

The Trouble & pains in getting these Seeds Over is amply Compensated by the Success that has attended them besides the pleasure it gives Mee that I can Oblige my Curious Friends as well as Improve (or at least Embelish) my Country.

I am with Due Respects and acknowledgments for the favourable Reception you gave Mee & my Friend Allen [not identified] last Tuesday.

Your Graces Friend, Yours &c   PC

137 ❧ TO CARL LINNAEUS

ALS:LS
London, July 20, 1759
[continued July 25 and 26]

I have the Pleasure to salute my Dear Linnaeus by the Hands of my Valuable Friend Dr Bierken.[1] The loss of his Company I much regret, but cannot forget the many agreeable conversations Wee have had in Examening my Cabinet. Botany was not his favourite So I could not tempt Him to make my Garden a Visit, which is Enriched with many Rare Plants & Trees not to be seen Elcewhere.

You may Blame Mee for not answering your Queries concerning the Hominum Troglidy [Homines Troglodytes], but as our Friend Ellis undertook to do It, I thought it needless to repeat It over again as He was a perfect Master on that Subject.

Dr Fothergill is much pleased with your Letter. Your Plan of procuring the Chinese

Specifics is a good one, if it could be Carryed into Execution. Many Difficulties attends it from Us (that is from England), for Wee are not permitted to go up into the Country, and it requires a Great Length of Time to be well Versed in their language.

A Jesuit well Skilled in Physick & Medicine is the only Man that can attain this great Discovery, for He has access to the Emperor's Court may very Easily get acquainted with the Chinese Physicians.

Or If the Court of Russia would adopt this Scheme & permit Two Skilfull Swedish Physicians to go in their Carravan to Pekin & procure them a Licence from the Chinese Court for their tarrying there Some years to Learn the Language & make Acquaintance with their Apothecaries & Physicians, then Wee might Hope to attain the Knowledge of their Art of Healing & of their Materia Medaca. I don't see any Other Way to attain It. [continued on the same sheet]

London, July 25, 1759

I Lament the Long Absence of poor [Daniel] Solander.[2] What can be the Meaning of this Delaye. Is no certain Advice come of his Fate? Is not the name of the Ship known & the Port from whence She sailed?

I thank you for yours of May 31st. Wee had the Mildest Winter ever known. Our Spring was Early & very Agreeable and our Summer the the finest & Warmest Since the year 1750. Great plenty of all Sorts of Grain & Fruits. New Wheat of this year's produce has been the 21st Instant at Market.

For all Sorts of News I recommend you to Dr Bierken who is well acquainted with the Curious People Here.

I have Two Species of what is called Rhuberbirum Vera, the One broad Leaves, the other Long narrow Curl'd Leaves. The one was sent Mee from the Jesuits at Pekin, the other was from my Dear Friend Dr Amman. But I Observed a very different plant of Rhubarb in the Chelsea Garden, which Mr Millar tells Mee was sent Him (I think) from Holland

Daniel Carl Solander. William Parry. The Linnean Society of London.

has all the Characters of the True Rhubarb. I here send you some Good Seed gather'd July 18 in the Chelsea Garden.

Having so convenient an opportunity I send you the Money Due you after I had paid for Dr Browns Specimens which Is Six of our shillings.

In one of your Letters you mention sending Mee your New Edition of Systema Natura, but I have not yett received It, which is a great disappointment to Mee.

I am glad you received the papiliones [butterflies].

Lett Mee hear from you, which always gives Sensible Pleasure to your affectionate Friend
P. COLLINSON

My address is to Mr Peter Collinson Merchant in Grace Church Street, London.

[Separate sheet, but probably a continuation of the same letter]

July 26, 1759

Pray my Dear Friend, don't forget to Tell Mee what certain Discoveries have been made on the Migration of Swallows. What is said by your self, and other Curious People, to my Paper on that subject? I fully Expected to have heard Something on It before this Time.

1. Possibly John Berkenhout (1730–1801), physician, naturalist and writer. Educated in Germany and attended Edinburgh University to study medicine in 1760. (DNB)

2. Daniel Carl Solander (1736–1782), FRS, botanist born in Sweden, studied under Linnaeus who "cherished him as a son" under his own roof. (Smith, J. E. *A Selection of the Correspondence of Linnaeus*. London, 1821)

In 1756 Collinson wrote Linnaeus asking him to send someone to help him catalogue his garden according to the Linnaean system. Solander arrived in England in 1760 with introductions to John Ellis and Collinson. Elected FRS 1764, he was reputed to have a phenomenal memory for plants and helped popularize the Linnaean system of classification. With Collinson's help (see PC to William Watson, October 5, 1762) he was appointed assistant librarian in the British Museum. In 1768 Solander accompanied Joseph Banks on Cook's voyage in the *Endeavour;* in 1772 he visited Iceland with Banks; in 1773 he was made keeper of printed books in the Museum. (DNB; Rauschenberg, Roy Anthony. "Daniel Carl Solander, Naturalist on the Endeavour." *Transactions of the American Philosophical Society* New series 58 Part 8 (November, 1968); Marshall, John Braybrooke. "Daniel Carl Solander, friend, librarian and assistant to Sir Joseph Banks." *Archives of Natural History* II (3) (1984): 451–456.

138 ❧ TO ARTHUR DOBBS

Draft AL:LS

August 10, 1759

Peaches are in Great Plenty in Our Colonies yett it is much Doubted (tho it is affirmed) by Others to be an original American Fruite, but most likely to be carried from Europe by the Spaniards under John de Ponce[1] anno 1521 but more likely by the French under Mon Ribalds[2] who attempted for 2 or 3 years or more to Settle Florida. In Order to It, brought over animals, Horses, Cows, Hoggs, goats &c, all manner of vegitable Seeds etc, Grains & Fruits.

Peaches are most Easily raised from Stones & when they was Drove off by the the Spaniards, probably left such Improvements behind them. The Indians though a people not Curious probably Introduced the Peach tree into their plantations.

But its plain they was Little Cultivated for Don Fer De Soto[3] in the year 1539 He with His Spaniards rambled above a thousand Miles backward & forward all over Florida for 2 or 3 years, is perticular in Mentioning all the Fruits He mett with in that Long Journey, but mentions not any Peach found, and Father Henepen in anno 1680 First Navigated the great River Messesipi near the Center & principal River of all Florida, visited the Indian Nations for some hundreds of Miles on both banks of that River & was Long a prisioner in that Country yett takes no notice that He saw any Peaches in Fruit or Dry, or in Cakes. Under his great Necessities so remarkable a Fruit & Food could not Escape Him.

This consider'd there is no reason to believe it an American Fruit but brought & Left by the French or brought over by the English, First to Virginia, for it was Customary for Every Nation that made new Settlements to carry over their native Country Seeds & Productions. At no doubt the first Settlers of Carolina in 1664 did the Same in that fertile Soil & fine Climate. The Fruit Increasing & falling down Spring up from the Stones & bear fruit 2 or 3 or 4 years at most. By this means it was soone Spread all the country Over & being a Juicy Fruit Suited the Climate better than apricot or nectarines.

The Indians soon became acquainted with them and adopted them an Article of their Food, for Mr Lawson in his History of Carolina[4] tells us he was treated by the Indians with Peach Cakes or Bread & dryd Peaches.

I am told that there is a Sett of White Indians now on Hatteras Island being Supposed to be the Offspring of the Fifty Men left on that Island by Sr Richard Grenville[5] anno 1585

Collinson noted in his Commonplace Book following this draft, "I have had no answer to this Letter. I apprehend it Miscarried."

1. Juan Ponce de Leon (c. 1460–1521), Spanish explorer, discoverer of Florida.

2. Jean Ribaut or Ribault (1520–1565), French mariner and colonizer in Florida.

3. Hernando De Soto (1500–1542), Spanish explorer in the present United States who led an expedition to Florida in 1539 and moved halfway across the continent, wintering near Tallahassee, then moving north through Georgia and the Carolinas into Tennessee, before turning South into Alabama. In the spring of 1541 he made the first sighting and crossing of the Mississippi by a Euro-

pean. He led his company up the Arkansas River into Oklahoma before turning back to the banks of the Mississippi, where he died. He was buried in the Mississippi.

4. Lawson, John. *The History of Carolina.* London: W. Taylor, 1714. In the passage referred to Lawson observes, "It is very much doubted if Peaches are an American fruit. It is more probable it was brought by the French who for some years attempted a settlement in the Bay of Mexico on the Coast of Florida in Lat. under John Ribalds anno 1562."

5. Richard Grenville (1542–1591), English naval officer, cousin of Sir Walter Raleigh, commanded a fleet of seven vessels carrying the first colonists to Roanoke Island in 1585.

139 ❧ TO JARED ELIOT

ALS: Yale

London, August 30, 1759

In March Last I wrote my Dear Friend of the Sasonnak, Capt Johnson[1] & sent what I could collect relateing to the Virtues of Salt. A Little leisure gives Mee Times to consider some other parts of your obliging Letter of the 8th of Augt. I shall be pleased to heare the Sicily Wheat is increased. I am glad to find it does not degenerate.

Your agent Mr. Ingoldhol [Ingersoll][2] was so Obliging as to Call on Mee but did not impart to Mee the Nature of his Business, So I could not show my inclination to serve Him or Your Colony, whose prosperity I have much at heart.

Yours of Sep: 2 has been fully Answer'd by Mine of the Accompanying Duplicates of the Instructions from the Society for Incouragemt of Arts & Commerce, which I forwarded by Two Ships for fear of Accidents. These I hope at least one of them is come Safe to hand & proves Satisfactory & will encourage the Silk Manufacture which can't fail in process of Time to Enrich your province.

White Mulberry Seed may be Easily procured from any of your Southern Colonies, as I hinted in my Letters. Mulberrys are of very quick growth Either from Seed or Layers. The only Way to Make it a General Case is to give a Bounty to those that raise a Certain Number of Mulberry Trees & plant them out in plantation Every year the Bounty to Increase, until they are of Seven Years Growth, but this I submit to the Wisdom of Your Legislatureship.

I am concerned there should be Such narrow minded principal prevail amongst your people not to plant because they themselves may not enjoye the fruits of their Labours. If their ancestors had embraced those principles what would their Situation have been at a Time they most wanted the Necessaries & Conveniences of Life.

The present of Silk from the Fair manufacturer was a happy presage of what may be expected when It becomes universal. I sent it to the Society who received it with great pleasure, for by a Little they saw What might be produced in Time.

Thus have I hudled a few Lines together to testify the respect of your Sincere Friend,

P. COLLINSON

Pay my Respects to our Worthy Friend Dr [Thomas] Clapp.

Pray write Mee Soone for it will give Mee great pleasure to hear the Instructions from the Society are come Safe. I hope to have your Remarks on them & their practibility.

What you relate of your Wild Cherry of which I have Some fine Trees, tho the Leaves etc may have So pernitious an Effect & yett I have Eat the fruit without any ill consequences. Like as our Laurel which though an Evergreen is of the Same family, being the Evergreen cluster Cherry, the Fruit I have often Eat without any Hurt & the Simple Distilled Water is a certain Poison.

If our Cattle Eat our Yew Tree it has the Same Effect as your Wild Cherry. The Simple Distil'd water from our Native Black Cherry was once in the highest Vogue for convulsive fitts in young Children, has been lately found of a Poisonous Quality So is expurged from our last Dispensatory, to the great Loss of the owners of the Black Cherry Orchards, but they are yett used in Brandy.

I have not the *London Magazine* for July 1757[3] so cannot tell what the proposal Was to make pott-ash, but this I know, one [Thomas] Stephens was Encouraged by the Government to communicate his methods of making pottash to the Colonies & accordingly went over to New England & I heard say had sett up Works, but with what Success I know not.

Would not raiseing of Hemp turn to Account in your Deep rich Strong Lands, which comes Sooner to Market to turn the Penny than Vines.

But no doubt Wine would turn to a good Account. A Light pleasant Wine would sell well in all our Sugar Islands. The Rhenish Grape I am apt to think would succeed best. It would produce a Good Mossell Wine if not a Rhenish Wine, & by Length of Time old Hock, but this requres time & Experience.

What I am surprised att, that So Many Germans comeing from the Country along the Rhine to Pensilvania, none should attempt makeing of their own country Wine if it was but for their own Drinking. And if Some ingenious Men in your Colony would plant a Quarter of an Acre of Vines in a VineYard, in a Warm Stoney Soil declineing to the South by way of experience to try their Skill & bring their hands In & make it of Such European Grapes as they can gett & Improve that Sort that Succeeds best, but if amongst the Number of Germans they could procure one only to Introduce them into the Methods they well sett out with better Hopes of Success. But [if] this affair is [not] undertaken in Earnest, with a resolution that no disappointment shall discourage, it is in vain to begin, for that I am Informed has been the Case of all the Colonies to the Southward, they have attempted Wine Makeing Butt because it did not presently succeed, they was disheartened & So all their past Labour & pains thrown Away.

1. "Sassenach"—Gaelic word for "Saxon" or English (OED). Sir William Johnson (1715–1774) Irish Superintendent of Indian Affairs in North America.

2. Jared Ingersoll (1722–1781), lawyer, public official, born Milford, Connecticut. In 1758 he was commissioned by the Connecticut government to act as their London Agent in order to recoup monetary losses suffered in the War between England and France. He was successful.

3. *London Magazine* Vol. XXVI (July 1757): 318–19 contains a footnote on the problems of producing pot-ash in the colonies. It does not mention Thomas Stephens.

Stephens published *The Rise and Fall of Pot-Ash in America; Addressed to the Right Honourable The Earl of Halifax.* London, 1755.

140 ❧ TO BENJAMIN COOK

Draft ALS:LS
Goodwood, October 1, 1759

This Fine Weather gilds the Charming Scenes about Goodwood, which Draws Us out to ramble over the Lofty Downs. With a Longing Eye I survey your fertile spott from one End to the other & see St Rook stare old Kate in the face.[1] But O the Gulph between & the many Matters that Clogg my Mind & Check my Ready Steps from wandering Further. The Magnet from my Little Flock at Mill Hill attracts Mee Home too powerfully to be resisted.

Pray my dear Cousen explain this Introduction, Why to tell you truly the young Duke and Duchess of Richmond have brought Mee down to Goodwood where my Stay is so Short & so much Business, to Crop the Luxuriency of Nine years Vegitation, that I can not now contrive to trip over to the Isle of Wight to make my dear Cosen a Visit.

How soone nine years slides away, for so many it is Since I accompanied My Dear Friend, the old Duke of Richmond down Heither. He was extreamly fond of planting and had at that Time the best Collection of Exotic hardy Trees that was then in England. These as I said before had Grown so freely that they Incumbered one another.

This Work the present young Duke[2] reserved for Mee to curtail & Lop. You know my Dear Cosen my Task so you' conclude I had great pleasure in these Operations as I remembered their first planting, and between whiles we was projecting new Schemes & plans for the future Improvement & ornament at Goodwood.

The Duke & Duchess great Friendship and cordial treatment added to all the Other Delights made this Journey perfectly agreeable.

It would have been more so if I could have paid my Respects to my Dear Cosen, but you had the Sincere Inclination of your aff Cou   PC

BENJAMIN COOK (d.1774) surgeon and antiquary at Newport on the Isle of Wight and Collinson's cousin. Supplied "Ancient Weapons" to Sir Hans Sloane through Collinson. See MacGregor, Arthur, ed. *Sir Hans Sloane.* London, 1994, p. 182.

1. St. Rook is above and behind Goodwood; "Old Kate" is St. Kathrine's Hill, from which one could look across to Goodwood and St. Rook.

2. Charles Lennox, third Duke of Richmond (1735–1806), married Lady Mary Bruce April 1, 1757.

Above: Proposals for The Aurelian. *Moses Harris. Natural History Museum, Entomology Library, London*

Right: Scarlet Tiger Butterflies. Moses Harris. The Aurelian . . . , *plate XL—dedicated to Peter Collinson. Natural History Museum, Entomology Library, London.*

MARY LENNOX, Duchess of Richmond (d. 1796), wife of Charles, the Third Duke of Richmond. The Duke and Duchess did subscribe: plates XIX and XX are dedicated to them.

1. Moses Harris (1731–1788), English entomologist, watercolorist, and engraver, Secretary of Society of Aurelians, 1762, published *The Aurelian or Natural History of English Insects; Namely, Moths and Butterflies. Together with the Plants on which they Feed* (1766) (with plate XL dedicated to Collinson), and *Exposition of English Insects* (1782).

143 ❧ TO PAUL GREGORIVITCH DEMIDOFF

Draft ALS:LS
March 5, 1760

To Mr. Greg: Demidoff, proprietor of the Iron Mines in Siberia, a letter of Recommendation to my friend Mr. Blackburne.

My Dear Friend

Your regard for the English and your Benevolent Disposition are prevailing Motives with Mee to recommend my Valuable Friend Mr. Blackburne to your Favour. He is a gentleman of an unblemished Character, with so ample a fortune as might place Him above the rank of a Merchant.

But you know the Active Genius of the English Inspires them with the Love of Trade and Business.

He visits Petersburgh with some Views that Way.

Your assistance will be Esteemed as a singular favor shown to Your &c,

PC

PAUL GREGORIVITCH DEMIDOFF (1738–1826). Wealthy Russian mineowner; traveler; went to Uppsala where he became acquainted with Linnaeus and his system; "natural history, formed his favorite study." Had a rich cabinet of natural curiosities and a botanical garden. (*Nouvelle Biographie Universelle* . . . Paris, 1852–66)

144 ❧ TO THOMAS BIRCH

ALS:BL
May 23, 1760

Dear Dr

I Submitt to you if the Remarks beneath will not be proper to be added by way of Postscript as they are pertinent to the Subject, from yours,   P. COLLINSON

PS Since my writeing the Above paper[1] on the Migration of Swallows, it may Deserve Notice that there is four Distinct Species of Birds, that go under the General Name, vizt

The Swift or Black Martin

The Swallow that builds on Chimneys

The Martin that builds against Houses

The Sand Martin that builds in Sand banks

I hope I have clearly proved that Some of these Species are Birds of passage. But Some of my Friends assert they pass the Winter in Cliffs or Caverns of the Earth, on Banks, or precipices.

What is much to be regretted that the Gentlemen were not curious to distinguish the particular Species they found in the Torpid State. And Mr Adanson at Senegal is Guilty of the like Omission.

So nothing Certain can yet be pronounced, which Species Stays, or which goes.

The Note on the Other Side [not given] I hope will putt people for the Time to Come to be more Carefull to Note the Species which may bring it to a Certainty.

1. "A letter to the Honorable J. Th. Klein . . . concerning the migrating swallows. *Philosophical Transactions* LI, part II (1760): 459–464. The contents of this letter appear as an "Additional remark" on p. 464.

Draft ALS:LS
London, September 25, 1760

To his Excellency the Right Honourable the Earl of Kinnoull, our Ambassador att Lisbon.

My Lord if you please to reflect on your Love for plants & planting, you will not be Surprised if excited by the like Ardour I take the freedome to address your Lordship & submitt some hints to your Consideration.

I have long taken Notice of the Latitude of the Islands of Azores from 36 to 40 N. Lat & how Little Wee know of them & their productions, as they lay near Mid Way between the Old World & the New. They seeme a Little World by themselves & highly probable abound with Trees, Shrubs & Flowers not to be found in Either. Most of these Islands are related to be covered with Woods &c &c.

The Island of Fayall [Faial] is said to take its Name from the Great number of Beeches or Some Trees like them. As Wee know the Beech is a Northern Tree & thrives well in climates more North than ours, why should not the other Trees & shrubs of those Islands do the like?

The Island of Flores [is so named] from the great Quantities of Flowers observed to grow there.

Could not your Lordship form some plan to gett certain Intelligence of the Vegitable State of these Islands & procure Seeds from Thence?

The Portuguese are very incurious, but as frequent opportunities must offer from Lisbon thither, is but a Short voyage, I wish your Lordships present Situation & Interest could be made subservient to the purpose & permission granted for a proper person to go & search those Islands & collect what He Could. But as they are great Bigots & hate protestants, If an Irish papist could be found that had a Botanic Turn its probable He would succeed better than any other.

Besides Vegitable rarities, there is no doubt but these Islands have many others, which would highly gratifie a Curious Mind, vizt shells & corals & other Marine productions unknown to us, besides Birds, Insects &c and perhaps Some Animals.

This Rude Essay my Dear Lord is with great Diference submitted to your more Mature Judgment.

By your Sincere & Affectonate Friend,   P. COLLINSON

THOMAS HAY, 8th Earl of Kinnoull (1710–1787), statesman, and ambassador to Portugal, 1759.

146 ❧ TO RICHARD WALKER

Draft AL:LS
[circa March 19, 1761]

My dear friend Doctor Walker

It gives Mee great comfort of Mind to think I could be any ways Instrumental to prompt your Benovelent Heart (always disposed to Good Works) Generously to Purchase the Ground & settle a plan for a Botanic Garden att Cambridge for 1600 pounds.

I wish it was in my power to give you that assistance so great a Work requires, but I shall contribute my Mite & by tomorrow Wagon send a Basket of some fine perennial Ground Plants, but I have no Duplicates of Shrubs & Evergreens, but I am not without hopes you will be supplyed if my poor Eloquence can move the Hearts of my Friends Mr Gordon, Mr Gray, and Mr Williamson[1] to be Generous & send you a Collection of Trees, Shrubs etc.

RICHARD WALKER (1679–1764), Professor of Moral Philosophy at Cambridge, purchased the property on July 16, 1760 and gave it in trust "for the purpose of a public Botanic Garden" on August 25, 1762. (Walters, S. M. *The Shaping of Cambridge. Botany,* Cambridge, 1981, 40–41)

This draft is written on the open sheet of Walker's March 19, 1761 letter to Collinson describing the planned garden. Walker wrote, "But to have a notion of the Garden you must come and see it, and I believe it will please you who was the first Author of the designs and I believe had not been undertaken without your encouragement & expectation of its usefulness to the knowledge of Botany."

At the foot of Walker's letter Collinson wrote, "Dr Walker was & is Sub Master of Trinity College, Cambridge. The good Man possess'd of a Considerable Estate that has Enabled Him to Purchase the Ground for the Botanic Garden and at his Death Interest to Endow a Botanic professorship, which both Garden & a professor is that been Much Wanted, To the Great Scandal of the University who spend so much in Gormandising there was nothing to spare for so usefull an Institution."

Collinson published "Some account of a physic garden at Cambridge." *Gentleman's Magazine* XXV (May 1765): 212.

1. John Williamson (fl. 1755–1780), acquired in 1756 Kensington Nursery founded by Robert Furber. (Desmond)

147 ❧ TO JOHN STUART, 3RD EARL OF BUTE

Draft ALS:LS
October 29, 1761

The very Gracious reception our good King & Queen was pleased to give our Friends today begets in our Minds a True & Gratefull Sence of that high Favour, & Wee my Dear Lord (my Self in particular) are not Insensible of the Obligations Wee lay under to you that the Interview was concluded with so General a Satisfaction.

This my Lord is intended to be acknowledged in a proper manner the First Oppertunity.

The King was so Indulgent to hint to Mee (I may say ask'd Mee) to see Kew Gardens & the Princess Wales favoured Mee with a particular Invitation.

So when your Lordship will please to Honour Mee with a Note, when it would be suiteable, I shall with pleasure see your wonderful operations & the Improvement those Gardens have rec'd from your great Skill in Every Branch of Science.

I am &c

P. COLLINSON

JOHN STUART, 3rd Earl of Bute (1713–1792), politician, noted patron of botany and horticulture, amassed a remarkable botanical library and had gardens of botanic significance at Luton Hoo, Bedfordshire, and later at Highcliffe, Dorset. He advised Princess Augusta on the development of her garden at Kew, acting as the Dowager Princess's "principal manager." (Henrey, Vol II, 241–2; Desmond). The genus *Stewartia* is named in his honor.

At the foot of this draft Collinson wrote, "1761—This 29 Oct went up with a deputation of 24 Friends with adresses [to] the King, Queen & Princess of Wales [expressing loyalty to George III who had recently assumed the Crown]. After the addresses was read, the King & Princess indulged Mee with a conversation on Kew Gardens & planting &c &c.

"Lord Bute's influence & Example & Advice has had a happy Effect on the King's uniform Conduct whilst Prince of Wales.

"From His Lordships great knowledge in the Science of Botany the Gardens at Kew have been furnish'd with all the Rare Exotick Trees & Flowers that could be procured.

"This summer 1761 the Princess of Wales built a high pagoda Summer house in Kew Gardens."

148 ❦ TO CARLO ALLIONI

ALS: University of Turin
London, November 25, 1761

I have the pleasure to acquaint my Learned Friend Dr Allione that his kind present of Seeds came Safe but Wish they had come Sooner in the year. However, Wee have raised Several of Them which adds to my Collection.

The american Seeds are not Yett arrived. But what few Seeds ripen'd in my Garden are here Inclosed.

I have great Variety of American Trees, Shrubs, & Flowers in my Garden, but few bring their Seeds to perfection for want of a Warm Italian Sun.

Inclosed is a list [not given] of Seeds that Will be very Acceptable to your Friend

P. COLLINSON

I want the Cortusa Mathiolii & Chamaepitys austricace & any others.

CARLO ALLIONI (1708–1804), "the Piedmont Linnaeus," Professor of Botany at the University of Turin, author of *Flora Pedemontana* 2vols., 1785 and other works.

149 ❦ TO CARL LINNAEUS

ALS: LS
[circa 1762]

My Dear Friend Dr. Linnaeus

As this is like to be the Last Ship for your Ports, I could not ommitt giveing you a Testimony of my Respect & for your Amusement Have sent you the progress of this Year's Spring in My Garden Situate on a High Hill north of London, but in the Warm Vales South of London the Spring is generally Two Weeks Before my garden.

Wee had very Temperate Warm Weather January, February & March Last, but our Summer has been pretty warm, but attended with much Rain which retards the Harvest but now fine Weather is sett in so I hope all will be well.

In this Magazine [*Philosophical Transactions*] you will see more of Mr Ellis Observations. I doubt but you have seen His History of Coralines.[1]

Pray in your Next Letter give Mee your Opinion of It without Reserve.

I am your Sincere Friend

P. COLLINSON

The Kalmias have flower'd finely this year.

Pray Tell Mee how many Books has Dr Kalm printed of His Voyage & His Journey to America.

When ever you see or write to Dr Kalm Tell Him He has quite forgot Mee.

You will Soone have your Deploma finely Ornamented.

1. Ellis, John. "Account of an Encrinus or Starfish" and "Account of the Male and Female Cochineal Insects . . ." *Philosophical Transactions* LII (1762), 357; 661.

ALS:PRO
Mill Hill, February 1, 1762

These Hints [the enclosed "Memorial" which follows] relateing to St Augustine [Florida] Copied by my Son are Humbly submitted to your Ldships better Judgement by yours, very Respectfully,   P. COLLINSON.

I Long for the Warmer Months that I may have the Honour of Visiting Kew Gardens with your Lordship.

Memorial relating to St Augustine by   P. COLLINSON

As I have been for 40 years well acquained with our colonies, being connected with them in a continued course of trade, and correspondence, it has given me frequent opportunities of knowing many interesting circumstances relating to them.

I beg to revive to your Lordship some particulars relating to St Augustine and its importance, which I am persuaded, has not escaped your vigilence. It is hoped from your Lordships influence we shall avail ourselves of this rupture with the Spainards, to get immediate possession of it, as it always has been and ever will be, a thorn in our sides, if they keep it, to the great detriment of our colonies, for to this asylum repair many of our bad people, who run away for debt, to cheat their creditors, and enrich the Spainards.

Then it is an harbour for runaway servants, and negroes, to their emolument. From hence, an illicit trade is carried on with our people, to other Spanish settlements, to the great loss of the fair trader, and his Majesty's customs.

Unless it is timely reduced, our infant colony of Georgia, this is exposed to Spanish depredations and even Carolina is not secure from them, and whilst it remains in their hands they will always spirit up a party of Indians, all along that coast to strip and slaughter, the unfortunate mariners ship wrecked on it.

If that headstrong Admiral Vernon[1] had obeyed his orders, given by Sr. Charles Wager, who knew its great consequence, it had not now been in Spanish hands. I need not add further to your Lordship the necessity of its being in ours, as it is the only check to the extending our settlements on that side, and will secure to us, a long range of coast, and country to the Cape of Florida; besides, it is the nearest Spanish port from whence we can be greatly annoyed with their privateers, who no doubt will distress a sort of inland navigation amongst their islands, all along that coast and ravage the settlements on them, unless some strong small vessels, are stationed on that quarter, and men of war besides, to protect Carolina, and Virginia &c.

P. COLLINSON.

A draft of this letter appears in Collinson's smaller commonplace book at the LS. Following the draft he wrote, "Happyly for England the French by their Family Compact, Drew the Spainards into a Warr with Us, Wee prosecuted it Gloriously & took the Havanna & their Fleet & all the Kings Treasure anno 1762. The French being obliged to Make Peace, & the Spainards to gett back the Havanna amongst other Articles, Surrendered St Augsteen & all Florida to us as farr as the R: Messesiepi, so fortunately all the purposes of my Memorial was answer'd. Feb 9, 1763."

See Anderson, Fred, *Crucible of War: The Seven Years' War and the Fate of Empire in British North America, 1754–1766.* New York, 2000.

(See Collinson to The Society for the Encouragement of Arts . . . , November 10, 1763.)

1. Edward Vernon (1684–1757), admiral. On 19 July 1739 Vernon received instructions "to destroy the Spanish settlements in the West Indies and to distress their shipping by every method whatever." After early successes including the capture and destruction of the Spanish Fleet at Porto Bello, an effort to capture Cartagena failed (April 1741). That failure is more fairly charged to the commander of the ground troops. (DNB)

151 ❧ TO CARLO ALLIONI

ALS: University of Turin

London, February 10, 1762

I am greatly Obliged for th favour of Dr Alione Letter & Thanks to Him for the Seeds He Intends Mee. They are not Yett come to my Hands, the Casia Poetica [*Cassia?*] Wee wanted. Pray Send More next year with what other Italian or Alpine Seeds you can Spare.

Some years agon I had the Cortusa Matthioli. I am not Sure it Grows in your Country, but I am told about Verona. If you correspond with the professor there, pray Desire Him to Send you Some Seed of It for it is a pretty plant.

Here with you will receive Some Seeds from Pensilvania &c with which I wish you Success. They come up best in the Shade in a Bed under a North Wall, but Lett no Trees hang Over them, for the Dripping of Trees kills the Tender Seedling plants.

I am with much Respect, Your Sincere Friend   P. COLLINSON

Seed of the Chamaepytis Austriaci

Pray my Love & Respects to my Dear Friend Dr [Joseph] Bruni.[1]

1. Giuseppe Lorenzo Bruni, (d.1775) FRS, physician and professor of anatomy, Turin.

152 ❧ TO PETER THOMPSON

Draft ALS: LS

Ridgeway House on Mill Hill, Hendon

March 15, 1762

So much Business engages Mee in town that I am glad to find here an Evening leisure to answer my Dear Friends Letter of the twenty-seven ulto.

In the Article for the Culture & Improvement of Land, overflowing or Watering with the Sea has always been recommended Spring & fall for a great fertilizer of the Ground.

Perhaps it may be 30 years agon that I used Salt water with success to kill the Worms in my grass plotts at Peckham. Slack Lime in Water or Walnut Leaves will have the Same Effect. If your Borders are wide where the Fruit Trees are planted, I think no prejudice can accrue to them, for I apprehend one watering, well done, will do the business. Trye a Small Space at first, next month may be best, for in Cold or Dry Weather the worms lay deep. Lett it be done Late in the Evening in moist Warm Weather for then they come out of their Holes & spread the Surface.

Every thing after its Nature. The Lugg Worm breeds in Salt Sands, is replenished by the Sea that kills the Land Worm. What's ones Meal is anothers Poison sayes the old proverb.

If your Field is a Dry Sandy Soil there is not doubt but Lucern will thrive, but if Moist the Roots are apt to rott in Winter. Sow it beginning of Aprill, not too thick in Rows Two feet a Sunder. Must be carefully Weeded by Hand, while it is Young, after ward Howing will Do. Lett the Surface of Ground be made fine & Smooth before the Seed is sown. If it takes a likeing to the Soil it is the most profitable of all Grasses, if it may be allowed that Name.

The next Article that requires my Notice is to tell my namesake if He had thought to Inquire of his Old School fellow He would not have been so many Hours as years before he had received a Satisfactory answer on the Migration of Woodcocks. I have long known from certain Intelligence the Rout of these Woodcocks, but I will Quote from the Celebrated Naturalist Professor Linneas a Swede by birth, from Ameonites Academici page 591.

The Woodcocks lay their Eggs & hatch them in the Swampy Swedish Woods, but at the approach of Winter they leave that Country & chiefly Fly over to England & Ireland & return again in the Month of Aprill or May to Breed. Doctor Cramer in his Natural History of Austria[1] remarks the Same Thing of the Woodcocks, that they breed in the Woods of Austria and return Annually to the warmer climate of Italy to pass the Winter.

Yours and your Friends anecdotes relateing to the Swallows will be highly acceptable. The least Intelligence is worth knowing that will reflect any Light on that Intricate Subject.

You see my Dear friend my Penn tires & you may be so too, therefore I Will relieve you by assuring you that I am your affectionate Friend,   P. COLLINSON.

I hope I stand Well with my old Friend your Dear Sister, because you omitt giveing Mee the Satisfaction of hearing how she does.

In my next you will heare what I have to say to yours about J. Valens [not identified].

PETER THOMPSON (1698–1770), FRS, FAS, Merchant, Kt, 1745. In another letter (undated, probably 1761, ALS:Cambridge University Library) Collinson refers to Thompson as a childhood friend, and in his October 27, 1742 letter to Thompson (ALS:Cambridge University Library) he describes a large shipment of fruit trees and bushes and gives instructions for planting.

Thompson replied to Collinson's swallows query on April 16, 1764, to which Collinson replied in turn on April 25, 1764: "I am pleased with Mr Gilberts Sensible Letter, but by the Sailors Observations & his own he agrees with Mee, Some Swallows are but birds of passage." (Draft ALS:APS, written at the foot and open side of Thompson's to Collinson).

1. Kramer, Gulielmus Henricus. *Elenchus Vegetabilium et Animalium per Austriam Inferiorem Observatorum*. Vienna, 1756.

153 ❧ TO JOHN BARTRAM

ALS:HSP

London, April 1, 1762

I had my Dear Johns Letter of November 12 which is always acceptable. I really believe my Honest John is a Great Wagg & has Sent 7 hard Stoney Seeds. I have a Vast Collection of Seeds but none like them, Something Shaped like an acorn to puzzle Us for there is no name to them, I do Laugh at Gordon for he guesses them to be a species of Hickery. Phaps I may be laughed at in my Turn for I think they may be what I Wish, Seeds of the Bonduc Tree [*Gymnocladus dioica,* Kentucky Coffee Tree] which thou picked up on thy Rambles on the Ohio. This Elegant Tree has Large Leaves divided into many Portions, very much Resembling the Angelica Tree. It bears Its Fruit in Pods Like the West India

Bonduc or Nickar Tree but what Blossom I could never Learn. This is the Only fine Tree in which the French Rival Us.

Thy Hypothetical Systems on the Phenomena in Nature shows a firtile Conception & a Fruitfull Genius but I have neither Leisure or Inclination to Oppose thy Sentiments. I subscribe to them, and if I had it would be frutiless for when we had both said our Saye out it would be all Conjecture.

What I Desire to See is thy Diary which Consists of facts that cannot fail to give Sensible pleasure by Instilling some knowledge into the Mind & Inlargeing my Ideas of the Inconceivable power & Wisdom of the Great Creator.

The Dearest of Friends must part, I Regret to Lose So Valuable a member of Society. I see Our Friend Franklin prepareing to depart. By Him I Send the Magazine & Two Books which will give Entertainment to thy Speculative Genius.

Thou must take this Letter as an Instance of Great Friendship for I am so Hurried in Business that I write a bitt & a Scrap Now & then to show thee how much thou hast the Esteem of they Real friend,

P. COLLINSON

My love to thy Wife.

When thou writes by the packet always Inclose it to my Friend Alexander Colden Esqr Post Master at New York & then it Costs Mee Nothing.

154 ❧ TO CARL LINNAEUS

ALS:LS
London, May 20, 1762

Some Years are passed Since I sent to my Dear Linnaeus my Dissertation on the Migration of Swallows, but I have received no Satisfactory answer.

As you have Asserted (I conclude from the Report of others) that they live under Water all Winter, I Did Expect & all the World did expect that You would Verifie the Fact from your own knowledge or from Some of your Pupils on Who's veracity you could Depend.

My Dear Friend, Your Honor, Your Experience, Your Knowledge calls upon you to prove this Fact, which most of the Greatest Naturalists of this Age absolutely deny As a Thing contrary to Nature and Reason.

What has been related by former authors, Men of good Credit, is Doubted because it is suspected they was too Credulous, so Easily Deceived, But this Enlightened Age will not be Imposed On. Our Beliefe must be Established on undeniable Proofs before Wee can receive a Relation So contrary to the Course of Nature for Real Truth.

Your Reputation is so high in the Opinion of the Learned & Curious of this Age, that what you assert is taken & Allowed to be a Real Fact, for when I have been reasoning on the Improbability of Swallows Living under Water it has been replyed, Dr Linneaus sayes so, and Will you Dispute his Veracity?

As it may be Difficult to come at the Certainty of this Fact, I shall propose & recommend these Two Experiments. If they do not positively Determine it, They will at Least go a great Way Towards It.

I thank you my Dear Friend for your Kind letter of Dec 11, 1761 and am with Great Respect & sincerity your Affectionate Friend,   P. COLLINSON

The First Experiment I propose is, to Verifie that Swallows live under Water by Dissecting these Birds, and Demonstrating that there is an Internal Apparatus provided & plainly to be seen to Enable Them to undergo so great a Change.

My Next Experiment that I recommend to be tryed is, As near as can be to The time of Swallows going away (or Time of Migration) Lett half a doz or more be Caught, which may be Easily done in th Night with a Nett as they sett at Roost on the Reeds & Willows. Have a Large Wide Tub ready filled a foot Deep with Mud or Sand, then fill it with Water within a foot of the Brim. Lett a Broad Board float on the Topp of the Water. On this Board putt the Swallows & then Cover the Tub with a Nett . So leave them in Quiet. This should be repeated every Day with Swallows until no more can be found, & if after a Month or Twos Time they are taken out of the Water alive, then the Fact is proved.

As you are very Certain of the Period of the Swallows Going & Comeing, some persons of Probity should be sett to watch their Motions. As their numbers are Great it is unlikely all could conceal their going down in the Water (if they do). Some in so many must be discover'd & soone after Fishermen employed to Drag them up again.

In the Spring at their return Some should be appointed to Watch their comeing out of the Water in their Languid Wet State & how long Time after that they Lay Drying before they was fit for Flight.

See PC to J. T. Klein, March 6, 1758.

155 ❧ TO PETER TEMPLEMAN

ALS:RSA
June 24, 1762

My good Friend Dr Templeman

I have Long Intended to submit a few Hints on the Premiums for America to the consideration of the Society [for the Encouragement of Arts, Manufactures and Commerce], but being diffident of their Importance delayed to do It untill I received the Inclosed Letter from a Gentleman whose experience & knowledge of the State of the Colonies concurring with my sentiments which are:

That too Large Quantities are Exacted of the Several Usefull productions to which premiums are anexed.

Large premiums on Smaller Quantities may be a much likelier Methode to Tempt them to make the Experiments. When once the Thing is done & known to be practicable then increase the Quantitiy & the premium on proportion.

With Submission to the Society they seem to fail in the First Setting Out for the Improvement of our Colonies. They offer premiums for the Raiseing various Profitable Articles, not considering the Slender Acquaintance & Knowledge the Colonists have with these productions, who when they read the proposals & Rewards &c (May Reason) Wee that know so little of Europe, How can we tell where to apply for the best Vines to make Wine, the best Olives for Oyle? How are we to procure Them?

Neither are Wee informed where the Aloe Succrotina, Saff Flower, Silk Grass [Yucca] &c is to be found, nor the Scammony, nor the Methodes of Cureing Either & yett we are offer'd premiums for productions Wee barely know the Names off. This is tantalizing Instead of Instructing Us.

Rather premiums should first be given to Those that will procure & Introduce the best of Each Kind into Our Colonies, with the Methodes of their Culture & prepareing them fitt for Use & Sale. Then we should have Materials to work with all and if we did not use them the fault would Lay at our Door.

In Opium the Society has most Laudably instructed Us to prepare It for the Market, But no care to Supply us with seed of the True & best Kind.

As the Colonies may be said to be just emerging out of their Infant State & begin to Walk alone, Works should be proportioned to their Circumstances, but by the Large Quantities required of Every Article, it would seem as if the Society thought that they abounded with Multitudes & was grown to Maturity.

But as this is farr from being the Case, Especially in all the Southern Colonies, the premiums should therefore be given on Small Quantities.

I have much to Observe on the articles of Wine, Olives, Raisins, Hemp &c &c, how Impracticable it is at present for the Colonies to come up to the Expectations of the Society, but I cease to be further Troublesome then to assure you

I am your Friend

PETER COLLINSON.

The "Inclosed Letter" was from Jared Eliot to Peter Collinson, March 20, 1760, an extract of which is preserved in the Society for the Encouragement of Arts' Guard Books: "I am now without hopes that the vineyard culture will succeed in time in this colony; not long since being fifty miles from home I called to see a friend who said I am glad to find the Society disposed to encourage raising silk; he wished that they would give a Premium upon wine for he had planted a vineyard; I sent him a copy of the society's Premium on that article; though I can not think that Premium as it now stands will be an inducement, five ton of wine looks like a mountain; for a poor man if he should undertake the planting and culture of such a vineyard sufficient to produce five ton of wine, he must starve and be undone, and what we call a rich man will not care to run so great a venture; for we small people must creep before we can go. If the Society should give a Premium of five pounds for the first barrel at the Port of London, such as shall be approved by those appointed by the society to examine the same, its being the produce of the country; that the first pipe of wine sent attested and approved as before shall draw a premium of twenty pounds; and that when the five ton is produced, and one ton of it arrive at London, and be approved of; that then the planter who thus imports shall be entitled to the whole hundred pounds, there first being a defalcation of twenty five pounds already paid; it is already probable if not morally certain that the planter who shall grow the grapes for the first barrel will be able the first to send a pipe and so on to the five ton.

"A gentleman who has been at Georgia and there got himself fully instructed by a German overseer in the whole culture of the vine tells me that he had raised grapes from 3 or 4 stocks to full perfection; but having removed to a distant town so left his vines, but is determined to set about it according to his ability, and increase till he shall have planted an Acre; he tells me that the heat is so intense, the thunder so frequent and violent that he thinks that colony will never do for wine, but this colony will do well."

"The grapes which the above gentleman praise are white grapes and sweet."

156 ❧ TO JOHN STUART, 3RD EARL OF BUTE

ALS: Archive of Mount Stuart, Rothesay, Isle of Bute

London, July 17, 1762

I was lately at a Capital Merchants House in this Citty, our conversation Turn'd on the three Indians. I was desir'd Two or Three hints relating to them might be Humbly submitted to your Lordship.

That their Stay here may be Short, for they contract bad habits, in their Intemperance have no government, & may do rash things, as I am told like to happen at Faux Hall Gardens.[1]

If with high Irregular Living they should be taken with a Fever or Small Pox, what Effect it may have on their Nation is uncertain, for they are a very Suspicious people, & if they take it in their Heads it was contrived, it is impossible to convince Them otherwise. Their Revenge is Slow but Sure. Our people may feel it to their Cost.

When they take their leave of the King, lett it be with all the State & Dignity possible, for such an appearance strikes their Minds with awe & reverence that will never be forgot & which they will communicate [to] their confederacy chiefs.

Presents to them & the Other Warr Captains must not be omitted, robes of distinction, for they Love Show & finery.

I am very Respectfully yours,   PC

My Sons best Respects.

---

1. Vauxhall Gardens, a fashionable garden resort in London with walks "so intricate that the most experienced mothers often lost themselves in looking for their daughters," private groves, supper boxes and a music-room. Boswell observed, "Vauxhall Gardens is peculiarly adapted to the taste of the English nation; there being a mixture of curious show,—gay exhibition, musick, vocal and instrumental, not too refined for the general ear;—for all which only a shilling is paid. And, though last, not least, good eating and drinking for those who wish to purchase that regale." The Gardens were closed in 1859 and built on. (Weinreb, Ben and Christopher Hibbert, eds. *The London Encyclopedia*. London: Macmillan, 1983, pp. 910–911)

157 ❧ TO JOHN BARTRAM

ALS: HSP

London, July 25, 1762

I cannot Lett our Dear Franklin pass over without a Line to my Dear John. In my Last of July 9th by pacquet I acknowledged the receipt of thine 10th May.

I know thy Many avocations therefore will patiently wait thy own Time for thy Journal to Pittsburgh. There is no End of the Wonders In Nature, the More I see the More I Covet to See, not to gratifie a trifleing Curiosity but to raise my Mind in Sublime Contemplation of the Unlimited Power & Wisdom of the Great Creator of all things.

I forgett if I ever Mention'd Two Monstrous Teeth I had sent Mee by the Governor of Virginia. One Tooth weights 3 lb 3/4 18 Inch round, the other 1 lb 3/4 13 In 1/2 round. One other has Doctor Fothergill & T. Penn Another. One Greenwood,[1] well known

The Pittsburgh Iris *(*Iris cristata?*). Georg Dionysius Ehret. Natural History Museum, Botany Library, London.*

"Pittsburg Iris from P Collinson May 24, 1767."

to B. Franklin an Indian Trader, knock'd some of the Teeth out of the Jaws & George Crogan [Croghan][2] has been att the Licking Place near the Ohio where the Skeletons of six Monstrous Animals was standing as they will Inform thee. Crogan is well known to B. Franklin. To Him I have wrote a Long Letter which I have Desired Benjamin to show thee before He sends it to Crogan of which Thou may tak a Coppy.

The Indian Tradition is that the monstrous Buffaloes were all struck Dead by Lightening at the Licking Place, but is it likely to think all the Race was Here Collected & was Extinguished at one Stroke?

P. COLLINSON

1. Joseph Greenwood, Indian trader and mapmaker. (*Franklin* X, 246n)

2. George Croghan (d. 1782), Indian trader and Deputy Superintendent of Indian affairs.

See PC to Emanuel Mendes Da Costa November 15, 1767.

158 ❧ TO HENRY FOX, 1ST BARON HOLLAND

Draft ALS:LS

August 2, 1762

As I am but a demy Conjurer at best, It is lucky for Mee as well as for You my Dear Friend that the Grand Conjurer Doctor Franklin is not yett return'd Home to Philadelphia in Pensilvania to whome I shall impart your Letter & request.

He first asserted the Doctrine of Points & their Effects in Electricity & their application to Houses.

Would you think it Possible that a Pointed Iron Rod fixed to the highest part of an House should disarme a Cloud pregnant with distruction, ready to burst on Some lofty Building or Towering Oake?

The Good People in our Colonys will assure you it is a fact, which Dayly Experience Verifies, for it is well known all Houses that have the protecting Rod Elevated on their Tops have escaped the fatal terrifying Effects of their Tremendous Thunder & Lightening, which much exceeds ours by what I have often Heard.

I have requested Doctor Franklin to send you proper Instructions how to erect the Pointed Rod.

May it under the protection of Providence Avert all Dangers from falling on your Salubrious Abode is the Sincere wish of Yours,   P. COLLINSON

At the bottom of this draft Collinson wrote, "In about a Week after Doctor Franklin saild for Pensilvania America."

HENRY FOX, First Baron Holland (1705–1774), Paymaster general and leader of the House of Commons, instrumental in passing the peace treaty that ended the Seven Years War. The lightning rod referred to here was installed on Fox's home at Kingsgate Kent. Franklin sent the directions two days later (*Franklin* X, 138n).

During the Revolutionary War, George III ordered Franklin's pointed lightening rods replaced with rounded ones. This inspired the London wags:

While you great George for knowledge hunt
And sharp conductors change for blunt
The Empire's out of Joint.
Franklin another course pursues
And all your thunder heedless views
By keeping to the point.

(Franklin XXV, 5)

159 ❧ TO CARL LINNAEUS

ALS:LS

September 2, 1762

My Dear Linnaeus cannot easily conceive the pleasure of this afternoon. There was our beloved Solander seated in my Museum, surrounded with Tables cover'd with an Infinite Variety of Sea Plants, the Collection of many years. He was Digesting & Methodizing them Into Order, & for his pains He shall be rewarded with a Collection of them, which no Doubt you will see.

Afterwards at Supper Wee remembered my Dear Linnaeus & My other Swedish Friends over a Chearful Glass of Wine.

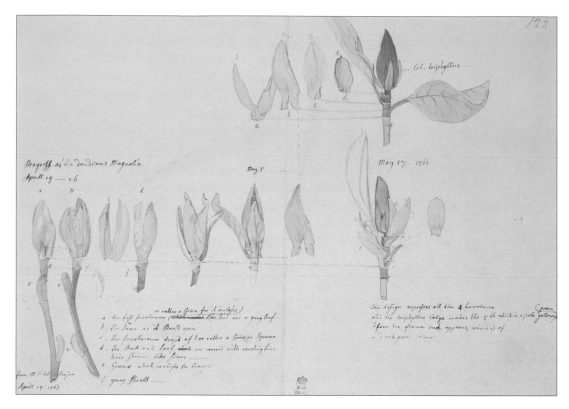

Magnolia. Georg Dionysius Ehret. Wellcome Trust Library, London.

My Son who is a great Lover of plants, as well as my Self, are greatly disappointed that the Betula nana [a dwarf Birch] is not sent us, as it is our Favourite plant & has been long promised to be sent to us.

And what I do not take friendly (is) that Every Friend has been obliged with your Systema Natura but my Self. Must your Oldest Friend be served last? That is not Kind.

I thank you for your Letter of Congratulation on taking of Martinico[1] & with It the True Cinamon but alas I am fearfull this Rich aromatick Tree will be given up again with the Island, without securing the Tree to our Selves, for Soldiers mind nothing but slaughter & plunder.

Solander is very Industrious in makeing all Manner of Observations to Enrich Himself & his Country with Knowledge in Every branch of Natural History.

We have had a Delightfull Warm Summer, all the Fruits of the Earth very good & in great plenty, & what Crowns all, the Blessing of Peace is Like to be Added.

That you may long Enjoye Health of Body & Mind is the Sincere Wish of your Affectionate Friend.

I am glad the Bulbous roots [Iris?] Please you. More Species will flower next year.

My Great Magnolia [*Magnolia grandiflora*] is now finely in Flower.

1. Martinique. Collinson's prediction proved correct. The island was returned to Spain under the terms of the Peace of Paris, 1763.

"Progress of the deciduous Magnolia, Aprill 19–26. Georg Dionysius Ehret. Natural History Museum, Botany Library, London. "From Mr P Collinson, Aprill 19, 1763."

160 ❧ TO WILLIAM WATSON

ALS: The British Museum Archive
London, October 5, 1762

As I know my Valuable Friend has the prosperity of the British Museum at Heart, Is the reason I adress this Letter to Him, and as I was honour'd with the Esteem of its great Founder [Sir Hans Sloane], & haveing a propensity to Love Natural History, I can not help feeling a concern that so Immense a Collection May become more universally Useful.

It will be to the Honour of this Nation as well as the Curators, that the World may be acquainted with Its Riches that all Students In Natural History may know where to Resort to improve their knowledge.

The Gentlemen whose department belongs to Natural History, are well Quallified to give a Descriptive Catalogue of Them, but if it is considered from their long and Constant Attendance, the necessary Time required for their own private affairs, It cannot be expected, nay I think impossible for Them to compleat so long & Laborious a Work, in any reasonable Time, if Ever.

By these unavoidable Delays, the Philosophick World is deprived of an Inconceivable fund of Knowledge, as it is the most extensive collection of Animals in all Europe, which are Dayly Decaying, so ought to be taken whilst in some tolerable Preservation.

An oppertunity now offers that may never happen Again for the Assistance of a Learned Gentleman who is now Here, and every way Quallified for this Vast Undertaking. Natural History hath been the Study of his Life, under the Greatest of Professors Doctor Linnaeus. By his great application He has attained to a Thorough Knowledge of It in all its Branches. This Gentleman is Dr Solander who you know & I believe you are Sensible of his Great Abilities.

I am perswaded from the Bent of his Mind He would undertake this Arduous Task. I Heartyly Wish It may meet with the Encouragement & approbation of the Curators.[1]
I am with much Respect
Your Sincere Friend

P. COLLINSON

WILLIAM WATSON (1715–1787), physician, elected FRS 1741 for his proficiency in botany, and later became a noted electrician. Sir Hans Sloane nominated him trustee of the British Museum.

Collinson drafted this recommendation with care. An earlier, somewhat longer draft appears in his larger commonplace book at The Linnean Society, London, along with the draft of a covering letter he sent Watson on October 4: "I Submit the Inclosed to your consideration. If I am so happy to have your Sentiments correspond with Mine, pray lay it before the Curators. Neither Dr Solander nor any in the Museum know any thing of my Letter. As Dr Solander is a very moderate Man I believe would want no great Matter, but if your fund is not Sufficient, what if a Deputation was to wait on Lord Bute requesting to beg the Kings assistance or He may Do it Himself.

But this I Submitt & am Your affectionate Friend" (ALS: The British Museum Archive)

The incumbent curator, William Empson, resisted Collinson's suggestion. When the trustees invited his comment he replied, "Notwithstanding somewhat more appears to be wanting to extend the uses of this great collection and to open in a more enlarged & diffusive manner the Contents of this Repository, with this Intention Mr Empson for some time past has been referring the several parts of the Collection to Dr Linnaes's System in order to compile a work of this kind . . . yet he has made some advancement in his Design which he presumes his early and long Acquaintance with the Collection joined to his Observations & Anecdotes imparted to him by Sir Hans Sloane will enable him to finish in a more perfect Manner than might be done even by a Person of Superior Abilities." (undated ALS: the British Museum Archive)

See also Collinson to Linnaeus, November 16, 1762.

1. At the foot of Collinson's draft of this letter he noted later, "This letter had the desired effect on the Curators, for Dr Solander was chosen March, 1763 on my representation." [Draft ALS: LS]

ALS:LS
London, November 16, 1762

My Dear Linnaeus,

I am informed there is proposals from the Academy of Sciences at Petersburg to engage our Dear Solander for a Botanic Professor.

For the Love and Esteem I have for the doctor, I cannot forbear expressing my Concern, for many Reasons, First, from the Uncertain Situation of the Publick Affairs in that Kingdome, for it is impossible Learning can flourish in Tumults & Riots. Who knows in a Revolution which may soon Happen, How farr the person of a Stranger may be safe & his Pension Secure.

Next If Wee consider the Russian Empire is Inland & those Countries sufficiently Explored Its Vegitable & Mineral productions Discover'd by the Indefatigable pains of Gmelin, Staler[1] & Others, besides, this Country has no commerce with the West or East Indies to bring New and rare productions from Thence. Pray what is here to Exercise Solanders great Talents, which He has been with so much pains & Industry Improveing. Am I not Witness to His Dayly Labours, do I not know of my own Knowledge his unwearied Application to attain competent Skill, in Every Branch of Natural Philosophy? Must all these fine Accomplishments be Lost & Sunk into Supiness for want of proper Subjects to exercise his Aspiring Genius?

Can you my Dear Linnaeus advise Solander to be confined for years, no longer a free Agent, But Buried & Lost in Obscurity & Confinement? If any Good & Advantageous Station Should Offer as a person of his Abilities will not want Friends, He is Here confined & Cannot Accept of It untill his Time is out. How hard is this?

Should it please God, my Dear Friend, to take you from Us, Who is there you could wish to be your Successor, but Solander? Who is there could fill your place with so much propriety & so well accomplished? But if He accepts the Professorship on the Old Conditions, His Hands will be tied, & his feet Fetter'd, that will prevent his accepting any Advancement.

No Doubt But you my Dear Friend know Persons less Eminent, but Every Way Quallified in Botanic Science to teach Russian Bears. I heartily Wish Wee could Here give Solander the Encouragement He Deserves.

Some of his friends have proposed a Scheme for that Purpose. The Success will be Known before the End of this year.

If after all I have said, you have determined Dr. Solander for Petersburgh, pray do not give a positive answer to the Academy there, until you Hear from your Affectionate Friend,[2]

P. Collinson

I presume my leter of the 20th of May relateing to the Swallows you have received. I expect the favour to a Satisfactory Answer, For to my first Letter, Three years agon on that Subject you never did Mee the Honour to take the Least Notice of It.

1. Johann Georg Gmelin (1709–1755), German botanist, published a "masterwork of scientific survey," *Flora sibiricá sive historia plantarum Sibiriae.* 4 vols. St. Petersburg, 1747–1769 and *Reise durch Sibirien von dem Jahr 1733 bis 1743.* 4 vols. Göttingen, 1751–1752.

Georg Wilhem Steller (1709–1746), German physician and natural historian. Steller traveled extensively in northwestern Russia and was the first natural historian to reach the coast of Alaska. Gmelin and Steller carried on an extensive correspondence. (DSB)

ALS:HSP
Mill Hill, December 10, 1762

I am here all alone & yett I have the Company of my Friends with Mee. This will be no paradox when I tell thee on the Table lays their Speaking Letters in that Silent Language which Conveys their most intimate thoughts to my Mind.

In Course thine my Dear John comes First. I thank thee for thine of the 15 August. I have in my former Letters acknowledged the receipt of thy Journal which is a lasting fund of Entertainment to Mee & my son these long Evenings.

I am pleased to Hear thou has gott the Loblolly Bay [*Gordonia lasianthus*]. I had it formerly. I know it is a Charming Tree. I have one now at Gordons who has been Some years Increasing It.

My Umbrella [Magnolia] flower'd this year & the flower Buds are strongly Sett for Next.

Whilst the Frenchman was readdy to Burst with laughing, I am ready to Burst with Desire for Root, Seed or Specimen of the waggish Tipitiwitchet Sensitive. [*Dionaea mus-*

cipula, Venus' Flytrap][1] I wish Billy when he was with thee had taken but the least Sketch of It to save my Longing. But if I have not a specimen in thy next Letter, never write Mee more, for it is Cruell to tantalize Mee with relations & not to send Mee a Little Specimen in thine of the 15th of August nor in thine of the 29th. It shows thou hast no sympathy or Compassion for a Virtuoso. I wish it was in my power to Mortifie thee as much.

Don't use the Pomegranate inhospitably, a stranger that has come so farr to pay his respects to thee. Don't turn him adrift in the wide world, but plant it against the South Side of thy House. Nail it close to the wall. In this manner It thrives wonderfully with us & flowers Beautifully & Bears Fruit this Hott year. I have 24 on One Tree & Some well ripen'd. Dr Fothergill says of all trees this is the most Salutiferous to mankind.

I am Glad the Portuge Laurels Thrive. Thou will be Delighted with them when it comes to Flower.

Dionaea muscipula, *Venus's Flytrap, "Tipitiwitchet Sensitive." John Ellis. The Linnean Society of London.*

I heartyly wish Billy & [blank in original] may have every Way Success at Carolina. Could they pack up some Insects in that hott Country that you have not.

Thy letter my Dear John of the 29 August I am much Obliged to Thee for taking so much Pains to informe Mee in so many Interesting Articles. It is fortunate for thee & Mee through this Means to have so Curious Man as Col Bouquet.[2] I hope He will continue There, now Peace is Securred under they Instructions to Observe & Colect [illegible].

I have often Seen they are a pretty domestic native animals such as your Wolf, differs from our European I am not able to Saye. Wild Catts must be a Curiosity as they is of the Tiger Species. Send a Short description, but I want to know more of what you Call the Panther. Now all Panthers are spotted, but yours is not, therefore It will be called A Linx. I have been regaling my Mind Every Evening I am Here, in reading over & Makeing Abstracts from they Entertaining Letters, beginning with the first & so on. I have collected all thou sayist of your Panthr but no mention is made of his Colour, his Size, Length or Height, shape of his head & ear, Length of his Tail &c.

By my beloved Friend Benn Franklin I wrote a Long letter relateing to the Skeletons of the Animals who are standing in the Licking place down the Ohio. I Desire Him to show it Thee for There In is all I have been able to collect relateing to the Existence of thos Surprising Animals, that thou might collect what thou thought deserving Notice before The Letter as Delivered. I have Three of the Monstrous Teeth, but Thou well Observed Teeth [illegible] to Determine what these Animals are, or what Class they belong not, [illegible] is there Hoffs & Horns, if they had any. The Good Colonel thought them Elephants Teeth but they have no relation to them for I saw Elephants' Teeth & they are in the British Museum and can be certain on that point, but what they really are is [impossible] to Determine unless there was the strictest Examination by a Man well Qualified & then is more then [likely] they may be found to be an unknown Creature, unless it may be the Rhinoceras whose teeth I have not Seen.

Thy Queries sett by J Wright to the Indians [illegible].

It is very probable that Colo Bouquet may have under Him Junior officers, espetialy in the Artillery, that can design & draw animals, I know that all the officers of that department have drawing Masters to learn them to take all manner of Designs. Now as I before observed there will be Leisure & nothing to fear in a profound peace with the Indians, now the French are striped of all that Fruitfull Country [illegible] the Re Maping. The Colo being a Gentleman of Curiosity & to bring one of the Wonders of the World to Light, may be excited to go & take a Survey of these Amazing Subject [illegible].

I was much comforted with thy good wife's postscript, that thou was got to the Congaree [River, South Carolina] in health, September 14th. I trust that a good Providence will be with thee in so laudable an undertaking as to explore and discover the wonders of his creative power and bring thee home in safety to the joy of thy wife and family and in particular of thy affectionate friend,

P. COLLINSON

Now my dear John, look on the map and see by this glorious peace [of Paris] what an immense country is added to our long, narrow slip of Colonies, from the banks of the Messisipi to Terra Labrador and Newfoundland &c. See what a complete empire we have now got within ourselves. What a grand figure it will now make in the map of North America.

1. On August 29, 1762 John Bartram wrote Peter, " I had A sensitive plant sent mee from the congaree. One came up before harvest but the hot weather killed it tho I watered it every night & since harvest I have two more come up but I [don't] dare let A drop of water touch the plant but I make A hole in the ground A little distance from the fibers of its root & fills the hole full of water in the evening & thay grow yet well. It differs much from the sensitive bryer which onely closeth its leaves at the touch & from the humble plant both which is very prickley but this is quite smooth slender stalked & both closeth its leaves & gently prostrates: my little tipitiwitchet sensitive stimulates laughter in all the beholders. There was lately a french gentleman from Montreal which was so agitated that he could hardly stand & said it was enough to make one burst with laughing. It seems to grow as well as in Carolina. How it will bear the winter I can't say. . . ." (ALS:HSP)

Bartram had discovered it and sent over dried specimens and seeds, but it was Bartram's great competitor, William Young Jr. (botanist to the Queen for £300 a year compared to Bartram's £50 as botanist to the King) who introduced living tipitiwichets to England. He packed his plants tight in a box of damp moss and carried them over himself in 1768. After exhibiting his sensational vegetable beasts he sold them to James Gordon, the nurseryman at Mile End. John Ellis wrote Alexander Garden in October that year, "I have sent Linnaeus the characters of it, which gave him infinite pleasure, as the manner of its seizing and killing insects, exceeds any thing we know of in the vegetable kingdom." (quoted in Kinch, Michael P, "The Meteoric Career of William Young, Jr (1742–1785), Pennsylvania Botanist to the Queen." *The Pennsylvania Magazine of History and Biography,* CX, 259, July, 1986.)

2. Henry Bouquet (1719–1765), Swiss officer in the British army. Commander at Fort Pitt, and known for adapting the discipline of European armies to warfare in the wilderness of Western Pennsylvania.

163 ❧ TO HENRI-LOUIS DUHAMEL DU MONCEAU

ALS:APS

London, March 6, 1763

Wee have too many Magazines in England and yett they are of Publick Utility.

Subjects that are too trivial to appear in the Transactions, & yett of use & proper to be known, are communicated all Over England & America (that is possessed by us) in the Gentlemans Magazine, to which I am perswaded my Friend DuHamel is no Stranger. I send the Inclosed that you may read my Observation on the Peaches & Nectarine growing together and another Letter signed Harrison on the Numerous Nests of Insects that Load the Trees & Bushes with advice to Destroye them in Time before they spread their Legions of Devourers.[1]

To these Little Essays I never subscribe my Name, because I do not Love Popularity, but sometimes I add a fictitious name.

I have known Three Instances of Peach Trees bearing Nectarines. Pray my good Friend, tell Mee your Obvservations on the Same Subject, & what is the Natural Cause & reason for Peach Trees produceing Nectarines. And Further, I shall be much Obliged to you to informe Mee The First Authors that mention the Nectarine and in what year it was published.

I am with much Respect, your Sincere Friend,   P. COLLINSON

Very fine Weather, my Garden full of Flowers which are my Delight. My Early Hyacinth has been [in] flower some Time & narces Polyanthis, which I shelter'd dureing the Frost, apricot very near in Blossome & some Peaches against a South Wall.

Mr Bombarde [not identified] has been so Obligeing as to send Mee a Box of your fine anemonies, which will give Mee great pleasure. In my Turn I shall Endeavour to Oblige Him.

You see by the Inclosed Weekly Bill the price of Bread from November to March. The moderate price was of great benefit to the poor dureing the Frost. Coals from Newcastle imported for the Use of London 570,774 Chaldrons for year 1762, which is near Double what it was Fifty Years agon, which shows the Increase of the Citty & its Inhabitants.

The finest Cargo of Seeds from J. Bartram is Taken by the Spaniards, & Carried into Bilbao, who you know have no Curiosity, so will throw them Overboard. The Ships Name is the Carolina, Captain Friend. Could you no ways procure them for your Self or the Kings Garden?

Weekly bill. By Wheaten is to be understood the finest Whites Meal By Household. Next Sort Courser Meal or Flower.

HENRI-LOUIS DUHAMEL DU MONCEAU (1700–1781), French General Inspector of the Fleet, published *Traité des Arbres . . .* Paris, 1755; *La Physique des Arbres.* Paris, 1758; *Traité de la Culture des Terres.* Paris, 1761; *Elements d'Agriculture.* 2 vols. Paris, 1762; *Historie d'un Insecte . . .* (with M. Tillet) Paris, 1762.

1. Collinson's observations appear in the *Gentleman's Magazine* vol XXXIII (1763): 82. The letter signed "J. Harrison" appeared in the same issue on pp. 85–86.

164 ❦ TO CARLO ALLIONI

ALS : University of Turin

London, March 11, 1763

I thank my Good Friend Mr Allioni for the favour of his Sons Letter of the 13 January.

Mr Alstromer[1] has been so kind to send to Mee the Packet of Seeds, but how great was my Disappointment when I found no Seeds of Cassia Poetica nor Cortusa.

This was a great Neglect & I do not take Friendly, for you positively say in your Letter vizt vous y Trouveris plusiers des plantes demandois. I did not find any one plant I desired, but trifleing things. And you add et entre autres les Semenees de Cortusa et Casea Poetica. These was Intirely forgot, which Carelessness Discourages Mee from a Correspondence that is so Negligent. For these Two plants, the Cassia & Cortusa I had sett my Heart upon.

All the seeds you have Sent are very trifleing & Common Here & not Worth my Sowing. I gave them away.

I Don't desire a great Number of Seeds, but those that are Ornamental plants.

Only 4 Seeds of Paliurus, 6 Seeds of Cascis—these are very Common in our Gardens, but they Seem with you Great rarities to Send only 4 & 6 Seeds of Each. It really makes Mee Smile to See your great Generosity.

Your Packet could not be Robbed, for It came to Mee Sealled up & not broke open or Else I Should Guess half the Seeds had been Stole.

Pray My Love & Respects to my Dear Friend Dr [Joseph] Bruni.

1. Probably Baron Claus Alstroemer (1736–1794), Swedish botanist and friend of Linnaeus. The Alstroemeria flower was named for him.

165 🐄 TO JOHN HAWKESWORTH

Draft AL:LS
September 14, 1763

Mr. Urban, I here Inclose to you some curious articles sent Mee from my Late Worthy Friend, the Reverd Mr. Jared Elliot of Killingsworth in Connecticut, New England. This Publick Spirited Gentleman's Memory Deserves to be transmitted to Posterity through your universal Intelligent Canal [the *Gentleman's Magazine*] who died the 22nd Aprill last 1763 in the 78 year of his age.[1]

As a clergyman he Discharged his Office with a Zeal becoming that Function.

He was Eminent in his charity & Benevolent in relieving & Comforting the Distressed in Body & Mind. A Blessing attended his Administrations, wether as a Surgeon or a Physician.

In a Publick Character He frequently printed practical essays on Field Husbandry, for the Benefit of his Country. He made the Experiments & then recommended them.

But what He most availed Himself on was the Discovery of the Great use that may be made of Black Iron Sand found in Such Quanityes on Neighboring Sea Coasts.

He sayes in one of his Letters (October 4, 1762) he mett with great Discouragements in attempting to Smelt the Black Iron Sand, yett He had Such a perswation of the Probability of It next to Enthusiasm that He could not rest from making more tryals, and it Pleased Providence to Prolong his Life to See it brought to such great Perfection that from 83 pound of Black Iron Sand, Fifty Pound of Iron hath been repeatedly Made.

Samples of the Iron hath been sent over which prove of an Excellent Texture for making Steel &c. The Society of Arts are so well Satisfied with the Reallyty and Usefulness of the Discovery and application [to perpetrate his Discovery] in finding & bringing so profitable a Comodity to Light [into use] for the Benefit of His County & in Time will undoubtedly Extend Hither.

Mr Elliot writt an Essay on the Raiseing of Mulbery Trees & Makeing Silk, was appointed by the Society of Arts to pay the premiums to Encourage the makeing Silk in that Province.[2]

JOHN HAWKESWORTH (1715?–1773), LL.D, contributor and reviewer for the *Gentleman's Magazine,* published *The Works of Jonathan Swift,* wrote several plays and translated *The Adventures of Telemachus.* (DNB)

1. *Gentleman's Magazine,* XXXIII (1763): 433–435 contains an expanded version of this letter.
2. Eliot, Jared. *The Sixth Essay on Field-Husbandry.* New Haven, 1759.

166 🐄 TO CARL LINNAEUS

AL:LS
London, September 15, 1763

To The Rt Hon. Baron Linnaeus, F.R.S. &c.

After reading my Dear Linnaeus's letter of the 23d November, 1762, How can I any longer Doubt that Swallows live under Water all Winter?

But what would confirm that surprising Phaenomenon, If my Dear Friend could any ways contrive to examine Anatomically what wonderfull Aparatus there Is at that Period of time at their going under Water in the Structure of the Heart of the Swallow, to Quallifie It to undergo a Change of Elements so contrary to Nature for animals that are Breed & Live on Earth and Air, to continue to Live & Breath so many Months under Water.

If this desirable Discovery is impracticable to be performed by your Self, I wish you would recommend, nay Enjoyn, some of your Numerous Disciples that may have Dwelling not too remote from these Lakes, to apply themselves diligently to catch these Birds & examine Them as near the Time they absconde Themselves as Possible.

I really Think it is an Inquiry Worthy of Dignity of the Great Philosopher, Linnaeus, and it should be His ambition to give Satisfaction to many Great & Learned men, that doubt, others absolutely Deny, the possibility of Swallows liveing so long under Water, By showing & explaining the reason of It anatomically.

For undobutedly the All Wise & Powerfull Creator hath Occasionally (for that End & Purpose of Living in Water) provided or Substituted some Vessells, or Organs, near the Heart, to Supply a sufficient means for respiration & prevent the Birds from drowning. If this can be happily found Out, It will Establish the Veracity of your assertion, and the more likely to be meet with in Birds that have laid some Time to the Lakes. It may facilitate this Inquiery, if rewards was offered to the Fisherman, when they took up any Swallows in the Water or from under the Ice, to bring them to you or your Disciples.

I have another Material Reason to recommend to you for Procuring Swallows in the Winter from the Lakes at any Reasonable Expense, that the particular Species may be certainly determine that Lives under Water, for if one Species only takes residence in that Element, the Hypothesis of another Species migraeting to distant Countries will not then be Doubted. For I am as certain that I twice saw them Takeing Their Flight Thither, as you are Certain you saw them taken from under the Water & Revive & Live.

It is a Remark that strikes Mee when I consider that all the Rivers and Lakes of England, Wales, Scotland, and Ireland, are not without their Fishermen, & yett neither Tradition, nor any Relation, nor yett any of the Books I have read of these Kingdoms, have the least Intimation or Record that Swallows have been found, & taken up, from under the Water, in the Winter Months. Can you, my Dear Friend, account for This, or Show Mee that your Swallows are of a Different Nature from Ours?

I have proposed more than Once Two Experiments to be Made in Hopes of Elucidating the Subject in dispute. Possibly some interesting Inferences may be drawn from Them, But I am not so happy to be regarded or favour'd with any Account of Them, which I shall beg Leave again to repeat. At the Time the Swallows are nearest absconding, they resort in vast Numbers to the Reeds & Bushes on the Sides of Rivers & Lakes, so may be Easily taken in the night with a Nett, to make the Tryal.

Experiment First, take 5 or 6 Swallows & tie a Weight to their Leggs & sink them under Water. If they survive after Laying there in Seven Days, who will doubt their Living in the Lakes.

But it may be Objected, this is forcing Them against Nature. To Obviate this, Make Experiment Second. Take a Large Deep Wide Tubb, put a foot Deep of Sand at the Bottome, then fill it with Water to within a foot of the Brim. Then place a thin broad Board on the Water. On this Board putt some Swallows, then Cover the Tub with a Nett. If they Immerge under Water & live, this will Establish my Dear Linnaeus's assertion.

You are my Dear Friend the Great & Good Man who Your Sagacious King and Queen Delight to Honour.

Your Long Life spent in the most arduous Studies, your unwearied application to Improve Mankind as well as your Own Country very Deservedly Intitle You to the High Honours so Lately conferred On You.[1]

May you Live Long to Enjoye Them with Health of Body & Tranquility of Mind, is the Ardent Sincere Wish of Your Affectionate Friend,

P. COLLINSON

P.S.   It is now Five years since my Good Friend Told Mee I should receive His Systa Natura. What a tedious while it is for a Philosopher to wait, & yett I have hoppes my Longing Eyes shall see It.

Pray when you see my Dear Friends Dr Back & Dr Biorkin, my Love & Respects to Them.

As soon as the Great Tall Siberia Larkspur [*Delphinium elatum*] has done flowering, I then cutt it down close to the Ground. It soon shoots up New branches, and is now again in flower. This I do every Year. Thus it flowers Twice in a year.

Almost every Day Rain Since the Middle of July. The Spring & Summer very Dry to this Middle of July. Very Great plenty of grass & all Sorts of Corn, but the Weather unkindly for the Harvest.

My great Magnolia hath been finely in Flower this Year. What is remarkable of the Species of the Magnolia, they do not Flower all at one & the Same Time Like Other trees, But continue flowering for Two or Three Months.

Regarding swallows, see PC to J. T. Klein, March 6, 1758.
1. In 1762, Linnaeus was elevated to the nobility as von Linné.

167 ❧ TO THE SOCIETY FOR THE ENCOURAGEMENT OF ARTS, MANUFACTURES AND COMMERCE

ALS: RSA
November 10, 1763

In all our extensive Continent of North America if the Latitude, Soil and Situation of West Florida is well considered, no Part seems better adapted for a Provincial Garden than the Country 30 or 40 Miles or more on some of the Rivers of that Province. For in this Climate it is reasonable to conclude all the Plants that grow on either Side of the Tropicks will find a genial Warmth to ripen their Fruits, seeds &c equal to that from whence they came.

Certainly no vegetable Production deserves more our Care and Culture, than the Tea Tree,[1] for which we pay annually such immense Sums. The Province in which the Tea grows in China is so near in Latitude to West Florida that there is not the least Reason to doubt its thriving well in that Country. But as the introducing this valuable Plant will be a

Work of Time, it is very requisite that a Garden be settled and in some Order to receive it, well and securely fenced, and under the Direction of a Person skilled in the Culture and increasing of it, for it will be some years before a Stock can be raised to supply the Publick.

That this Garden may not lay idle and useless (whilst Tea Trees are procuring) let the Ground be applied to the raising of Olive Trees in Nurseries for publick Plantations as a free Gift to those who will come under Covenant to secure and preserve them.[2] The French brot Olive Trees into this Country, where we are told they grow surprisingly; some Trees a Foot and half diameter and 30 feet high. Some grow also in Carolina. From these a Stock may be soon procured to raise Nurseries. For though the Olives and Oyl were Articles not encouraged by the French because they would interfere and possibly in time sink the Price of their Home Productions, yet they will highly deserve the Attention and Cultivation of English Planters because they are Commodities for which we pay considerable Sums yearly. But there must be great Plantations of these Olive Trees to raise a Quantity to make an Article of Commerce.

As new Settlers first employ themselves to raise such Productions as are immediately necessary to support Life, next those Annual Ones, as Cotten, Indigo, Opium & Rice, these are perfected the same year they are sown, and come directly to a London Market, to make returns from hence in a multitude of Articles wanting in a Planters Family. For it cannot be expected they can go on raising Productions that require several Years to bring them fit for Plantations. Therefore a Provincial Garden is more immediately necessary to the increasing and bringing forward every Vegitable that can be suggested as becoming in Time profitable Branches of Commerce.

For the raising and cultivating profitable Plants from more temperate Climates, a Provincial Garden for this End may not be better settled than in Pensilvania, if that of West Florida should prove too hot.

Vineyards are quickly raised from the Cuttings of Vines, so need not the Assistance of a Provincial Garden.

As the producing of Silk in our Colonies is of such great Importance to the Interest and Trade of Great Britain, such vast Sums being paid in ready Money for the same, to encourage so profitable a Production is in the first Place to raise Mulberry Trees from Seed.[3] This can be done nowhere so effectually as in a Provincial Garden, by Way of Nurseries; but as some Years are required to train them up fit for transplanting, Here the proper Means is found to do it, That whilst the Colony is increasing the Mulberry Trees will be growing. And when fit for transplanting, let the Publick Share in them under proper Restrictions, giving Security. Care shall be taken of them, and that they shall be applied to the feeding the Silk Worm.

For the further Promotion of the Article of Silk, if the Society for Arts & Commerce was to petition the King for Tracts of Land in Florida, And divide those Tracts into smaller Ones, into Farms or Plantations, And a considerable certain Portion of each Plantation to be planted with Mulberry Trees, for feeding Worms, These will be growing to Maturity whilst Inhabitants are increasing. Each Farm being known to have such a Mulberry Plantation on it, will not long want Purchasers or Tenants.

These Hints it is hoped may deserve the Consideration of the Society.

PETER COLLINSON

On or near the Sea Coast the Cochineal Indian Figg, Aloes-Succotrina, and Capers may be cultivated with Success, a suitable Improvement for barren lands. Scammony loves a higher Ground and richer Bottom.

As it is a tedious and difficult Work to get the Seeds out of Cotton, Has the Society any Engines for this Purpose?

1. The cultivation of tea was not attempted in America until 1848, and then without commercial success.

2. Olive culture was never commercially successful in the American colonies. (Hillhouse, Augustus L. "*An Essay on The History and Cultivation of the European Olive-Tree,*" Paris: L.T. Cellot, 1820, pp 48–49).

3. Collinson encouraged silk culture in the American colonies in his February 4, 1764 letter to Benjamin Gale and thirty years earlier in his April 22, 1737 letter to Samuel Eveleigh. For reasons of climate and the costs of labor, silk cultivation never reached commercially successful levels in America.

168 ❧ TO HENRIETTA MARIA GOLDSBOROUGH

ALS: MdHS
London, January 2, 1764

I am really ashamed to think that I can make no better returns then My Sincere acknowledgments for Mrs Goldsboroughs Noble Present of Five Delicious Hams. I must express it So, for your Sweet food makes the Fatt tast like Marrow. By the Capts care they came in excellent Order. I thank you for the Yucca Seed. It is a charming plant in flower & its Leaves are very Singular for the filaments or Threads that hang from Them.

Formerly a Strong thread & Cloth was manufactured from the Leaves, which used to be called Silk Grass and made the strongest fishing Lines.

I wish the few Seeds you Desired may be Worth your Acceptance. They are Put in a Box committed to the Care of Capt Brooke.

I wish you Success with them.

I have Putt in a Little Seed of St Forine [Sanfoin]. If you have any High Dry Ground it will then thrive and make a long enduring Fodder for Cattle, Its Leaves are not like Grass Leaves but on a Stalk are Divided & bears red flower not unornamental in a Garden.

It gives Mee Pleasure to hear that the Peach Stones have born Fruit. Your's is the Delightful Country to bring them to Perfection. Wee are Obliged to the best brick Walls, whose warm reflection & much art used in Pruning, to have them in a tolerable ripeness, but your fine Climate without So much trouble gives you to tast their Delicious Fruit, Spontaneously. I happened to save but few stones this year but expect more Next. This answers your kind Letter of Sept. 20th.

I am with Gratefull Acknowledgements for the kind tokens of your Regard For your old but Sincere Friend   P. COLLINSON.

The Seeds, Desir'd in your other Letter Will Come by Mr Hanburys Ship.

Inclosed in the Box is the Methods how to Cultivate & manage Lucern [Alfalfa]. It is a very Profitable Food for Cattle, it grows So fast & is cutt So often in a Summer. We never Suffer Cattle to feed on it but always keep it mowed one Plat under another.

LS:MdHS
February 1, 1764

It gives Mee Pleasure if any thing I have Sent can give you Entertainment & help to Divert Reflections on Past Occurences that is Better forgot than remembered, as Wee cannot alter the unerring Decrees of the Almighty.[1]

Lett us look to our Selves, that ought to be our Principal concern to Secure an Inheritance in Everlasting Happyness.

The State of those that are gone ought to be no more admitted into your mind, for as the Tree falls So it Lies. Sorrow not as without Hope but rely on the Infinite goodness & Mercy of God & Despair not of his Loving kindness & the Workmanship of his hands.

It Delights Mee to hear that from some of the Peach Stones Some Fruit have been Produced worth your Notice. It is from Setting the Stones that Wee have Such Variety but for one Real good one, many Indifferent is to be expected, but those are Easily taken away. Yours is the Country for Peaches, & what are Good Here will be excellent with you. As you like this Pretty amusement I will this year save of the best Sorts & Send you. As they soon come to Bearing with you, the Pleasure of Expectation is not too Long Delayed.

I Sent you a Box of Seeds by the Capt that brought the Hams, which came in very good Order & was excellent.

Amongst those Inclosed Seeds you will find Some Pyracantha or Evergreen Thorn [Firethorn] which in Flower & Berry make a fine Show, but as this rarely comes up untill next year it must be sowed where it must not be disturbed where it is sown. Fence in the Place thick with sticks a foot long & make a Little Palissado [palisade]. This you must be sure to Keep Clear from Weeds for it may Lay another year, for I have often Seed Especially your Cedars, White Fringe tree, that Lays untill 2d or third Spring before it rises.

The Fraxinella [*Dictamnus alba,* burning bush] is one of the finest Flowers but this Seed may Lay untill the 2d year. Sow it thin, for it requires room, & Palisadoe it about & keep it Clear of Weeds, for they Choak the Seed & Deprive & rob it of its nourishment. When this comes up, it Looks Like a young Tree or Shrub. Where too thick, remove them asunder the 2d or 3d year. They root Deep & Continue Many Years.

The other Seeds may be all Sown. If they come not up this year they may Next. That you may know for Certain, have Sticks a foot or 2 long & as thick as 2 fingers. Lett the top part of one Side be cutt Smooth, on that Part write the Seeds name in Ink; lett it be well Dyed in the Sun & then Stick in the Place the Seed is Sown & then you Will not forget what is there Sown & Watch its coming up & Watch every Weed & as Soon as it appears pull it up.

I am respectfully yours   P. COLLINSON

I thank you for both your Letters with the Yucca Seed &c. It is a handsome Flower & the Green Leaves remarkable.

---

1. Her son Thomas by George Robins died in 1761 of "a bilious fever" at the age of 22. He had been sent to a school in London under Peter's care and had graduated from Edinburgh as a physician.

170 ❧ TO BENJAMIN GALE

Extract of ALS : Yale

February 4, 1764

I am glad to find you are intent on raising mulberry trees [for the silk culture]. If they is came up from Seed they make the best trees. They should be first sewed in beds in a garden until three or four years old and then transplanted into a proper place well fenced until they are out of the reach of cattle. But they arise quick from laying down the young root chutes in the ground in autumn. To make this feasible cut down a tree within a foot of the ground in the winter. The next summer it will shoot out a great number of branches round the stem. Lay these down next autumn in the earth digging it well and the next autumn following they will be fit to remove. Continuing this practice annually, in a few years a great number will be raised. Transplant them first into a nursery in your garden in rows two feet asunder, each plant nine inches or a foot distant. Let them stand two or three years and annually transplant the thriftiest best grown where they are always to remain.

The mulberry tree will also take from twigs two feet long. Set two thirds deep in beds of good rich mold.

BENJAMIN GALE (1715–1790), physician and political writer. Studied with Jared Eliot, married Eliot's daughter, Hannah, and eventually took over Eliot's medical practice in Connecticut. Corresponded with many English & Continental scientists on agriculture. His "Historical Memoirs, relating to the Practice of Inoculation for the Small Pox" was read before the Royal Society in May 1765 (see *Phil. Trans.* LV (1766): 193–204). Gale was following Eliot in attempting to cultivate mulberry trees in America.

171 ❧ TO CADWALLADER COLDEN

ALS : N-YHS

Ridge Way House, February 25, 1764

I am Here Retired to my sweet & calm old Mansion, from its High Elevation Look 40 or 50 Miles round Mee on the Busie Vain World below, Envying No Man but am truly thankfull for the undeserved Blessings Good Providence hath pleased to conferr on Mee.

With a Pious Mind filled with admiration I contemplate the Glorious Constellations above, and the Wonders in the Vegitable Tribes below. I have an Assemblage of Rare Plants from all quarters, the Industrious collection of forty years. Some or other of them all the year round & all the Seasons through are delighting my Eyes, for in the Depth of our Winter, the plants from the Alps, Siberia & the mountains of Asia exhibit their pretty flowers and anticipate the Spring: the Black Hellebore with its Large white Flowers, the acconite with its Golden Clusters, these show themselves before Xmas. For that reason the First is called the Xmas Rose. Primroses & Polyanthus, Wall flowers & some Violets & single anemonies flower all Winter, unless a snow happens to fall, which is seldome. It seems a Paradox (considering our Latitude) to tell Foreigners that Vegitation never ceases in England.

I am this Instant come in from seeing your Skunk Weed (arum Beta fol). Its Early ap-

"Ridgeway House," Peter Collinson's home at Mill Hill. Drawn by "Mr. Renton." Courtesy of Mill Hill School.

pearance & its singularly spotted flowers attracts the notice of Everyone. It hath been now a month in flower. By this you may Guess the difference of seasons with you & Us.

But this Winter (if it may be called so) is very different from all that has been remembered. Wee have had as Mild & Warm, but then it hath been Dry, Suney & pleasant. Whereas This hath been continued (I may say dayly), Rains, if a few frosty Mornings, certainly Rain at Night, Moist & Warm but attended with Hurricane Winds & the air so beclouded it was rare to see the face of the Sun. The consequences of such Inclement Weather hath been more Shipwrecks & Inundatins then ever was known in One Winter. It is very affecting to read the very Deplorable accounts from Time to Time.

The Loss of Sheep & Cattle drowne'd advances much the price of Provision, but Thank God from the plenty of Last year (tho' a bad Harvest) our Bread keeps under 12d a peck Loafe and Wee have been able to supply vast Quantities to our Indigent Neighbours. I am assured some Weeks 8 & 10 Thousand Quarters of wheat has been shiped off for France, Portugal, Spain & Italy. This Trade brings in Great Riches, being a Surplus that Wee can spare without Prejudice to ourselves.

When I look back & consider the Poor state of Agriculture Here in the last Century, it affords a pleasure I can't express to see our extensive Improvements made in This Age. Then the Citty of London imported annually Polish wheat from Dantzick (to the Enrich-

ing foreigners) to fill Our Graneries, for Our culture of wheat was so spareing, that if a Crop failed, a Famine was like to Ensue. To prevent this Terrible Calamity the Citty prudently sold it out One year under another but the Dantzick Corn Trade hath been long left off. Instead of buying Wee annually sell to Our Neighbors.

As often as I survey my Garden & Plantations it reminds Mee of my Absent Friends by their Living Donations. See there my Honorable Friend Governor Colden how thrifty they look. Sir, I see nobody but Two fine Trees, a Spruce & a Larch, thats True, but they are his representatives. But see close by how my Lord Northumberland[1] aspires in that Curious Firr from Mount Ida [in Turkey; possibly *Abies nordmanniana*] but Look Yonder at the Late Benevolent Duke of Richmond, His Everlasting Cedars of Lebanon will Endure when you & I & He is forgot. See with what Vigor they Tower away, how their Stems enlarge & their Branches extend. But pray what are those pines, Novelties rarely seen, That Elegant one with five Leaves is the Cembro Pine from Sibiria, the other Tall Tree is the very long Leaved Pine of 10 or 12 inches from So. Carolina [*Pinus palustris*]. They stand mementos of my Generous Friend the Late Duke of Argyle. That Gentle Tree so like a Cypress looks uncommon, thats the Syrian Cedar [Cedar of Lebanon?]. The Seed was gave Mee by Sir Charles Wager first Lord of the Admiralty, gather'd in the Isle of Iona, in his Voyage to convey Don Carlos (the Now K of Spain) to Naples.

But those Balm Gilead Firrs grow at a surpriseing rate. It is pleasant to see, but they renew a concern for my Dear Friend Lord Petre. They came young from his Nurserys, with all the species of Virginia Pines & Cedars, but that Firr that grows Near them is remarkable for its Blewish Green. That was a present from my Worthy Friend Sir Harry Trelawny.[2] It is called the black Spruce. He had it from Newfoundland. It grows delightfully.

Regard but the Variety of Trees and Shrubs in this plantation as mountain Magnolia, Sarsifrax, Rhododendrons, Calmias & Azaleas &c &c &c, all are the Bounty of my Curious

Botanic Friend J. Bartram of Philadelphia, and those pretty Fringe Trees, Halesias & Stuartia, all Great Beauties I must thank my Friend Mr Clayton the Great Botanist of America.

How Fragrant that Allspice, how Charming the Red flowered Acacia, Great Laurel Leafed Magnolia & Umbrella Magnolia & Loblolly Bay—these Charming Trees are the Glory of my Garden & the Trofies of that Friendship that subsists between Mee & my very obligeing Friend T. Lambol Esq[3] of South Carolina.

Thus Gratitude prompts Mee to Celebrate the Memory of my Friends amongst whome you have long Claimed the Respect & Esteem of yours Sincerely

P. COLLINSON

1. Hugh (Smithson) Percy, First Duke of Northumberland (1715–1786), FRS, developed gardens at Syon House, donated plants to Royal Botanic Garden at Kew. Philip Miller dedicated 8th edition of *Gardeners Dictionary* to him. (Desmond)

2. Henry Trelawney (fl. 1750s) of Butshead, Plymouth, Devon, particularly successful in raising pines. (Desmond)

3. Thomas Lamboll (1694–1774), Quaker planter of Charlestown, S. C., friend of the Bartram family, had a country seat on James Island, sent the Loblolly Bay to Collinson. (See Berkeley and Berkeley. *Dr. Alexander Garden of Charles Town.* Chapel Hill, 1969, p. 77)

172 ❧ TO ALEXANDER COLDEN

Draft ALS : Yale
June 1, 1764

I am glad to hear Sr Wm Johnson has concluded a peace with the Cheneses [Genesee Indians]. Hope it will have a good effect, for if Wee can but divide the Mocans [Mohawk] & engage them to take up ye Hatchet against those Bloody Villains the Delewares etc.

But what Justice shall be done to those eveel Irish & Scotch Presbeterians in Pennsilvania that came down & broke the prisons & place of Residence of so many helpless Innocent Indians and Murthered both Men Women & Children in Cool Blood that Fled for protection & would not Joyn the other Indians in their barbarously Killing the white people on the Frontiers.[1]

What a notoriously Wicked example is this to the Indians of the Five Nations, who have kept Neater [behaved better] Who Wee have accused of Barbarity & Crulty for Exerciseing the Like on our People. What will the Five Nations say to Such Merciless proceedings. Wee must never more talk to them of the Butcheries of their People. Yours   PC

Possibly ALEXANDER COLDEN (1716–1774), son of Cadwallader Colden, postmaster of New York, or the son of James Colden who had an interest in science and was a protégé of Collinson's. (*Franklin* VII, 263n)

This draft appears (along with two others to Franklin, one dated April 1, the other June 1, 1764) on Franklin's letter of February 11, 1764 to Collinson.

1. During the summer and early autumn of 1763 hostile Indians repeatedly attacked isolated settlements and farms along the Pennsylvania frontier. Public sentiment against Indians was high.

On December 14, 1763, fifty armed men from Paxton, a town on the Susquehanna, attacked a small settlement at Conestoga, near Lancaster, killing the six Indians they found there and burning the village. Fourteen other Indians were spared because they were away on the night of the raid. On December 27 "the Paxton boys" as they came to be called struck again, attacking the remaining Indians in the place of safety where they had been placed and murdering them all, men, women and children. The victims were known to be friendly. (See " Pennsylvania Assembly: Reply to the Governor, January 20, 1764," and the note preceeding it in *Franklin* 11, 22–30)

173 ❧ TO BENJAMIN FRANKLIN

Draft ALS: Yale

London, June 1, 1764

At the Same Time that I commend the Zeal of my Dear Friend & his compatriots for the checking the Unjust Incroachments of proprietary Power I lament the Inefective Diversions of a Province founded on principals of Peace & Equity.

I am much obliged to my Friend Colden for Sending Mee your Gazet of the 29 th March.[1] It has been perused by Many Friends. Wee all are pleased to See your Spirit'd Repolastions, as they are fully Founded & the Noble Stand against the unreasonable artifice of a Family that have deviated from the paths of Justice by forsaking the upright intentions of their Great Ancestor.

When a proprietary House [the Penn Family] is blinded to its interests by Avarice & Seeks to continue in authority by Oppression, its no longer worthy of Dominion, Lett it Center where it ought to be in the Crown, which will be more Beneficial to the Province.

Yett when I Say the Governmt ought to Cease It is On presumption it will be for the Benefit of the province. There may be weighty Objections against It Such as will readly Occur to One So well Acquainted with Colony Governmt & Interests. Such a Measure is not to be entred into precipitately, the advantages and disadvantages of Each are to be well weighed before the Casting Vote is given least the Old Proverb is made Good out of the Frying pan into the Fire.

Pray who is it that draws up the Governrs exchanges, there is some artifice in them that His Talents Seem not capable off, but if I am Mistaken I ask His Excuse. I have been Since informed the Dictator that holds the Governr in Leading Strings is Sam Chew,[2] a Shrowed Fellow but He is out in His Politicks, His pupil & his Family may repent the Choice of Such a Director. Vale

P. Collinson.

This draft appears (along with another to Franklin dated April 1, 1764 and a draft to Alexander Colden dated June 1, 1764) on Franklin's February 11, 1764 letter to Collinson.

1. The March 29, 1764 issue of the *Pennsylvania Gazette* is comprised of statements from the Governor and the Assembly concerning "An Act for granting to his Majesty the sum of fifty-five thousand pounds, etc." also referred to as "The Supply Bill." The problem arose from the taxation of unimproved land.

2. Collinson probably meant Benjamin Chew (1722–1810), Attorney General of the Province of Pennsylvania. Samuel Chew was a physician, not involved with politics to this extent.

174 ❧ TO PETER SIMON PALLAS

ALS: Staatsbibliothek, Berlin

London, June 9, 1764

I now have the pleasure to Acquaint my Dear Pallas that He was yesterday Chosen a Member of the Royal Society & wish He Long Live to enjoye that Honour.

I received your Curious Letter of Aprill 30th. Am glad to hear all the percells arrived Safe to your Hands & that Dr Bohadsch's[1] was dispatch'd to him with Letter of advice.

I am glad to hear Professor Gleditch[2] will Enter into those Inquiries that are to Mee so very interesting.

As the Season returns I hope not to forget Some American Seeds, but pray tell Mee how I shall send them to Him. I wish He could give Mee the Names of those He most particularly Desires.

Thy abstract of Mr Jacobi[3] Experiments is very curious. It Establishes for certainty that Salmon do not enter into Contact or Copulate together. His remarks on the Eggs & their Hatching with other Phenomena may give very usefull & Improving Hints & the Stocking or replenishing ponds with the embryos of Salmon & Trouts may Succeed to great advantage provided those Ponds have Springs of Running Water passing thro them, but it is very Doubtfull if it succeeds in Ponds of Stagnant Water.

His Blending Salmon with Pike has not a probability of Succeeding as they are of a Different Genus, however it is well to Trye.

I am afraid my Poor Dear Gronovius is not So well as I could Wish because you mention nothing of your intended expedition Heither.

Pray tell Him when you write to Him that I received his obligeing Letter of the 15th May, but that Mr Shrubbe [not identified] has not been with Mee.

I am with respect Sincerely Yours,   P. COLLINSON

Is not the Turkish Dye made from the Cocos Polonicus, which is an Insect found att the Roots of Several plants in Poland, the Tormentilla &c &c,[4] but if your people Succeed pray Lett Mee know. I am told the Turks keep it a great Secret. Wee want the art of Dying Cotten wool Scarlet. There is a considerable Sum offer'd by our Society of Arts[5] for discovering that Secret.

If you know that Mr Gronovious writes French that [then] hint to Him that his Letters to Mee may be in French, which is more Familiar than Latin. But if he does not write French Easily then do not mention this to Him.

I am concern'd So Ingenious a Man as Geastne [not identified] contents himself with Such a poor professorship. Perhaps wee should not Censure Him if wee knew his Motives & family connections.

I intend communicating Mr Jacobi's Experiments to Our Society.

My Friend Dr Solander was Elected the Same Day you was. You have heard he is settled at the British Musaeum by my Instigation.

PETER SIMON PALLAS (1694–1770), FRS, born in Berlin, Professor of Surgery at the Berlin Medical-Surgical Academy, at one time employed at the Russian Academy of Sciences by Empress Catherine II (the Great).

1. Johann Baptist Bohadsch, published *De quibusdam animalibus marinis eorumque proprietatibus.* Dresden, 1761.

2. Probably Johann Gottlieb Gleditsch (1714–1786), German botanist. Published *Catalogus Plantarum.* Leipzig, 1737; *Systema plantarum,* 1764; *Methodus Fungorum,* 1753 and many other works on botany.

3. Stephen Ludwig Jacobi (1711–1784). "Method of breeding fish to advantage." *Hannoverische Beyträge zum Nutgen und Vergnügen* 1763, no. 23; also "On the breeding of trout by the impregnation of the ova." *Hannoverische Magazin, worin kleine Abhandlungen . . .* 1765, no. 62.

4. The Turkish dye was a deep red dye made from the root of the *Rubia tinctorum,* also known as common madder. It was one of the most sought-after colors well into the nineteenth century. The dye process originated in India and spread to other parts of the East, especially Turkey.

5. Society for the Encouragement of Arts, Manufactures and Commerce. During the period 1762 to 1764 the Society offered a premium of £100 "for the greatest improvement in dying cotton to answer the purposes of Turky or India red." (See: Dossie, R. *Memoirs of Agriculture . . . ,* Vol. 1. London, (1768) p. 183.

175 🐾 TO CADWALLADER COLDEN

ALS:N-YHS
London, October 7, 1764

I acknowledged the favour of my Dear Friends Letter of August ll & forwarded Dr Whyts.[1] An affair has happen'd in your province which hath Given Our Society [of Friends] much Concern. A young Man of your Citty, was called as a Wittness & refused to take an Oath, was threatned with fine & Imprisonment if He dont, being Intimidated He took it, contrary to his conscience & our Christian principle.

Our Friends Here are much troubled to be informed of such Harsh proceedings, in a Country where all profess Liberty of Concience.

I here Inclose for my Dear Friends perusal a Coppy of a Letter from our Society to One In your Citty In which will be seen how the Case Stands Here and Wee hope for the Same Lenity from your Legislator.

I know your Own Generous Principals and what a Friend you are to Liberty. Therefore I am the more perswaded of your kind Influence to Metigate the Rigour of such proceedings, and what will be an additional Mark of your Tenderness, & Regard, to discourage as much as may be our Friends being summoned on Juries in Cases in which they can not Act consistent with their principles (I never was summoned on a Jury). These Hints are submitted with great difference to your prudence & Discretion by your Sincere & affectionate Friend.

P. COLLINSON

1. Possibly Dr. Robert Whytt (1714–1766), FRS, president of the Royal College of Physicians, Edinburgh.

176 🐾 TO CARL LINNAEUS

ALS:LS
[circa 1765]

Can there be got no seed of the Cimicifuga?[1]

As Mr Edwards has presented Baron Linnaeus with a Colour'd Print of Dr Fothergill's Great Pheasant from Tartary,[2] I procured some Feathers to give Some Idea of Its Wonderfull Plumage.

In the first place, the Chinese made an excellent painting of this Most beautifull Rare Bird on a Sheet of paper Six feet Long. But least Wee should suspect there was More Art and Ingenuity than Nature, they most carefull packed Up all the Feathers of this Wonderfull Bird to Verifie their Performance to be Genuine.

It is the Size of a Large Cock Turkey, the Two Feathers of its Tail are full Three Feet Long, it has all the Characters of the Pheasant.

Mr Edwards from the Eyes in the Wings names it the Argus.

As it comes from Chinese Tartary It would Thrive Well in our Climate.

But what is remarkable In all the Chinese paintings Neither I nor my Friends Ever saw this Charming Bird which would make so glorious a Figure. [Several lines missing]

Argus Pheasant. George Edwards. Trial plate bound in Gleanings of Natural History. *The Linnean Society of London.*

The size of the Chinese Argus or Luen is, from the tip of the bill to the end of the tail in a straight line, seven feet and a half; from the top of the back to the legs, one foot three inches and a quarter. The leg and foot 10 inches and a quarter.

1. Probably *C. racemosa* (black snake root, a North American plant used as an emetic).

2. Great Pheasant from Tartary: This is probably the Argus Pheasant or Argusianus Argus. The wings contain rows of round, gold colored "eyes" and it measures about 72 inches. Found in Indochina, Malay Peninsula. See also PC to Linnaeus, April 20, 1767.

177 🐦 TO CARL LINNAEUS

ALS:LS
London, May 1, 1765

What a Comfort it is to Mee that I hope I can salute my Dear Linnaeus in Health, having So Happly Escaped a Threatening Sickness.

You have, my Dear Friend, Infinitely Obliged Mee with your most acceptable Letter of December the first. I felicitate on your Recovery & on your Daughters Nuptials. May happiness attend them. I am thinking what a Many & Variety of Ocurrences have Happened since I saw my dear Baron [Linnaeus] at my House in London. It is amazeing in our Short Lives what a few years Brings about.

I did not in the least Imagine but you had received the Account of the Penna Marina from Our Friend Ellis because I know He sent It to you as soon as it was published. How

It Miscarried I know not. I am glad I sent It to Dr Back, that you might have the Opportunity to see It, but had I known you had been without One I should have sent it to you.

Wee all Deplore the Loss of the Excellent Mr Forskohl,[1] but it rejoices Mee that He Lived to send you the Opo-balsamum on which Botanists was so Divided.

It is Surprising with what Address you can Dispatch Such Great, Curious & Critical Works, as the Kings & Queens Museum &c, But the Exalted pleasure you Enjoye in Surveying the Riches of the Creation is an ample Gratification, suited to your Noble Mind, replenished with such Eminent Learning & Knowledge. Pray is there any Hopes of seeing published the Non-descript-Insects Engraved? For discriptions without Figures convey but imperfect Ideas of the Subjects.[2]

You are happy my Dear Linnaeus that you can sett at Home & Receive the Annual Tributary Collections from all Parts of the World. May you Long Live to Enjoy the Fruits of your Labours.

Dr Kuhn[3] is With Us, translateing your Travels, which I long to peruse.

Dr Solander goes on very Successfully at the Museum, has been lately much Engaged in surveying the Dutchess of Portlands Museum where there is a very Great Collection of Shells and Marine Productions, Gems & precious Stones.

I Desire your Acceptance of some Seeds from Maryland which I hope will afford you some Speculation. Where there is to Much of a Sort for the Upsal Garden you May Divide them amongst your Friends.

Now is the Delightful Season. Flora appears Bedecked with Great Variety of Beautifull Attire, altogether Charming. The Long approaches of our Spring Make our Gardens very Entertaining, for Vegetation never Ceases in our Temperate Climate.

Some Body told Mee that you Doubted the Flowering of the Sarracena in England. I can Assure my Dear Friend for many years past, Both Species of Saracena, the Same that are figured in Catesby's Nat Hist flower annually in my Garden. The Flower Buds now appear about an Inch high. It is certainly One of the Wonderful Flowers. They are finely painted by Mr. Ehret. It is a Bogg plant, and I know their Culture. I have now the Ledum Palustre [crystal tea] very finely in Flower, & that is a Rare Bogg Plant. If you desire It I will give you my Methode. The Leaves of the Two species are as Surpriseing as the Flowers, for they are Open Tubes, contrived to Collect the Rains & Dews to Nourish the plants in Dry Weather.

A Very Curious work began to be published in the year 1763 Intitled British Zoology, the principal Editor Thomas Pennant, Esq. a Gentleman of good Estate & Great Learning.[4] There is 3 parts already Done, a fourth will be finished Next Winter. The Inclosed Blew Covered Book will give you Some Idea of the Work & the Authors Abilties. Each book conts 25 plates, is Two Guineas.

Now my Dear Friend I wish you all Happyness & am Affectionately yours,

P. COLLINSON

I am Impatient for the arrival of your Ships that I may happily See your Systema Nata that I have waited so long to see.

The Martins always come 2 or 3 Weeks before the Swallows. Is not this a Demonstration that they go not both to the Same place, If they did, they would come away all together.

Can there be got no seed of the Cimicifuga?

1. Pehr Forsskål (1736–1765), one of Linnaeus's "apostles," those of his students sent abroad to investigate the plants of distant lands. (Blunt)

2. Linneaus spent several years cataloguing the natural history collections of the King and Queen of Sweden. The King's collection was published in 1754 as *Museum S.R.M. Adolphi Friderici* with illustrated plates. An unillustrated second volume was published in 1764. The Queen's collection appeared in 1764 as *Museum S.R.M. Ludovicae Ulricae*, about two thirds of it devoted to insects, but with few illustrations. (Blunt)

3. Adam Kuhn (1741–1817), Philadelphia physician.

4. Thomas Pennant (1726–1798), *British Zoology,* 1766. He also wrote several books of travel with a scientific interest.

178 ❧ TO CHARLES LYTTELTON, BISHOP OF CARLISLE

ALS:BL
July 20, 1765

To Lord Lyttleton

By this time I presume all Compts. are paid & visits made, & now my Dear Lord can attend to the request of an old Friend & give Mee leave to remind Him of what I propos'd to Him, that his Botanic Friend should make Him a Hortus Siccus of all the rare plants in the County.

Then I shall see if there is any that has escaped the vigilence of Ray & other Botanists.

I waited in hopes an able Penn like yours, would celebrate our Great & Worthy Deceased Friend Dr Stukely[1] but non appearing, the Duties of Friendship called on mee to offer my mite in the Gents Magazine for May & when my Hand was in, I could not forget my old Friend Dr Walker of Trinity College Cambridge who bought the Ground & gave it to the University for a Physick Garden. A Tribute of Praise is due to such Benefactors to Mankind and in Ages to come these Magazines will be rummaged into for the Accuracies of the Times, as Great Numbers are regularly bound up annually so that at present I dont know a better record.[2]

In Aprill I gave a Dissertation on the Plane Tree[3] which I believe will please you.

To-morrow I sett out to Goodwood, was willing to testifie my Respect before I go and to assure my Dear Lord I am his Sincere and affectionate Friend.

P COLLINSON

I doubt it is well with you but wee are so burnt up I don't Remember the like, our field are brown Russet no after Hay can be expected, when the Fields from Day to Day from morning to night scorch when a burning Sun & piercing Easterly Wind, in 2 months but 3 rainey Days, yett the Town & Country is very Healthy.

But Dr Ducarel[4] read Mee a letter from his Brother in Normandy in a large Town 12 Miles from Roan [Rouen] a Meliary purple Fever carries off such Numbers that the Bishop forbids the Bells tolling either for Deaths or Burials for fear the people will be Discouraged & leave the Town, & Spread the infection.

No doubt you hear from your Good Brother[5] of strange Alterations at Court.

CHARLES LYTTELTON (1714–1768), antiquary, Bishop of Carlisle (1762), FRS., and President of the Society of Antiquaries, 1765.

1. William Stukeley (1687–1765), antiquary and physician.

2. "Some Account of the life of the late Dr. Stukeley" and "Some Account of a Physic garden at Cambridge." *Gentleman's Magazine* vol XXXV (1765): 211–212.

3. "An account of the Eastern plane-tree, or sycamore." *Gentleman's Magazine* vol XXXV(1765): 159–160.

4. Andrew Coltee Ducarel (1713–1785), DCL, FRS, antiquary, Keeper of the library at Lambeth Palace.

5. George Lyttelton, First Baron Lyttelton (1709–1773), became a Member of Parliament in 1735.

ALS:BL
London, August 30, 1765

Just as I returned from a Hott Dusty Disagreeable Journey From Goodwood in Company with the Duke of Argyle[1] I mett with my Dear Lords acceptable favour of the 25th ulto.

The Country & Parks are so burnt up & Exhausted that there is not a Verdant Spott to be seen, but all looks like the Sunburnt fields of Asia. The Distress is great. In some places they have no food, nor Water, for their Cattle. The Parks at Goodwood are so Russet & Bare that the Duke ordered them to Cutt Green Boughs to sustain the Deer. So you may believe Venison this year is not overloaded with Fatt, but then you are compensed with better Flavour.

But under this General Distress Wee had the Great Consolation to see every Where such plentifull Crops of Wheat, the Ears Pendant with heavy Grains. The Harvest began last Week reaping Wheat & Some Corn had been Carried In & high harvest Weather continues, a Long Day of Burning Sun without Clouds to screen the fainting Reaper. Must be Intolerable, but the Cooling East Wind is some refreshment. Its Excessive Hott, Birds Thermometer[2] was up at 80 to Day.

In our Journey Wee saw not a bad Crop of Barley & Oats all ripe for the Sicle, for this constant Weather hurries on Harvest at Great Rate, so I hope Corn will soon come to market to relieve the Poor & Lower the price of Bread.

It gives Mee great pleasure that you have Drank the Waters at Scarbrough. I hope the good Effects will continue.

As the Composeing an Hortus Siccus requires Time to perfect It so it must be done gradually as rare plants offers for common plants may be the Last Work.

So that if you can bring a Decade or Two of what plants can be collected of Such as are not over common may such better with Mr Parishes [not identified] little Leisure to Collect them & yett in Time may be a compleat Collection.

My Way of Drying Plants is Easie. I gather the Plant in full Flower or in perfect Seed, both is best when can be conveniently Had, Display the plant, smooth the Leaves & flowers on a sheet of White or rather Whited brown paper (for Brown paper spoils the plants). When this is Done press It Down with a Large folio Book or Two.

Next Day Look at It & see if any of the Leaves &c wants rectifieng, & the Third Day Change the plants into Fresh Paper, Drying the Other well, & the fifth Day return them to the first paper, & then they will keep to any Time, unless the plants are very Succulent, then they may require another Changeing. Remember allways to keep a Weight on them. To bring them to Town, Tie them up in Two Thin boards the size of the paper, & then nothing can Hurt in their Conveyance.

I am pleased to hear He has been so fortunate to find the Sisymbrium Monense [*Coincya monensis,* Isle of Man Cabbage]. It is a Sweet plant, one of My Favourites. I formerly had it growing in Great perfection but in removeing my Garden lost It. I wish I could have some Seeds.

I am Glad to Hear so Judicious a Measure hath the Desired Effect & that your Poor can be relieved from our [illegible] Kingdome. Wee Here share in the Advantage to the Great Reliefe of the Lower Sort of People.

I am my Dear Lord with my best Wishes for your Preservation, your Sincere and Affectionate Friend,

P. COLLINSON

1. John Campbell, 4th Duke of Argyll (d. 1770).   2. John Bird (1709–1776), London instrument maker.

180 ❧ TO CARL LINNAEUS

ALS:LS
London, September 17, 1765

The Sight of my Dear Linnaeus's well Known Characters revives my Heart, and gives Mee pleasure I cannot express.

To you, To Whome Nature pays tribute from all parts of the World, could I expect to offer any Thing New? I am glad to find the China Argus proved So.

As you So Justly Admire the Saracena as one of the Wonders in the Vegitable Kingdome, that you may have a More perfect Idea of the wonderfull Reservirs that Retain the Water to Supply the plant in great droughts, I send you Two Leaves. I have filled them with Moss within to keep them to their Size & Shape, which may be easily taken Out, & I have packed them in Moss, so hope they will come fresh & plump to your hands & give you a Satisfaction that the best description cannot so well Do. I have added the Seed Vessels of this years Flowers.

I think the Dipsacus hath perfoliated Leaves down the Stalk, that holds Water to Replenish the plant & the Viscums of the West Indies, in their concave Leaves, retain a great Deal of Water to refresh the plant, whose Roots spread on the old rotton Bark of Trees, & do not Incorporate with the Tree as our Viscums do.

You, my Dear Friend, Surprise Mee with telling Mee of your Cool & Wet summer, whereas our Summer has been so much on the Extreams the Other Way. For all May, June & July was excessive Hot & Dry, but 6 or 7 Rainey Days in 3 Months, so that all our Grass fields Looks like the Sunburnt Countrys of Spain & Africa. Our Fahrenheits Thermometer frequently 84 and 85 in the Shade in the Open Air, but in my Parlor frequently at 95.

I do assure you I have had Little pleasure of my Life this summer, for I cannot bear Heat. I have longed to be on Lapland Mountains.

The beginning of August Wee had some fine Rains, but that did not recover our Usual Verdure, (Since) to this present writeing, Hott & Dry Weather, not a drop rain for 14 days past. Our Hay is very Short & Oats & Barley but a Midlin Crop, but Wheat which Wee Most Wanted, Good Providence has favoured Us with a plentifull Crop, & a Good Harvest, which began Two Weeks Sooner then in Common Years. Peaches, Nectarines, Figgs & Grapes, Pears, &c. are Early ripened, and are Richly Flavoured, & many Exotic Shrubs & plants flower finely this year.

My Garden is now a Paradise of Delight, with the Variety of Flowers & plenty of Roses now in Bloom, as if in May & June.

But to obtain all this pleasure, great pains have been taken to keep the Garden continual Water'd every Evening.

That you, my Dear Friend, may long Enjoye Good Health & Tranquility of Mind, is the Sincere Wish of your affectionate Friend,

P. COLLINSON

P.S. Must I not have the pleasure of Seeing your Noble Work the Systema Natura before I Die which you have given Mee the Expectation off some years Agon.

Pray my Respects to your Son. I also have a Son who loves Botany & Nat Hist as well as my Self.

[on cover sheet:]

Many Leaves grow round the Center Budd of the Scarracenits, which makes a pretty appearance with their Mouths open to catch the Rains & Dews; but many poor Insects loose their Lives by being drowned in this Cisterns of Water.

The Two Leaves now Sent, are the Leaves of Last year, So are in Little Decayed.

The Leaves of this year are not attained to Maturity.

Inclosed are Specimens of the Erica Cantabrica [*Daboecia cantabrica,* St. Dabeoc's Heath], &c. now in flower in my Garden, which was Raised from Seed sent mee last year from Spain. It is an Elegant plant, & makes a pretty show.

Erica cantabrica. *Georg Dionysius Ehret. Natural History Museum, Botany Library, London.*

ALS:Glos. Rec. Off.
London, December 1, 1765

I am not Able to Saye how much I am Obliged to my very Kind Friend John Player for So many Marks of his Regard. I Scarse know amongst such numbers which to Acknowledge First.

But as thou has delighted my Eyes with a favourite Object I never hoped to See. It Attracted my Thoughts to consider its Duration which I have Drawn up & Submit to thy Candid Perusal. In Such calculations one is obliged to take things at large & in round Numbers, for to King Stephens Reigne all is conjecture.

My Friend Lord Petre[1] has in his Park at Writtle near Ingatstone [Ingatestone] in Essex Another of these Ancient of Times. By his Capacious Trunk & a Lofty Head of four Great Arms like four Towers He overlooks all His Subjects and proclaims Him King of the Woods all round Him. I carefully Measurd this Stately Chesnutt and found It full 45 feet in Girth 4 feet from the Ground. It is Above 30 years Since I Saw it first. Then to appearence it was Sound. Lately I saw it & to my Griefe Saw it hollow within, yett by its Vigorous Head it may Stand a Century or Two.

When I have leisure thou will hear farther from thy obliged Friend

P. COLLINSON

The Drawings are prettyly executed & give a Good Idea of the Trees. The Elm is Superior to all I ever Mett with. Pray canst recollect what Species, if not our London Elm than some Species of Witch Elm are 3 or 4 sorts distinguished by their Leaves.

A Probable computation of the Age of the Great Chesnut Tree in Lord Ducies[2] Garden at Tortsworth

As it was a remarkable large Tree in the Reigne of King Stephen, It might rise from a Nut about the year 800 in the Reigne of King Egbert[3].

From this Date to Attain Such Maturity & Magnitude to be a Signal Tree to fix the Boundary of the Manor & Then long (but how long is uncertain) be a Mark of Eminence in the Record, the Great Chesnutt Tree of Tamworth now Tortsworth, cannot allow less than this brings it Down to the first year of King Stephen anno 1135—335 years.

From this Reign Wee are Certain of Its age Down to the year 1765—630 years
Must be total—965 years

If any Regard is to be had to the Three Periods Given to Oak & Chesnut it favours my Computation that they are

300 years Growing
300 years Standing
300 years Decaying

It seems to Mee this Venerable Instance of the Great Effort of Vegitation is little less than a Thousand years Old and may possibly be More & may yett last another Hundred years before it is totally Extinct.

JOHN PLAYER lived at Stoke near Bristol, farmed, and was an amateur geologist.

1. Robert Edward, 9th Baron Petre (1742–1787)

2. Matthew, Moreton Second Baron of Ducie (d. 1770), created Baron Ducie of Tortworth in 1763.

3. King Stephen reigned 1135–1154, Egbert 828–839.

ALS:N-YHS
March 20, 1766

I had the pleasure of my Dear Friends Letters of October 16 & January 14. It gives Mee great Satisfaction that you have made a safe Retreat to your little Town where you can calmly look back on the Late Mad & Tumultuous Scenes that Distressed your Mind and embarrassed your Government. Our Newspapers are full of the frantick Tricks of a Riottus Mobb. I was truly concern'd for you, yett I was persuaded of your unshaken Mind, in persueing the paths of Equity & Moderation.[1]

As the Act is repealed, I hope all Animosities will Cease & Trade & Business be restored to its right Channel.

I think it highly reasonable that Governors & officers that have suffer'd from a Rebellious Crew of Banditi should be Indemnified. I have heard it hinted that Instructions will be sent to every Government where such ravages have happen'd that the province shall make good the Damages. I have not yett had an Oppertunity to wait on Sr J: Amherst but hope to do it in a few days, & then you may expect to hear further on that Article.

Immediately on Reciving Yours of December 17 I went & bespoke you a Chariot & this 25 March they assure Mee it will be ready in 3 Weeks. I shall then take first Ship, but shall give Davis the preference.

Mr. Godard remitted Mee a Bill for 81:15:0 on Mr Henry Potts of the Post Office which is accepted.

You need not been in a Hurry to send Money as I owe you Some. As soon as the Chariot is ship'd & all Charges paid, then I will send your account Currt.

In the Mean Time I am with Sincere Love & Respects your affectionate Friend,

P. COLLINSON.

P. COLLINSON thanks to his Friend D: Colden,[2] is obliged to Him for the hints on Breeding Sheep. This Difficulty of rearing Sheep in the No: Eastern Colonies may always retard their Increase, but when the Oeconomy of Spain comes to Obtain in the So: Western Colonies, by feeding them on the Mountains in Summer & In the warm Savanas under them in the Winter, then England may Dread Her American Rivals as all Arts seem to be travelling Westward. As you may have Woolens &c for family Use through my Hands, why should you pay an advance price for them at N. York.

If you go to Coldenham at proper Season think of a few Seeds &c.

1. Over great opposition in America the Stamp Act became effective in November 1765. The Stamp Act Congress convened in New York in October, and throughout the colonies the Sons of Liberty organized opposition to the Act's enforcement. When Lieutenant Governor Colden ordered a major in the Royal Artillery to "cram the Stamps down their throats" an angry mob confiscated the stamps, destroyed Colden's coach and hanged and burned him in effigy along with a devil.

In January 1766 Colden wrote Collinson, "In my last I desired to give you the trouble of buying a Post Chariot for me with the harness & other necessary furniture & begg'd you would send it over to me by the first opportunity. . . . I cannot now ride on horseback & it is necessary for my health frequently to take the air. . . . I should not give those who are unfriendly the pleasure to see me reduced to a mean method of going abroad after their having had the pleasure of seeing my Chariot burned by the Mob in a most insulting manner on Government. . . .

"I have suffered considerably in my private fortune by my strict adherence to my Duty at this time. I am in hopes of obtaining some recompense & a reward for my past services for which purpose I have wrote to Mr Secretary Conway & to the Plantation & [obscure] to Sir Jeffery Amherst who on all occasions has done me friendly Good offices." (ALS:Huntington Library) See Anderson, Fred, *Crucible of War: The Seven Years' War and the Fate of Empire in British North America, 1754–1766.* New York, 2000, pp. 608–610.

2. David Colden (1733–1784), Cadwallader's son. Appointed Weight Master of the Province of New York, January 21, 1764.

ALS:LS
London, September 25, 1766

By the Spring ships 1765, May 1 and by the last in the Autumn, September 17, 1765, I wrote to my Dear Linnaeus, and sent Him the Leaves of the Saracenia which he so much admired, that He might see its Structure & Two Specimens of the Erica Cantabrica.

A year is now passed & not a Line from my Dear Friend. This is treating Mee unkindly, considering our Long Friendship.

You have promised More then Once to send Mee your Master piece of Nature, the Last Edition of the Systema Natura. Is not my eyes to be blessed with a Sight of that Universal Pinax before I Die? Year after Year I have not failed to remind you of your promise. If you doubt it, I will send your Letters. It give Mee concern to Urge the Affair so far, but pray excuse it, for it is the Last Time I will ever mention it to you.

Some Time agon I saw what I think a Surprising Curiosity. On a Large Peach Tree full of Fruit, there was a Twig about Two Inches Long, on one side grew a Peach, and on the Other Side a Nectarine. They grew so close together that they touched each other. I stood long with Admiration reviewing this Wonder. The Nectarine had the shineing smooth Surface with a Red complection, the Peach was rough & Downey, as peaches are.

Wee have had Two More remarkable Instancs of peach Trees naturally & without Art, producing Nectarines, so I reasonable Conclude, The Peach is the Mother of the Nectarine. Where this Lusus Natura has happend, Ingenious men have improved the Accident, by budding, or with Grafting, from the nectarine branch, and Thus the Race of Nectarines began.

The Variety Wee have in our Gardens have been produced by sowing the Stones, I will tell my Dear Baron an Instance in my Garden.

Some person Eating a nectarine threw the Stone away. Next year it came up. I suffered it to grow, supposing it to be a Peach, but as it grew up to the fifth year, to my Great Pleasure it Showed it to be a Nectarine, & this year, at this present writeing, has near Three Dozen of Ripe fruite on It, as Rich & High Flavour'd as those against the Wall.

Dr Solander came down to Mill Hill to Fill His Belly with Nectarines & he saw this fine Tree full of Fruit, which ripens a Week or Two later than those against the Wall.

This Accident confirms what many doubted, that a Nectarine Tree can be produced from the Stone without Grafting or Budding.

As you my Dear Friend, have the Largest Botanic library, pray Lett an Ingenious pupil search it carefully & answer the following Queries, for I want to be satisfied about the Origin of nectarines. 1st. Was the Nectarine known to the ancients? 2nd. Who are the First authors that Mention It? 3dly. Do they take any Notice of its Origin, and Mention the Country Whence It Came? [1]

Wee have had a most uncommon Rainey Summer, which was no way propitious to the Growth of the Wheat, but it pleased good providence to send us the finest hott Dry Harvest ever known, yett the Warm Constant Rains drew up the Wheat so much to Stalk, that the Ears are very Light, yett I hope there will be Sufficient to support the Nation. Now Wee have prudently stoped the Exportation, for so great are the Wants, & demand for foreign Markets, It was so great and so pressing, that it advanced the price so considerably that

ARBUTUS (Andrachne) frutescens, Spica erecta, foliis ovatis integris, et serratis, Bacca tuberculosa polysperma.

Occasion'd Insurrections in Many parts of the Kingdome, to stop by force the Corn from being Exported, but now a proclamation is come out to prevent It, I hope all will be Quiet again.

Much wett has made great Crops of Grass, so that every Where we have had Second Crops of Hay almost as large as the first & a Glorious Autumn to make it.

The Fields have a most delightfull Verdure & the Gardens are in the Highest Beauty, being Cover'd with the great Variety of Autumn Flowers, haveing not had the least frost to October 4, I have Housed none of my Succulent Exotics, for the Weather is so Hot, Dry, & fine, they are better abroad than in the House.

I survey my Garden with Raptures, to see the Infinite Variety with which the Great Creator has enriched the Vegitable Word.

A few days Agon Professor Hope of Edinburgh[2] came to see my Little Paradise. He was highly Delighted to see so many New & Curious plants he had not seen else where. I loaded him Home with Specimens.

Was it possible to see my Dear Linnaeus, what Joys it would give Mee, but if I cannot see the Father, I hope the Son will be Tempted to Make England a visit, and to see his Dear Fathers Old Friend.

In the Princess of Wales Garden at Kew the Protea Major is in fine flower & the Andrachne [*Arbutus unedo,* Strawberry Tree] has been finely in flower last May, in Dr

Fothergill's garden. Mr Ehret has painted It. As soon as it is engraved I will send you a print.

It will Give Mee great pleasure & Comfort to hear you Enjoye your Health. That it may long Continue is the ardent wish of your Sincere & Affectionate Friend,

P. COLLINSON

Pray my respects to your Son.

October 4, 1766, Your last letter was August 15, 1765. As the Seals or Phocoe have an Opening in their Hearts called the Foramen ovale, and a passage called Ductus arteriosus Botalli which being both open, they can keep a long time under Water.

If a Provision or Contrivance, something of the same Nature, could be Discover'd in the Structure of the Hearts of Swallows, then I should no longer doubt of their Continueing under Water all Winter.

This I have by Letter after Letter proposed to my Dear Baron; but he turns his Deaf Ear to all my proposals to Elucidate this Dark affair, who has so many Ingenious Men under Him Capable to Do It, to clear up this great Point, for Land Birds to be Qualified to live More than half the year under Water.

We have Several New Animals from America, which I presume Dr Solander will give you an account of Them.

1. *Prunus persica* var. *Nectarina* were known and consumed in China over 2,000 years ago.
2. John Hope (1725–1786), Professor of botany at Edinburgh University, King's botanist for Scotland and Superintendent of the Royal Botanic Garden at Edinburgh.

184 🎋 TO CARL LINNAEUS

ALS:LS
Ridge-Way House on Mill-Hill
Tenn Miles North of London
March 16, 1767

I am Here Retired to a Delightfull little Villa to Contemplate & admire with my Dear Linnaeus the Unalterable Laws of Vegetation. How ravishing to See the Swelling Buds Disclose the Tender Leaves.

By the Publick news papers Wee was told that with you in Sweden the Winter was very severe by the Sound being Frozen Over. I have no conception of the Power of that cold that could fetter the rowling Ocean in Icy Chains.

The Cold was what Wee call Severe, but not So Sharp as in the year 1740. It lasted about a Month, to the 21st of January, & then the Thaw began, and Continued on. February the 1st & 2d, Soft, Warm, Sunny Days, as in Aprill, & so Continued, Mild & Warm, with Southerly Winds all the month. This brought on the Spring Flowers, Feb 8th the Helleborus Niger Made a fine show, the Galanthus & Acconite Vernal the 15th cover'd the Garden with Beauty, with Some Crocus and Violets & Primula veris &c,

How Delightfull to See the Order of Nature, O How obedient the vegitable Tribes are to their Great Law Giver. He has given this Race of Flowers a Constitution & Fibres to resist the Cold. They Bloom in Frost & Snow Like the Good Men of Sweden.

These flowers have Some Time made their Exit, & now, March 7th, a Tenderer Tribe Succeeds. Such my Dear Friend is the Order of Nature.

Now the Garden is covered with More than 20 Different Species of Crocus, produced from Sowing Seed, and the Iris Persica, Cyclamen Vernalis Polyanthos.

The 16th March, plenty of Hyacinthus Coeruleus et albis in the open Borders & Anemonies & now my Favourites, the Great Tribe of Narcissus & Polyanthos Shew all over the Garden & Fields. Wee have Two Species Wild in the Woods that now begin to Flower. Next the Tulipa precox are Near Flowering, & So Flora Decks the Garden with Endless Variety (Ever Charming).

The Progress of our Spring, to the Middle of March, I perswade My Self, will be acceptable to my Dear Baron.

Now I come to Thank Him for his most Acceptable Letter of the 8th of October last. I am extremely Obliged for your Kind Intentions to Send me the Work of Works, your Sys Nat. I hope it will please God to Bless my Eyes with the Sight of it.

I feel the Distress you must be under with the Fire.[1] I am glad, next to your own & familys Safety that you Saved your papers & Books. By this Time I hope all are settled & in Order. So pray now, at your Leisure, Employe Some Expert Pupil to Search into the Origin of the Nectarine, who are the first Authors that Mention how & when it was Introduced into the European Gardens.

It is Strange & Marvelous that a Peach Should Naturally Produce or Bear Nectarines, a fruit So Different, as well in its exterior Coat as well as Flavour, from a Peach, & yet this Nectarine will produce a Nectarine from the stone, & not a Peach. This remarkable Instance is from a Tree of a Nectarine raised from a Stone in my own Garden, which Last Autumn had Several Dozen of fruite on It, finely ripened. For more particulars I refer to my Last Letter.

Pray tell me Who Perses Was, what Country Man, & who is the Author that relates His Introducing Peaches into the European gardens.[2]

That Batts as well as Flies lay as like Dead all Winter is True, but they do not Change Elements & go & Live all that Time under Water. Swallows cannot Do It without a provision & Contrivance for that End, which it becomes your great Abilities to find out, for it is not Sufficient [to] Assert but to Demonstrate the Internal Aparatus God Almighty has Wonderfull Contrived for a flying animal Bred on the Land & in the air, to go Volontaryly under Water & Live There for So Many Months.

Besides, Wee are not informed which Species Lives under Water, as there are Four Species.

You, my Dear Friend, have raised my admiration & that of all my Curious Acquaintance, for Wee never heard before that Mushrooms were of an Animal Nature & that their Eggs are Hatched in Water. Wee must Suspend gratifeing our Curiosity untill this Phenomenon is more particularly Explained to us Here. Dr Solander is also a Stranger to It. Very probably some Acount has been Published In the Swedish Tongue. If that is sent to Solander then Wee shall be made acquainted with that Discovery.

I here with Send you a Print of the Andrachne which Flowered for the First Time in Doctor Fothergill's Garden last year. Was raised from Seed from Aleppo Sent to the Dr in the Year 1756. You See it's Manner of flowering is very Different from the Arbutus [*Arbutus unedo*]. I have a Large Tree raised from the Same Seed that Stands Abroad in the Garden but never Blossom'd. It is now beginning to Shed its Bark, as Mr Belon or Belonius well Describes,[3] which is a peculiar Difference from the Arbutus and nearly agrees with the Platanus.[4]

I am my Dear Friend with my Sincere Wishes for your Health & preservation, your affectionate friend P. COLLINSON, now Entered into my 73 Year, in perfect Health & Strength in Body & Mind, God Almighty be praised & adored for the Multitude of his Mercies.

Pray present a print of the Andrachne to my Worthy Friend Dr Beck with my Sincere Respects.

Pray Send Mee Seeds of the Alstromeria figured & Described in the Amoenitat Acad.[5]

1. In April 1766 a large fire destroyed about one third of the town of Uppsala and threatened Linnaeus's home. He soon built a small unheated building on a knoll above his home at Hammarby to house his books and collections, away from the dangers of future fires. (Blunt)

2. Collinson, along with many others, was confused by the botanical name for the peach—*Prunus persica*. It was thought that peaches came to Europe from Persia or were discovered by Perses.

Actually, they came from China, by way of Persia, via trade routes through Asia and the Mediterranean.

3. Pierre Belon (1517–1564). Probably *Portraits d'oiseaux, animaux, serpents, herbes, arbres . . . d'Arabie et d'Egypte*. Paris, 1557.

4. *Platanus orientalis*. Belon's work included woodcuts that were the first to show several plants of the Near East including *Platanus orientalis*.

5. Linnaeus, *Amoenitates Academicae*. Leyden, 1749.

185 ❧ TO CARL LINNAEUS

ALS:LS
April 20, 1767

Pro Memoria

The Andrachne was Raised from Seed by My Advice procured from Aleppo in the Year 1756, sent over by Dr Russell to Dr Fothergill, and Flower'd, for the First Time in the Garden of Dr Fothergill Anno 1766.

I preseume this is the First plant that Ever Flower'd in Europe, Stands abroad & Flower'd in the Open Ground.

My tree in my Garden is much Larger than Dr Fothergills but has not yett Flower'd. It sheds its Bark Every Year as is well describ'd by Belon in Travels.[1]

The Adrachne in Full Flower that 17th 2ay 1766.

The Size [of] The China Argus or Luen[2] Is From the Tip of the Bill to the End of the tail in a Streight Line Seven Feet & half. From the Top of the Back to the Legs one Foot 3 Inches & 1/4.

The Leg & Foot 10 Inches & 1/4.

P. COLLINSON

1. Pierre Belon (1517–1564), *Les observations de plusieurs singularités et choses memorables trouvées en Grèce, Asie, Judée, Égypt, Arabie . . .* Paris, 1553.

2. Argus Pheasant or Argusianus Argus. See also PC to Linnaeus [circa 1765].

ALS: Erlangen
June 30, 1767

After so many Years expectation, I have the pleasure to Receive My Dear Friend Dr Trews Kind tokens of Respect. As they are long a comeing Makes them the More to be Valued, but my Motto is & will be Bis Dat, qui cito Dat [He gives twice who quickly gives].

I Dare say I have as many Occupations, in Different Ways, as Dr Trew, but yett I allways took Care I would never Suffer in my Friends Esteem by my Neglect to be reciprocal.

Therefore I have Given Notice to Mr Ehret & Mr Millar to gett their Paccages ready to Such a Day & my Few Things was also Ready & come in Two Boxes, Millers Things are in his own Box, packed by Him Self Marked CT No 1.

Mr Ehrets Parcell & Mine & Books [from the] Royal Society Come in Box CT No 2.

Sent this 10th July to Mr Grote & Co to send by First Ship to Hamburg &c.

Now I hope my Dear Friend will not be Tired out with Expectation.

I Deliver'd in Your Name your Present of the Curious Works to your List [and] to the Royal Society. That Learned Body Desired Mee to present their Thanks for so many Curious peices, in Natural History, & Desires your acceptance of the Transactions to the Last printed Number.

Now my Dear Friend I come more particularly to acknowledge your Favours confer'd on a Friend that Honours and Esteems you, for your Noble, Publick Spirit in promoteing every Branch of Natural Knowledge. You are the Linnaeus of Germany, your Name that will never be forgot because You will Ever Live in all your Numerous & Learned Works.

I am much pleased with Knorrs Lapides & Museum Bayreath [Bayreuth] Fossils, Birds &c &c.[1] I wish I could make ampler Returns, But really my Dear Friend, I must tell you with Concern you have lost many Curious articles for want of Keeping Up a regular annual Correspondence, for as you Seemed very Indifferent about It I was equally So.

I have collected a great Variety of Seeds & Seed Vessells. I wish any of them may answer your purpose. I also sent your List [to] The Princess of Wales Garden at Kew Which *I*s the Paradise of England, I may say of Europe, for from all Parts of the World flows in Vegetable Treasures every year. All that Art or Expense can do is Here Exhibited. This is the Place for Plantae Selecta Et Rariores.

But I had your list return'd with only Two Specimens of Seeds. I sent your List, as on the other Side [not reproduced here], to other Curious Gardens, but without Success.

You will find I have added Vol 2 of the London Essays[2] & have added some Modern, Interesting, Physical Works which I hope will prove acceptable. Dr Dimisdales account of our present Methode of Innoculation is the best Book on that Subject.[3] The Numbers & Success are wonderfull.

As Wee could not prepare Good Specimens of the Tulipa Montards [Montana] Flore Rubro et Luteo I have sent you some Roots of Each so next year you may expect to see them in perfection. They Require the Same Management as other Tulips.

You will find a Good Collection of american Seeds, the Seed Vessell and Leafe of the Faba Egyptica. By placing the Leafe in a Hair Sive over the Steam of Hott Water it may be expanded & Dri'd between Papers. This Rare Plant grows in Deep Waters in New Jersey North America.

Now my Dear Friend I bid you Hearty Fare well, Live Long, Healthy & Happy Is the ardent Wish of your Friend   P. COLLINSON

My Letter to Mr De Murr is in the Box.

Pray tell Mr De Murr that I received a Letter from Professor Walch[4] but as I am retired from London it doth not suite Mee to commence a new Correspondence.

1. George Wolfgang Knorr, (1705–1761). Probably *Recuiel de monumens des catastrophes que le globe de terre* . . . Nuremberg [1767]–1775 with another t.p. reading "Lapides . . . diluvii tectes." Museum Bayreath may refer to *Bayreuthische wöchentliche auszüge aus den neusten kirchen—, gelehrten—, natur—, und Kunstgeschichten.*

2. *Medical Observations and Inquiries.* vol. 2 (1764).

3. Thomas Dimsdale (1712–1800), physician. Published in 1767 *The Present Method of Inoculation for the Small Pox,* which passed through many editions. "In 1768 he was invited to St. Petersburg by the Empress Catharine to inoculate herself and the Grand Duke Paul, her son. The empress herself seems to have placed perfect reliance on the Englishman's good faith, but she could not answer for her subjects. She had relays of post-horses prepared for him all along the line from St. Petersburg to the extremity of her dominions, that his flight might be rapid in case of disaster. Both patients did well. The physician was created a councilor of state with the hereditary title of baron, now borne by his descendant. He received a sum of £10,000 down, with annuity of £500, and £2,000 for his expenses. (DNB)

4. Possibly John Walsh (1725?–1795), FRS, studied the torpedo fish and corresponded with Franklin.

187 ❧ TO EMANUEL MENDES DA COSTA

ALS: The Fitzwilliam Museum
Mill Hill, November 15, 1767

P. COLLINSONS Respects to my Kind Friend Mr Da Costa

I expect against Next Meeting of the [Royal] Society Our Ingenious Friend Dr Franklin will Send the Elephants Teeth &c Lately found in North America.[1] As they are cumbersome things & are not fitt to Lay Long on the Table before the Society—though

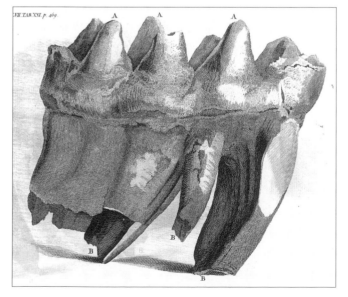

Fossil Teeth, engraving from 57 Phil. Trans. *464–469 (1767).*
American Philosophical Society.

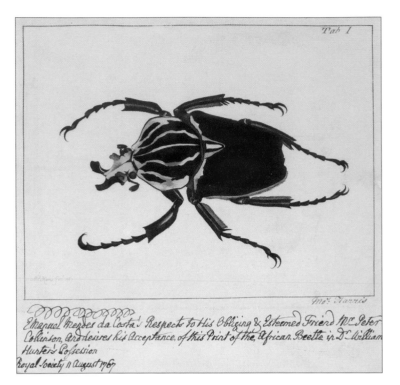

the Greatest Rarities that Ever was laid before them.

I have drawn up the Inclosed Account of them, (Copied by Son) in plain Letters for our Secretary Better reading It. Be so good to attend (for I cannot) & Show the Society the Two Species of Teeth, for you know what Novices Wee have amongst us, & you know how Deletory our Secretary is. So pray dispatch the affair, by my acct; a reader that doth not See the pronged-Teeth, can have no Idea of them. So I hope the Society will Engrave Them & add to my Acct in the Transactions.[2] I hope nothing will prevent Mee Dineng with you on St Andrews Day. Till then

Adieu my Good Friend

Pray my respects to Mrs Da Costa.

One Thing I beg of you when the Teeth &c come Lay them on Table before the Society & then the Secretary cannot Shuffle of reading my paper about Them. Which you will please to give to Him.

My Idea of Them Is, that they are the Remains of Some Monstrous animals that Have the Long Teeth or Tusks of Elephants, with the Molares and Biteing Teeth Not Like to any Animal yett known, But are Peculiar to that Species; when Ever & Where It Exists. This I hint to you, but Leave to Our Wise People to find out.[3]

After the Meeting is over at which they was Shown, do favor Mee with a Line to Mill Hill in Hendon, How our Noble President & Great Men received Them and their Wise Observations on Them which will much oblige yours.

P. COLLINSON

1. The fossil teeth were collected by George Croghan in June 1766, near the Ohio River at Big Bone Lick, Boone County, Kentucky. Croghan sent specimens to England as gifts to Lord Shelburne, Secretary of State, and to Benjamin Franklin. Collinson saw and commented on Franklin's set. (See *Franklin* XIV, pp 25–28, and see Bell, Whitfield J. "A Box of Old Bones: A Note on the Identification of the Mastodon, 1766–1806." *Proceedings of the American Philosophical Society* 93 No. 2 (May, 1949))

2. Collinson's account was published in the *Philosophical Transactions,* LVII (1767): 464–467; sequel to the foregoing account, *Philosophical Transactions* LVII (1767): 468–469.

3. Collinson correctly surmised that the "Monstrous animal" was herbivorous: it was the *Mammut americanum,* the American mastodon.

"Collinson avoided the shocking idea that the animal might be extinct, but he seems to have been on the verge of this great innovation. He explicitly made three important and brilliant contributions: the tusks and the grinders belonged to the same animal; this animal was of a species perhaps elephantine but distinct and known only from fossils; by analogy of affinity and structure this animal was herbivorous. It was many years before these correct and well-reasoned conclusions were generally accepted." Simpson, George Gaylord, "Beginnings of Vertebrate Paleontology." *Proceedings of the American Philosophical Society* 86 (1) (1942).

ALS: Glos. Rec. Off.

Mill Hill, January 1, 1768

As my Friend Player is pleased with new discoveries in the Fossil Kingdome & Delights to exercise his Hypothetical Genius, the following Relation will Gratifie both So I perswade my Self will not be unacceptable.

George Croghan Esquire Who is Deputy of Sir William Johnson, the Kings Superintendant of Indian Affairs in America, In the Course of his Navigation down the Great River Ohio, after passing the Miame River, in the Evening He came near the place where the Eliphants Bones are found about 4 Miles South East of the River Ohio and 600 Miles distant from and below Pitsburgh. From the nearest Sea Coast at least 700 Miles. Next Morning He Mett with a large Road which the Bufalloes had Beaten wide enough for 2 Wagons to go abreast Leading Straight into the Great Licking Place, to which the Bufalloes and all the Species of Deer resort in the Heats of Summer to Lick the Salt Earth and Salt Springs, whether to Clense and Cool their Stomachs or for What other purpose is uncertain.

Esquire Croghan had been Here Some years before and gave Some account of the monstrous Bones & Teeth found at this Place called by the Indians the Great Bufaloes Lick.

But now being more at Leisure, He carefully examined all Its Surrounds and Discovered under a Great Bank on the Skirts of the Lick, Five or Six feet below the Surface Open to View a prodigious Number of Bones & Teeth belonging to Some of the Largest Sized Animals. By the Quantity He Computes there could not be less than thirty of their Skeletons.

By their Great long Teeth or Tusks of fine Ivory Some of the Length of Six feet, Every One that Views Them will not hesitate to conclude that they belong to Eliphants.

But it is very Remarkable & worthy observation None of the Molares or Grinding Teeth of Eliphants are found with these Tusks. But a great Number of very large Pronged Teeth (one of Mine Weighed near 4 lb) of Some Vast Animals are only found with them, Which have no Resemblance to the Grinding Teeth of Eliphants or of any Other great Animal yett Known.

As no living Eliphants have ever been Seen or heard of in all America Since the Europeans have known that Country, nor any Creature like Them, & there being no probability of their haveing been brought from Africa or Asia & as it is Impossible that Eliphants could Inhabit the Country where these Bones & Teeth are now found, by reason of the Severities of the Winters, it Seems incomprehensible how they came There.

I conclude my Ingenious Friend Player may have heard of the Fossil Eliphants Teeth annually found in Siberia Lodged in the Banks of the Great River Oby [Ob'] & Other Rivers of that Country.

On the System of the Deluge it has been conjectured that as the Extensive Kingdom of Siberia lays behind the Native Country of the Eliphants in Asia from West to East and to the North, By the Violent Action of the Winds & Waves at the Time of the Deluge, these Great floating Bodies, the Carcases of Drowned Eliphants, Were driven to the Northward and at the Subsideing of the Waters, Depositied, Where They are now Found.

But What System of Hypothesis can with any Degree of probability account for these remains of Eliphants being found in America where these Creatures are not known ever to have existed is proposed to thy Consideration By the Sincere Friend

P. COLLINSON

Thy Curious papers I Left with Friend [not identified] as thou Desired.

The Bishop of Carlile presented to the Royal Society of 7th February 1766 Some Portions of Large Long Fossil Teeth & Bones from Peru which have Some Similitude to the Above Mentioned by no So Recent, more Petryfied, the pronged Teeth are like to Agate.

A List of the Teeth and Bones of Eliphants Sent over by George Croghan Esquire February 7, 1767 from Philadelphia

To Lord Shelburne[1]

Two of the largest Tusks or Teeth, one whole and Intire above Six feet long, the Thickness of Common Elephants Teeth of that Length

Several very large Forked or pronged Teeth

a Jaw bone with Two of Them In It

To Doctor Franklin

Four Great Tusks of Different Sizes one broken in halves near Six feet Long

One Much Decayed, the center looks like Chalk or Lime. A Part was cut off from one of these Teeth that has all the Appearance of fine White Ivory

a Joynt of the Vertebra

Three of the large pronged Teeth. One has four Rows of fangs.

Captain Burry [not identified]

an Officcer Who Served in the late Warr in America Brought from the Same Lick a Tusk or Tooth of a Calf Eliphant, the Surface a fine Shining Chesnut Colour & a Recent look about 2 foot Long and a very Great pronged Tooth larger then any of the Above.

Thank a Snowey Day for this Long Scrawle

1. William Petty, 1st Marquis of Lansdowne, 2nd Earl of Shelburne (1737–1805).

189 ❧ TO CADWALLADER COLDEN

ALS:N-YHS
London, February 10, 1768

I had the pleasure of my Dear Friends Letter with the Pacquet for Ld Shelbourn which was Deliver'd. Now there is Lord Hillsborough[1] appointed Secretary for the Colonies, for the future of your application will be to Him. Wee may now as the Colonies are his peculiar Care the Publick Greivances will be redressed, yours in perticular. So the sooner your application to Him the better & if it was conveyed by your Friend Sr Jeffery Amhurst it may have more Weight for I have no Acquaintance with Him.

I wrote you by last Pacquet that My application to Lord Clare[2] was ineffectual for it was not in his Department.

I will take Care & send the Sattin of which I will give you advice, but what need was there to send money as the Ballance in my hands is in your Favour.

I presume you have heard of the Wonderfull Discoveries Near the Ohio about 600 Miles below Pittsburgh & 4 from the River. In a Great Licking place, George Crogan Esqr found a Great Quantity of the Great long Elephants Teeth & Bones. He sent over of these Great Long Teeth or Tusks 6 or 8 which I have seen & handled, some above Six feet Long & the same thickness of Recent Elephants Teeth of that size, & what is remarkable some are not in the least Decayed. The Ends cutt off show as fine white Ivory as Recent Ivory.

Now is not this Wonderfull a Small Tooth about 2 foot Long of a Chesnutt Colour hath a fine Natural Polish as if Just taken out of the head of the young animal.

As there never was any Elephants in America neither could they subsist for the severe Long Winters, where they are now found near the Ohio.

What Hypothesis can be formed to account for these being found there under a Bank on the side of this Great Lick where some portions of the bones & Teeth Lay exposeed to View (700 Miles from the Sea). Mr Crogan believes from the Quantity of the Bones & Teeth there could not be Less then 30 Animals. He sent the Teeth to Ld Shelbourne & Benn Franklin.

Portions of the Like Elephants Teeth found in Peru was sent Last year as a present to the Royal Society.

Mr Franklin talks of Comeing over by some of the Summer Ships. He is very Well, much Carressed & Admired Here.

Pray Give my Kind Respects to Your Son David. I shall be greatly obliged to Him for the Information He Intends Mee on the Rattle Snake. Any Remarks in natural History will be very acceptable to your Sincere Friend   P. COLLINSON.

I am from Home but willing to send [by] first Ship to Pensilvania.

I thank Good Providence I have Lived to see a pair of your Great Moose Deers Horns, sent to the Duke of Richmond. There is not a pair in the British Museum, which is a great Loss to that Grand Collection which is the Wonder of the World.

It was always said, the Great Deers Horns found in the Bogs of Ireland, some 10 feet from Tip to Tip, was the same of the Great Moose Deers of N. England & Canada. But this pair shows there is no affinity, but your Moose Horns are very Like the Elk of Germany & Russia.

So that the Animal that produced the Irish Horns is not now Known to Exist in all your Discover'd World and it is not in our 3 parts, but possibly it may have being in Terra Australis, or no where, but that is not agreeable to the plan of Providence.

---

1. Wills Hill Hillsborough, 1st Viscount Hillsborough (1718–1793). Appointed Secretary of State for the colonies January 20, 1768.

2. Robert Nugent Clare (1709–1788), Viscount Clare.

Draft ALS:LS
March 25, 1768

It is Ingenious to confess Faults but Its better to mend them. It is our duty both in a Moral & Religious Sence.

Never think of the Gratifications of London. If Innocent, these are Transient, if Illicit, is the Pain Suffer'd in Body or Mind a compensation for such momentary Joyes. The Gay Scenes of Youth quickly pass away. Happy are they that can reflect on Them with that Peace & Serenity of Mind which is the Result of Temperance & Moderation in all our Actions.

But what do I hear whisper'd about that Dr Clayton is a Gentle Clever Fellow & knows His business, but gives way to Such an Indolent Lazy Habit, Lays a Bed & Loiters about, is very Indiferent of going any where when Sent for, a Poor recompense for so Liberal an Education. Are these things so—you know best—if not, they do you Injustice.

Consider how well Quallified you Enter into the first Scenes of Life. Now is the Time to lay the foundation of future Happyness & Prosperity. Then Exert your Genius, be Indifatiguable in your Application, give Proof of your Abilities & Lett the First Acts of your Life meet with a General Applause. It gives Mee a Peculiar Satisfaction to hear you have Meet with Success, to some Advantage.

My Dear Dr, it is all in your own Power. You cannot accuse your Father, he has done his Part; do you but yours and All will be Well. You that are so well Accomplished, it will be a disgrace to Human Nature, Ingratitude in the highest Degree to the Great Author of your Being, for those fine Endowments, if you Suffer your self to hide your Talents & sink into Supiness, and Stupidity, In the Prime of Life, in the Vigor of Youth, when Reason, when Interest, when Duty calls on you to Quit the Couch of Ease & fly on the Wings of the Morning, to Assist & Relieve your fellow Creatures in Distress.

To One of your Good understanding much less might be Said, but if proceeds from the Respect I have for you and an Anxiousness for your Welfare. Accept of these overflowings of Good Will, with that Candor with which they was Dictated, & believe Mee to be what I really am, your sincere friend,

P. COLLINSON

THOMAS CLAYTON, M.D., son of John Clayton of Virginia, a clever, cheerful, indolent fellow, received his medical degree from Edinburgh and practiced in London for a short time before returning to Virginia where he established a successful practice and became "a gay and amusing companion for his father." Berkeley and Berkeley, *John Clayton.* Chapel Hill: The University of North Carolina, 1963, 155–156.

191 ❧ TO HENRY BAKER

Copy of ALS: Yale
Mill Hill, April 2, 1768

My Dear Friend

It is mortifying to be detained here by an intruding Visitor that I can not easily gett rid off [gout]. So am obliged to practice Patience and Flannel that if you see me not on St Georges Day [April 23] you may guess the reason of it if my Seat is empty.

As very probable you see [Charles Lyttleton] the Bip of Carlile once a week I request you'l be so kind to give this Pacquet to Him, Left by my Son. For your amusement you may survey the Contents & then tie them up again & present them to our Worthy president in my name.

They come from Paul de Demidoff Esq who sent the Sepulchral Antiquities. I proposed Him for an Honorary Member & you was so obliging to Carry it to the Society [of Antiquaries], which I presume was read, accepted & hung up according to Custom. I request the favour of your Vote & Interest and am with much respect & Esteem my Dear Friend Sincerly Yours

P COLLINSON

If you have Occasion to favor me with a Line leave it at Somerset Coffee House for my Son calls there every Week on a Tuesday. A Little News will be acceptable to a Recluse.

HENRY BAKER (1698–1774), FRS, naturalist, poet, devised a method for the education of deaf mutes and thereby made his fortune, wrote *The Microscope Made Easy,* London, 1742, and *An Attempt towards a Natural History of the Polype:* London: R. Dodsley, 1743.

At the foot of this letter Baker wrote, "Mr Collinson's Packet to the Bishop of Carlisle contained several Paintings done in the East Indies of the different Idols worshipped by the Gentoos (your collection of Devils). They were painted well, but frightfully ugly," along with this draft of his answer: "My Dear Friend Collinson, alias Iron-Man, Assume yourself: kick out the intruding visitor: send Patience to the Starving Poor; lay by your Flannel, and pay your usual Respects to St George, to the Dragon and to me. You were deficient in your duty to St Andrews [the Royal Society; annual meeting for election of officers was held on St. Andrews Day, November 30] and a new omission will endanger your Charter."

192 ❧ TO WILLIAM BARTRAM

ALS: HSP
Mill Hill, July 18, 1768

It Rains Hard & so it does Every Day
More or Less at a Time

This Morning Dr Fothergill came and Breakfasted Here. As I am always thoughtfull How to make Billy's Ingenuity turn to some advantage, I bethought of Mee showing the Doctor His Last Elegant performances. He Deservedly admired them & thinks so fine a Pencil Is worthy of Encouragement, & Billy may Value Himself in Having such a Patron, who is Eminent for his Generosity & his Noble Spirit to promote every branch in Natural History.

He Desires Billy would employ some of His Time in Drawing all the Land, River & Sea Shells from the very Smallest to the Largest. When very small, 8 or 6 in a half Sheet.

As they grow larger 6 or 4, then 2 or 1 (without any Shade, which often Times confounds the shape of the Shell) & the place where found & add if any thing peculiar to them besides.

He is not in hast and Desires nothing may be Done in a Hurry. When two or three shells is Done to send them when there is Convenient Oppertunity.

I further proposed to him, as you have such a variety of Water & Land Terrapins or Turtles that Billy would take a fitt Oppertunity to Draw them all, good full-grown Subjects as may for size be contained in a half sheet of paper & if there is any Difference between Male & Female to give Both & also be sure to give the under & upper shells & all from Live Subjects & give their Natural History, as farr as can be Collected.

I Doubt not but thy Father &c will assist thee. As these animals, of a proper Size & Growth are to be Mett with casually, so it will be a Work of Time. So send now and then One or Two, as it Happens, & in Time Lay out to procure good Subjects of those three new Species found in West Florida, the Soft Shell, Shovel Nose & &c & that other Species of Soft Shell found in the R Ohio.

Sett all thy Witts & Ingenuity to Work to Gratifie so Deserving a Patron.

A few Weeks Agon I gave my Friend Billy orders to send a Drawing of the Faba Egyptica Like that sent Mee & as Many Land, River & Sea Shells as He can afford for Twenty Guineas for the Dutchess of Portland.[1] Don't crowd the Shells, but a few in a sheet shows better & be sure no shade. This She Does by way of Specimen. If she Likes thy performance She will give Orders to keep drawing on until all the Shells are Drawn.

Send all to Mee, rouled on a Rowl & putt in a Little Box for fear of getting Wett.

I am thy Sincere Friend,   PC

I Doubt not but thy Brother Moses[2] as He walks the Fields & Woods & River Sides He will assist & Brother Johnny[3] also will Look out for Land Shells, of Snails & &c &c when he goes abroad to Collect Seeds.

My Respects to thy Good Father. I wrote him a Long Letter July 7th in answer to his of 15th May.

Draw on Good Paper for then the Subjects show better.

WILLIAM BARTRAM (1739–1823), John Bartram's fifth son. He too was an avid naturalist, artist, and author. Best known for his *Travels,* 1791.

This is the last known letter from PC to the Bartrams. Collinson died on 11 August. The drawing project he initiated succeeded wonderfully. See Ewan, Joseph, *William Bartram: Botanical and Zoological Drawings, 1756–1788.* Philadelphia: The American Philosophical Society, 1968.

1. Bentinck, Margaret Cavendish, Duchess of Portland (1715–1785), owned the finest shell collection in England.

2. Moses Bartram (1732–1809), John Bartram's fourth son, merchant seaman and businessman.

3. John Bartram, Jr. (1743–1812) John Bartram's sixth son, eventually took over his father's business and was the first to catalogue the garden. See "Bartram's Garden Catalogue of North American Plants, 1783," *Journal of Garden History,* Vol. 16, No. 1, January–March, 1996.

Bibliography

Allen, David Elliston: *The Naturalist in Britain*. London, 1976.

Ames, Oakes, *Economic Annuals and Human Cultures*. Cambridge, MA., 1939.

Anderson, Fred. *Crucible of War: The Seven Years War and the Fate of the Empire in British North America, 1754–1766*. London, 2000.

Andrews, Charles M. *The Colonial Background of the American Revolution*. New Haven, 1924.

Aubrey, John, *Brief Lives*, Oliver L. Dick, ed. London, 1950.

Bailey, Liberty Hyde. *Manual of Cultivated Plants*. The MacMillan Company, New York. 1951.

Bayne-Powell, Rosamond, *Eighteenth-Century London Life*. New York, 1938.

Bell, Whitfield J. Jr. *Patriot-Improvers*. 2 vols. Philadelphia, 1997, 2000.

Berkeley, Edmund and Dorothy Smith Berkley, *The Life and Travels of John Bartram*. Tallahassee, 1982.

———. *The Correspondence of John Bartram*, Gainesville, 1992.

———. *John Clayton, Pioneer of American Botany*. Chapel Hill, 1963.

———. *Dr. Alexander Garden of Charles Town*. Chapel Hill, 1969.

Boswell, James, *The Life of Samuel Johnson, LL.D.* Oxford, 1951.

Brett-James, Norman G., *The Life of Peter Collinson*. London, 1925.

Brewer, John, *The Pleasures of the Imagination: English Culture in the Eighteenth Century*. New York, 1997.

Bridson, G. D. R., Valerie C. Phillips and Anthony P. Harvey. *Natural History Manuscript Sources in the British Isles*. London, 1980.

———. *The History of Natural History: An annotated bibliography*. New York, 1994.

Britton, Nathaniel Lord and Addison Brown. 1913. *An Illustrated Flora of the Northern United States and Canada,* 2nd Edition. A 1970 reprint by Dover Publications, Inc., New York.

Byrd, William II, *The Correspondence of the Three William Byrds of Westover, Virginia, 1684–1776*. Marion Tinling, ed. Charlottesville, 1977.

Calmann, Gerta, *Ehret—Flower Painter Extraordinary*. Boston, 1977.

Canny, Nicholas, *The Origins of Empire*. Vol I in the Oxford History of the British Empire. New York, 1998.

Catesby, Mark, *Natural History of Carolina, Florida and The Bahama Islands*. 2 v. London, 1730–1747.

Coffey, Timothy. 1993. *The History and Folklore of North American Wildflowers*. Houghton Mifflin Co., New York.

Colden, Cadwallader. *The Letters and Papers of Cadwallader Colden,* vols 50–56, 67–68 of New-York Historical Society *Collections*. New York, 1917–1923; 1934–1935.

Collinson, Peter, "An Account of the Introduction of American Seeds into Great Britain." *The Journal of Botany,* Vol LXII. London, 1924, pp 163–165.

Corner, Betsy C. and Christopher Booth. *Chain of Friendship: Selected Letters of Dr. John Fothergill of London, 1735–1780*. Cambridge, 1971.

Custis, John. See Swem, Earl G., *Brothers of the Spade,* Worcester, MA., 1947.

Darlington, William, *Memorials of John Bartram and Humphry Marshall*. Edited with an introduction by Joseph Ewan. New York, 1967.

Davis, P. H. *Flora of Turkey,* Vol. 1. University of Edinburgh Press, Edinburgh, 1965.

Desmond, Ray, *Dictionary of British and Irish Botanists and Horticulturists*. London, 1994.

————. *Kew: The History of The Royal Botanic Gardens.* London, 1995

Dictionary of American Biography. Edited by Allen Johnson and Dumas Malone. 20 v. New York, 1928–1936.

Dictionary of National Biography. Edited by Sir Leslie Stephen and Sir Sidney Lee. 63 vols. London, 1885.

Dillwyn, L. W. *Hortus Collinsonianus.* Privately printed. Swansea 1843.

Ewan, Joseph, *A Short History of Botany in the United States.* New York, 1969.

————. *John Banister And His Natural History of Virginia, 1678–1692.* Urbana, 1970.

Fothergill, John, *Some Account of the Late Peter Collinson . . . In a Letter to a Friend.* London, 1770.

Fox, R. Hingston, *Dr. John Fothergill and His Friends . . .* London, 1919.

Franklin, Benjamin, *The Papers of Benjamin Franklin.* New Haven, 1959–.

Frick, George F. "Peter Collinson" in *The Dictionary of Scientific Biography.* New York, 1971, Vol III, pp 349–351.

Fry, Joel T, "Bartram's Garden Catalogue of North American Plants, 1783" in *Journal of Garden History,* Vol 16, No 1. London, 1996.

George, Mary Dorothy, *London Life in the Eighteenth Century . . .* London, 1951.

Gipson, Lawrence H., *The British Empire Before the American Revolution.* 12 v. New York, 1958–1965.

Gleason, H. A. and A. Cronquist. *Manual of the Flora of Northeastern United States and Canada.* New York Botanical Garden, Bronx, 1991.

Green, John Richard, *A History of the English People.* 4 v. London, 1877–1880.

Grigson, Geoffrey, *The Englishman's Flora.* London, 1955.

Grist, D. H., *Rice.* London, 1959.

Harvey, John, *Early Nurseymen.* London, 1974.

Henrey, Blanche, *British Botanical and Horticultural Literature before 1800.* 3 vols. London, 1975.

————. *No Ordinary Gardener: Thomas Knowlton, 1691–1781.* London, 1986.

Herbst, Josephine, *New Green World.* New York, 1954.

Hindle, Brooke: *The Pursuit of Science in Revolutionary America.* Chapel Hill, 1956.

Honor, Hugh. *The New Golden Land.* New York, 1975.

Hughes, Edward, *North Country Life in the 18th Century.* London, 1952.

Jacob, Margaret C. *The Cultural Meaning of the Scientific Revolution.* New York, 1988.

Leighton, Ann, *Early American Gardens.* Boston, 1970.

————. *American Gardens in the Eighteenth Century.* Amherst, 1986.

Luer, Carlyle A. *The Native Orchids of the United States and Canada.* New York Botanical Garden, Bronx.

Mabberley, D. J. 1987. *The Plant Book.* Cambridge University Press, New York.

Marshall, P. J. ed. *The Eighteenth Century.* Vol II in The Oxford History of the British Empire. New York, 1998.

McBurney, Henrietta, *Mark Catesby's Natural History of America.* London, 1997.

McLean, Elizabeth P. "A Preliminary Report on the 18th century Herbarium of Robert James, Eighth Baron Petre. *Bartonia* No 50: 36–39, 1984.

———— and William R. Buck, "'Mosses' in Lord Petre's Herbarium collected by John Bartram." *Bartonia* No 51: 17–33, 1985.

———— and Alfred E. Schuyler and Ann Newbold, "Vascular Plants in Lord Petre's Herbarium Collected by John Bartram," *Bartonia* 53: 41–43 (1987).

———— "John and William Bartram: Their Importance to Botany and Horticulture," *Bartonia* 57: 10–27 (1992).

Meyers, Amy R. W. and Margaret Beck Pritchard, *Empire's Nature: Mark Catesby's New World Vision.* Chapel Hill, 1998.

Morgan, E. S., *Prologue to Revolution . . .* Chapel Hill, 1959.

Morgan, Edmund S and Helen M. Morgan, *The Stamp Act Crisis.* Chapel Hill, 1959.

Namier, Lewis B., *England in the Age of the American Revolution.* London, 1961.

Nelson, E. Charles: *Aphrodite's Mousetrap: a biography of Venus's Flytrap.* Aberystwyth, 1990.

Nichols, John, *Literary Anecdotes of the Eighteenth Century.* 9 v. London, 1812–1816.

O'Malley, Therese, and Joachim Wolschke-Bulmahn, editors, *John Evelyn's "Elysium Britannicum" and European Gardening.* Washington, 1998.

O'Neill, Jean: "Peter Collinson, Friend of Linnaeus—'Plants for an Intire Stranger'" *Country Life,* May 21, 1981.

————. "From American to Peat Garden" *Country Life,* August 30, 1979.

————. "Peter Collinson's Copies of Philip Miller's Dictionary in the National Library of Wales." *Archives of Natural History* (1993) 20 (3): 373–380.

————. "Peter Collinson and the American Garden" *Garden,* published for Garden Society Members. July/August, 1984.

Rastrick, Arthur, *Quakers in Science and Industry.* London, 1950.

Raven, Charles E., *John Ray, Naturalist . . .* Cambridge, 1950.

Reveal, James L., George F. Frick, C. Rose Broome and Melvin L. Brown, "Botanical explorations and discoveries in colonial Maryland: An introduction." *Huntia* 7, 1987.

Reveal, James L., *Gentle Conquest.* Washington, 1992.

Reveal, James L. and James Pringle, "Taxonomic botany and Floristics," pp. 157–192 in Flora of North America Editorial Committee (ed), *Flora of North America north of Mexico.* New York, 1993.

Ridgeway, Christopher, and Robert Williams, editors, *Sir John Vanbrugh & Landscape Architecture.* Sparkford, 2000.

Slaughter, Thomas P., *The Natures of John and William Bartram.* New York, 1996.

Smallwood, William Martin, *Natural History and the American Mind.* New York, 1941.

Smith, James Edward, ed., *A Selection of the Correspondence of Linnaeus and other naturalists from the original manuscripts.* 2 vols. London, 1821.

Stearnes, Raymond Phineas: *Science in the British Colonies of America.* Urbanna, 1970.

———. "Colonial Fellows of the Royal Society of London, 1661–1788" in *Notes and Records of the Royal Society of London,* 8 (1951).

———. "James Petiver, Promoter of Natural Science . . . : *Proceedings of the American Antiquarian Society,* 62, 1952, p 243–365.

Stephen, Leslie, *History of English Thought in the Eighteenth Century.* 2 v. London, 1876.

Swem, Earl G., "Brothers of the Spade. . . ." *American Antiquarian Society Proceedings,* 68 (1948).

Tolles, Frederick B., *Meeting House and Counting House: The Quaker Merchants of Colonial Pennsylvania, 1682–1763.* Chapel Hill, 1948.

Trevelyan, George Macaulay, *Illustrated English Social History,* v. III: *The Eighteenth Century.* London, 1951.

Weigley, Russell F, editor, *Philadelphia: A 300-Year History.* Philadelphia, 1982.

Woodward, John, *Brief Instructions for Making Observations in All Parts of the World—1696.* Republished by the Society for the Bibliography of Natural History with an introduction by V. A. Eyles. London, 1973.

Personal Name Index

(numbers refer to letter numbers, "intro." refers to the introduction)

Adanson, Michel (1727–1806), id: 132; 144

Albin, Eleazer (1713–1742), id: 58

Alexander, James (1691–1756), id: 44; letters: 103; 53, 60, 62, 100, 120, 125, 127

Alexander, Mrs., 135

Allen, Mr., 136

Allioni, Carlo (1708–1804), id: 148; letters: 148, 151, 164

Alpino, Prosper (1553–1617), id: 96

Alstroemer, Baron Claus (1736–1794), id: 164; 184n

American Philosophical Society, id: 67; 64

Amherst, Jeffrey (1717–1797), id: 135; 112, 135, 182, 189

Ammann, Johann (1707–1742), id: 25; 137, 141

Argyll, Duke of, see Campbell, John

Armstrong, John, 93

Ascanius, Peter (1723–1803), id: 110; 111

Bäck (Beck), Abraham (1713–1795), id: 70; 73, 75, 110, 166, 177, 184

Baker, Henry (1698–1774), id: 191; letters: 191

Baltimore, Lord, see Calvert, Charles

Banks, Joseph, intro., 137

Bannister, John, 11, 73

Barclay, Henry, id: 77; 39

Barrére, Pierre (1690?–1755), id: 97

Bartram, John (1699–1777), id: 8; letters: 8, 12, 14, 15, 16, 17, 19, 20, 21, 23, 24, 28, 32, 49, 51, 153, 157, 162; intro., 7, 9, 18, 22, 29, 34, 39, 44, 48, 55, 57, 60, 61, 63, 64, 65, 67, 73, 78, 87, 90, 92, 94, 95, 100, 108, 111, 112, 114, 116, 119, 120, 122, 126, 163, 171, 192

Bartram, John Jr. (1743–1812), id: 192

Bartram, Moses (1732–1809), id: 192

Bartram, William (1739–1823), id: 182; letters: 192; 108, 111, 112, 162

Bauhin, Gaspard (1560–1624), id: 110; 22, 110

Bedford, Duke, see Russell, John

Belcher, Jonathan (1682–1757), id: 77

Belon, Pierre (1517–1564), 184, 185

Bennett (of Kingshead), 80

Bentinck, Margaret Cavendish, Duchess of Portland (1715–1785), id: 192; 65, 192

Berkenhout, John (1730?–1801), id: 137

Best, Mr., 97

Beurer, John Ambrose (1716–1754), id: 58; letters: 58, 59; 65, 69, 89, 93, 94, 109

Bevan, Silvanus (1691–1765), id: 57

Bevis or Bevans, John (1693–1771), id: 107; 112, 113, 125, 127, 135

Bianchi, Giovanni Battista (1681–1761), id: 81

Birch, Thomas (1705–1766), id: 94; letters: 128, 144; 94, 132

Bird, John (1709–1776), id: 179

Bjork, Tobias, id: 45; 73, 78, 166

Blackburne, John (1690–1786), id: 55; letters: 55; 52, 69, 143

Blackstone, John (1712–1753), id: 79

Blackwell, Elizabeth (1700–1758), id: 94

Bland, Elias, id: 85; 81

Boerhaave, Hermann (1668–1738), 36

Bohadsch, Dr. Johann Baptist, id: 174

Bolling, Capt., 18

Bombarde, Mr., 163

Boscawen, Edward (1711–1761), id: 125

Boswell, Capt., 3

Bouquet, Henry (1719–1765), id: 162

Boyle, John, 5th Earl of Orrery (1707–1762), id: 93

Bradley, James (1693–1762), id: 31; 77, 107; 113

Brander, Mr., 131

Bream, Capt., 67

Breintnall, John, id: 16

Breintnall, Joseph (d.1746), id: 8; letters: 30, 72; 7, 8, 12, 15, 16, 20, 24, 30, 32, 49 72, 74

Brewer, Samuel (1670–1743), id: 50; letters: 50; 52

Kruger & Grote, 89, 93
Kuhn, Adam (1741–1817), id: 177

Lamberg, Mr., 108
Lamboll, Thomas (1694–1774), id: 171
Lawson, Isaac (d. 1747), id: 61; 36, 70, 75
Lawson, John, 5, 138
Leclerc, Georges Louis, Comte de Buffon, (1707–1788), id: 108; 89, 108, 134
Lee, Thomas, 87
Leigh (at Totridge), letters: 129
Lennox, Charles, 2nd Duke of Richmond (1701–1750), id: 23; letters: 80; intro., 33, 51, 52, 124, 140, 171
Lennox, Charles, 3rd Duke of Richmond (1735–1806), id: 140; 92, 142, 189
Lennox, Mary, Duchess of Richmond (d. 1796), id: 142; letters: 142; 140
Lewis, Richard, id: 6
Library Company of Philadelphia id: 7; letters: 7, 13; intro., 8, 12, 13, 15, 20, 30, 49, 72, 81
Lierthon, Dr., 65
Lindsay, Capt., 21
Linnaeus (Linné), Carl (Carolus von) (1707–1778), id: 36; letters: 36, 45, 61, 70, 73, 75, 78, 79, 104, 106, 110, 119, 131, 137, 149, 154, 159, 161, 166, 176, 177, 180, 183, 184, 185; intro., 8, 22, 23, 30, 34, 39, 44, 60, 61, 62, 65, 69, 75, 78, 79, 82, 86, 94, 101, 104, 106, 108, 110, 111, 120, 143, 152, 153, 159, 160, 161, 162, 186
Lister, Martin (1638–1712), id: 4
Lloyd, Robert Lumley (d.1730), id: 9
Lockyere, Charles, 58
Logan, James (1674–1751), id: 23; 12, 24, 32, 36, 72, 78, 79
Logan, Jr., William, intro.
Lom d'Arce de, baron de Lahontan, Louis Armand (1666–1715?), id: 68
Lonsdale, Lord, see Lowther, Henry
Loudon, Earl, see Campbell
Lowther, Henry, 3rd Viscount Lonsdale (1713–1751), id: 77
Lyttelton, Charles, Bishop of Carlisle (1714–1768), id: 178; letters: 178, 179; 188, 191

Lyttelton, George, First Baron Lyttelton (1709–1773), id: 178

Macclesfield, Earl, see Parker, George
Manby, Mr., 93
Manduet, William, 32
Marsh, Thomas, id: 27; 37
Martyn, John (1699–1768), id: 75; 110, 119, 120, 125
Mason, Charles, 35
Mather, Cotton, 125, 127
Mathews, Admiral, 62
Mead, Richard (1673–1754), id: 108; 65, 93, 108, 111
Mesnard, Mr., 81
Mettford, Mr., 37
Middleton, Christopher (d. 1770), id: 60; 33, 62
Miller, John, 8, 80
Miller, Philip (1691–1771), id: 12; intro., 7, 8, 11, 12, 20, 26, 30, 36, 50, 51, 55, 65, 75, 78, 94, 108, 110, 119, 124, 136, 137, 141, 171, 186
Mitchell, Capt., 100
Mitchell, John (1711–1768), id: 61; 63, 65, 69, 70, 75, 78, 81, 84, 93, 101, 109, 110, 141
Monk, Mr., 22
Montagu, John, 2nd Duke of Montagu (1688–1749), id: 37
Montagu, John, 4th Earl of Sandwich (1718–1792), id: 125
Moreton, Mathew, 2nd Baron Ducie (d. 1770), id: 181
Morris, Lewis (1671–1746), id: 49
Mortimer, Cromwell (d. 1752), id: 90; 81, 94

Newton, Sir Isaac (1642–1727), 7, 66, 107
Nolet, Abbe, Jean Antoine, id: 88
Norfolk, Duke, see Howard, Charles
Norris, Jr., Isaac (1701–1766), id: 12
Northumberland, Duke of, see Percy, Hugh
Nugent, Robert, Viscount Clare (1709–1788), id: 189

Oakes, Abraham (1686?–1756), 116
Oglethorp, James Edward (1696–1785), id: 77
Orrery, Lord, see Boyle, John

Osborn, Sir Danvers (1715–1753), id: 101
Osborne, Thomas (1738–1767), id: 77; 93, 94, 100

Pallas, Peter Simon (1694–1770), id: 174; letters: 174
Parish, Mr., 179
Parker, George, 2nd Earl of Macclesfield, (1697–1764), id: 68; letters: 68; 93, 101, 107
Parkinson, John (1567–1650), 23, 24, 76, 94
Parsons, James (1705–1770), 93
Pastorius, Francis Daniel (1651–1720), 12
Payne, John, 86
Pearce, Capt., 24
Pelham, Henry (1695?–1754), id: 100
Pelham-Clinton, see Clinton, Henry
Pelham-Holles, Thomas, 1st Duke of Newcastle (1693–1768), id: 113, 118; letters: 118; 127
Pemberton, Jr., Israel (1715–1779), id: 14; 19, 20, 21
Pembroke, Lord, see Herbert, Henry
Penn Family, 173
Penn, Hannah (1671–1726), 35
Penn, John (1700–1746), id: 35; letters: 35; intro., 30
Penn, Richard, intro., 30, 35
Penn, Thomas (1702–1775), intro., 30, 35, 44, 157
Penn, William (1644–1718), 6, 23, 35
Pennant, Thomas (1726–1798), id: 177
Percy, Hugh (Smithson), 1st Duke of Northumberland (1715–1786), 171
Perkins, Dr., 50
Petiver, James (1663–1718), id: 96; 94
Petty, William, 2nd Earl of Shelburn (1737–1805), id: 188; 187, 189
Petre, see Robert, 8th Baron Petre
Pitt, William, 1st Earl of Chatham (1708–1778), id: 123; letters: 123; 125, 127
Player, John, id: 181; letters: 181, 188
Plukenet, Leonard (1642–1706), id: 30; 11, 70, 73
Plumstead, Mr., 47
Ponce de Leon, Juan (c.1460–1521), id: 138
Potts, Henry, 182

West, Capt., 39

Wettstein, Caspar (1695–1760), id: 99; letters: 99

Whiston, William (1667–1752), id: 77; 74

White, John (fl. 1740s), id: 17; 19, 32

Whitworth, Mr., 58

Whytt, Robert, id: 175; 93

Wilkins, John (1614–1672), id: 76

Williams, Lawrence, 24

Williamson, John (fl. 1755–1780), id: 146

Willoughby, Francis (1635–1672), id: 41

Wilmer, John (1697–1769), id: 110

Wilmington, Lord, see Compton, Spencer

Winchester, Lord, 125

Winkler, Johann Heinrich, 81

Witt, Christopher (1675–1765), id: 12; 14, 17, 19, 24, 30

Woodward, John (1665–1728), id: 76

Wright, Capt., 8, 14, 15, 16, 17, 30, 31, 49, 132

Wright, Edward, MD, id: 115; letters: 115

Wright, J., 162

Plant Index

(numbers refer to letter numbers)

Brassica rapa, 16, 102
Bromelia piguin, 94
Buckthorn, 63
Bulbous root, 11, 159
Bulbs, 11
Burning bush, 169
Burr weed, 61n
Butneria, 119
Buttonwood, 17

Cactaceae, 61, 70, 71
Caesalpinia bonduc, 101, 153
Calamintha, 12
Callistephus chinensis, 14
Calycanthus floridus, 15, 23, 32, 171
Calycanthus, 119
Camellia japonica L., 8n
Camellia sinesis, 42
Canada tree, 101, 153
Cane wood, 8, 12, 21
Canna indica, 18
Cannabis sativa, 155
Capers, 167
Capparis spinosa, 167
Carolina allspice, 15, 23, 32, 171
Carolina tea, 18, 63
Carpinus caroliniana, 21, 32
Carthamus tinctorius, 124, 155
Carya, 18, 21, 23, 32, 153
Carya glabra, 32
Caryophellata avens, 12
Caryota L. Palmae, 61
Caryota urens, 61
Cascis, 164
Cassada pudden, 63
Cassava, 63
Cassia poetica, 151, 164
Castanea pumila, 11, 14, 18, 26, 63
Castanea dentata, 14, 32, 92, 21, 181
Catalpa bignonioides, 52
Ceanothus americanus, 12n, 19
Cedar, 23, 55, 92, 171
Cedar, Red, 14, 21, 22, 23, 32, 71
Cedar, Siberian, 25, 171
Cedar, Syria, 14, 18, 171
Cedar, White, 14, 21, 22, 32, 71, 169
Cedar of Lebanon, 14, 18, 171
Cedrus libani, 14, 18, 171
Cedrus, 23, 55, 92, 171
Cedum, see, Sedum
Celtis occidentalis, 24
Cembro pine from Siberia, 25, 171

Centaurea, 14
Cercis canadensis, 18, 21
Cereus, 61, 70, 71
Cetalpha , 52
Ceterach, 22
Chamaecyparis thyoides, 14, 21, 22, 32, 71, 169
Chamaelirium luteum, 12, 16
Chamaepentas austricace, 148, 151
Chamaerhododendron, 32, 87
Cherimoya, 94
Chermolia of Seville, 94
Cherry, 14, 21
Chestnut, 14, 92, 21, 181
Chestnut, Spanish, 14, 32
China flower, 42
Chinese rhubarb, 114, 120, 137, 141
Chinquapin , 11, 14, 18, 26, 63
Chionanthus virginicus, 11, 55, 169, 171
Christmas rose, 171, 184
Christophoriana, 61
Cimicifuga racemosa, 176, 177
Cimicifuga, 176, 177
Cinchona, 90, 94
Cinnamomum verum, 159
Cinnamon, true, 159
Cistus ladanifer, 61n
Cistus ledon, 41
Citrullus lanatus, 25
Claytonia virginica, 70
Claytonia, 70
Clematis, 61
Clinopodium, 14
Clover, 84
Cochineal Indian Figg, 167
Cock Spurr thorn, 12, 32
Coincya monensis, 179
Colchicums, great, 16
Cole seed, 102
Collinsonia, 60, 61, 78, 96, 104
Collinsonia canadensis, 60, 61, 78, 96, 104
Comfrey, 94, 109
Cone wheat, 102
Convolvulus scammonia, 94, 110, 155, 167
Coreopsis altissima, 61
Corn, 6, 79, 88, 101, 122, 123, 133, 171, 179, 183
Cornus florida, 11, 21, 23
Cortex Peruvianus, 90, 94
Cortusa matthioli L., 148, 151, 164
Cotton, 167
Cottonweed, 12

Cowslip, Jerusalem, 18, 94
Cowslip, Mountain , 11n, 18, 26
Cowslip, true, 23, 131, 184
Crabapple, 32
Crabs, wild, 32
Crackberry, 76
Cranberry, 61, 65, 76, 110, 111, 112
Crataegus monogyna, 12, 32
Creeping Jenny, 8
Crocus, 61, 184
Crowberry, 76
Crystal tea, 177
Cucumber, muscovy, 25
Cucumber, Turkish, 25
Cucumber root, 94, 110
Cunila origanoides, 16
Currants, white, 39
Cyclamen persicum, 61, 184
Cyclamen, 16, 39, 61, 184
Cyclamen, vernal, 61, 184
Cynanchum, 12
Cypress, 6, 8, 23, 26, 92
Cypripedium, 12, 14, 19

Daboecia cantabrica, 180, 183
Date, 18
Delphinium elatum, 166
Devil's Bit, 12, 16
Devil's Walking Stick, 101
Dictamnus fraxinella, 169
Diervilla lonicera, 8
Diffenbachia seguire, 41
Dionaea muscipula, 87n, 162
Diospyros viginiana, 18, 21
Dipsacus, 179
Dittany, 16
Dodecatheon meadia, 73n
Dogwood, 11, 21, 23
Dracaena draco, 71
Dragon tree, 71
Dumb cane, 41

Echium Masinum, 22
Echium, 70
Ehretiana, 104
Elm Hedge, 86
Elm, dark green, 92
Elymus, 61, 61n
Empetrum nigrum, 76
English elm, 181
Eranthis hyemalis, 171
Erica Bac procumbens nigra, 76

Erica baccefera, 76
Erica cantabrica, 180, 183
Eruca vesicaria?, 18
Eryngium, 12
Erysimum cheiri, 171
Euonymus, 12
Euphorbias pilulifera L., 130
Evergreen thorn, 169
Evergreen, 111, 136

Faba Egyptica, 96, 186, 192
Fagus grandiflora, 21, 32
Ferns, 16, 107
Ferula gabanifera, 12
Ficoides, 22
Ficus carica, 180
Ficus, 71
Fig, 180
Fir, 8, 16, 32, 92, 135
Fir, Cornish, 92
Fir, silver, 39
Fir from Mount Ida, 171
Fir, yew-leafed, 71, 92, 139
Firethorn, 169
Fragaria chiloensis, 26
Fragaria moschata Duschesne, 26
Fraxinella, 169
Fraxinus, 21, 32, 92
Fringe tree, 11, 55, 169, 171
Fumaria bulbosa, 70

Galanthus, 16, 184
Galega, 12
Galium palistre, 37
Gentian, Officinal, 58
Ginseng, 89
Ginseng, American, 32, 34, 94, 101
Ginseng, Chinese, 34, 70
Gladilous, cape, 22
Gladiolus, white melody, 16
Gleditsia, 133
Gleditsia triacanthos, 18, 21
Goat's Rue, 12
Golden rod, 14, 16
Gordium, 12
Gordonia lasianthus, 50n, 162, 171
Gossypium, 167
Grapes, 3, 6, 17, 19, 78, 101, 155, 167, 180
Ground cherry, 39
Ground Cypress, 12
Guarambanus, 94

Guava, 61, 71
Guelder rose, 8, 12, 21
Gum, black, 21, 32
Gum, sweet, 21, 23, 32, 71
Gymnocladus candensis, 153

Hackberry, 24
Haematoxylum campechianum, 124
Halesia carolina, 171
Halesia, 171
Haw, black, 21, 32, 39
Hawthorn, 21, 32, 39
Heath, Black berry bearing, 76
Helianthemums, 71
Hellebore, 12, 16, 60, 61
Hellebore, black, 171, 184
Helleborus albus et Vindis flora, 61
Helleborus niger, 171, 184
Hemp, 155
Hepatica flo pleno, 61
Hepatica, 131
Herb Christopher, 61
Hermaphrodite flower, 16
Hernandia, 61
Hibiscus rosa-sinensis, 61, 71
Hibiscus, 23, 47
Hickory, 18, 21, 23, 32, 153
Hickory, pignut, 32
Hickory, sweet, 21
Hickory, white, 21
Hicoria alba, 21
Hicoria glabra, 32
Holly, 22, 92
Holly, varegated, 92
Honeysuckle, 8, 16, 17, 19
Honeysuckle, shrub, 8
Hop tree, 21
Hordeum, 179, 180
Hornbeam, 21, 32
Horse chestnuts, 11, 39, 92
Horsebalm, 60, 61, 78, 96, 104
Hyacinths of Peru, 16
Hyacinths, 16, 163, 184
Hyacinthus, 16, 163, 184
Hybiscus syriacus, 41

Ilex vomitoria, 18, 63
Ilex, 22, 92
Imperatoria, 12
Imperial, yellow, 39
Indian corn, 79, 88
Indian fig, 167

Indian frill, 18
Indian iris, 11n
Indian shot, 18
Indian turnip, 16, 63, 63n
Indigo, 167
Ipomoea purga, 27n
Iris, 11, 159
Iris persica, 184
Iris verna, 11n
Isle of man cabbage, 179
Ivy, 11, 18, 19

Jacea, large, 14
Jack-in-the-pulpit, 16, 63, 63n
Judas tree, 18, 21
Juglans nigra, 21, 23
Juniper, 6, 22, 92
Juniperis, 6, 22, 92
Juniperus sabina, 22
Juniperus virginiana, 14, 21, 22, 23, 32, 71

Kalmia angustifloria, 87
Kalmia hirsuta, 8, 11, 16, 18, 32, 39, 149
Kentucky coffee tree, 153
Ketmia, 23

Lacnanthes tinctoria, 12n
Ladies tresses, 12
Lady finger grass, 70
Lady's Slipper, 12, 14, 19
Larch, 39, 135, 171
Larix laricina, 39, 135, 171
Larix kaempferi, 136
Larkspur, Great Tall Siberian, 166
Lathryus latifolius, 12
Laurel, 8, 11, 16, 18, 32, 39, 149
Laurel, Bay, 11
Laurel, Mountain, 32, 149
Laurel, Portuge, 162
Laurel, silver, 22
Laurel, swamp, 21, 32
Laurus Indica Aldin, 52
Laurus nobilis, 11
Laurustinus, 11, 61, 131
Ledum palustre, 177
Leonurus canadensis, 73n, 94
Leptospermum, 52, 167
Leucojum, 131
Leucojum autumnale, 131
Liatris spicata, 12, 14, 16
Life everlasting, 12
Lilac, Persian, 39

Lilac Peruvianus flore Coccineo, 90
Lilio Narcissus, 69, 94
Lilio narcicis, white, 71
Lilium, 12, 16
Lilium canadense, 12, 14, 24, 39, 64
Lilium superbum, 122
Lily, 12, 16
Lily, Gurnsey, 18, 39
Lily, Red Mexica, 69
Lime tree, 17, 21
Linaria, 16
Linden tree, 17
Lindera benzoin
Liquid Amber Tree, 71
Liquidambar orientalis, 71
Liquidambar styraciflua, 21, 23, 32, 71
Liriodendron tulipifera, 21, 23, 32
Loblolly bay, 50n, 162, 171
Locust, Honey, 18, 21
Logwood, 124
London elm, 181
Lonicera, 8, 16, 17, 19
Lords-and-ladies, 63, 63n
Lotus, 24
Lucern, 168
Lychnidea, 64, 94
Lychnis, 64, 94
Lysimachia nummularia, 8

Magnolia, 50n, 63, 71, 122, 133, 171
Magnolia, great, 133n, 159, 166, 171
Magnolia glauca, 8, 11
Magnolia grandiflora, 133n, 159, 166, 171
Magnolia tripetala, 29, 32, 39, 63, 122, 162, 171
Magnolia virginiana, 32, 87
Malabaricus, 71
Mallow, 23, 47
Malus, 45
Malus coronaria, 32
Manihot esculenta, 63
Maple, bay, 22
Maple, sugar, 17, 19, 21, 23, 24, 32, 43
Marsh bedstraw, 37
Marsh pea, 12
Martigon, 12, 14, 24, 39, 64
May apple, 12
Meadow lily, 12, 14, 24, 39, 64
Mecca balsamae, 177
Medea, 94, 110
Medeola virginiana, 94, 110
Medicago sativa, 168

Medlar from Naples, 12, 19
Melia azedarach, 39
Melocactus, 59
Melon, african, 26
Melon, calmuc, 25
Melon, Italian, 25
Melon, Muscoy, 25
Melon, Sir Charles Wager's, 25
Mertensia virginica L., 11n, 18, 26
Mespilus germanica, 12, 19
Metroxylon, 55, 61, 61n
Monarda didyma, 73n, 94
Morus, 39, 139, 167, 170
Mulberry, 39, 139, 167, 170
Mullen, 16

Narcis. Camparelle, 90
Narcis. Nana Minor, 90
Narcisso Leucoium, 61
Narcissus, 39, 90, 131, 184
Narcissus Campernelli, 90
Narcissus, China, 69
Nectarine, 17, 19, 24, 45, 138, 163, 180, 183, 184
Nerine sarniensis, 18, 39
Nettle tree, 24
New England Pine, 117
New Jersey tea, 12n, 19
Nicker tree, 153
Nothofagus solanderi, 12, 21
Nymphaea, 8
Nyssa sylvatica, 21, 32

Oak, 92, 108, 111, 117
Oak, Evergreen , 6
Oak, narrow leafed, 23, 26
Oak, swamp spanish, 21
Oak, white, 21
Oak, willow leafed, 32
Oak bark, 55
Oats, 179, 180
Oats, black, 102
Obscoletheca, 52
Olives, 155, 167
Onobrychis viciifolia, 168
Opium, 167
Opo-balsamum, 177
Optunia ficus-indica, 167
Opuntia, 101
Orange Tree, 52
Orchis, 12
Orpine seed, 20

Oryza, 27, 167
Osmond Royal, 37
Osmunda regalis, 37
Oswego tea, 73n, 94
Otanthus maritimus, 12
Oxydendrum arboretum, 18, 39

Paeonia, 16
Paliurus, 164
Palm, Large, 61
Palmae, 61
Palms, 71
Panax, 12
Panax pseudoginseng , 34, 70
Panax quinquefolium, 32, 34, 94, 101
Pansy, 131
Papaver somniferia, 27n
Papaw (Pawpaw), 61, 63, 71
Paradise plant, 63
Passiflora, 70
Passion flowers, 70
Pea, perannual, 12
Peach, 11, 12, 17, 24, 45, 138, 163, 168, 169, 180, 183, 184
Peach, double blossom, 11, 39
Peach, Katherine, 14
Pear, 17, 19, 180
Penguin, 94
Pennywort, 16
Pensilvania martigon, 122
Peony, 16
Periwinkle, 61
Perle tree, 18
Persicaria, 26
Persicary, oriental, 26
Persimmon tree, 18, 21
Peru Bark, 90, 94
Petrea L., 8n
Philerea, 92
Phillyrea, 92
Picea, 16, 21, 92, 135, 171
Picea mariana, 171
Pigellium fleawort, 12
Pignut, 32
Pilewort, double, 16
Pimpernella saxifraga, 12
Pine, 6, 16, 21, 22, 32, 71, 80, 92
Pine, five leaved, 117
Pine, long-leaved, 171
Pine, scotch, 92, 117
Pine, southern, 171
Pine, stone, 32, 63

Pine, virginia, 171
Pine, Weymouth, 171
Pine, white, 117
Pine cones, 16
Pineapple, 87
Pinus, 6, 16, 21, 22, 32, 71, 80, 92
Pinus cembra, 25, 171
Pinus palustris, 171
Pinus pinea, 32, 63
Pinus strobus , 117
Pinus sylvestris, 92, 117
Pinus virginiana, 171
Pistachio, 18, 63
Pistacia vera, 18, 63
Pitcher plant, 107, 111, 112, 135, 177, 180, 183
Plane, eastern, 17, 19, 178
Plane, western, 17
Plantago Musa x *paradisiaca,* 61
Plantain, 18, 71
Plantain vel Musa, 61
Platanus occidentalis, 17, 19, 178
Plum, 17, 19, 21, 24, 39
Podophyllum peltatum, 12
Polianthes tuberosa, 39
Polyanthus, 61, 91, 131, 163, 171, 184
Pomegranates, 131, 162
Poplar, 17, 92
Poppy anemone, 61
Populus alba, 92
Portugal laurel, 162
Potentilla erecta, 174
Prickly ash, 101
Prickly pear, 101
Prickwood, 12
Primrose, 171
Primula veris, 23, 131, 184
Primula vulgaris, 171
Primula x *polyantha,* 61, 91, 131, 163, 171, 184
Prunus, 14, 21
Prunus armeniaca, 14, 17, 19, 24, 88, 138
Prunus avium, 139
Prunus dulcis, 11, 12, 17, 39, 63
Prunus lusitanica, 162
Prunus persica var. *Nectarina,* 17, 19, 24, 45, 138, 163, 180, 183, 184
Prunus persica, 11, 12, 17, 24, 45, 138, 163, 168, 169, 180, 183, 184
Prunus spinosa, 32
Prunus americana, 17, 19, 21, 24, 39
Psidium, 61, 71
Psyllium fleawort, 12

Ptela trifoliata, 21
Puccoon, 12n, 16, 18
Pulmonaria, 18, 94
Pulsatilla , 61, 93, 163
Punica granatum, 131, 162
Pyracantha, 169
Pyrus communis, 17, 19, 180

Quercus, 92, 108, 111, 117
Quercus alba, 21
Quercus Phellos, 32
Quina , 90
Quinine, 90

Ranunculaceae, 61
Ranunculus, 16, 30, 70, 90
Ranunculus, Virginia wood, 30
Ranunculus Ficaria , 16
Red bud, 18, 21
Red root, 12n, 19
Rhamnus, 63
Rhamnus infectoria, 124
Rhenish grape, 139
Rheum palmatum, 114, 120, 137, 141
Rhododendron, calmias, 50n, 171
Rhododendron maximum, 32, 87, 149
Rhododendron tomentosum, 177
Rhubarb, Chinese, 114, 120, 137, 141
Rhubarb, Siberian, 31
Rhubarbum Chinense, 114, 120, 137, 141
Rhuberbirum Vera, 137
Ribes rubrum, 39
Rice, 27, 167
Robinia hispida, 111, 122, 171
Rock rose, 61n, 71
Rocketts, Double, 18
Rosa, 180
Rosa Chinesis, 61, 71
Rose, 180
Rose, Christmas, 171, 184
Rose, wild, 21
Rose, yellow, 39
Rose acacia, 111, 122, 171
Rose laurel, 87
Royal fern, 37
Rubia tinctorum, 174n
Rubiaceae, 148, 151
Rubus articus, 119
Russian Larex, 136

Safflower, 124, 155
Sago Palm, 55, 61, 61n

Sainfoin, 168
St. Forine, 168
St. Timothy's grass, 70
Sanguinaria canadensis L., 12n, 16, 18
Sanicula canadensis, 12, 29
Saracena, 107, 111, 112, 135, 177, 180, 183
Sarracenia, 107, 111, 112, 135, 177, 180, 183
Sarsaparilla, 12, 22
Sarsifrage, see, Saxifrage
Sassafras, 14, 21, 22, 23, 71, 171
Sassafras albidium, 14, 21, 22, 23, 71, 171
Satureja, 14
Satyrion, 12
Savin, 22
Saxifrage, double white, 16
Scammony from Aleppo, 94, 110, 155, 167
Scilla peruviana, 16
Sedum, 8, 16, 20
Sedum, wood, 16
Sedum spathulifolium, 16
Sedum telephium, 20
Senna marilandica, 12
Senna, wild, 12
Service, 21
Service, dwarf, 16
Service, sweet, 87
Sheep laurel, 87
Sheep turd, 32
Shooting star, 73n
Siberia White Fir, 136
Sida hermaphrodite, 16
Silk grass, 155, 168, 169
Silver bell, 171
Sisymbrium Monense, 179
Sisyrinchium, 12, 94
Skunk weed, 8, 16, 63, 63n, 171
Skunkwort, 8, 16, 63, 63n, 171
Smilacina racemosa, 12, 16
Smilax, 12, 22
Snake root, 12, 29, 176, 177
Snowdrop, 16
Solidago, 14, 16
Solomon's Seal, 12, 16
Sorrel tree, 18, 39
Sourwood, 18, 39
Spanish nuts, 14
Spice bush, 21
Spindle Tree, 12
Spiranthes, 12
Spiranthes spiralis, 12

Subject Index

(numbers refer to letter numbers)